Linda K. Fuller, PhD

Sportscasters/Sportscasting
Principles and Practices

Pre-publication
REVIEWS,
COMMENTARIES,
EVALUATIONS . . .

"This book provides both strategies for writing about sports and also the big picture of understanding the impact sports has on society. Beginning sports writers can benefit from tips on preparing to cover sports—from interviewing to pre-game preparation. Seasoned sports writers and those interested in better understanding the big business and impact of sports will benefit from the discussions of issues of race, gender, and the development of sports in the United States. It provides helpful resources, including sports-related Web sites and an extensive reference list of studies and research about sport."

Julie E. Dodd, EdD,
*Professor, College of Journalism
and Communications, University of Florida*

Sportscasters/Sportscasting
Principles and Practices

Sportscasters/Sportscasting
Principles and Practices

Linda K. Fuller, PhD

Routledge
Taylor & Francis Group

NEW YORK AND LONDON

First published 2008
by Routledge
270 Madison Ave, New York, NY 10016

Simultaneously published in the UK
by Routledge
2 Park Square, Milton Park, Abingdon, Oxon OX14 4RN

Routledge is an imprint of the Taylor & Francis Group, an informa business

© 2008 Taylor & Francis

Printed and bound in the United States of America on acid-free paper by
Edwards Brothers, Inc.

Excerpts from *Oh My!* (Enberg and Perry, 2004) reprinted by permission.
Sports Publishing LLC.

Library of Congress Cataloging in Publication Data
   Sportscasters/sportscasting: principles and practices / Linda K. Fuller.
      p. cm.
   Includes bibliographical references and index.
   1. Radio broadcasting of sports. 2. Television broadcasting of sports. I.
Title.
   GV742.3.F85 2007
   070.4'49796—dc22

                                                        2007046833

ISBN10: 0-7890-1825-X (hbk)
ISBN10: 0-7890-1826-8 (pbk)
ISBN10: 0-2038-8926-6 (ebk)

ISBN13: 978-0-7890-1825-0 (hbk)
ISBN13: 978-0-7890-1826-7 (pbk)
ISBN13: 978-0-20388-926-8 (ebk)

Frank Schmidt—sports pundit extraordinaire, longtime sporting friend of our whole family who, by a stroke of luck, was able to proof the bulk of this book in the Bahamas and Wilbraham. Heartfelt thanks.

CONTENTS

Preface and Acknowledgements

Even though I grew up in an era when girls weren't supposed to play games that made them sweat, I have always been interested and involved in the sporting world. So, when I was invited to participate in a conference on the Olympic Movement and the Mass Media at Calgary, Canada, the year before it was to host the 1988 XV Winter Games, I pulled out an article I had saved by Marilyn Hoffman: "Women sports stars tackle broadcast journalism," (*Christian Science Monitor,* August 2, 1984, p. 27). It inspired me to research women's roles in the Olympic Games—an eye-opening exercise that ended up in my analysis of women as athletes, organizers, and sports journalists (Fuller 1987a and b). That led to my being invited to an International Conference on Sports Business at the University of South Carolina in 1989, where I presented a paper on "The business of sportscasting"—later published (Fuller 1994c). Next, it seemed like an easy step to offer a course on sportscasting, but since there was no text available I had to make up my own plans. This book is a result of that experience.

Over the years, a number of people have helped me form the basis of what you will find here Whether students, colleagues, sportscasters, sports and/or media professionals, family, or friends, they are listed here alphabetically: Dale Arnold, "Voice of the Patriots"; David Banville; Alina Bernstein, Film and Television, Tel Aviv University, Israel; Chris Bjork; Bill Braney; Dan Cahill, radio and television columnist, *Chicago Sun Times;* Robert Callahan; Sungwook Choi, Communication Studies, Portland State University; Kevin Collins; Bob Cousy; Lindsey Dean, WTAG/Worcester; Frank Deford; Chad Dell, Communication Arts, University of Wisconsin-Madison; Mike Delmonico; Lou Dimizio; Mark Domeij; Richard Dones; John Finn;

Rob Fredette; WCAP/AM 98 and WHDH's *Sports Huddle,* Boston; James Dones; Bruce Garrison, School of Communication, University of Miami; Isaac Greaney, University of Chicago; Bud Greenspan; Linda Grodofsky, Springfield Central Library; William J. Guilfoile, Director of Public Relations for the National Baseball Hall of Fame & Museum, Inc.; Russ Haddad; David J. Halberstam, President, Word-Picture Sports; Pat Haverty; Patty Hickey; Mary A. Hums, Professor of Sport Administration, University of Louisville; David Keyes; David A. Klatell; Jim Klein, Sports Director of Springfield's WGGB-TV/Channel 40; Demetrios Kyriakis; Richard Lapchick, formerly with the Center for the Study of Sport in Society at Northeastern University; Kara Laurence; Susan Leppanen; Dean Lindsey, WTAG; Bob Lobel; John Mackiowiecki; Paul Madao; Steve McCarthy; Mike McDade; Bob McMullen, Manship School of Mass Communication, Louisiana State University; Barry Meade; Steve Nidetz, *Chicago Tribune;* Douglas A. Noverr, Department of American Though & Language, Michigan State University; Michelle Oliviera; the late Jack O'Neill, Springfield (MA) sportscaster and on-air announcer of University of Massachusetts sports; Billy Packer; Tim Piper; Arlinda Quinones; Bill Rasmussen, founder of ESPN; John Rezendes; Mark Rossi, WGAW/Radio 1340 Worcester; Katie Savignano; Louis O. Schwartz, President and Founder, American Sportscasters Association; Tom Shaer, WXRT "The Score"/All Sports Radio, Chicago; John Sweeney, Sports Communication, University of North Carolina/Chapel Hill; Mark A. Tudi, Sports Careers; Jeff Turgeon; Terry Warburton, Department of Communication Studies, The Behrend College, Pennsylvania State University; Ken Weingartner, Sports Media Workshop; and Ken White, Mass Communication, Northwest Missouri State University.

In addition, enormous appreciation goes to my many friends and fellow sports researchers whose presentations at various conferences over the years have been inspirational. They include members of the North American Society for the Sociology of Sport (NASSS), the Popular Culture Association (PCA), and the International Association of Media and Communication Research (IAMCR), and it is particularly exciting to be part of getting sports divisions for the National

Communication Association (NCA) and the International Communication Association (ICA).

My lengthy relationship with The Haworth Press has always been terrific, but I especially want to single out Rebecca Browne's support in this project. Martin Manning and Frank Hoffman encouraged the project and everyone in the production process worked well to coordinate both this book and its accompaniment, *Exercises in Sportscasting*.

Special acknowledgement goes to my husband, Eric Fuller, his brother David Fuller, as well as to Frank Schmidt for reviewing parts of the manuscript—good sports all. Thanks, too, to our son Alex Fuller for technical help. And of course this endeavor owes everything to our many outstanding sportscasters, professionals in an ever-evolving field.

Chapter 1

Introduction to Sport, Sportscasters, and Sportscasting

The importance of sports to contemporary American culture is manifest. It can be measured by the many hours that fans spend riveted to television screens, by the column inches in newspapers devoted to sports, to their presence in sports bars, and by the samples of cocktail conversations. Novelists, poets, and dramatists increasingly turn to sports for motifs, and scholars are beginning to execute minute investigations of the psychological, philosophical, and social significance of sports. As in the past, twenty-first century sports mirror, sometimes reinforce, and sometimes challenge fundamental social divisions. Simultaneously sports have joined the electronic media, bureaucratic structures, and mass consumption as one of the new sinews holding together modern society.

(Rader, 2004, p. 363)

This book has been a long time in the making. It dates to my search for textbooks to teach sportscasting—only to find that there were none available. So, although it seemed only natural to write one myself, the path to that end certainly has been circuitous; along the way, it made me realize that there is a wide audience for this topic. Although demographically geared to students—of both genders and any ethnicity, who are considering careers in the sportscasting field, it has evolved into a critical reference tool, with stories sprinkled throughout by and about sportscasters and their sports industry counterparts.

Sportscasters/Sportscasting

1

ORGANIZATION

Format-wise, *Sportscasters/Sportscasting: Principles and Practices* includes an overview of the lucrative sports industry, defining and describing how its role in broadcasting operates. The history of sportscasting is outlined, along with discussions of its economic base (advertisers and advertising, sports tourism, sports marketing and management, the sports-media complex, sportscaster earnings, and sports sponsorship), audience(s)—U.S. and international sports spectators and audiences for special events, and the role of sportscasting relative to the media: print sports media (sportswriters/sportswriting, sports journalism/sports journalists), sports television, including case studies, sports broadcasting controversies, and topics beyond broadcasting. Subsumed under the chapter on media is a special section on sportscasters: sportscaster recognition, the "jockocracy" issue, sportscaster celebrityhood, sportscaster signature statements, sportscasters as newscasters, sportscasters in the media, and in-depth profiles of more than 200 sportscasters. Sociological perspectives on sports and sportscasting consider discussions on the pervasiveness and salience of sports (the sociology of sport, the language of sport, sport and religion, and sport in popular culture), role modeling/ heroes (sport and identity, sport celebrityhood, and sport mentors), and some sociocultural issues relative to sportscasting (gender, gender orientation, race, drugs/doping, gambling, and sports violence). A practicum on sportscasting rounds out the book, including sections on becoming a sportscaster (sportscasting skills, sportscasting jobs, sportscasting preparation, sportscasting how-tos, and internships), sports journalism writing and broadcasting (the latter including sections on career moves, interviews, specific sports, and sports psychology). Finally, the future of sportscasting takes on technology and topics such as sports stadiums, politics and legalities, ethics, and your role in sports and sportscasting. As you can see, this is a multifaceted, user-friendly volume.

Positioned to be more applied than theoretical, although clearly situated in critical studies since it concerns itself with political economy, narratives, reception studies, and ideologies, this book opens a new area of study by going beyond concentrations of news and entertainment programming to include sports broadcasting (Morse, 1983). Although sports journalism in general draws upon the philosophies of Aristotle, Kant, Mills, and Rawls, ethics here becomes a subject onto itself, and overall it calls on work by Giulianott, 2004; Graham, 1994; and Morgan, 1994. John Vincent (2005, p. 2) suggests several theoretical approaches for explaining mediated coverage of sport: "Feminist sport scholars claim that female athletes are marginalized and exploited . . . Cultural studies scholars view the media as playing an important role in the construction and reconstruction of hegemonic ideologies such as capitalism, patriarchy, and heterosexuality, by creating and naturalizing social reality . . . Political economy scholars claim newspapers are driven by the financial considerations of circulation and advertising revenue." What makes this study of sportscasting so exciting is how multidisciplinarian, multitheoretical, and multiapplicable it is.

What you should particularly enjoy here are profiles of a number of sportscasters, along with their perspectives on the profession. Sprinkled throughout are some of their stories, along with incredible insights into the industry. Because we all have our own preferences, you will learn how some sports spectators like individual sportscasters, while others like teams (Curt Smith, p. 84 cites Ken Coleman and Warren Lahr, Curt Gowdy and Paul Christman, Dick Enberg and Merlin Olsen in his 1998 book), and yet you may prefer sportscaster foursomes.

Beyond that, you will undoubtedly be interested in the many appendixes at the end, including the following:

- Acronyms
- Autobiographies, biographies, and books about sportscasters
- Glossary
- Sportscaster profiles
- Sportscasting-related journals, periodicals, magazines, newspapers, and e-zines
- Sportscasting-related resources for racial minorities
- Sportscasting-related resources for women
- Sportscasting-related schools, libraries, museums, and archives
- Sportscasting-related Web sites

- Sports halls of fame
- Sports networks
- Sports and sportscasting-related organizations
- Worldwide sports

EXERCISES IN SPORTSCASTING

Exercises in Sportscasting, a supplement to this book, contains exercises to enhance learning not only about the business but also about your own relationship to it. For example, this introductory chapter's exercise concerns your own definition/description of sportscasting; for history, you are encouraged to talk to older people about their memories of early sports reportage. For financial issues, you might consider the $500+ billion sports tourism business, along with product placement in sports venues and retail areas. As a sports audience member, it behooves you to analyze some of your fondest memories, as well as to critique various players, teams, and/or events in terms of your role as a spectator. Relative to radio, you can count how many are in your household—a really fun exercise that you can ask others to do, too. Sociology and sport exercises encompass a range of subjects, such as culture and social relations, gender, race, homosexuality, and the like, while Chapter 7 encourages you to dive right in. Last, exercises for the chapter on future concerns and considerations of sportscasting stretch your imagination.

Several exercises suggest further reading on certain subjects, such as globalization of sport, the economics of sport, sport audiences, media and sport, sport sociology, laws and legalities relative to sport, and dealing with issues such as drugs and doping, gambling, and technology. Encouraging you to be a media critic, these book reviews encourage you to consider the author's credentials, main point(s), proofs, contribution to the field, and your own personal evaluations.

Sport, as you continue to learn, is a "Big Business"—a multibillion dollar business. Globally, according to the Sporting Goods Manufacturers Association (http://www.sgma.com), this translates into more than $350 billion, not counting another $170 billion for sporting goods. Between athletes' salaries, corporate sponsorship, media coverage, and related fields of advertising and public relations, the sports marketing industry has actually become a business unto itself.

As the electronic media become evermore our preferred source of sports information—so much so, in fact, that radios and televisions are becoming continually more noticeable at actual sporting events, the practice of sportscasting needs to be factored in. While a number of books have been written about specific sportscasters, even more by specific sportscasters, to date nothing has been written combining the craft of sportscasting with a wider socio-political-economic perspective. My main purpose is for you to get a sense of sportscasting.

Perhaps the eminent writer James A. Michener (1907-1997), author of a number of best-selling epic novels, as well as the controversial expose *Sports in America* (1976), says it best. Revealing how, as he was listening to a football game on the car radio between two teams whose names and players he didn't know, he got sucked in:

> The announcer was breathless in his excitement over the performance of his heroes. Then the game ended and he revealed the score. His miracle players had lost, something like 42-0, and I realized for the first time that the announcer's job was to create suspense, sustain tension, and give the listener the feeling that he had participated in a game which had been decided only in the final seconds. (pp. 383-384)

In traditional broadcasting, such as radio and television, sportscasters write, read, and simultaneously analyze, critique, report, and dramatize sporting events. Whether they are covering amateur or professional sports, whether they are covering them live or after an event, they bring their own perspectives and personal baggage to the job. Mainly, they adjust to being part of a team, bringing their own perspectives to the broadcast booth. Dick Stockton (cited in Smith, 1998, p. 91) provides a particularly intriguing worldview to the topic:

> It's amazing the variety of people you team with over the years. I have worked with quarterbacks Roger Staubach, Len Dawson, John Unitas, Terry Bradshaw and Dan Fouts, all Hall of Famers, and linemen such as Dan Dierdorf and Randy Cross. I have

worked with linebackers such as Wayne Walker and Matt Millen. Coaches? Hank Stram and John Madden, who worked with a lot of announcers in his first years with CBS. The interesting thing is the different approaches these analysts took. Coaches looking at the big picture. Quarterbacks looking at receivers and the passing lanes. Defensive people looking at the line of scrimmage to see how to stop the running game. Offensive linemen looking at pass protection. Old habits die hard. I'm glad they do.

Although we might mostly think of a sportscaster as working at radio and/or television stations, giving commentary and play-by-play at sporting events, and sports news anchors reporting sports-related news, we need to step back and realize that he or she is a link between us, the fans, and our favorite players and teams. Together, we form a bond, making us feel as if we are right there at an event. Relative to baseball, Roberta E. Pearson (1988, p. 11) puts it this way: "Rather than simply asking 'Who will win this particular game?' the announcers dramatize the conflict, placing the game within the narrative structure of the season as a whole." She continues:

> The announcers, among their other functions, serve as keepers of the flame, relating a particular game not only to the current and recent seasons, but to baseball's legendary past. They compare active to past players, tell anecdotes about the game's great and famous and reminisce about their own careers. They also contrast the contemporary game to its previous incarnations, commenting on alterations in rules and playing conditions and not invariably valorizing the present. This invocation of baseball's pervasive nostalgia perhaps serves to reinforce the game's residual values. (p. 12)

Think of it this way: Play-by-play persons call the action, while "color commentators" might host a pregame show or intermission, or fill in gaps between breaks in the play; sometimes, of course, the jobs are one and the same.

The basic idea is announcing action, in "real time." Sportscasting, by the way, is mainly an American English term, not necessarily used as a blanket phrase around the world—which brings me to a disclosure of perspective. At the risk of being accused of Western ethnocentrism, it must be admitted that most of this book is U.S.-oriented, even if many of its themes can hopefully be transferred to other countries and cultures. As we well know, globalization in sport continues to be an area of interest to many scholars and practitioners (Allison, 2006; Amis, 2005; Andrews, 2006; Bairner, 2001; Chandler, 1988; Cronin and Mayall, 1998; Eitzen, 2004; Foer, 2004; Gems, 2006; Houlihan, 1994; Maguire, 1999; Majumdar and Hong, 2006; Miller, Lawrence, McKay, and Rowe, 2001; Roche, 2001; Szymanski and Zimbalist, 2005; Tomlinson and Young, 2006; Van Bottenburg and Jackson, 2001; Wenner, 1998; Westerbeek and Smith, 2003; Whannel, 1992; Wilson, 1994).

Sometimes, admittedly, it does not go as well as it should. "The art of sports broadcasting, from a play-by-play and commentary standpoint, has devolved to Neanderthal level, a rollicking circus of forced enthusiasm and excess," Brian Lowry (2006, p. 1) levels in his criticism. He offers as an example ABC's "planned 3 ½ hour Super Bowl pre-game show featuring its ESPN crew, meaning the amount of babble about the game will run as long as the game itself."

Much of sport, as you know, crosses borders. Much as *Hockey Night in Canada* might be a national phenomenon, many American audiences also participate in it, just as people around the world catch our Super Bowl. But this all should make us feel funny about calling our annual baseball final the World Series.

Lots of sportscasting involves humor. Read these examples, from sportscasters who might not necessarily have tried to be funny:

- Dizzy Dean: "Fans, don't fail to miss tomorrow's game."
- Giant's broadcast announcer Ron Fairley: "He fakes a bluff."
- Padres broadcast announcer Jerry Coleman, attempting to tell radio listeners about a fly ball hit by a member of the opposing team: "Winfield goes back to the wall. He hits his head on the wall and it rolls off! It's rolling all the way back to second base! This is a terrible thing for the Padres."

- Jerry Coleman again: And Kansas City is at Chicago tonight, or is that Chicago at Kansas City? Well, no matter, Kansas City leads in the eighth, 4 to 4."
- Ralph Kiner, announcer for the New York Mets: "We are experiencing audio technicalities." Also, "Today is Father's Day, so everyone out there: Happy birthday!"
- Curt Gowdy: "Folks, this is perfect weather for today's game. Not a breath of air."
- Unnamed golf broadcaster, during a tournament: "Arnie [Palmer], usually a great putter, seems to be having trouble with his long putt. However he has no trouble dropping his shorts."

At this point, then, you realize that you are about to engage in a book that has wide-ranging perspectives, ranging from a historical review to predictions about the future. It is meant to involve you, the reader, and it is meant to evolve, so your participation is highly encouraged.

The Web site, eHow, offers several steps on becoming a sportscaster. These steps include attending a school of journalism and taking courses in writing and sports history, and reading about sports.

If only you could just follow some magic steps to become a sportscaster. As you will find, it is wondrously more complicated than that.

"Sport is not socially, politically, economically, culturally, or historically neutral," Martin Polley (2007, p. xiv). "Sport is always linked to the wider settings in which it is played, and to think that it can float free of them—as in, for example, the claim that 'sport and politics should not mix'—is an obstacle to your understanding of sport."

Chapter 2

The Historical Development
of Sports and Sportscasting

As might be expected, the evolution of sportscasting began quite
soon after the earliest broadcasting media came into being, rooted
first in sportswriting, then radio dating from the 1920s, television at
mid-twentieth century, and moving into new technologies such as
Web sites, blogs, and podcasts (Fuller, forthcoming). The chronology
includes a number of "firsts," such as the fact that the first professional team in the United States was the Cincinnati Red Stockings,
established in 1869.

Radio telegraphy was used as early as 1920 to report some baseball, football, and prizefighting scores, such as WWJ's first broadcast
of a prizefight (Jack Dempsey versus Billy Miske, September 6,
1920), or WTAW's first radio play-by-play broadcast of a collegiate
football game (Texas University versus Mechanical College of Texas
on November 25, 1920), but it was all pretty primitive. Curt Gowdy
(cited in Poindexter, 1966, p. 135) has a classic recollection:

> Football is a complicated game, but there wasn't anything very
> complicated about covering it until television came along. When
> I first began doing college football in Oklahoma, all it took was
> an engineer and a couple of announcers, one for play-by-play,
> the other for color. On long trips the color man was sometimes
> left home to save expenses.
>   The engineer would set up one mike on the roof, suspend an-
> other below the roof for crowd noises, and put one or two in the
> radio booth. We were supposed to do a certain number of com-

mercials per game, but used our own judgment as to exactly when. There were no producers, directors, technicians, agency men, nor any of the other reinforcements who now work a big college or professional football games on television.

In answer to arguments as to when the very first sportscast was actually made, the year was 1921 can be etched in stone. Several key events occurred in 1921:

- Johnny Ray and Johnny Dundee were contending parties in a boxing event that took place on April 11, 1921, at Motor Square Garden in Pittsburgh, and a blow-by-blow description of it went out over local "crystal sets," which is what early radios were called.
- The "battle of the century," a boxing match between Jack Dempsey ("The Manassa Mauler") and Georges Carpentier, champion of France, took place on July 2, 1921, carried by WJZ of Jersey City. It was announced by Major Andrew J. White, considered to be the first major sports broadcaster.
- On August 5, 1921, the first Major League baseball game was broadcast on Westinghouse Electric's radio station KDKA, the home team, the Pittsburgh Corsairs, won 8 to 5 over the Philadelphia Phillies. Harold Arlin provided the play-by-play from Forbes Field, his voice transmitted by telephone from the press box to the broadcast studio and on to the audience (Smith, 1992).
- The next day (August 6, 1921), Arlin officiated at the first radio broadcast of a tennis match: Australia versus Great Britain for the Davis Cup, on KDKA.
- The 1921 World Series, between the New York Giants and the New York Yankees, at the Polo Grounds in Manhattan, was broadcast from October 5-14 on radio station WJZ (Towers, 1981, p. 4). Sandy Hunt, a reporter for the *Newark Sunday Call,* provided the play-by-play—via telephone lines to the station.
- Arlin again appears in this history, as on November 5, 1921, he announced the first college football game—again on KDKA, Pittsburgh versus West Virginia. Word is, though, that he got so

excited on one touchdown that he knocked the station off the air. Yale versus Princeton was more successfully broadcast on November 12, 1921.

Interest in sport, and reportage of it, dates from the earliest days of the founding of America—beginning with the print media, which expanded once its economic value was made apparent. Jon Enriquez (2002, p. 198) points out how early examples dealt more with announcement about events rather than describing them: "One of the earliest known sports stories appeared in the *Boston Gazette* on March 5, 1733. It was a description of a prize fight held in England, and it was copied from a London newspaper—a practice typical of the day." Soon, we had specialization, such as for specific sports, specific audiences, and of course specific advertisers.

Early on, any number of experimentations took place. Journalism professor Frank Luther Mott (1962, p. 579) informs us about the importance of the telegraph, in 1844, precursor to the establishment of the Associated Press: "Wireless was first used for news reporting in connection with the international yacht races of 1899." None other than Guglielmo Marconi, the man generally recognized as inventor of the radio, handled the transmission for the Associated Press. Newsreels, too, played a part: "Among the most popular newsreel features were clips from sporting events, and sportsreels helped nationalize sports by visualizing major sports heroes who had never before been seen by sports fans outside of the cities where they played" (Bryant and Holt, 2006, pp. 29-30). The telegraph, it turns out, was used to broadcast the first college sporting event, at the University of Minnesota, in 1912—the same year wireless telegraphy played such a significant role during the sinking of the Titanic. Ronald A. Smith (2001, p. 14) explains how the university experimented with the technology, a spark transmitter: "Professor F. W. Springer and a young instructor, H.M. Turner, began an experimental radio station with the call numbers 9XI-WLB. As part of their investigation, Springer and Turner broadcast accounts of Minnesota's home football games to a sparse audience."

As to radio's first wave of sportscasters, names like Grantland Rice, Graham McNamee, Ted Husing, Harold Arlin, Ford Frick,

Haywood Hale Broun, France Laux, and Tommy Cowan come to mind. Grantland Rice (1954) made history in 1924 with his often-quoted depiction of Notre Dame's football team as the "Four Horsemen" (of the Apocalypse). Following is a description of their October 18 battle against Army, the "Dean of American Sportswriters" wrote:

> Outlined against a blue-gray October sky the Four Horsemen rode again. In dramatic lore they are known as famine, pestilence, destruction and death. These are only aliases. Their real names are: Stuhldreher, Miller, Crowley and Layden. They formed the crest of the South Bend cyclone before which another fighting Army team was swept over the precipice at the Polo Grounds this afternoon as 55,000 spectators peered down upon the bewildering panorama spread out upon the green plain below.

The second group of best-known radio sportscasters might include Mel Allen, Red Barber, Lindsay Nelson, Jack Brickhouse, Clem McCarthy, Ernie Harwell, Harry Caray, and Bill Stern, and, Ronald "Dutch" Reagan, began his career doing sport re-creations in Davenport, Iowa as a football announcer.

Although sports history continues to be a burgeoning area of interest (Andrews and Wagg, 2006; Phillips, 2005; Rader, 2004; Zang, 2004)—whether seen in terms of ethnicity and/or demographics (Eisen and Wiggins, 1994), sociocultural concerns (Guttman, 1991; Hargreaves, 1994), language, media reportage, nationalism, commercialism, violence, and/or specific sports, academics are pleased to see it being taken seriously (Booth, 2006, Crawford, 2004, Dunning et al., 2006, Fuller, 2006a, Gems, 2006, Gorn and Goldstein, 2004, Houlihan and White, 2002, McComb, 2004, Munslow and Phillips, 2005). For example, there are now thriving divisions and subdivisions of sports interest groups in the International Association of Media and Communication Research (IAMCR), the National Communication Association (NCA), the North American Society for the Sociology of Sport (NASSS), the Popular Culture Association (PCA), and a push for them in the National Communication Association (NCA) and International Communication Association (ICA). Separately, if associatively, there are list-serves and chat groups such COMM-SPORT and an affiliation with the Olympic Games.

It is a particularly good sign that scholarly interest in sport is taking place on a global basis, as individual countries analyze and appreciate both leisure and competitive activities indigenous to their cultures. At the same time, it is encouraging to know that these studies include minorities and otherwise underrepresented and underutilized sporting participants. As we move away from models involving power plays of elitism, hegemonic masculinity, sexist and racial biases, it becomes particularly appropriate to discuss the mouthpieces of these events.

RADIO

At the end of the nineteenth century, moving image technology was being applied to sporting events. Since then, newsreel and wireless coverage of sport from the 1920s, and then television coverage, means that there is a vast archive of film and sound news-based materials on sport. As we get closer to the present, this includes entire events—whole matches, full marathons, and so on—as well as highlights. Through these media, we can literally see the events happening and, in many cases, hear the real noises of the crowd, while also hearing how contemporary commentators reported on sport. (Polley, 2007, p. 94)

Once it was recognized that sports could was a commodity, the rest was history. Although at first it was thought that the only way money could be made was from the sales of radio receivers, it did not take long for entrepreneurs to discover radio as an ideal source for advertising.

But before getting into the commercial aspects of radio, let's return to the 1921 Dempsey-Carpentier fight. David Sarnoff, general manager of the Radio Corporation of America (RCA), created radio station WJZ at Boyle's Thirty Acres in Jersey City for the occasion, "with an antenna strung between a steel tower and the clock tower of the Lackawanna railroad terminal" (Gleason L. Archer, 1971, p. 213). Played before an over-capacity crowd of some 91,000 fans, its gross of $1,789,238 was more than double that of any previous fight (Kahn, 2000). Theodore Roosevelt's children were in attendance, along with luminaries like John D. Rockefeller, Jr., William H. Vanderbilt, Vincent Astor, Henry Ford, Al Jolson, George M. Cohan, H.L. Mencken, Damon Runyon, Ring Lardner, and about 2,000 women. Despite opposition from some political quarters, church groups, and the Board of Temperance and Public Morals worried about the fight's possible effect on young people. Telephone lines and a radio transmitter helped broadcast the event to an estimated audience of 300,000. If you are interested, by the way, Dempsey won by a knock-out in the fourth round.

Let's revisit the 1921 World Series. Broadcasting historian Erik Barnouw (1966, p. 85), describes its importance for WJZ, emphasizing the role of "announcer" Tommy Cowan (based on his 1950 book *Reminiscences*):

> Like the Dempsey-Carpentier fight it was really a relay. During the first game Tommy sat in the shack holding a telephone receiver to one ear; at the other end of the line, at the Polo Grounds, was a reporter from the Newark *Call*. When Tommy heard, 'Strike one,' he quickly repeated, 'Strike one.' After 'Ball one,' he said, 'Ball one.' The hand holding the receiver became bloodless, the shell of his ear raw. The thing seemed to go on for hours. At the end he did not know who had won. For the second game he was given a headset.

Ted Husing's 1935 autobiography describes a funny story about a University of Pittsburgh sophomore providing play-by-play for a 1922 game, which he had money on, but that was not going his way. With thirty seconds to go, he still claimed, "It's enough. Only inches to go. One buck by Big Jack Hoozis and it'll be all over. Old Jack Hoozis will be the hero on the Pitt campus tonight, all right. Time in—they're coming out of the huddle—they're lining up—double wing-back formation, and Hoozis will take it. Signal—here comes the play—Hoozis has his arms out for it—the ball's passed—and . . . O-o-oh! The goddam bonehead fumbled it" (pp. 55-56). Apparently he then dropped the mike and never held the mike again.

In 1923, Hal Totten announced daily baseball games from Chicago ballpark station WMAQ— the first announcer to do so. Soon, baseball and other sports were being carried on radio stations throughout the country, and audiences were not only being entertained, they were being educated about rules and regulations, players, and performances. "Undoubtedly, to hear a broadcaster describe a home run hit by the New York Yankees' Babe Ruth or a steal of second base by the Detroit Tigers' Ty Cobb were dramatic moments that enticed individuals and families to tune in games on the radio and cheer for their favorite players and teams," Frank P. Jozsa, Jr. (2003, p. 121).

Unlike college football coaches of the 1920s, most of whom were paid more than full professors—some even more than university presidents, campus sports announcers were simply part of stations that carried a range of radio fare. As commercial radio grew, so did stations at institutions of higher learning; yet many educational groups wanted to distance themselves from athletics, the best-known example being that of the University of Chicago, where there were athletic dorms, special meals, and a training table facility (Lester, 1995).

Although home games might be broadcast live, road games often brought their own special issues, and "re-creations" were rampant. Embellishments and fabrications became the norm. Radio ruled as the nation's dramatic storyteller, and its sportscasters filled many voids as they entered peoples' homes.

As the first national live broadcast of a sporting event, the 1927 Rose Bowl featured legendary announcer Graham McNamee behind the mike. Although he was formidably formal, even histrionic, his musical voice training and sports experience helped in his being hired by WEAF in New York in 1923. Amateur boxing helped him be familiar with "details like hooks, jabs, roundhouses, feinting, ducking, and clinching," according to his 1926 autobiography. "The 'infectious excitement' of his announcing was considered a success from the first broadcast' (Smith, 2001, pp. 24-25), and after his announcing the 1922 World Series, the station reportedly received 1,700 pieces of mail. That number went to more than 50,000 within two years; *Radio Digest* gave McNamee a cup inscribed with notice of his being "the most popular radio announcer." His only competition, Ted Husing, who also had a background in athletics but was about a dozen years younger, was described as fast-talking, dramatic, and accurate, aided by his invention of "the annunciator board."

Thanks to radio, sports easily infiltrated into mass culture in the 1920s—the era of stars like Babe Ruth, Knute Rockne, Jack Dempsey and other sporting household names. Hollywood, developing around this same time, took on subjects such as the sports hero or the sports underdog (Fuller, 1991), and any number of celebrities, like "The Sultan of Swat" (Fuller, 1995b) have appeared in movies either as themselves or other athletes.

Sportscasting was cultivating its own stars around this time, many sportscasters becoming associated with specific teams and specific products. Mel Allen was the voice of the Yankees, Bob Prince for the Pittsburgh Pirates, Jack Buck for the Cardinals, and Curt Gowdy for the Red Sox. In the advertising arena, Don Dunphy was the voice of Gillette.

Predominantly, radio is regional, and an instant source for local news. For its first four decades, radio predominated as the source for sports coverage—both live and after-the-fact, for those who might have missed various events. Although it built an audience in the 1930s, during the Depression, radio had to dedicate much of its airtime to war news in the 1940s, and then in the 1950s it featured classical music to the rise of disc jockeys. "The period produced a strange flowering in sportscasting: the "re-created" baseball game" (Barnouw, 1968, p. 289):

> It built a short-lived chain, the Liberty Network. Saving the expense of pickups from baseball parks, entrepreneur Gordon McLendon staged hair-raising play-by-play descriptions in a Dallas studio from information on a news-agency ticker while an engineer, like an organist selecting stops, faded sound-effects records in an out: quiet crowds, restless crowds, hysterical crowds. His selections stimulated the announcer, who invented reasons for any sudden crowd excitement: a fan had made an unbelievable one-hand catch of a foul, or a peanut vender had fallen downstairs . . . The McLendon broadcasts were often more exciting than the ball games.

By the 1960s, radio shared the airwaves with yet another war, but its role as a mass medium remained secure. Radio announcers broke with traditional journalism, though, in a startling way: they promoted sports, instead of merely reporting them. For the next four decades, radio revolved around music, talk, news, and other forms of infotainment until being recently catapulted by the likes of Sirius satellite radio and any number of twenty-four-hour sports radio outlets.

As a classic example, in 1987, the first all-sports radio station was started when WFAN of New York began broadcasting on July 1. Formerly famous in media history as the first station to take on advertising, as WEAF, on October 28, 1922, it broadcast a football game between Princeton and the University of Chicago via long-distance lines from Stagg Field (Chicago) to New York, and a month later it did the same for the annual Harvard-Yale rivalry. You can check out its Web site (www.wfan.com) to see how a single station can become so diversified, albeit still dedicated to sports.

In an interview on Bob Costas' *Coast to Coast,* Red Barber reported,

> When I began I think there were three commercials for nine innings. So it meant you were on the air all afternoon. You had opportunity. You had room on the air to tell stories. Now, as you well know, you gotta hustle at the end of every third out. You're not allowed any talking time between innings. You're not allowed any feature time. If you're doing television today, you don't have an opportunity to tell a feature story. You don't have an opportunity really to be much of a personality. (cited in Edwards, 1993, p. 74)

Clearly, Red Barber enjoyed the luxury of time in storytelling, as did Vin Scully—as opposed to Lindsay Nelson, who didn't like to overdo his telecasts.

Hailing from Tennessee, Lindsay Nelson early on was so taken by radio that he determined to make it his career; he reminisces in his autobiography (1985, p. 21): "I remember the night we gathered in the living room of our home to listen to Graham McNamee's broadcast of the 1927 heavyweight championship fight between Jack Dempsey and Gene Tunney at Soldier Field in Chicago . . . McNamee saying he was so close to the ring that he could reach out and touch the canvas with his hand." Nelson was like another, later, Southerner—Keith Jackson, who made his name doing collegiate football telecasting, moved on to ABC, and had this view about announcers: They should "amplify, clarify, punctuate, and then get out of the way" (cited in Smith, 2001, p. 128).

Johnny Most (cited in Carey, 2003, p. 34) reveals how, early in his career, he covered the Dodgers without actually traveling with them: "Instead I recreated live broadcasts of the away games off the Western Union ticker tape, which gave a short description of each hit, steal, out, and personnel change." It worked well until the tape broke—you can only imagine the stalling and improvising that was required.

TELEVISION

> Televised sports in the United States got underway late in the afternoon of May 17, 1939, when someone threw a switch in the RCA Building in downtown New York City. The picture impulses picked up by the bulky Iconoscope television camera located at Columbia University's Baker Field traveled through a transmitter in a nearby truck and up an antenna fastened to the top of a flagpole, which then catapulted them through the sky to the 85th floor of the Empire State Building. From there the signal leaped to the RCA Building, and NBC's experimental station W2XBS was on the air. 'Good afternoon, ladies and gentlemen!' came the nasal twang of Bill Stern, the famous radio broadcaster. (Rader, 1984, p. 17)

Although at first television had some technical troubles covering sports such as football or baseball, where the action takes place on a wide field with lots of participants, it did not take long for consumers to get used to wanting visuals. Some sportscasters, too, might have had difficulty with the transition to television, but they too quickly crossed over.

Whereas radio was portable, and installed in most cars since Paul Galvin invented car radios in 1929, television actually was first popular in bars—haunts of male sporting fans. But that was before games moved to nighttime, so radios at work remained popular until around the 1960s as a source for sporting events and sporting news. Even today, though, you see people bringing radios to ballparks, wanting a voice to fill them in on what they might be seeing in real time.

"And now we add radio sight to sound," intoned David Sarnoff in 1939 when he introduced the notion of television at the New York World's Fair at the RCA Pavilion. Field production for mobile television production then, as described by Bill Molzon (n.d.) of Waynesburg College, included, "Two Telemobile trucks, in order to do 'outside pick-ups. One contained standard rack-mounted equipment for two cameras and the other housed a 159 megacycle, 300W transmitter. Each unit was about the size and shape of a twenty-five-passenger bus and weighed 10 tons."

This was also when television's first live sporting event took place—on May 17, 1939, for the second game of a baseball doubleheader between Columbia and Princeton. A single camera on third base was set up to cover everything. Sports journalist Leonard Koppett, from Columbia's class of 1944, revels in the fact that it all began at his alma mater's Baker Field when the National Broadcasting Company set up an experiment to send the show, hosted by Bill Stern, to some 400 sets with receivers. Pleased with the results, NBC began broadcasting from Brooklyn's Ebbets Field five months later. The *New York Times* writer notes how his newspaper duly noted the event, but how the whole process was soon put on hold as attention turned to World War II—explaining the hiatus in why television did not dominate for several more decades (Koppett, n.d.).

But before moving on, there is an interesting saga you should know regarding Bill Stern. Prior to this pivotal opportunity of being television's first sports announcer, when given the chance to broadcast the Army-Illinois football game on NBC radio, Stern asked some of his family and friends to send telegrams to the network praising his work; problem was, some arrived prior to the event, and he was fired. Luckily, he was later rehired (Poindexter, 1966). Let this be a lesson for you. That 1939 Columbia-Princeton contest, by the way, was not so easy: "As dramatic as was the voice of Bill Stern, the limitations of one camera angle and the poor quality of the picture on snowy screens detracted from the scene," (Ronald A. Smith, 2001, pp. 49-50). "Only by listening to the announcer could one follow the action. The cameraman focused on the pitcher during the windup and attempted to follow the ball to the plate. Whenever the ball was hit, Stern would describe the flight of the ball, but the cameraman had difficulty following it."

Just as 1921 was a key year for radio, so was 1939 for television. On May 20, just three days after the first intercollegiate telecast, NBC covered a six-day bicycle race at Madison Square Garden, and the first telecast of a boxing match (Lou Nova versus Max Baer) took place June 1, 1939, at Yankee Stadium. August 26 dates the first television broadcast of a pro baseball game—the Cincinnati Reds versus the Brooklyn Dodgers, by Red Barber, on W2XBS; next, September 30 saw the first televised American football game—Fordham versus Waynesburg College (see Molzon, n.d.). October 22 featured the first television broadcast of a pro football game, the first coverage of an NFL game—this time, the Brooklyn Dodgers versus the Philadelphia Eagles, at Ebbets Field, brought by NBC.

Hockey (February 25, 1940—the New York Rangers versus the Montreal Canadiens), basketball (February 28, 1940—Pitt versus Fordham), track and field (March 2, 1940, from Madison Square Garden, telecast on W2XBS), and other sports followed soon thereafter. It might be noted that television sets were enormously expensive when they premiered—about as much as an automobile, so very few households could afford them. Perhaps this also explains why taverns, like today's sports bars, reigned.

When the veterans returned home after WWII and America settled into a new lifestyle, telesports took over and technology improved enough to encourage viewers to move beyond the novelty of seeing their favorite sports. More cameras were used, and their clarity and reliability were greatly improved. "Early cameras were heavy and cumbersome and needed bright light to produce even a passable picture," Stanley J. Baran (n.d.). "Boxing and wrestling, contested in confined, very well-lit arenas and baseball and football, well-lit by the sun and played out in a familiar, well-defined spaces, were perfect subjects for the lens."

Screens were soon made larger; color was introduced, multiple camera angles were incorporated, as well as slow motion. "Instant replay," first introduced when Lee Harvey Oswald was shot by Jack Ruby the month before, appeared on December 7 for the 1963 Army-Navy game and forever changed the face of production. Barnouw (1970, p. 245) describes the process:

> While one camera showed the over-all action "live," other cameras followed the key players in close-up, with each camera linked to a separate videotape machine. Within seconds after a play, its crucial action could be re-examined in close-up, or even unfolded in startling slow motion. This accomplished incredible transformations: brutal collisions became ballets, and end runs and forward passes became miracles of human coordination. Football, once an unfathomable jumble on the small screen, acquired fascination for widening audiences.

"This is not live! Ladies and gentlemen, Army has not scored again!" announcer Lindsay Nelson informed audiences, but we have never seen sports quite the same since. Basically, television needed to distinguish itself from radio, and it needed to educate audiences to the medium. Appealing mainly to men, industry executives decided to go for, as broadcasting historian J. Fred MacDonald (1979, p. 9) called it, the "excitement of sport contests."

Boxing became a natural choice, both for visuals and viewers, but also for advertisers. Gillette had sponsored the sport since radio days, and Don Dunphy's move to television brought lots of fight fans along with him for what was called *The Gillette Cavalcade of Sports*—a program that lasted until 1964. But boxing was dealt something of a death knell when, on March 24, 1962, Emile Griffith KO'd welterweight Benny "Kid" Paret on *The Fight of the Week;* carried unconscious from the ring, Paret died soon thereafter—along with regular boxing broadcasts.

Wrestling was popularly introduced to television, both because it was cheap to produce and because there was lots of it available (Morton and O'Brien, 1985). In 1947, *Howdy Doody* had to make way for Gorgeous George—a high-profile wrestler not unlike some of today's outlandish performers, along with others with lively names like Skull Murphy, Nature Boy, or The Mighty Atlas. "Television helped perpetuate the carnival atmosphere of wrestling by allowing the announcers to throw away any semblance of objective reporting and become part of the antics themselves," (Jeff Neal-Lunsford, 1992, p. 68). "DuMont's Dennis James, for example, provided sound effects to match the action in the ring. If a wrestler had an opponent in a hammerlock, James would draw his fingernail across an inflated balloon in imitation of a cry of agony. To reproduce the sound of breaking bones, James would employ a rubber dog bone, which, when bent, emitted a sharp cracking noise."

The 1950s, often called the "Golden Age of Television," featured stars such as "Uncle Miltie" Berle, Jack Benny, Lucille *(I Love Lucy)* Ball, and Jackie Gleason. It also saw a number of sports shows, following the success of Gillette's venture, such as *Sports Special, Sports with Joe Hasel, Sportsman's Quiz, Pabst Blue Ribbon's Bouts, Fishing and Hunting Club, Game of the Week, Pro Football Highlights,* even a fifteen-minute show on NBC called *Sportswoman of the Week.* And, would you believe, in 1949 *Roller Derby* played on ABC for four hours each week during prime time, the network's most popular show. But the key term here is *prime time.* Expanding audiences soon wanted other entertainment fare during that time, and sports moved to other scheduled slots.

Professional football in the 1950s was starting to emerge from the shadows of the college game. On December 23, 1951, the first network NFL game was braodcast on the DuMont network; the problem was, compared to CBS and NBC, (the other emerging networks), DuMont had the fewest affiliates. A seminal game took place between the New York Giants and Baltimore Colts for the NFL Championship in 1958, which especially recalled for its overtime thrills. Football soon reigned on the airwaves—and its history continues to fascinate fans around the world. You will read here later about the role, for example, of *Monday Night Football,* which made its debut on September 21, 1970.

If the 1920s began the first boom period in American sports, the second one dates to the 1960s, when it became clear that sports needed television just as much as television needed sports. One of the prescient moves made by the networks at this time—albeit as a "stop-gap summer fill-in show," was ABC's decision to begin a program called *Wide World of Sports,* on April 29, 1961. Hosted by Jim McKay, the program took an anthology/magazine format, covering both the familiar and the unfamiliar, and bringing sports such as skiing, track and field, luge, tennis, curling, and the like to interested audiences. According to Jim Spence (1988, p. 69), who spent more than a quarter century with ABC Sports, "Ground rules were simple: if something is visually exciting, let's try it." As television was building its own identity, sports provided some already-known athletes to audiences.

As is turns out, the story of ABC Sports is a special one in the history of sportscasting. Key to it all was producer Roone Arledge, a "behind the-scenes superstar" according to boxing writer Bert Sugar (1978). He explains how Arledge took the perspective of the spectator, taking in all the surroundings—checking out fellow fans, players on the sidelines, and the action all around (p. 77). "In addition to bringing the viewers to the game—as well as bringing the whole game to viewers—Arledge revolutionized the production components of the game," add Bryant and Holt (2006, p. 34).

> He placed microphones on the field; he doubled and then tripled the standard number of cameras used to cover the game; he accentuated the personalities of players and coaches; he oversaw the development and implementation of the instant replay; he allowed the play-by-play and color commentators much more freedom to dramatize and personalize the event, as well as to use replay and graphics to underscore analysis; and he made *Monday Night Football* (MNF) de rigueur viewing in sports bars and homes throughout America, thereby extending the weekend one more day for avid football fans. Most memorable of all, it was

Arledge, the programming whiz, who coined the term "The thrill of victory, the agony of defeat."

What seemed like a single, silly event in 1968 turned out to have implications for sports programming to this day. With only fifty seconds left in a close NFL game between the New York Jets (32) and the Oakland Raiders (29), on November 17, NBC opted to air a (pre-)scheduled made-for-TV movie, *Heidi*. After some 13 million furious fans crashed the network's switchboard letting it know how upset they were about what was an upset by Oakland, what became known as the "Heidi affair" has hardly been repeated; since then, most sports events are allowed to run their course. From a perspective of more than three decades of reporting Red Sox spring training, Len Berman (2005, p.74) looks back at the early days, before live shots: "We'd shoot our material on film, drive it to the airport, get it on a plane, fly it to Boston, have it driven to the TV station, process it, edit it, and then play it on air."

Recognizing the symbiotically needy relationship between sports and media, Robert McChesney (1989) notes how, at first, "sport was generally considered vulgar and disreputable among a large portion of the American reading public" (p. 51) but, as it became organized and commercialized, it "emerged as a prime source of entertainment and communal bonding" (p. 55). He notes how television changed the landscape:

First, television came to penetrate the overwhelming majority of American homes; it was now clearly a mass medium. Second, the technology for sports broadcasting radically improved with the advent of color television, videotape (with its slow-motion and instant-replay capacities), satellites, and portable cameras. Third, Congress passed the Sports Broadcasting Act of 1961, which permitted professional sports teams in a league to negotiate as one unit with broadcasters. This had previously been considered an infringement of antitrust laws. Fourth, the networks and stations began to purchase broadcast rights directly from the teams and leagues and then sold time on those telecasts to advertisers. These two developments made sports broadcasting potentially a far more lucrative operation for sport owners and broadcasters alike. But the most critical factor was simply that certain advertisers discovered that sports provided access to a very desirable market—not only for 'blue collar' products like beer and razor blades, but for big-ticket items like automobiles and business equipment. (pp. 61-62)

The increasing penetration of cable television, along with expanded broadcast rights, had huge financial implications for the 1970s and 1980s (Powers, 1984); furthermore, it figures enormously into our discussion of sportscasting. Later in this book, we will learn about the incredible changes in sports programming that began in 1979 with the establishment of twenty-four-hour televised sports on ESPN (Entertainment & Sports Programming Network). By the 1990s and into the new millennium, we see a proliferation of specialized channels devoted to sport, and we see astronomical fees for sponsoring them.

Bruce Garrison (1987, 3/9) of the University of Miami reviewed "The Evolution of Professionalism in Sports Reporting" some decades ago and discovered the following:

1. Movement toward more process-oriented reporting rather than exclusively event-oriented reporting.
2. Increased use of innovative reporting methods, including use of new technology, for investigative and public opinion reporting.
3. Sports story topics of a wider range—such as courtroom litigation, high finance, and international politics.
4. Participation in sports reporting by women, both in print and on the air.
5. Increase in sports newsmaking by women.
6. Reduction of "cheerleading" of local teams and reporting of the good and the bad activities by teams.
7. Sensitivity about professional behavior standards through creation and enforcement of codes of ethics by groups such as APSE.
8. Concern for reporting credibility.

9. Reaction by print sports media to the impact of the instantaneous coverage by electronic media.

10. Adoption of new computer-based technologies for faster and more accurate coverage of sports in print and on the air.

11. Spot and feature photography of sports action at a higher level of quality through better talent and better technology.

12. Better use of available print space and air time for sports reporting.

13. Large news holes for newspapers and, probably, for television networks and local stations.

14. Reduction of bias against coverage of women's sports, primarily at amateur levels.

15. More common use of features about sports people and their activities.

16. Concern for credibility, ethics, and professionalism in behavior of sports reporters.

17. Recognition of sports topics by the Pulitzer Prize Committee for excellence in reporting.

Do you see any parallels between sports in print and sportscasting? How would you characterize these professions today? Rather than reviewing the entire history of sportscasting here, several important points are the economic, political, and sociocultural concerns for the practice, and the fact that oftentimes, sportscasters themselves have become more the focus of audience concern and comment than the sporting event itself. "The great sportscasters always realized what should be emphasized, and the media seems to be coming around to sharing that point of view as well," wrote Warburton in 1987; we can only hope that his comment continues to have validity.

Technically, production improvements aided by such developments as videotape, instant and slow-motion replay facilities, multiple cameras, digital editing, computer graphics, statistical data processors, and the like have further changed sports, making them both more sophisticated and specialized. Neal-Lunsford (1992, p. 75) cites the "TV time out" as an example, with starting times for games being routinely adjusted to fit television schedules. Technology has also impacted the role of the sportscaster from that of simple blow-by-blow announcer to that of complex analyst and showperson.

Today, as you know, we have any number of all-sports media venues. Battalions of personnel cover events such as the Super Bowl, the World Cup, the Tour de France, the Olympic Games, even the X Games. Still, although we have advanced from wire to wireless connections from the sporting spot for the interested audience(s), the art and the craft of sportscasting continue to depend on people.

Chapter 3

The Economics of Sports, Sportscasters, and Sportscasting

As the sports industry continues to grow in terms of participants, spectators, and overall industry size, the economics associated with sport media coverage have escalated accordingly. As networks continue to encounter technological changes in an effort to maintain financial viability, the role of televised sporting events will undoubtedly be a major factor. Soaring rights fees paid for major sporting events and advertising broadcast revenues are two examples of the economic influences of television on sport-media relationships.

(Mondello, 2006, p. 227)

The monetary aspects of sportscasting are discussed in this chapter (Fuller, 1989, 1994c). "At all levels, sports has become big business," (Peter E. Mayeux, 1991, p. 331). "Sports news is important and taken seriously by a growing number of people." In this chapter, you will be introduced to the notion of sports advertisers and advertising, sport tourism, sports marketing and management, the sports-media complex, sportscaster earnings, sports sponsorships, and so much more. Sports have become Super Sports, featuring Super Stars, and funded as a Super Business.

The burgeoning popularity of electronic and portable media have become prevalent. Broadcast and telecast media are more noticeable at actual sporting events, and the $213 billion dollar sports business demands our attention. According to Street & Smith's *Sports Busi-*

ness Journal (www.sportsbusinessjournal.com), the business of sport in the United States is one of the largest and fastest-growing industries—more than double that of the auto industry, and seven times that of the movie industry. It is divided into these categories:

- *Advertising* ($27.43 billion, 14.1 percent), including billboards, arena/stadium signage, ($16.39 billion), national network television ($4.69 billion), radio ($2.34 billion), national cable television ($1.78 billion), sports magazines ($1.45 billion), regional television ($570 million), and national syndicated television ($210.1 million).
- *Endorsements* ($897 million, .5 percent)
- *Sporting goods* ($25.62 billion, 13.2 percent)
- *Facility construction* ($2.48 billion, 1.3 percent)
- *Internet* ($239.1 million, .1 percent)
- *Licensed goods* ($10.50 billion, 5.4 percent), including $2.5 billion for the NFL, $2.5 billion for colleges, $2.3 billion for MLB, $1.2 billion NASCAR, $1 billion NBA, $900 million NHL, and $100 million for "other"
- *Media broadcast rights* ($6.99 billion, 3.6 percent): Big Four plus NASCAR $5.29 billion, colleges $1.06 billion, other $640 million
- *Professional services* ($15.25 billion, 7.8 percent), such as facility/event management $6.75 billion; financial, legal and insurance $5.81 billion, marketing and consulting $2.30 billion, and athlete representation $385 million
- *Spectator spending* ($26.17 billion, 13.4 percent), a toss-up between ticket sales of $11.74 billion and concessions, parking, on-site merchandise sales of $10.70 billion, and premium seating revenue of $3.73 billion
- *Sponsorships* ($6.40 billion, 3.3 percent), *medical spending* ($12.60 billion, 6.5 percent), and *travel* ($16.06 billion, 8.3 percent)
- *Multimedia* ($2.12 billion, 1.1 percent), *gambling* ($18.90 billion, $14.69 billion for pari-mutuels, $2.17 billion on the Internet, and $2.04 billion for legal sports books, 9.7 percent),
- *Operating expenses* ($22.98 billion, 11.8 percent)

SPORTS ADVERTISERS AND ADVERTISING

The bottom line of infotainment is sales. Advertisers do all they can to ensure they can be aware of how their products will be offered, by whom, when, and where. The real game, it turns out, is ratings— and the media battle for those ratings have led to unprecedented costs for sports broadcasting rights; sport serves as bait for sales. So it certainly comes as no surprise to learn that television executives and advertisers are extremely interested to know which sporting events and which sportscasters can draw and sustain audiences. Advertisers may not be invested in a particular sportscaster's level of expertise in technical, sport, and/or television issues—what they do concern themselves with is how well he or she can garner ratings points for particular target niches and programs. Also, they may or may not really care, either, whether audience members like or do not like a specific sportscaster, as long as they tune in—a classic case of "Cosellitis," (Howard) when large numbers of people admitted to tuning in to the man they loved to hate.

Interdependence between media advertising and sport can be dated to the earliest days of broadcasting. "Because sporting events already existed there were no sets to build, no writers and actors to hire. This made sports inexpensive to produce, a primary concern when the audience was small and not yet generating large advertising revenues," Stanley Baran (n.d.) reminds us. "The economic value of media rights fees and luxury suites in professional sports are enormous." Lee and Chun (2002) state, "As a result of increasing revenue in professional sports, team values have risen and will continue to rise to unpredictable levels." Currently, professional sports team revenues include $5.34 billion for the National Football League, $4.26 billion for Major League Baseball, $3.03 billion for the National Basketball Association, and $2.20 billion for the National Hockey League.

A classic example comes from NBC's *Gillette Cavalcade of Sports.* Owned not by the network, but by the razor advertiser, the show knew its audience for "Friday Night Fights" from Madison Square Garden, and remained a staple for some two decades after its start in 1943. As much as people thrilled to the antics of boxing greats like Sugar Ray Robinson, Rocky Marciano, Rocky Graziano, Archie Moore, Willie

Pep, and others, old timers report mostly remembering how Sharpie the Parrott would scream the sponsor's signature "Look sharp! Feel sharp! Be sharp! With Gillette razor blades!" (Fuller, 1992b). The original announcer for the pugilistic program was Bob Stanton, joined in 1948 by Ray Forrest and later replaced by Jimmy Powers. Like *Blue Ribbon Bouts* and cigarette-sponsored shows, sportscasters became associated with specific products. Ken Coleman (cited in Smith, 1998, p.166) remembers:

> In the 1950s and '60s, one company could afford more sponsor time on your game. In our case, Carling controlled things. We had them for quite some time. People will come up in Ohio— "Hey, Mabel!" Or in Boston, it's "Hi, neighbor, have a 'Gansett"—for all the Red Sox' years with Narragansett Beer.
>
> A broadcaster got identified with a product, particularly beer— which was good, except if the team changed sponsors. Then the identification hurt, and they'd fire you—*you,* but never Mabel.

Advertising, we know, is at the core of the sports industry. Whether print, electronic, or online, it is a $250+ billion dollar business in the United States, $324 billion worldwide (Schaaf, 2004; Andrews, 2004); teams contract with companies both locally and globally. It is just the way sports work. This is not a new phenomenon, either. Consider that more than a century ago, during the days of "yellow journalism" in the United States, the French newspaper *L'Auto* decided to stage a bike race as a publicity stunt; as circulation increased, the Tour de France was born.

Based on Nielsen Monitor-Plus data of 2004, and led by Anheuser-Busch's $293.4 million, the top fifty companies spent a combined $4.1 billion on sports advertising. Next in line: Chevrolet ($219.9 million), Cingular Wireless ($164.5 million), Ford ($143.1 million), Coca-Cola USA ($142.7 million), Visa International ($136.1 million), Miller Brewing Co. ($131.8 million), Proctor & Gamble ($130.6 million), Nissan North America ($111.1 million), and IBM Corp. ($105.4 million), followed by Dodge, McDonald's, Toyota, Capital One, Coors, Southwest Airlines, Home Depot, Subway, Nextel, and Allstate Insurance.

Also in 2004, TMS Media Intelligence (www.tms-mi.com) reported televised sports advertising at $8.05 billion. Led by professional football at $2.06 billion, that figure includes the Athens Olympics ($1.30 billion), then college basketball ($618.0 million), golf ($609.8 million), professional basketball ($584.8 million), auto racing ($584.1 million), professional baseball ($494.7 million), college football ($480.3 million), general sportscasts ($450.9 million), other sports shows ($442.1 million), tennis ($151.0 million), and hockey ($119.0 million). Specifically, ads for *Monday Night Football* sold for about $325,000 in 2004, about the same as spots for the NBA Finals, while for Fox's 2004 World Series, ads went for about $300,000 a unit.

NFL and ESPN constructed an eight-year (2006-2013), $8.8 billion deal for *Monday Night Football,* replacing ABC with a contract worth nearly double what it had been worth—allowing ESPN to go wireless and to offer Spanish-language telecasts. Prior to this broadcasting rights deal, another blockbuster negotiation took place in November of 2004, when the NFL announced agreements worth $11.5 billion, with CBS, Fox, NBC, and DirecTV.

Still the market leader in sports cable network services, ESPN remains incredibly profitable for its parent company, Walt Disney. Begun by the father-son team of Bill Rasmussen in 1979, the Connecticut-based sports channel set a new standard in programming. Today, the twenty-four-hour network boasts equity stakes in nineteen foreign networks, Internet service, ESPN Sports bars, and a theme park. ESPN-2, the decade's fastest growing cable channel, in nearly 40 million households, features live-event coverage. Other key sports broadcasters include the Fox Sports Network and Turner Broadcasting System's CNN/SI, under Time Warner, Inc.

Although television still commands the most money in terms of sports advertisements, do not discount radio, which draws in more than $2 billion annually for sports. Arbitron (www.arbitron.com) reports that some 41.8 million people listen to sports radio at least once a week; its annual advertising revenues are $2.2 billion, its broadcast rights fees $443 million. With about 150 all-sports radio stations around the country, 65 percent of the listeners being male, the format continues to be successful. Boston's WEEI-AM continues to walk away as the nation's top-rated sports radio station, peaking when the Red Sox won the World Series in 2004. Satellite radio has added yet more listeners.

For magazines, a full-page, four-color ad in *Sports Illustrated* costs $247,000. In addition, direct mail, billboards and other outdoor advertising, like bus wraps, video games (have you played "NASCAR Thunder"?), and embedded advertising are all reliable sources for sports promotions. One of the newest players in sports-related advertising is the Internet. Although networks, teams, and sponsors promote their Web sites, the possibilities for advertising are almost endless. Look at the role of wireless communications; our cell phones and PDAs can be rigged to get instant news about our favorite teams.

Most advertising comes as part of a bundle, such as having a network purchase a series or time slot. Much of it is event-specific; in 2002, for example, *SportsCenter* was getting $11,000 for a thirty-second ad while the U.S. Open finals commanded $175,000 and *Monday Night Football* was able to charge $325,000. Interest generally grows during the particular sporting season: a Major League Baseball (MLB) Division Series charged $90,000, which increased to $175,000 for a league championship; the World Series might go for $300,000 or more. Reviewing rights fees for the Winter Olympic Games provides a clearer case:

Year	Place	Network	Fee
1960	Squaw Valley	CBS	$50,000
1964	Innsbruck	ABC	594,000
1968	Grenoble	ABC	2.7 million
1972	Sapporo	NBC	6.4 million
1976	Innsbruck	ABC	10 million
1980	Lake Placid	ABC	15.5 million
1984	Sarajevo	ABC	91.5 million
1988	Calgary	ABC	309 million
1992	Albertville	CBS	243 million
1994	Lillehammer	CBS	300 million
1998	Nagano	CBS	375 million
2002	Salt Lake City	NBC	555 million
2006	Torino	NBC	613 million

Or, look at how rates for Super Bowl have escalated. The first one, January 15, 1967, (Green Bay, 35 to Kansas City, 10), ran simultaneously on CBS and NBC, the former charging $42,400 for a thirty-second ad, the latter $37,500. We can recall the tremors about "a million dollars a minute," but by now we just take it for granted that fees will continue to grow—to the point where Super Bowl XLI, February 4, 2007 (Indianapolis, 29 to Chicago, 17) had sticker-shock advertising rates of $2.6 million for thirty seconds. You may be interested in Bernice Kanner's *The Super Bowl of Advertising: How the Commercials Won the Game* (Bloomberg Press, 2003), as well as the results of a CBS/AOL (2004) report on the "Top 10 Greatest Super Bowl Commercials":

1. Coke (1980)—"Mean Jo Green"
2. Budweiser (2003)—"Replay/Jackass"
3. McDonalds (1993)—"Jordan vs. Bird"
4. Apple Computer (1984)
5. Tabasco (1998)
6. Pepsi (1992)—"Boys on beach"
7. Mountain Dew (2000)—"Cheetah"
8. Levi's (2002)—"Crazy legs"
9. Noxema (1973)—Joe Namath, Farah Fawcett
10. Xerox (1977)—"Miracle"

Sport finance involves many different sources of revenue, such as from concessions, broadcast rights, merchandising, ticket sales, parking and entry fees, luxury boxes and club seating, and much more. From the most recent data available, figures for advertising from sports includes $1.33 billion for ABC, $1.43 billion for CBS, and $472 million for NBC. Fox reportedly had $1.18 billion worth of sports-related advertising, ESPN $1.16 billion and ESPN-2 $219 million, Fox $1.18 billion, and specialty channels such as The Golf Channel had $88 million, The Speed Channel $63 million. Programming-wise, professional football leads the pack with sports revenue of $2 billion, followed by professional basketball at $579 million, golf nearly tied at $578 million, college basketball $521 million, auto racing $472 million, on down to $21 million for soccer and $11 million for rodeo (Miller, 2005).

Of course we, the fans, pay the price(s) for ridiculous players' salaries and related costs. Although the term "average" can be questionable, we have been told that the average annual salary for major league players was $2.9 million in 2004, those in the NBA coming in the highest at $4.9 million per player and those in the NHL coming in the lowest at $1.3 million. The NFL claims the highest average team payroll and MLB sits in the middle with salaries averaging $2.5 million per player. Add to this other financial issues such as league and team revenue sources, franchise value, gate receipts, media contracts, international sales, revenue sharing, and more and you begin to get the bigger picture.

In 2004, Team Marketing Report (www.teammarketing.com) found that, while baseball tickets have more than doubled in the past decade—some three times more than the Consumer Price Index has grown, ticket prices across the board are horrendously high. The National Football League, for example, averaged ticket prices of $54.75, the National Basketball Association $44.68, the National Hockey League $43.57, and Major League Baseball $19.82. Don't discount the secondary ticket market, worth some $20 billion, where scalpers and online ticket brokers can make money without hardly any regulations to prohibit them from adding to the economic impact of the sports world. Broadcasting rights for 2004 amounted to $7 billion, mostly made up of the Big Four leagues and NASCAR, which account for $5.3 billion, with televised sports advertising equaling about $8 billion.

Yet another form of advertising, a subject worthy of a book all on its own, is the notion of product placement in sport (Fuller, 1997c, 1999c). A multimillion dollar industry, it involves everything from promos for movies on MLB bases to logos for products at sports venues. Small wonder that our favorite athletes quaff our favorite sodas, or that sportscasters drive our dream cars. Or, that franchises such as Disney's Mighty Ducks are featured in Disney movies and media. Action sports, dominated with advertisements by Mountain Dew, are also associated with ESPN—which has recently signed on with Nielsen Media Research's Sponsorship Scorecard, to track sports product placements (Eggerton, 2005). Then again, it might all be virtual. People from different geographic locations see products placed just for their regions, sometimes in odd places, such as on the first-base line, on the field, even in the stadium.

SPORT TOURISM

The multibillion dollar sport tourism business, reported by Sport Business Associates (www.sportbusinessassociates.com) is "one of the fastest growing areas of the $4.5 trillion global travel and tourism industry." This statistic helps explain why cities and countries spend so much time, effort, and money to be chosen for events such as the Olympic Games, World Cup, and more; it helps us understand why sportscasters are encouraged to encourage us to want to be "live" at key sporting events. They hope, as you view gorgeous golf courses, luxurious beaches where volleyball might be played, challenging ski slopes, regular rugby towns and such, that you will want to visit that venue.

As an example of sports tourism's popularity, a simple Google search offers more than 52 million hits. You will note that areas as disparate as South Africa, Ireland, Greece, Fiji, India, Mexico, Cote d'Azur, Canada, Korea, Nepal, Abu Dhabi, Scotland, Malaysia, Moldova, Kenya, Sri Lanka, and so many more are encouraging tourists to partake in various local activities.

Academically, sports tourism is a fairly new discipline (Brabazon, 2006; Gibson, 2006; Higham, 2004; Hinch and Higham, 2004; Hudson, 2002; Ritchie and Adair, 2004; Robinson, 2004; Robinson, Gammon, and Jones, 2003; Rowe and Laurence, 2000; Ryan, 2003; Scarrott, 1999; Standeven and DeKnop, 1999; Turco, Riley, and Swart, 2002; Van Der Wagen, 2002; Weed and Bull, 2003); sports tourism mainly wants to discuss the impact and implications in a global frame. Sports tourism has its own journal, *The Journal of Sports Tourism,* which reports on historical, social, economic, and psychological determinants involved in the movement. Whether participatory or event-based, the notion of sports tourism can be significantly determined by sportscasters' comments.

ESPN offers a classic "virtual tour" for visitors to New York City on its Web site ESPN Sports Travel. Following a brief description of the Big Apple, and suggestions for transportation, it suggests sports experiences such as watching a game from the Yankee Stadium bleachers, catching some hoops at Madison Square Garden (the "World's Most Famous Arena"), watching the start of the New York Marathon from Brooklyn, attending the U.S. Open at the Arthur Ashe Stadium, biking the Central Park loop, and ice skating at Rockefeller Center, along with listing major attractions, local media, and lots of sporting ideas.

Sometimes, sheer numbers make the difference. Think of how many people enroll in marathons; Boston, the world's oldest annual marathon, dating to 1897, has 38,000 runners, while New York has a starting field of 30,000. Multiply those numbers by family and friends, along with regular rooters, and you get the idea. Baseball's spring training is a more recent entrant into the sport-destination category, especially since, in 2000, the Florida Sports Foundation reported that it brought $490 million to the local economy.

In the United States, sports-related travel is a $44.5 billion industry, broken down this way: $40.8 billion spent by spectators in general, $1.1 billion for colleges, $295 million for Big Four professional teams, and $2.3 "other." The Travel Industry Association of America (www.tia.org) reports that, in the past five years, 38 percent of American adults, or 75.3 million, "attended an organized sports event, competition, or tournament either as a spectator or participant while traveling 50 miles from home." Of these, 52.7 million adults, or 70 percent, took their most recent sports trip in the past year. Their favorites? Some 17 percent (33.7 million) said baseball or softball, 15 percent (30.3 million) football, 9 percent (18.8 million) basketball, 7 percent (15 million) auto racing, and 6 percent (1.1 million) favored golf.

SPORTS MARKETING AND MANAGEMENT

Another important area of study involves sports marketing and management. "Sports marketing," a term coined by *Advertising Age* describing consumer and industrial product use of sports as promotional vehicles, reports it is a $27.4 billion industry, broken down as follows:

- Billboard, arena/stadium signage: $16.4 billion
- National network television: $4.7 billion
- Radio: $2.3 billion
- National cable television: $1.8 billion
- Sports magazines: $1.4 billion
- Regional television (network and cable): $570 million
- National syndicated television: $210 million

Both sports marketing and sports management are popular fields of study, at undergraduate and graduate levels. There is a great deal, and growing, scholarship in the discipline (Brooks, 1994; Cuneen and Sidwell, 1994: DeSensi and Rosenberg, 1996; Graham, Goldblatt, and Neirotti, 2001; Howard and Crampton, 1995; Jones, 2003; Masteralexis, Barr, and Hums, 2004; McDonald and Milne, 1999; Miller, 1997; Milne and McDonald, 1999; Mullin, Hardy, and Sutton, 1993; Parkhouse, 1991; Parks, Zanger, and Quarterman, 1998; Pitts and Stotlar, 1996; Schaaf, 1995; Schlossberg, 1996; Scully, 1995; Shank, 1999; Stoldt, Dittmore, and Branvold, 2006; Stotlar, 1993; Thoma and Chalip, 1996; VanderZwaag, 1998; Wascovich, 1993), this brief list only meant to get you started in exploring more about it.

Sports Marketing

There's probably one thing you couldn't help but notice—lots and lots of ads. Gatorade is scrawled across the court floor in gigantic letters. Big Budweiser and Coke signs festoon the arena walls. Prominent players wear uniforms with equally prominent corporate logos, like those of Nike or Adidas. And it doesn't stop between quarters. You see dozens of television commercials featuring star basketball players pushing everything from cars, to shoes to life insurance to breakfast cereal. Even the sports arena is named after a bank, a group of stores, or some other corporation that agreed to sponsor the care and upkeep of the facility.

Although we may think of sports as fun and pure pleasure, sports is nothing if not a big business. Each year, sports organizations pull in billions of dollars from fans and corporate sponsorships, enough to reward their players with handsome multimillion dollar contracts.

Sports marketers are the people who handle the business side of sports. Some work for a league or sports association, like Major League Baseball or the National Basketball Association. Others work for teams, like the LA Lakers, the New York Yankees, or the Detroit Pistons. Some work on behalf of major companies, like Coca Cola or Budweiser, managing promotional campaigns and sponsorships of domestic and international sporting events. Others work as sports agents, representing professional athletes, negotiating contracts and endorsements, and otherwise managing an athlete's career. Still others organize sports-related events on behalf of sports organizations, associations, teams, or companies. (*Overview of Careers in Sports Marketing,* www.careerprospects.org)

This quotation best describes the wide range of sports marketing, demonstrating how it can involve both sport and nonsport products. Applying principles of marketing, it encompasses planning, consumer demographics and psychographics, endorsements, negotiations, the planning and/or coordination of sporting events, market research, promotions, merchandising, fund-raising, public relations, sponsorship strategizing, overseeing sports facilities, checking on ticket pricing and sales, and generally following the field of sport, alert to trends that might affect individual athletes, teams, and organizations. Careerwise, sports marketers might major in business, economics, communications, or even in the discipline itself. Entry-level employees working for a professional team might make about $30,000, but with experience that number can increase to $75,000 or more, and of course key sports marketers can earn double that or more.

In their own way, sportscasters are a form of sports marketer, keeping up with the field and its participants, attending events, and making sure they are aware of many stories beyond mere statistics. Mary A. Hums (2001) points out how, in the very competitive sport industry, "It's not what you know it's who you know" and who knows you. To get in the door, she suggests KEYS: Knowledge, Experience, Your hard work, and Skills. Other good advice can be found in Field, 2004, Heitzmann, 2004, and Plunkett, 2006.

Mark H. McCormack (1930-2003), the visionary pioneer of the field of sports marketing who founded IMG and a billion-dollar-a-year business, began by turning Arnold Palmer into golf's first television celebrity athlete. Clients returned 20 percent of their endorsement salaries, 10 percent of their prize money, and 3 percent of their salaries to the company, yet they lined up to be part of the program. In addition to athletes, sporting events (Wimbledon, U.S. Golf, U.S. Olympic Committee), and other events (e.g., the Nobel Foundation, Oxford University, the Grammys, the Kennedy Space Center, the Smithsonian), sportscasters John Madden and Bob Costas are affiliated with the company.

Sports Management

Another vocation dealing with sport business, sports management might set you up to study and then to practice a range of occupations from dealing with professional or college sports, recreational sports, events or facility management, sports information, and/or working with sports marketing. There actually has been quite a bit of concern over how college sports can get too caught up in commercialism (Sperber, 2001; Zimbalist, 2001; Porto, 2003), so their management at this level is particularly important.

THE SPORTS-MEDIA COMPLEX

Missing from much of the discussion of the economics of sport is an analysis of the extent to which corporate sport—from schools, to universities, to the pros—is an institution with wildly distorted spending priorities. The vast, *vast* majority of funds are spent on creating, supporting, and promoting a very small number of sports: in the United States, sports' economic center is boys' and men's basketball, baseball, football, and (to a lesser extent) ice hockey. Women's sports and men's marginal sports receive far less economic support than these 'big four' do, and this fact as much as anything else helps to explain the continued hegemony of these central men's sports. (Messner, 2002, p. 76)

Looking back at a century of sports business, Phil Schaaf's *Sports, Inc.* of 2004 traces what he considers the first phase of the modern era as the period between the 1896 (modern) Olympic Games and the 1975 ruling granting free agency to baseball players. Today, we have evolved into what can be called a "Corporate-Sports Complex," wherein sponsorship influenced by multinational companies such as Nike, Anheuser-Busch, Visa, IBM, Gillette, FedEx, and others goes far beyond simple promotion of products and services. Variously referred to as "MediaSport," "sportainment," or simply the "sports-media complex," it is clearly an area worthy of study.

The symbiotic relationship of the sports-media complex has been well-documented. A number of books have been written about the interdependence between television and sports (Guttman, 1988; Hofmann and Greenberg, 1989; Klatell and Marcus, 1988; Koppett, 1981; Lipsky, 1981); Noverr, 1983; Powers, 1984); Rader, 1984; Real, 1989).

Led by *Madden NFL 2005* for PlayStation 2 (which sold 1.3 million copies the first week of its release, at $46 a pop), sports video games average around $1 billion annually; other popular titles include *ESPN NFL 2K5* for PlayStation 2 and *NBA Live 2005* for PlayStation 2. As David Rowe (1999, p. 67) states, "Sport and the sports media, as cultural good par excellence, are clearly a central element in a larger process (or set of processes) that is reshaping society and culture."

It is easy to see why some people say we live in a time of, as Sungwook Choi (2005) calls it, "hyper-commercialism" in sports media. As a case study, he analyzed ads from one day in the 2004 World Series (Boston Red Sox versus St. Louis Cardinals); the game lasted nearly three-and-a-half hours, it also included pre- and post-game shows, with commercials before, during (between innings, during changes of pitchers, etc.), and afterward. Choi's findings: "Of this time, two hours, 29 minutes and 12 seconds were devoted to the game and the introduction of players. And 45 minutes and 25 seconds were allocated to commercial advertisements. Including Fox's advertising of their own programs, which took up four minutes and 15 seconds, the total advertising time increases to 49 minutes and 40 seconds" (p.18). Actual advertising time, then, is about 28 percent of the broadcast.

SPORTSCASTER EARNINGS

Although of course there are enormous differences between where a sportscaster works and what his or her experience may have been in terms of salary, about a decade ago they ranged from $12,000 to $400,000 (Lainson, 1998b). To date, it is tough to match John Madden's 2002 salary of $7.5 million for NFL games on Fox—making him the highest-paid sportscaster in the world, wealthier even than most of the players he called.

Drawing on data from Chronicle Guidance Publications and the Occupation Outlook Handbook, Knight Ridder (www.krponline.com/pdf/Sports_Broadcasting.pdf) the following is a chart showing "Jobs in the Field" of sports broadcasting from 2003:

Job title	Place of work	Kind of work	Average salary
Local TV sportscaster	TV studio, local sports venues	Writes and delivers sports news; interviews sports figures, and covers sporting events.	$68,900 (weekday) 37,200 (weekend)
Local radio sportscaster	Radio studio, local sports venues	Writes and delivers sports news; interviews sports figures, and covers sporting events.	$12,500-30,600
Play-by-play announcer, color commentator	Sports venues coverage; tapes interviews and stories relating to the event.	Provides live game	$50-7,500 per game

Sportswriter salaries might range from $19,000 to $24,000; those working for daily newspapers or monthly magazines earn from $23,000 to $85,000 plus (Field, 2004, p. 127). The good news is that employment prospects for sports reporters are good. Sports columnists have a salary range from $15,000 to more $1 million, but prospects there are only fair.

"When you have a sports broadcaster make ten times the salary of the president of the United States, it's difficult to argue against the contention that the tail is wagging the dog, and that's exactly what has happened in network television" (Spence, 1988, p. 328).

SPORTS SPONSORSHIP

One of the most visible aspects of modern sport is its strong links to commercial enterprise. Stadiums and arenas bear the names of businesses that pay to buy the naming rights to these venues. Commercial sponsors' logos appear on athletes' clothing and equipment, on the facilities in which they play, and in the titles of the vents in which they compete. Media companies spend vast sums of money on rights to broadcast sporting events, and advertisers pay to promote their products and services in the commercial breaks during the screening of these events. . . There are few businesses today that do note have, or have not had, some link to sport and there are even fewer sports leagues, teams, events or organizations that do not have some commercial aspect to their operation. (Slack, 2004, p. xxii)

According to IEG Sponsorship Report (www.sponsorship.com), sports sponsorships in 2004 were valued at $7.7 billion—an increase of more than 8.6 percent. The infrastructure for sport sponsorship has changed dramatically from the days when sales of admissions and sales of food for fans were bottom-line venues of support. Today, while on-site ticket sales are still important, television coverage and contracts, whether local, national, and/or on cable, reign supreme. Add to that, though, a range of other revenue streams, such as radio, licensing, team sponsorships, global marketing agreements, and stadium-related sources like parking fees, concession stands, various seating options, team products (well beyond banners), and clever billboards to remind us who is really paying big.

Dating to the 1960s, when groups such as International Management Group (IMG), (Bob) Woolf Associates, and ProServ started full-service sports marketing/sponsorship agencies, sports marketing grew during the 1970s and exploded with the excitement of the 1984 Olympic Games in Los Angeles. Advertisers like Coca-Cola became "official" sponsors. rEvolution (www.revolutionworld.com), based in Chicago, announced in 2005 that it had established a strategic partnership with the NCAA for its semifinal and final games of the Division 1 Men's Basketball Championship, marking a new hospitality plan in the sports marketing world.

Although we associate names like Tiger Woods, Lance Armstrong, and Michael Jordan as the mega-stars of sport, other sportscasters have become household names. Some examples that come to mind include the following: Mel Allen for White Owl cigars; Pat Summerall—True Value; Merlin Olsen—FTD; Bob Uecker as one of the "Miller Lite All-Stars"; Howard Cosell—Fruit of the Loom; Phil Rizzuto—The Money Store; Joe Theismann—Colonial Penn Life Insurance; John Madden—Ace Hardware, Outback Steakhouse, Verizon Wireless, Rent-A-Center, Miller Lite, Sirius Satellite Radio, and Tinactin; Don Meredith—Lipton Tea; Dick Vitale—DiGiorno pizza and Hooters; O.J. Simpson for Hertz, Jim Palmer for Jockey shorts; Terry Bradshaw—Radio Shack; Keith Jackson for Shoney's, Gatorade, and Ice Breakers' Ice Cubes; Keith Olbermann—Boston Market; Joe Buck for Holiday Inn, plus "Slamma-lamma-ding-dong!" for Budweiser. No doubt you can think of many more. It can work in reverse, too, as Harry Caray pointed out (cited in Smith, 1995, p. 246):

> Now, I love Budweiser. Once, I'd been sponsored by Falstaff—I had Bud in my refrigerator. I was sponsored by Meister Brau—had Bud in my refrigerator. I drank Budweiser for, number one, its taste. Number two, when I started working for Anheuser, I wasn't making much but bought about $5,000 worth of its stock. That stock has tripled 3 for 1 at least 15 times; 2 for 1, at least 10 times; 3 for 2 stock dividends, at least five. Anheuser-Busch made me rich with a lousy little $5,000 investment 40 years ago, and here I am drinking its competitor! People think I'm a smart investor. Little do they know how dumb I am and how smart I am by being lucky. They do know that to this day I drink nothing—well, almost nothing—but Bud.

Athletes' endorsements continue to be another major money source; coming in at about $900 million, the top sports stars include LeBron James, Yao Ming, and Dale Earnhardt, Jr. Of course you would have guessed the highest-paid athlete is Tiger Woods, at $87 million, followed by Michael Schumacher at $60 million. The list then goes to at least two dozen more males (Oscar De La Hoya, $38 million; Michael Vick, $37.5 million; Shaquille O'Neal, $33.4 million; Michael Jordan, $33 million, etc.) before reaching the highest-paid women athletes: Maria Sharapova ($18.2 million), Serena Williams ($12.7 million), Annika Sorenstam ($7.3 million), Venus Williams ($6.5 million), and Lindsay Davenport ($6 million). "Today, sports images bombard people from all angles, and color, creed, or nationality have almost no bearing," Phil Schaff (2004, p. 98) reminds us.

> Pepsi runs advertisements with Sammy Sosa and Ken Griffey Jr. Tiger Woods, in his twenties, is the most appealing pitchman in the world. Michael Jordan, the most important endorser prior to Woods, ruled spokesman territory for almost a dozen years. George Foreman signed the largest contract in the history of sports marketing when he sold the rights of his name to Salton for the George Foreman Grill.

In terms of sponsorship, probably motor sports dominate. "Some of the tracks have sponsor names, the cars are plastered with sponsor decals, and the drivers wear uniforms that often look like walking billboards—and they usually mention all of them, particularly in television interviews," (Dick Mittman, 2003, p. 79, Indianapolis Motor Speedway/Indy Racing League).

Whatever the distance being covered, it requires sports journalists who can be flexible in terms of both moving around to different places and being able to filter blatant promotion and public relations from general reportage. "Sportscasting would be the greatest job in the world, if only they *let* you broadcast," (Curt Gowdy cited in Len Berman, 2005, p. 61), who interpreted the statement to mean "all the outside pressures: the commercials, the promos, the ratings, management tinkering, personal appearances, sportswriters just waiting to pounce on every mistake." The real mistake is not realizing that sport really is just business—business as usual.

To learn more about the economic aspects of sports, sportscasters, and sportscasting, here are some suggested resources: Andrews, 2001; Aris, 1990; Berri, Schmidt, and Brook, 2006; Colangelo and Sherman, 1999; Conrad, 2006; Fizel, Gustafson, and Hadley, 1999; Fort, 2006; Goff and Tollison, 1990; Goldman and Papson, 1998; Gorman and Calhoun, 1994; Graham, 1994; Grant, Leadly, and Zygmont, 2007; Gratton and Solberg, 2007; Hamil, Michie, Oughton, and Warby, 2006; Hofmann and Greenberg, 1989; Horne, 2006; Jackson and Andrews, 2003; Jeanrenaud and Kessene, 2006; Jennings, 1990; Jozsa, 2006; Klatell and Marcus, 1988; Leeds and von Allmen, 2004; Lewis, 2003; Milne and McDonald, 1999; Quirk and Fort, 1999; Rosentraub, 1997; Schaaf, 2004; Sheehan, 1996; Shropshire and Davis, 2003; Smith and Westerbeek, 2004; Staudohar, 2000; Staudohar and Mangan, 1991; Weiss, 1993; Wenner, 1989, 1998; Yost, 2006; Zimbalist, 2003, 2006.

Chapter 4

Audiences for Sports and Sportscasting

Take me out to the ball game,
Take me out with the crowd.
Buy me some peanuts and Cracker Jacks,
I don't care if I never get back,
Let me root, root, root for the home team,
If they don't win it's a shame.
For it's one, two, three strikes, you're out,
At the old ball game.

(Lyrics by Jack Norwood, music by Albert Von Tilzer, 1908)

U.S. SPORTS SPECTATORS

The discourse of the TV sports commentators provides a model of sports consumption which reinforces the mode of attention demanded by postindustrial work. As with most television programming, the soundtrack of any televised sports event is addressed simultaneously to the attentive spectator and the distracted fan. In TV sports, the commentators in particular mediate between the flow of sports programming and the distractions of the viewing situation. The direct address of the commentators is thus central to the discursive organization of the sports narrative, and to the placement of spectators in relation to the sports metatext, and to each other (Rose and Friedman, 1997, p. 5).

Are you humming? Are you in the mood for ballpark goodies? Chances are that if you are reading this book you are a sports fan. But maybe you have never considered who "we" all are, and why we have been drawn to sporting events since the dawn of time. "Ironically, many of the apologias offered in defense of sports spectatorship have relied heavily if not exclusively on the alleged cathartic benefit of watching aggressive sporting events," Bryant and Raney (2000, p. 155). This chapter begins with U.S. sports spectators, and then discusses global audiences and special sporting events.

Chances are, you have thrilled at Don Larsen's "perfect game" in the 1956 World Series (his license plate is DLOOO—his initials, plus his no-runs, no-hit, no-errors score); "Broadway Joe" Namath's help with the New York Jets in beating Baltimore in Super Bowl III (1969); Billy Jean King's winning the tennis "Battle of the Sexes" by defeating Bobby Riggs in 1973; Secretariat winning the "Triple Crown" of thoroughbred horse races in 1973; Seattle Slew in 1977, or Affirmed in 1978 (both horses); the USA hockey team's "Miracle on Ice" in the 1980 Moscow Olympics; gymnast Mary Lou Retton's "Perfect 10" vault at the 1984 Los Angeles Olympics; Florence Griffith Joyner's ("Flo-Jo") being declared the world's fastest woman (note: as of 2006, her World Records in the 100- and 200-meter races still hold) at the 1988 Seoul Olympics; the Nancy Kerrigan-Tanya Harding "incident" at the 1994 U.S. Figure Skating Championships; boxer Mike Tyson's biting a part of Evander Holyfield's ear in 1997; Michael Jordan's being named the greatest North American athlete of the twentieth century by ESPN; boxer Muhammad Ali's (born Cassius Clay) being crowned "Sportsman of the Century" by *Sports Illustrated;* soccer player Brandi Chastain's bra-bearing celebration at the 1999 Women's World Cup final; Janet Jackson's "Nipplegate" halftime controversy at Super Bowl XXXVIII; Dale Earnhardt's last-lap fatal crash in the 2001 Daytona 500; Cal Ripkin's consecutive game "streak" (2,632 games, from 1982-1998) with the Baltimore Orioles; Bode Miller's becoming, in 2005, the first American since 1983 to win the overall alpine skiing World Cup title; golf champion Tiger Woods' earning record of $87 million in 2005—making him the highest paid professional athlete; Lance Armstrong's record-setting seven consecutive wins of the Tour de France (1999-2005); soccer player Zinedine "Zizou" Zidane's controversial penalty spot kick (and head butt) in the 2006 FIFA World Cup; and so much more. Chances are that you are a sports fan.

Back in 1982, Bryant, Brown, Comisky, and Zillman wondered whether the effects of sports commentary were stylistically dependent: Did audiences react to notions of hated enemies or enjoyable competition? What they found was, "Sports commentary can so dramatically alter the viewers' perception[s] of players and play is [sic] noteworthy in its own right . . . Sports commentary appears to be a very powerful tool in influencing viewers' perception[s] of play and their enjoyment of an athletic contest" (p. 118).

"The importance of mediated sports today is evident in both their scale and intensity," (Michael Real, 1998, p. 14). "The huge scale of media sports appears in audience sizes of many millions for televised sporting events and media contracts for billions of dollars. The scale is there in the explosion of sports talk radio, sport magazines, Internet sport sites, and consequent global sport marketing, inflated salaries and endorsement contracts." Real (2006) has expanded this notion about the role of the Internet: "From its explosive development in the last decade of the twentieth century, the World Wide Web has become an ideal medium for the dedicated sports fanatic and a useful resource for even the casual fan. Its accessibility, interactivity, speed, and multimedia content are triggering a fundamental change in the delivery of mediated sports, a change for which no one can yet predict the outcome" (p. 171).

Expanding on the notion of television in the mediation of our sport spectatorship, Duncan and Brummett (1987, p. 176) conducted baseline research, " what sports are for people is determined in part by the nature of the medium through which they are experienced." They consider, specifically, how television incorporates narrative, intimacy, commodification (interweaving commercials into content), and rigid time segmentation into sporting events. Later, they constructed a theory about visual pleasures that fans get from watching televised sports (Brummett and Duncan, 1990, p.240), concluding:

> Clearly, the spectators entered into the persona of the "fan" as they entered the house. This persona would *integrate* the pleasures and sources of pleasures derived from viewing the game.

The raw materials for *fetishistic* pleasure were provided by the commentators' discourse and by the usual technological devices, which allowed the spectator to unify the many passing scenes of the game into the gaze of fascination. John Madden and Pat Summerall kept up the usual constant patter of commentary, inviting the viewer to watch with observations about the ongoing game. Color commentator Madden called fans' attention to where key players were in the lineup and, at the end of the Vikings' first possession, told fans to look for a punt block.

"Television has essentially trivialized the experience of spectator sports," Benjamin G. Rader wrote back in 1984 (p. 5). "With its enormous power to magnify and distort images, to reach every hamlet in the nation with events from anywhere in the world, and to pour millions of additional dollars into sports, television—usually with the enthusiastic assistance of the sports moguls themselves—has sacrificed much of the unique drama of sports to the requirements of entertainment."

Not surprisingly, interest in fandom comes from a number of disciplines (Costas, 2001; Crawford, 2005; Elias and Dunning, 1986; Hughson Inglis, and Free, 2004; Hughson and Free, 2006; Rein, Kotler, and Shields, 2006; Sandvoss, 2003; St. John, 2004; Wann et al., 2001)—business, communications, sociology, physical education/human kinetics, among them. Sport spectatorship, as one of many media gratifications, draws on complex processes such as attitudes and behaviors. Roone Arledge's slogan, after all, was "Take the fan to the game, not the game to the fan" (cited in Johnson, 1971, p. 79). Ron Powers (1984, p. 18) has pointed out that, "The hallmarks of Arledge's style were a high respect for the power of *story* over the human imagination, a probing visual intimacy with the subject matter, a relentless, even obsessive preoccupation with the smallest detail." Because the fan has so many available outlets, though, marketers need to zero in on how to capture and maintain them. It is particularly exciting, though, when a sportscaster of Bob Costas' stature brings us his personal paean to baseball; although he worries about issues like superstar players, wild cards, payroll disparities, interleague play, and owners, he nevertheless presents a balanced view of his favorite sport.

American sports fans, according to a 2004 ESPN Sports Poll that was conducted by TNS Sports (www.tnsglobal.com), found some 67.5 percent followed the NFL, 60.1 percent MLB, 56.1 percent college football, 48.5 percent the NBA, 46.8 percent figure skating, 46.3 percent college basketball, 43.6 percent extreme sports, and 43.4 percent NASCAR. Following these came horse racing (37.4 percent), fishing (36.6 percent), the PGA (36.4 percent), boxing (38.2 percent), the NHL (32.7 percent), the WNBA (32.0 percent), and the WTA (31.5 percent). We obviously have wide-ranging fandoms. In terms of sports attendance, baseball led the pack with 120.3 million, followed by football (72.0 million), basketball (67.2 million), hockey (60.7 million), auto racing (35.9 million), horse racing (30.6 million), rodeo (23.6 million), golf (12.5 million), soccer (7.2 million), greyhound racing (6.4 million), action sports (4.1 million), tennis (3.4 million), volleyball (2.7 million), lacrosse (1.2 million), bowling (538,000), curling (458,000), and figure skating (349,000). Any surprises?

PGA Tour telecasts reach more than 68 percent of U.S. households. Generally considered the heir to Michael Jordan as the "world's most famous athlete," Tiger Woods draws attention to his sport like no other player in history— Arnold Palmer and Jack Nicklaus included. The average golf fan watches twenty-nine telecasts over the course of the season. The U.S. Tennis Association (USTA) had revenue of $221 million, and earned a record $26 million in 2005, its second year with a positive net income.

It may surprise you to learn that, according to *American Demographics,* about one-quarter of all kids interact with sports media on a daily basis (Miller, 2004). In a study of U.S. children ages eight to seventeen, Wilson (1999, p. 10) found that some 94 percent "watch, read about, or listen to sports using one of eight media—television, radio, newspapers, books, magazines, video games, the Internet, or the movies. Among boys, 98 percent use some form of sport media. The percentage among girls is 90." At the other end of the age spectrum, a woman from Chicopee Falls, Massachusetts, named Kathryn Gemme, who died recently at age 112, was recently declared the ultimate Red Sox fan—imagine living long enough to break Babe Ruth's "Curse"!

Sports audiences in the United States are the target market for greedy programmers who hope to sell them to greedy advertisers. Small wonder, then, that Daniel L. Wann and colleagues (2001, p. 2) also refer to sports spectators as "sport consumers." Allen Guttmann (1988), professor of English and American Studies at Amherst College, attributes our fascination with sport as a reflection of our culture due to the fact that they are "secular, bureaucratic, and specialized," theoretically democratic in terms of equality among competitors. Traditionally, when teams establish markets they try to expand fan bases not only for attendance but also to lure and then maintain periphery businesses such as in-stadium vendors, public relations firms, and sports marketers.

Niche markets, determined by demographics, are clearly important in the sports industry. It reminds me of a funny *New Yorker* cartoon by Mischa Richter (August 26, 1991) titled "Baseball reaches for the PBS audience." Two sportscasters are sitting in the booth, one commenting about a player, "He has the clean precision of Ingres." His counterpart responds, "Yes, and even more remarkable, he combines it with the swift emotional delivery of Van Gogh."

Back in 1983, sports historian Benjamin G. Rader declared that we were living in the "Age of Spectators." Radar saw television (Rader, 1984, p. 210), more than any other single force, as transforming spectator sports into trivial affairs. Sports would never again be an arena populated by pristine heroes. No longer are sports as effective in enacting the ritual embodying traditional American values, he determined, and no longer did they evoke the same intensity, the same loyalty, or the same commitment. For sports are no longer so transcendent in American life. This is how Leonard Koppett (1994, p. 2) paints the picture:

> As mass entertainment, intensively commercialized spectator sports play a larger role in American culture than in any other society, past or present. In no other country today do the amounts of money spent, tickets bought, games played, livelihoods involved, words printed, hours televised, or spinoff industries concerning sports match American totals, either by absolute or proportional measure.

In the early days, wrestling drew not just the barroom crowd; advertisers soon found that women were watching, too: "Attracted by the scantily clad and well-muscled grapplers, the female audience was not so much interested in wrestling technique as it was in watching their heroes pose and preen under the hot television lights. One eastern wrestling promoter, waxing optimistic, estimated that women comprised 90 percent of the whole audience (Neal-Lunsford, 1992, p. 67).

Today, the Super Bowl attracts some 130 million viewers—55 million of whom are women, mostly due to its massive hyping on television. Studies have shown that nearly one-third of Americans follow television sports daily and another 50 percent listen to it on the radio. Special sporting events in the United States such as the Indy 500, the Super Bowl, The Masters, the U.S. Open, NBA Finals, the World Series (which celebrated its 100th birthday in 2003), the Kentucky Derby, and any number of others make particularly interesting case studies in terms of sportscasting and its audiences.

Traditionally, when teams establish markets they try to expand fan bases not only for attendance but also to lure and then maintain periphery businesses such as in-stadium vendors, public relations firms, and sports marketers. When we want details on fandom in the United States, some of the best sources include Nielsen ratings, Scarborough Marketing, Inc., the Gallup Organization, and Harris Interactive, Inc. Nielson Sports (www.nielsensports.com), for example, bills itself this way: "This division tracks ad spending with sporting events, as well as national and local TV ratings for sports teams—by game, month, season, and league standing. Nielsen Sports gives clarity to audience demographics, brand preferences, and attitudes among sports fans."

Len Berman (2005, p. 3), who has hosted the sports "bloopers" program *Spanning the World* since 1987, claims that, "As a nightly sportscaster, at times I think I'm doing sports for the sports impaired." Yet, Americans know what they like and don't like in their sportscasters. The late Red Auerbach, general manager of the Celtics, describes how sportscaster Johnny Most served as a link between generations of Boston sports fans: "He was funny and entertaining, but don't misunderstand. Johnny Most was no clown. He understood the intricacies and theories of the game, and sure, he loved the Celtics, just as they loved him, and he made no secret of it. Only a phony would have denied that, and Johnny was no phony" (cited in Carey, 2003, p. viii).

American audiences form a unique breed, oftentimes enjoying sports that are not as popular in other parts of the world. For example, our national pastime of baseball is really only popular in parts of Asia, and Formula One rules in Europe, even if since 1999 it has taken place in Bahrain, China, Malaysia, Turkey, and the United States (Arron and Hughes, 2003; Collins, 2004; Hilton, 2003; Hughes and Arron, 2003; Matchett, 2000; McCarthy, 2003; Turner, 2005; Watkins, 1997). Also known as F1, or Grand Prix racing, it reportedly drew 54 billion viewers in more than 200 countries for the 2001 season. Resistant to women drivers, even if it uses scantily clad "grid girls," and looking for venues that will be supportive of cigarette advertising, Formula One is yet another classic example of sport as big business in the global sphere.

Yet in the United States, nothing matches our on-site enthusiasm for NASCAR. In its most recent annual ESPN Sports Poll, of approximately 21,000 U.S. sports fans surveyed, well over 40 percent report being fans; no wonder the networks paid $2.4 million for NASCAR broadcast races from 2001-2006. One of the largest wholly owned family businesses in the world, NASCAR was started at Daytona Beach in 1948 by Bill France, Sr., and the France family still owns its sanctioning body. Furthermore, Nextel's $750 million naming-rights pact for its top racing circuit signifies the largest sponsorship deal in sports history. Generating annual sponsorship revenues of $50 million and licensing fees of $35 million (licensed merchandise makes about $1.3 billion each year), NASCAR's Daytona 500 and Brickyard 400 are estimated to have local economic impacts of $240 million and $220 million, respectively (Miller, 2005).

The World Wrestling Entertainment (WWE), owned and operated by Vince McMahon, has eight weekly programs that include a three-ring action show, three highlights shows, and a magazine. Drawing about 24 million viewers per month, its pay-per-view events generated in excess of 7.1 million buys in 2003. "It is a fascist spectacle of male power, depicting a world where might makes right and moral authority is exercised by brute force," Henry Jenkins (1997, p. 76). "It engages in the worst sort of jingoistic nationalism. It evokes racial and ethnic stereotypes that demean groups even when they are intended to provide positive role models. It provokes homophobic disgust and patriarchal outrange against any and all incursions beyond heterosexual male dominance."

Minor league sports generate $1.6 billion annually. Sportscasters in the minor leagues, as well as for the many athletic teams sponsored by colleges and universities in the United States, generate $10.7 billion annually; sportscasters play a unique role in terms of linking fans with favorite coaches and teams (*Sports Business Journal;* Fulks, 1998).

Soccer, known as "football" to those outside the United States, dominates the globe as a favorite sport (Finn and Guilianotti, 2000; Foer, 2004; French, 2003; Garland and Rowe, 2001; Guilianotti, Bonney, and Hepwarth, 1994; Hamil, Michie, Oughton, and Warby, 2006; Murphy, Williams, and Dunning, 1990; Sandvoss, 2003; Szymanski and Zimbalist, 2005). Only recently, have American media begun to incorporate it into sporting clothing or to feature soccer star David Beckham in magazines (Cashmore and Parker, 2003). Beckham recently relocated to Los Angeles. The movie *Hooligans* (2005) with Elijah Wood is a good sign that soccer is slowly seeping into the United States. Some believe that our sports marketplace is already overloaded, yet the issue of boredom is brought up relative to why there isn't a wider audience for soccer (the "nothing happens" refrain).

American football, according to a Harris Poll (www.harrisinteractive .com) is our favorite sport, which can be a frightening statistic when one considers the many implications surrounding the sport. "Football's historical prominence in sport media and folk culture has sustained a hegemonic model of masculinity that prioritizes competitiveness, asceticism, success (winning), aggression, violence, superiority to women, and respect for and compliance with male authority" (Sabo and Panepinto, 1990, p. 115). Football fans obviously see the game differently, depending on their experience(s) with it. Former players, for example, might have a clearer eye as to what could/should/would work best, when and where. Adam Gopnik (2007, p. 39) shares an incredible insight into how the famous quarterback

Joe Namath responded to a question about another Jets quarterback: "I've only watched him this year as a fan, on television. I haven't had a chance to break down the passing game to see if Chad's going to the right spots or going to the wrong receiver." It makes us all wonder how much we really "watch" at all.

Approaching football as cultural text, Michael Oriard (1993, p. xxii) suggests:

> [football] can suggest more generally how meaning is produced in a mass-mediated society. Popular spectator sports such as football differ in important ways from related cultural representations; in contrast to movies and television dramas, for example, football games are unscripted, their action real. But . . . whatever the violence in football means to specific spectators, the issue of violence is inescapable.

Football certainly has drawn much academic interest (Barry, 2001; Benedict and Yeager, 1998; Jenkins, 1996; Fuller, 1992f, 1999, 2005a; Nelson, 1994; Oriard, 1993; Sabo and Panepinto, 1990; Schwartz, 1998; Trope and Delsohn, 1987; Welch, 1997). Fuller (2005a, pp. 3-4) deconstructs football rhetoric:

> Strategically, the goal of American football seems pretty basic: eleven players on each team, *offense* or *defense,* try to reach *end zones* where they can *score.* The team with the most points wins. The ball, sometimes (erroneously) referred to as a pigskin, is handled by a ballcarrier, who hopes to keep it away from ball hawks. So, there might be body blocking, butt-blocking, chop blocking, power blocking, roughing a kicker or passer, ball-stripping, zone blocking, flea-flicking, spiking, encroaching or eating the ball. A player might be a headhunter, a heavy hitter, a scrimmage kicker, a sledgehammer, a jumper, a monster, a punishing runner, or a punter. Opponents are always on the lookout for weak sides. He might deliberately spear a fellow player's helmet, make a sucker play, sack or shank the ball, make a plunge, or tackle a ball carrier. There are even some ghoulish terms, a coffin corner being one of four places where sidelines

and goal lines intersect, a dead ball one out of play and dead-man (or sleeper) play referring to an illegal pretense for passing. A dying quail, when a toss lacks speed and power, can also been called a duck ball. Skull sessions, also known as chalk talk, review and predict plays. At the other extreme, how does one explain that football lingo also includes "Hail Mary," a low-percentage desperation pass that appeals to a higher power for completion. It may not surprise you that there can be intentional grounding, intercepts, slashing, "unsportsmanlike conduct," and a disabled list. Or that possession is of prime importance.

Baseball audiences are intimate, declares Dick Enberg (2004, p. 102), especially on radio: "A baseball announcer on radio has a connection with an audience that no one else does, touching a fan base that cares deeply about the team." In the early days of baseball broadcasting, Red Barber was one of the best; according to his biographer, Bob Edwards (1993, p. 15), he "moved people. A microphone was his magic wand. Either he knew what people cared about or he made them care simply because he had raised the subject. It seemed to me that no one was indifferent to him or what he had to say. He knew how to reach listeners in a way that no one else on radio could." Miller (1997, pp. 245-6) entreats us to consider "any list of great baseball broadcasters. Each has or had a unique style, a different way of making the broadcasts informing and entertaining. But despite the wide variation in styles, they all come back to the same fundamentals: They tell the truth, give a good, accurate picture of the game, and they earned credibility with the fans." Between playoffs, the All-Star Game, World Series, and general broadcasts, our "national pastime" (Billet and Formwalt, 1995; Fuller, 1990a, 1991, 1995b, 2006b), despite insane ticket prices, continues to be a favorite.

Basketball, our third favorite fandom—especially during "March Madness," when the NCAA tournaments take place, has recently embraced women's college basketball among its followers. It, too, has received academic attention and sportscaster memoirs (Andrews, 2001; Boyd, 2003; Boyd and Shropshire, 2000; George, 1999; Reynolds, 2005; Vitale, 1988, 2003; Williams and Friedman, 1999).

Women's college basketball also has conference watchers, retail goods, trivia, blogs, and any number of assorted antics by fans.

Then there is hockey—a national pastime in Canada (Gruneau and Whitson, 1993; Howell, 2001; White and Young, 1999), but equally popular in the United States. In the United Kingdom, Crawford and Gosling (2004) have studied the "Puck Bunny" phenomenon— female followers of The Manchester Storm, and has found them to be similar in knowledge of ice hockey and commitment as their male counterparts. "Hockey is a terrific live spectacle, featuring lots of crowd-pleasing hits and the occasional scuffle between testy foes," writes Jeff Gordon (2003, p. 30). He continues:

But even seasoned fans can be left scratching their heads after a bang-bang scoring play. Sure, some goals result from the exciting end-to-end rushes and beautiful stick-to-stick passing that build anticipation before the climactic moment. But most goals result from broken plays. Hockey is a game of mistakes. An errant pass, a puck hopping over a stick, a funny bounce off the boards, a weird deflection in front of the goal . . . and the puck is in the net. What happened? Television replays are a beat writer's best friend, because you don't always have the time or opportunity to speak to the players involved in scoring plays.

Dick Enberg (2004, p. 226) had been warned the first time he was assigned to work at the sport of golf " [it]Attracts the most critical audience. There's nothing close. Golfers watch golf religiously, and then they go out and play. They truly understand the finer points of the game. The golf viewer has no patience for any mistakes." While most serious scholarship has focused on Tiger Woods, other analysts have written about golf in terms of various discriminations (Chambers, 1995; Crosset, 1995; Hauser, 2003).

Miller (1997, p. 252) questions whether broadcasters can really be considered fans, especially considering who and what they know; he cites Harry Caray, self-billed as the "ultimate fan," but claims that moniker just is not the case, despite his more than a half-century as a sportscaster: "Harry had had the best seat in the house. He's traveled on team charters. He's walked through clubhouses. He's played cards with some of the guys. Harry knows the game, and he knows the people in the game." Regular fans, he argues see players as just names on a scorecard—"It never enters the mind of a real fan that players are human beings, that players have families, outside interests, and responsibilities."

"In addition to the impact of higher average ticket prices and total family costs to attend regular season games, there are other market forces and human impulses and idiosyncrasies that influence how fans relate to and why they support specific professional sports, leagues and franchises," (Frank P. Jozsa, Jr., 2003, p. 161). He cites the work of Dr. Robert K. Passikoff, founder and president of Brand Keys, who conducts annual national surveys of sports fans, using a model that includes these four variables: pure entertainment value, authenticity, fan bonding, and a franchise's history and tradition.

Because it is a uniquely American activity, it is also worth noting that, according to the Fantasy Sports Trade Association (www.fsta .org), some 15 million adults participate in fantasy sports. Whether for football, basketball, baseball, hockey, golf, etc., it is a $500 million annual industry. "The power of television motivated me to slide headfirst into second, just like Pete Rose," (Keith Dunnavant, 2004, p. xiv). "The power of television left me struggling in vain to throw the long bomb like Joe Namath, sink the jumper from the top of the key like Jerry West, and serve from the baseline like Jimmy Connors. Watching sports on television filled my head with a million dreams shattered by the reality of my extremely limited athletic ability."

SPORTS SPECTATORS AROUND THE WORLD

Americans generally think of "sports" as baseball, football, basketball, and maybe hockey, golf, or tennis. Yet people around the world may think very differently. Consider, for example, the global interest in soccer that is only recently winning converts in the United States—albeit still a holdout for television networks, which find it difficult to insert commercial messages in continuous play. (See Appendix 12 "Worldwide Sports," to give you some idea of the plethora of play available to us all.)

In North America, Canadians are much more oriented to cold-weather sports like skating, hockey, and skiing than are most people in the United States; Broom Ball, a kind of hockey played in "sand-shoes" or sneakers, or curling are Canadian favorites. Cold climates are also conducive for sled-dog racing; consider, for example, the popularity of Alaska's Iditarod. Many of Canada's sports radio announcers have loyal followers and fans.

Baseball, it may surprise you, doesn't travel too well around the world. Although it has gained popularity in some Asian and Asian-Pacific countries like China, Japan, Korea, Australia, and Taiwan, it is also very popular in soccer-obsessed Venezuela and many recruits come from countries like the Dominican Republic and Cuba. The vaguely related sport of cricket is enormously popular in former British colonies such as India and Pakistan.

Soccer reigns in South America, eastern and western Europe, the Middle East, the Caribbean, Asia and Africa, but in Brazil there is also "futvolei" (foot-volley)—similar to Burma, Cambodia, Laos, Malaysia, and Thailand's "sepak takraw," a game where a woven, wicker ball is kicked around, hands being taboo. Kite-flying is a favorite sport in Thailand. Second only to soccer, Swedes love tennis. Avid athletes, they also have long been joggers, skiers, skaters, sailors, and general fitness buffs. Other European favorites include hiking, biking, skiing, and any number of outdoor sports.

It may surprise you to learn that swimming is the most common recreational activity amongst Icelanders—until you find out how they make use of the many active volcanoes surrounding the island that provide a constant thermal temperature perfectly suited to outdoor swimming pools. The famous Blue Lagoon draws lots of tourists.

Since my hometown boasts the Basketball Hall of Fame, its popularity in Brazil amazes me, but basketball is also big in Israel, Ghana, and Australia, and most recently the Chinese player Yao Ming has encouraged attention in Asia. With estimates of some 300 million Chinese people now involved in basketball, broadcasts of Yao Ming's games draw in some 100 million viewers overseas (Fuller, 2006c). When the Boston Celtic's legendary coach, Red Auerbach listed people who had most affected James Naismith's game, which was invented in 1891 at the YMCA in Springfield, Massachusetts, he chose:

Hank Luisetti, 1938 All-American from Stanford who perfected the one-hand jump shot that triggered today's high scoring. George Mikan of the old Minneapolis Lakers made the pivot a tremendous offensive threat, and the Celtics' Bob Cousy simply made plays and moved a club. Bill Russell, of the University of San Francisco and the Celtics, revolutionized the game's defensive side with his rebounding and shot-blocking. (Starr, 2006, p. 2)

Sports fans around the world are spend lots of time online; ESPN .com is the most visited sports Web site at 11.5 million visitors in 2005, but it was easily followed by FoxSports.com (9.2 million), Yahoo Sports (8.4 million), SI.com (7.3 million), AOL Sports (7.1 million), NFL Internet Network (6.3 million), MLB.com (4.3 million), CollegeSports.com (4.0 million), NASCAR.com (4.0 million), and NBA Internet Network (3.5 million). Furthermore, since they began with an NBA game on April 13, 2001, live sports Web casts continue to gain in momentum. According to RealNetworks (www.real networks.com), some eighty-seven countries have joined in, especially from China. In 2002, the Major League Baseball Web site (www.mlb.com) had its first live Web cast of a Yankees-Rangers game that attracted 30,000 viewers; while that one was free and subsequent games come with a fee, the Web site boasts more than 500,000 subscribers.

Clearly, as was brought up in the introduction to this book, sports audiences continue to grow globally (Ehrenreich, 2006; Garner, 2000; Guttman, 1986; Harris, 1994; Klatell and Marcus, 1988; Mandelbaum, 2004; Murphy, Williams, and Dunning, 1990; Peterson, 2000; Queenan, 2003; Sandvoss, 2003; Toma, 2003; Wann et al., 2001; Weiler, 2000). Miller (2005) reports how, in searching for international audiences, the major professional sports leagues have been playing exhibition and preseason games outside the United States. For example, he cites how Major League Baseball played regular season games in Tokyo, and the National Football League played a regular season game in Mexico City. The Open Wheel Racing Series staged seven of its sixteen races in 2004 outside the United States (in Mexico, Canada, South Korea, and Australia). NASCAR held its

Busch series races in Mexico. More and more players for these various teams are coming from other countries (20 percent for the NBA), and plans are in the works for preseason games against clubs from an increasingly global market.

Now, where does all this information about other sports cultures fit into your life as a future sportscaster? For starters, it behooves you to know other games, other languages, and other pronunciations of names. As a teaser, picture yourself announcing some of these various sports!

SPORTS SPECTATORS FOR SPECIAL EVENTS

With the advent of television, the fans at home rather than those in the stadium or the arena became the ultimate arbiters of organized sports. To attract more television viewers and meet the demands of commercial sponsors, television directors employed multiple cameras, replays, slow-motion shots, flashy graphics, catchy music, and announcers to create a sporting experience unavailable to the fan in the stands. (Rader, 2004, p. 249)

It is always exciting when sports fans around the world rally around a specific event, so this section concerns itself with both national and international audiences. Nationalism clearly plays a role in our rooting for a particular team (Bairner, 2001; Bale, 2002; Bernstein and Blain, 2003; Foer, 2004; Fuller, 2004b; Houlihan, 1994; Maguire, 1999; Miller, Lawrence, McKay, and Rowe, 2001; and Wilson, 1994). Mechikoff and Real (1990, p. 9) remind us: "Sport and media gatekeepers ensure that a national audience sees its own athletes in competition as much as possible. Ethnocentric and jingoistic announcer comments exacerbate the tendency to identify only with one's own team. Politicians jump on the self-promotional bandwagon of us-against-the-world mentality." Although we might interpret events according to our own frames of reference, it is interesting to analyze fandom for events like marathons, the Olympic Games, the Super Bowl, the World Cup, and Xtreme sports.

Marathons

A classic example of how the media can hype an event into becoming an international phenomenon comes from what was a simple, local field race in Boston. On April 20, 1897, fifteen runners decided to replicate what had been done in Marathon, Greece, by running the requisite 26.2 miles in a marathon. The *Boston Globe* reported that hundreds of spectators took trains to various points along the route to root for family and friends who had decided to undertake this seemingly silly venture. The audience for the event, which has since expanded to becoming an Olympic sport, has grown so large that nowadays more than 300 media outlets, and more than 1,300 hundred journalists, cover it—the Boston Marathon.

But Boston is only the beginning. The New York City Marathon, which draws more than 37,000 runners from around the world, is reportedly watched in person by more than 2 million people throughout this five-borough race; some 350 million more follow it on television in 150 countries. Especially during the fall and spring, numerous other marathons take place, premier field and track events offer enormous media coverage, exorbitant awards and endorsements to the winners, and certain exposure for sponsors. From his vantage point of covering the New York City Marathon since 1999, Len Berman (2005, p. 218) shares some other pictures of the event: "Even with our exhaustive coverage, though, there are some things we don't show. Of particular note, we don't show runners throwing up at the end of the race. There's a little area just past the finish line where many of the runners go. They lean over the fence and puke their brains out."

Olympic Games

The Olympic Games are the great Circus Maximus of planet Earth. They are now mounted every two years, involve roughly ten thousand athletes from over two hundred nations, and, in the 1990s, the price tag per Summer Games topped $2 billion per city. Thanks to television, radio, newspapers, magazines, and, more recently, the Internet, during the weeks of the Olympics billions of people venerate the athletes who become Olympic champions, and the host city gets to strut its stuff. The entire enterprise is swathed in tinseled layers of marketing and hype—by the International Olympic Committee (IOC), by the National Olympic Committees (NOCs), by the transnational corporations who pay tens of millions of dollars to sponsor the Games, by the television networks that pay hundreds of millions of dollars to broadast them, and by host cities and national governments who have invested hundreds of millions of taxpayers' dollars. All this marketing draws on the myth of the redemptive power of "pure sport" for athletes, for their spectators, and for local and national communities. (Burstyn, 2000, p. ix)

Drawing a great deal of scholarly interest, including an Olympics chat group, the winter and summer Olympic Games have been alternately celebrated two years apart since 1992 (Baker, 2000; Barney, Wenn, and Martyn, 2002; Daddario, 1998; de Morgas Spa, Rivenburgh, and Larson, 1995; Dyreson, 1998; Findling and Pelle, 1996; Fuller, 1987a, 1987b, 1990b, 1990c, 1996; Guttmann, 1992; Hoberman, 1986; Larson and Park, 1993; Lenskyj, 2000; Mandell, 1987; Preuss, 2000; Roche, 2000; Segrave and Chu, 1988; Senn, 1999; Simpson and Jennings, 1992; Tomlinson and Whannel, 1984; U.S. Olympic Committee, 1996; Wilson and Derse, 2001). Of course the Olympic games date to Olympia, Greece, of 776 BC, revived in 1896 to what are called the "modern" games. Today, millions of fans around the world tune in by whatever media is available.

Though women today form a large fan base, it was not always so— or even allowed. Today, it is almost amusing to recall the words of the Baron Pierre de Coubertin (1863-1937), founder of the modern Olympics, about female audiences:

Respect of individual liberty requires that one should not interfere in private acts . . . but in public competitions, [women's] participation must be absolutely prohibited. It is indecent that the spectators should be exposed to the risk of seeing the body of a woman being smashed before their eyes. Besides, no matter how toughened a sportswoman may be, her organism is not cut out to sustain certain shocks. Her nerves rule her muscles, nature wanted it that way. Finally, the egalitarian discipline that is brought to bear on the male contenders for the good order and good appearance of the meeting risks being affected and rendered inapplicable by female participation. For all thee practical reasons as well as sentimental ones, it is extremely desirable that a drastic rule be established very soon. (cited in Gerber, 1974, p. 137)

Although ABC is credited with turning the Olympic Games into a major spectacle, more recently NBC has hosted them. Paying $2.3 billion for the 2004 and 2008 Summer Games and the 2006 Winter Games, this is all part of a package NBC bought for $3.5 billion for five Olympics from 2000 through 2008. If you wonder why, consider the prestige such programming brings, along with ad sales and the space to sell "lead-ins" for future network shows. For the 2004 Athens Olympics, NBC averaged 16.17 million households per evening in prime time—the most-watched television network for each of its seventeen nights of Olympic programming. The top-rated program: gymnastics, including women's individual and team gymnastics, men's individual and team gymnastics, and individual gymnastic competitions.

As part of the Annenberg (University of Southern California) Olympics Research Project team, Eric W. Rothenbuhler (1988, p. 75) examined the notion of "celebration hypothesis" relative to the 1984 Los Angeles Summer Olympics, finding "that those watching the Olympics were still the most likely respondents to be in a group, to have visitors with whom they celebrated other holidays, to have food and drink, to plan their viewing, and to pay close attention to the television." My own audience study (Fuller, 1990c) of the 1988 Seoul Summer Olympics, a telephone survey of 1,168 persons in the northeast part of the United States, found some 90 percent of the participants reporting interest in the Games, nearly half watching several hours a day—despite conflicting press reports about the low ratings. You might be interested in replicating that audience survey (see Exercises 4-5 to 4-7, including directions, the actual survey itself, and a suggested coding scheme).

The 1996 Atlanta Olympics, as studied by David L. Andrews (2004, p. 17), drew this conclusion: "The drama of the Olympic Games as broadcast to millions of Americans by NBC has been neither unpredictable nor is it divorced from the pervasive commodification of sport. Instead, NBC's televisual Olympics are a 'media event' consciously designed, promoted and delivered to serve the network's profit-driven purposes." From her content analysis of sportscaster language of these Games, Lisa M. Weidman (1998) found encouraging signs that the announcers did not make female athletes seem too feminine. The 2000 Sydney Olympics, studied by Weiller, Higgs, and Greenleaf (2004, p. 19), found ambivalent comments, especially relative to female athletes by male sportscasters, focus on appearance for both genders, parity relative to gender marking, "narrative reflecting male-female comparison" as a hallmark of coverage, a hierarchy of naming, and focus on "personal lives/emotions of both male and female athletes."

Super Bowl

> Of all the sports that women may want to spectate—assuming that they want to buy into this supreme patriarchal experience— none better exemplified that nexus of Big Business, big stakes, and big boys than American football. And of all the football games that women and men alike are expected to watch, none can surpass the Super Bowl. A ratings leader, it has become an advertiser's yardstick, drawing as it does more than 140 million viewers and costing more than $2 million a minute. (Fuller, 1999c, p. 161)

Right away, it is obvious that this quotation is dated as, according to Fox (www.fox.com), some 133.7 million total viewers tuned in at some point to Super Bowl XXXIX—making it the network's most-watched evening ever. It is, annually, the biggest television event of the year, and Super Bowl ranks amongst the ten most-watched programs in television history. Recent ratings are as follows:

- Super Bowl XXXII (1998) 44.5 (NBC)
- Super Bowl XXXIII (1999) 40.2 (Fox)
- Super Bowl XXXIV (2000) 43.3 (ABC)
- Super Bowl XXXV (2001) 40.4 (CBS)
- Super Bowl XXXVI (2002) 40.4 (Fox)
- Super Bowl XXXVII (2003) 40.7 (ABC)
- Super Bowl XXXVIII (2004) 41.4 (CBS)
- Super Bowl XXXIX (2005) 41.1 (Fox)

The Super Bowl, watched mostly by a male audience, still has 43 percent of women in the United States, as well as a worldwide viewership estimated at 800 million. "Super Sunday," which is ranked as the second biggest day of food consumption (after Thanksgiving), is a major party event for spectators. If Roone Arledge revolutionized Mondays for football fans, then Pete Rozelle can be credited with taking it to the next level with Super Bowl Sunday. The Super Bowl, created in 1967, when Vince Lombardi's Green Bay Packers pummeled the Kansas City Chiefs at the Los Angeles Memorial Coliseum on January 15, that first AFL-NFL championship game has evolved into the quintessential sporting event.

World Cup

The World Cup, popular more around the world than in the United States (because, as has been noted here earlier, soccer is more popular elsewhere), it gets billed as "the biggest show on earth." In 2006, in Germany, the World Cup was estimated to have some 30 billion global viewers, making it the most watched event in television history. Sponsored by the Federation Internationale de Football Association (FIFA), the next staging of the quadrennial tournament will be held in South Africa in 2010.

Xtreme Sports

Although it is difficult to categorize Xtreme sports, or Extreme sport, or action/adventure sport as such, and the sports really don't have specific events, it somehow seems appropriate to include them here. The main idea is an adrenaline rush—pushing oneself to the limits, both for participants and for spectators. The Sporting Goods Manufacturers Association (SGMA), reporting a $68.6 billion year in 2009 (Arabe, 2004), looks to Generation Y (born from 1980-1984), who play team or extreme sports, like inline skating, cross-country skiing, surfing, biking, snowboarding, scuba diving, sky-diving, rock climbing, mountaineering, hang gliding, paintball, and much more.

Eric Dunning wrote a book in 1999 titled *Sports Matters: Sociological Studies of Sport, Violence, and Civilization.* Its main title says it all. Relative to the notion of sport-related violence, portions of the summary from Jennings Bryant's (1989, pp. 287-288) chapter in *Media, Sports, & Society* are worth repeating:

1. It has been reaffirmed that sports telecasts can be presented and manipulated to create different levels of enjoyment for viewers and listeners. Message factors in sportscasts and other sports presentations must be taken seriously, since it is so obvious that they can have robust effects on sports fans' perceptions and on their enjoyment.

2. Sports fans are not all alike. For example, viewers with a propensity for personal aggression tend to be particularly fond of sports violence. Those who are personally less aggression prone tend to have their enjoyment dampened by excess violence, or they may just not watch in the first place.

3. The disposition of fans toward teams and players is consistently a potent predictor of their enjoyment of sports violence. Violence, and particularly the harm resulting from violence, must happen to the right people if it is to be enjoyed to the fullest.

4. Moral judgmental factors are important mediators of the enjoyment of sports violence. Unsanctioned sports violence tends to result in impaired enjoyment, even if a disliked opponent is defeated via such unfair aggressive tactics.

5. Most avid sports fans seem to enjoy extremely rough, even violent, televised sporting events, so long as dispositional factors are aligned correctly, the viewers' moral judgment is not violated, and "macho" personality factors prevail.

Chapter 5

The Role of Media in Sports and Sportscasting

Through its many filters—visual, cultural, critical, psychological, sociopolitical, and of course economic, the media operate to encourage us to think we are participants in sports when we really are simply spectators. Providing us with a vision of the world, through images and interpretations of those images, the media aim to give us a sense of the wider world—albeit through the lens of a constructed, corporate reality. "Now that an entire generation has grown up assuming that life without television is an impossibility, it may be useful to remind ourselves that sportscasting began with radio, not with TV, and that sports journalism in print is older still," Guttman (1986, pp. 128-129). This chapter discusses print media (sportswriters/sportswriting, sports journalism/sports journalists, and sports print media), broadcast media, controversies, and emerging technologies, which leads to an examination of sportscasters themselves. Introducing the topic in terms of "jockocracy," we will consider sportscasters as celebrities, and include profiles of more than 200 prominent people in the field.

PRINT SPORTS MEDIA

Sportswriting in the 21st century can't be attributed to some Big Bang theory. The cynical style, often obese with humor, that we see today has gradually evolved from the matter-of-fact reporting that once defined sportswriting. There is no doubt that it is profoundly different today. The crusader style once used by

Sportscasters/Sportscasting

many early writers to promote sports has been swallowed by the critical approach to sportswriting that is now dominant. Still, since sportswriting has spanned across generations, everything that appears in print today is ultimately a product of the various styles used in years past. Each of the forefathers of sportswriting has left his stylistic mark on the art, reworking and restructuring it to fit his needs. (http://www.stolaf.edu/depts/cis/wp/malmgren/coursework/philosophyofsport.html)

Historically, as might be imagined, the first medium to deal with sports was print. Today, as can be seen in Appendix 4 of this book, there is a wide range of print sources for the sports fan. It is also encouraging to know that Wish Publishing (www.wishpublishing.com) was founded in 1999 as "the first book publishing company devoted exclusively to women's sports topics."

Dating to the days of the earliest printing press, in the fifteenth century, both businesspeople and the lay public have been interested in sports. Although our earliest newspapers were more focused on political topics, it did not take long before a mass audience was lured into reading and, by the 1830s, the emphasis on literacy took on such importance that we soon saw competition in terms of what became known as the "penny press." By the early twentieth century, we were a nation of newspaper consumers, even if the advent of broadcasting has drastically changed that pattern. Consider: in 1920, there were more than 2,000 newspapers in the United States, with a circulation of nearly 28 million; a year later, following the first sports radio broadcast, those numbers went precipitously down—and newspaper readership today is at an all-time low.

In 1895, the first professional sports section appeared in a local newspaper: William Randolph Hearst's *New York Journal.* It took another ten years before others joined, but soon sports news was included in the *Washington Post,* the *Commercial Advertiser,* and the *St. Louis Globe.* Thoroughbred racing was covered in John Stuart Skinner's *American Turf Register and Sporting Magazine,* founded 1929, while William T. Porter's *Spirit of the Times* (1831) was more general. Other key early publications included *Sporting Life* (1883), *The Sporting News,* founded by Alfred H. Spink in 1886 and published by his son, J.G. Taylor Spink from 1914 to 1962 (Reidenbaugh, 1985), *Sport* (1946), as well as pieces in the *New York Herald*, the *Sun*, and the *Tribune*. Imagine: more than a century later, the sports section is still a male bastion, an "old boys club," with severely limited female voices and/or stories.

Mike Sowell (2006, p. 65) has written about Winifred Black, one of the country's first sportswriters, who "infiltrated an all-men's club in 1892 to become the first woman to cover a prize fight for an American newspaper. She also wrote about football and interviewed heavyweight boxers." Using the byline "Annie Laurie" for the San Francisco *Examiner*, her writing style contrasted with her male counterparts, and she used the opportunity to comment on gender roles of the era.

Maria "Midy" Morgan is considered the first female sportswriter, covering horse racing for *The New York Times* in 1869 (Robertson, 1992), along with livestock news. Sadie Kneller Miller wrote about the Orioles for the *Baltimore Telegram*—using her initials as a byline to disguise her gender, daredevil Nellie Bly wrote for the *New York World* beginning in 1889, Pauline Jacobson covered sports for the *San Francisco Bulletin* in 1906, Eloise Young was sports editor for the *Chronicle News* in Colorado in 1908, and in 1916 Nan O'Reilly began a golf column in the *New York Evening Post*. Kelly Tilghman of The Golf Channel was announced as the PGA Tour's first female lead golf announcer only in 2007—co-anchoring with Nick Faldo. Pam Creedon (1994b, p. 75) provides milestones relative to women in newspaper sports journalism in what she labels "Sob Sisters and the Golden Age of Sports Writing" as follows:

1920: Mary Bostwick at the Indianapolis Speedway for the *Indianapolis Star*

1922: Dorothy Bough, sportswriter for the *Philadelphia Inquirer*

1924: Lorena Hickok— Big Ten football for *Minneapolis Morning Tribune;*Margaret Goss' "Women in Sport" column for *NY Herald Tribune;* Nettie George Speedy: sport news for the *Chicago Defender*

1929: Nan O'Reilly golf editor of the *New York Evening News;* Cecile Ladu sports editor of the *Albany Times Union*

1932:   Maribel Vison (Owen) covers sports for *The New York Times*

1942:   Lois Fegan reports on ice hockey for the *Harrisburg Telegraph*

1943:   Jeane Hofmann reports baseball training camps for the *NY Journal-American;* Zelda Hines is the women's bowling editor for the *Chicago Defender*

1944:   Mary Garber is sports editor at *Winston-Salem Sentinel*

1973:   Karol Stringer of AP enters the pits at the Indianapolis 500; Betty Cuniberti covers an NFL team from training to the Super Bowl for the *San Bernardino Sun-Telegram*

1976:   Betty Cuniberti becomes sportswriter for the *San Francisco Chronicle;* Lawrie Mifflin is a sportswriter for the *New York Daily News;* Leslie Visser covers NFL beat for the *Boston Globe*

1977:   Carolyn White is sportswriter for the *Akron Beacon-Journal*

1978:   LeAnne Screiber is sports editor at *The New York Times*

1979:   Alison Gordon covers American league baseball for *Toronto Star*

1982:   Claire Smith: *Hartford Courant*

1985:   Christine Brennan covers Washington Redskins for the *Washington Post*

1988:   Karen Hunter-Hodge becomes the only black woman sportswriter in New York *(Daily News)*

World War II brought the likes of Mary Garber as sports editor of the *Winston-Salem Journal-Sentinel,* even though, "She was banned from dressing rooms during post-game interviews and was forced to sit with players' wives instead of in the press box with the male reporters" ("AWSM tribute to Mary Garber"). Helene Elliott, a sports columnist for the *Los Angeles Times,* was the first female journalist inducted into the Hockey Hall of Fame; she covered every Stanley Cup since 1980, the New York Islanders' four consecutive championships, the 1980 "Miracle on Ice" U.S. defeat of the Soviet Union, Wayne Gretzky's rise, and more, it is well-deserved honor. "For decades women sportswriters faced intimidation and harassment from male athletes, coaches and even colleagues," Sherry Ricchiardi (2005) has observed. "Thanks to the perseverance of pioneers, the blatant sexism has subsided, and locker-room doors are open to both genders. But the battle for equality isn't over." At the very least, they have gone from being called "sluts and groupies" to actually being admired in many cases; still, women only account for 12.6 percent of all Associated Press member newspaper sports staffs (see Miloch et al., 2005).

As you will see from the extensive Reference section included with this book, a number of sports-related books have been written. When you go to a bookstore, you will find that most of them tend to be celebrity- and/or specific-sport-oriented, but since we are interested in integrating your knowledge of and probably love for sports with the profession, many citations and suggestions for further reading tend to take the subject to the next level. In particular, you will find a number of books about sports and the media (Andrews, 2001; Andrews and Jackson, 2001; Baker, 2003; Baker and Boyd, 1997; Boyle and Haynes, 2000; Boyle, Flood, and Kevin, 2004; Cocchiarale and Emmert, 2004; Creedon, 1994b; Davidson, 1993; Davis, 1997; Dinan, 1998; Fuller, 2006a; Klatell and Marcus, 1988; Nichols, Moynahan, Hall, and Taylor, 2001; Nicholson, 2006; Oriand, 1993; Raney and Bryant, 2006; Rowe, 1999; Tudor, 1997; Wenner, 1989, 1998; Whannel, 1992, 2002).

In 2002, *Sports Illustrated* (McEntegart et al.) compiled its list of "The top 100 sports books of all time." To get you started, here are the first ten: (1) A.J. Liebling's *The Sweet Science* (1956); (2) Roger Kahn's *The Boys of Summer* (1971); (3) Jim Bouton's *Ball Four* (1970); (4) H. G. Bissinger's *Friday Night Lights* (1990); (5) Ring Lardner's *You Know Me Al* (1914); (6) John Feinstein's *A Season on the Brink* (1986); (7) Dan Jenkins' *Semi-tough* (1972); (8) George Plimpton's *Paper Lion* (1965); (9) Ken Dryden's *The Game* (1983); and (10) Nick Hornby's *Fever Pitch* (1991). *TV Sports Markets* is a television-sports newsletter (see www.SportbusinessTVcom)–yet another example of print media about the very real world of active sports. Bill Simmons, the sports fan called "That Sports Guy" who writes the column by that name for ESPN.com, has brought renewed interest in reading for an online audience; Warren St. John (2005, p. 1) describes the phenomenon: "Writing from the perspective of an unabashed partisan—his teams are the Patriots, Red Sox, and the

Celtics—he has pioneered an intensely personal style of sports writing that draws on frequent references to movies, television sitcoms, music, video games, even his friends and wife (the Sports Gal of course), always with a side dish of mortar-thick sports history and analysis."

Still, the Association of Women in Sports Media (AWSM) has estimated that only some 3 percent of our 10,000 print and broadcast journalists are women. Chambers, Steiner, and Fleming (2002, p. 113) write: "Much of the homophobic, hyper-heterosexual, masculinist and often racist coverage of athletes can be attributed to the continuing dominance of sports journalism by men." Drawing on the work of C. A. Tuggle's 1997 analysis of *ESPN Sportscenter* and *CNN Sports Tonight,* replicated seven years later, found even less coverage of women's sports (Adams and Tuggle, 2004), Kimberly L. Bissell (2006, p. 172) reports in her study of sexualized language for women's professional tennis, how, "The inequity in coverage of male and female sports is manifested in column inches of stories, the placement of articles within the newspaper, the use of art on the page, and the range of sports and athletes depicted." Creedon and Wearden (2000, p. 2), realizing how "the overall amount of women's sports coverage in traditional media has decreased since the 1996 Olympics," at least see consistent coverage of it relative to high school and college women's sports. Typically, according to Alina Berstein (2002), only about 10 percent of print media coverage goes to elite female athletes—a statistic that has remained consistent for the last quarter-century.

SPORTSWRITERS/SPORTSWRITING

Irregular hours and tight deadlines are the price you pay for free entry into hundreds of sporting events a year. Reporting can be hectic—news can happen at any time and usually does. When news breaks and the editor calls, reporters must be prepared to drop everything at a moment's notice and run, notebook in hand, to the newsworthy event. This unpredictability and "always on call" condition attract many to the field, though it is also one of the most common complaints. New media writers experience largely the same stresses, as Web sites have deadlines just the same as print. Reporters covering a steady beat may develop some rhythm to their days, but it is precarious routine. Sporting events can extend beyond deadlines, and writing under time pressure is always a danger. Depending upon what area of sports they're covering, reporters may find themselves anywhere from a posh press suite in the Astrodome to at a dusty baseball field compiling all their own statistics for a high-school game. Despite all the demands of the profession, sports writers are involved with sports all day, every day.

(Miller, n.d.)

Whether they write for dailies, weeklies, monthly, or yearly publications, sportswriters aim to both inform and entertain their readers. Their stories might be anecdotal, personal, statistical, and/or critical; they might be little or large, local or national, personal or public, simple reportage or earth-shattering news. The single sportswriter might cover a soccer game in the morning, attend a press conference that afternoon, go to a hockey game that night, and report on a tennis tournament the following morning. "There's absolutely no job like being a sportswriter," (Christopher J. Walsh, 2006, p. 14). "We are the enemy; we are free publicity. We are valuable commodities; we are expendable. We have the greatest jobs in the world; we have no lives. We are not real journalists; we are the best journalism has to offer."

Some of the most notable early sportswriters include Ring Lardner (Bruccoli and Layman, 1976; Elder, 1956; Geismar, 1963; Yardley, 1977), Fred Lieb, Westbrook Pegler, Damon Runyon (Breslin, 1991), Quentin Reynolds, Paul Gallico, Ring Lardner, Grantland Rice, Red Smith (Berkow, 1986), Bob Considine, Joe Williams, and Arch Ward (Littlewood, 1990). The more current generation would include Dave Anderson, Roger Angell (1972), Harvey Araton, Pete Axthelm, Christine Brennan, Jimmy Breslin (1991), Frank Deford (1987), Peter Gammons, Frank Graham, Jr. (1981), Dave Goldberg, David J. Halberstam (1999), Halsey Hall, "Scoop" Jackson of *SLAM, ESPN .com's Page 2* and *ESPN The Magazine,* Sally Jenkins (1996), Leonard Koppett (1994, 2003), Robert Lipsyte (1975, 1991), Jim Litke, Mike Lupica (1988), Jim Murray (1993), Shirley Povich (2005), Rick

Reilly of *SI*, William C. Rhoden, Selena Roberts, Alan Robinson, Joan Ryan, Richard Sandomir (2001), Dick Schaap (2001), George Vecsey (1989), Mike Wilbon and no doubt many others who do not happen to have citations here.

"The only thing I know for sure about sports," Pulitzer Prize-winning sportswriter Jim Murray (cited in Elderkin, 1993) said, "is that they need dramatizing." As fans, we particularly thrill to "rags to riches" stories of sports heroes (Hank Aaron, Lance Armstrong, Roger Bannister, Wilt Chamberlain, Dorothy Hammill, Michael Jordan, Diana Nyad, Mary Lou Retton, Wilma Rudolph, Babe Ruth, Anika Sorenstam, Tiger Woods, and others).

Because they were so knowledgeable, a number of sports journalists became, if sometimes by default, sportscasters. A classic example here is Grantland Rice (Barber, 1970; Fountain, 1993; Harper, 1999; Inabinett, 1994; Poindexter, 1966), who wrote for the *New York Tribune*. "He was a logical choice to be a sportswriter-turned-broadcaster," declares Ronald A. Smith (2001, p. 20). "He had graduated Phi Beta Kappa at Vanderbilt, where he played football and baseball while majoring in Greek and Latin. He was probably the best-known sportswriter of his time, but he was also an early broadcaster of the baseball's World Series." It was not always so easy to have the mouth, but the mike, say what had flowed so simply from the pen. "After the crack of the bat, he would wait for the shout of the crowd, hesitate a few moments, and then describe what had happened" (p.21). Rice's style concentrated on making heroes out of athletes—his choices mostly being Babe Ruth, Jack Dempsey, Bobby Jones, Bill Tilden, Red Grange, and Knute Rockne; supportive of sports as a profession, he simultaneously railed against too much money spent on sports.

Some more recent well-known sportswriters include the following: Mitch Albom, author of the 1997 best-seller *Tuesdays With Morrie;* Pete Axthelm, who is also a sports commentator for *The NFL on NBC* and *NFL Primetime* on ESPN; Christine Brennan of *USA Today,* a specialist in figure skating; Heywood Hale Broun, son of writer/film critic Ruth Hale and columnist Heywood Broun; Murray Chass of *The New York Times,* inducted into the Baseball Hall of Fame in 2004; Dan Daniel, called "the Dean of American Baseball Writers"; Helene Elliott, the first female journalist to be inducted into the Hockey Hall of Fame; Peter Gammons of *The Boston Globe,* nicknamed "The Commissioner"; Mel Greenberg, who covers women's basketball; Ed Hinton—motor racing; Joe Hirsch, "the dean" of thoroughbred racing writers; Dan Jenkins, celebrated by many as "the best sportswriter in America"; Peter King, football columnist for *Sports Illustrated;* Frederick C. Klein, the *Wall Street Journal's* first-ever sports columnist, with "On Sports"; Tony Kornheiser, sportswriter for *The Washington Post,* radio analyst for ESPN's *Monday Night Football* since 2006, host of *The Tony Kornheiser Show;* Jane Leavy, award-winning sportswriter, author, and feature writer for the *Washington Post;* Mike Lupica, who wrote "The Sporting Life" column at *Esquire;* Will McDonough—until his death in 1992, he had attended every AFL-NFL World Championship game and every Super Bowl; Joe McLaughlin, "one of the true newspaper legends of the Southwest Conference"; James Patrick Murray, sportswriter at the *Los Angeles Times* (1961 to 1998), 14-time winner of Sportswriter of the Year award, he earned a Pulitzer Prize in 1990; Phil Mushnick, sportswriter for the *New York Post* who criticizes the world of sports as portrayed in the media; the late Shirley Povich of the *Washington Post,* recipient of the Baseball Writers Association of America's J.G. Taylor Spink Award; Rick Reilly, "Back-page" sportswriter for *Sports Illustrated,* who has won the Sportswriter of the Year award eleven times; George Washington Sears, sportswriter for *Forest and Stream* in the 1880s; Dan Shanoff, a former writer for ESPN.com's "Page 2" section who now runs his own sports blog; Dan Shaughnessy, sports columnist for *The Boston Globe;* Gary Smith, a senior writer for *Sports Illustrated,* called one of America's best sportswriters; Red Smith, said to be America's most widely read sportswriter; Wendell Smith, a noted African American sportswriter influential regarding Jackie Robinson; Bert Randolph Sugar, boxing writer, owner of *Boxing Illustrated* magazine, editor and publisher of *The Ring;* Roger Treat, editor of the first football encyclopedia; Anne Ursu, a novelist known as Batgirl, "the mistress of sass," and unofficial blogger for the Minnesota Twins; Peter Vecsey, sports columnist and analyst who specializes in basketball; Christopher J. Walsh, award-winning sportswriter and author of *No time outs: What it's really like to be a sportswriter today* (2006); King Solomon White, pioneer of the Negro Leagues who wrote the first definitive history of black baseball; Todd Wright, host of *Todd Wright Tonight* on Sporting News Radio; Diamantis Zervos, author of "Baseball's Golden Greeks"; and Paul Lionel Zimmerman ("Dr. Z"), football sportswriter for *Sports Illustrated.* You undoubtedly have your favorites.

There are also several sportswriters associated with various statistical methods, such as John Hollinger with APBRmetrics for basketball, or Bill James, Pete Palmer, and Alan Schwartz of "sabermetrics," the Society for American Baseball Research (SABR). Joseph S. Sheehan is one of the founders of sabermetric baseball forecasts, published by Baseball Prospectus. Michael Salfino is a nationally syndicated newspaper columnist who uses statistical analysis in predicting player and team performance for fans of the NFL and Major League Baseball, especially fantasy sports enthusiasts.

If you are interested in this topic, no doubt you have read Richard Ford's 1986 best-selling book *The Sportswriter;* chosen by *Time* as one of the 100 all-time novels, it concerns a guy who writes for a sports magazine (much like *Inside Sport,* where Ford once worked), undergoing a midlife/spiritual life crisis. Observing athletes simply living in the present, the antihero develops the philosophy, from following sports, that there are "no transcendent themes in life." Or, you might want to read Alyson Rudd's *Astroturf Blonde* (1999), about her evolution from football (U.K.-speak for soccer) player to sports journalist for *The Times.* You may even want to consult some sportswriting books (Bolton, 2005; Brookes, 2002; Koppett, 2003; Rappaport, 1994; Walsh, 2006; Wilstein, 2001; Wojciechoski, 1990).

"Like it or not," Staci W. Kramer (1987, p. S9) has commented, "sportswriting is no longer the art of writing about athletes as though they sprang from Zeus's head and live on Mount Olympus. The unwritten rules of the golden age of sportswriting have been rewritten by the double whammy of electronic media and tabloid journalism. Instead, we have the age of realism or what one observer calls the age of the human side of the athlete combined with the 'if I don't write it someone else will' school of journalism." Printwise, sports have been revolutionized with the advent of *USA Today,* whose in-depth pages of graphics, statistics, and wide-ranging sports coverage have spurred nearly all other newspapers to improve sports coverage.

SPORTS JOURNALISM/SPORTS JOURNALISTS

For a journalist, there is no such thing as useless knowledge. Every fact from every discipline has the potential to brighten style or strengthen substance. Journalism is a profession whose practitioners should know everything and pretend to know nothing. Too many people in the profession know nothing and pretend to know everything.

(Schaap, 2003, p. 80)

A profession that dates to the days of Homer's *Iliad* of the eighth century, which included athletic events, sports journalism in the United States probably dates to 1829's *American Turf Register,* which dealt with horse racing. Journalism historian Frank Luther Mott (1962) discusses *Spirit of the Times* (1831-1901) as an example of expanded coverage of sports. According to Raymond Boyle (2006, p. 1), a member of the Stirling Media Research Institute in the United Kingdom, sports journalism is a paradox: "In the hierarchy of professional journalism it has been traditionally viewed disparagingly as the 'toy department,' a bastion of easy living, sloppy journalism and 'soft' news." Yet, he argues, between globalization, digitization, and marketization, "the shifting boundaries of sports news, the rise in public relations and issues of access and the impact that the digital media environment is having" (p. 6), enormous changes are occurring. Predominantly a male-dominated profession (Coakley, 2003), where media content is edited and presented by gatekeepers in power positions, sports journalism can influence how readers and fans view athletes and athletics.

Wayne Wanta (2006, p. 105) would agree about the conflict about identity crises that print sports journalists undergo: "Newspapers editors often consider sports a necessary evil: Sports sections are among the most read, but sports are not viewed with the same respect as other newspaper staples, such as crime news, politics, and business. Add to this the impression by many editors that sportswriters do not take themselves seriously and sometimes engage in ethically questionable practices." Further, "Sports reporters are not supposed to root, but we cannot help having our passions and our opinions," George Vecsey (1989, p. 17) has confessed. His advice to would-be sports journalists: "Take at least a few of the most general journalism courses, backed up with courses in political science, law, economics, science, and a foreign language, of course" (p. 297).

As was mentioned earlier, there are a number of sports-media books, and sports journalism is no exception. Some are general journalism books containing a section on sports (Gibson, 1991; Mayeux, 1991; O'Donnell, Hausman, and Benoit, 1992), some deal with sports journalism—albeit most are print-oriented (Anderson, 1994; Andrews, 2005; Fischer, 1995; Garrison, 1990; Grafton and Jones, 2003; Helitzer, 1996), and a few are broadcasting-sport specific (Brown and O'Rourke, 2003; Catsis, 1996; Hedrick, 2000; Hitchcock, 1991; Kuiper, 1996; O'Donnell, Hausman, and Benoit, 1992; Scannell, 1991; Schultz, 2002).

Once photojournalism became popular with a population either unable or too busy to read, when magazines like *Look* and *Life* had such high circulations in the 1950s, it was obvious that print media could appeal to an entirely new target. Add to that great writers, coming from a heritage of a Golden Age of sports that included Heywood Broun, father of sports commentator Heywood Hale Broun, news reporter Frank Graham and his son Frank, Jr. Their story was detailed in "A Farewell to Heroes" (2003), and it was a winning recipe. This was also the era of writer/storyteller Paul Gallico, sports editor of the (New York) *Daily News,* who invented and organized the Golden Gloves—an amateur boxing competition.

Trying to answer the issue as to whether sports journalists cater to Major League Baseball officials, William B. Anderson (2001) of the Manship School of Mass Communication at Louisiana State University compared how labor situations in 1890 and 1975-1976 were handled in various newspapers. Questioning whether sportswriters should be cheerleaders, "hero worshippers," distant analysts, or simply storytellers, he relied on *Spalding's Official Base Ball Guide, Reach's Official American Association Base Ball Guide, Sporting Life,* New York *Clipper, The Sporting News,* and other publications to check for slanted language. Recognizing how both "sports journalism and sports journalists have changed since 1890," he nevertheless found similar influential factors: "For instance, the interests of media owners, the social-cultural environment, changes in the journalism industry, and the media strategies of organizational leaders impacted how an individual reporter might cover a story of comment on an issue" (p. 364).

SPORTS PRINT MEDIA TODAY

Currently, sports magazines generate $943.7 million in circulation revenue, and $1.45 billion in annual advertising revenue. Leading the pack is *Sports Illustrated* (Fleder, 2003), with a circulation of 3.22 million, for which sports journalist Frank Deford has written since 1962. Pointing out that it continues to be our most popular sports magazine, he has said that it changed our conversations by making teams and leagues a national topic, not just regional (Spanberg, 2003). *SI*'s circulation is followed by, according to *Sports Business Journal: Golf Digest* (1.56 million), *Golf Magazine* (1.40 million), *ESPN The Magazine* (1.38 million), *Road & Track* (780,000), *Sports Illustrated for Kids* (774,000), *Hot Rod* (708,000), *Tennis* (706,000), *The Sporting News* (584,000), *Runner's World* (521,000), *Ski Magazine* (454,000), *Skiing Magazine* (402,000), *Golf for Women* (381,000), Bicycling (283,000), *Golf Tips Magazine* (247,000), *USA Today Baseball Weekly* (234,000), *Slam* (224,000), *Stock Car Racing* (218,000), *Western Horseman* (217,000), and *Football Digest* (182,000). It won't surprise you that *Sports Illustrated* has the highest advertising revenues ($726.3 million), its swimsuit issue being the largest revenue-producing single edition in the magazine business (Davis, 1997); it surpassed $1 billion in advertising revenue for the first time in 2004. *ESPN The Magazine* has the next highest revenues, followed by various golf, fishing, running, and specialized sports publications.

Recently, a number of specialized sports-related tabloids have hit the newsstands, which is hardly surprising; as more than one person has commented, oftentimes sports stories hit the front pages of our newspapers and the "breaking news" segments of our television programs. Something about our psyches, it seems, draws us to disasters, "fallen hero" sagas, and "beautiful people." How else can you explain the media's fascination with people like Mike Tyson, John Daly, or Barry Bonds, Anna Kournikova, Maria Sharpova, or Natalie Gulbis?

In considering print and electronic media, there are a number of sports-related "fanzines" out there. These nonprofessional publications produced by and for fans, spurred on by sci-fi fans in the 1930s, can be found on the Internet. For example, in the wake of several disasters in the soccer world, as well as a reaction to growing hooliganism, British scholars Boyle and Haynes (2004) demonstrate their popularity, and Anders Svensson (2004, p. 26) has analyzed a Swedish ice hockey fanzine, concluding that, "Modern information and communication technologies today have made it possible to follow how supporters discuss sports, media, and themselves, so it will also be possible to closer examine whether the idea that fans' self-understanding includes senses of possession and making the events is salient for ice hockey supporters' comprehension of themselves." In their own way, a number of sports Web sites are forming whole new communities (Fuller, 2007a)—all part of our mediated culture.

"Broadcasting stories of games as the games go along is equivalent to a succotash party with neither corn nor beans," ran a 1925 editorial in *The Sporting News* (Reidenbaugh, 1985, p. 107). Next, we examine the veracity of that statement.

SPORTS MEDIA: BROADCASTING AND BEYOND

Besides newspapers, magazines and the radio, a lucrative, modern and vitally important medium—cable, network and satellite television programming—communicates all aspects of sports to a geographically dispersed and vast audience. For the viewers of professional sports programs, television combines motion, sight and sound. Moreover, similar to radio programs, television broadcasts have excellent mass-market coverage and a low cost per exposure.

(Jozsa, 2003, p. 118)

As defined by the Communication Act of 1934, broadcasting refers to the dissemination of communication meant to be directly received by the public or by the intermediary of relay stations, as found in radio and television. Traditionally, one, to many, communications, data, images, and sound can be transmitted either by print or electronic means as airwaves, via fiber, satellite links, and/or wire; here, the emphasis is on radio, television, and new innovations in broadcasting. The literature is rife with examples (Baker, 2003; Barnett, 1990; Boyle and Haynes, 2000; Boyle, Flood, and Kevin, 2004; Brown and O'Rourke, 2003; Cocchiarale and Emmert, 2004; Davidson, 1993; Dinan, 1998; Freeman, 2002; Halberstam, 1999; Klatell and Marcus, 1988; Nichols, Moynahan, Hall, and Taylor, 2001; Nicholson, 2006; O'Neill, 1991; Oriand, 1993; Patton, 1984; Powers, 1984; Rader, 1984; Rowe, 1999; Smith, 2001; Spence, 1988; Tudor, 1997; Wenner, 1989, 1998; Whannel, 1992, 2002). This section deals with the notion of sports broadcasting in terms of sport on radio, sport-radio, and television.

RADIO

Initially, radio men, known for their 'golden throats,' handled television's announcing chores. Even though viewers could see the games for themselves, announcers tended to talk too much, employ too many clichés, and risk their credibility by resorting to hyperbole.

(Rader, 2004, p. 251)

As noted in Chapter 2, once radio was introduced into American living rooms in the early 1920s, sports were popular programming. "The airwaves echoed with a collection of elegant performers and roughhewn troubadors, and their most artful themes blended reverberance, personal expression, and an often riveting beguilement," recalls baseball historian Curt Smith (1987, p. 3). "With no picture to assist them, announcers became the sole link between the happening and their public. If the broadcaster was indelible, so was the event."

Many people still think that sports reportage is best broadcast on the radio (Barber, 1970; Poindexter, 1966). Let's look at a timeline of some early radio sportscasts:

- November 25, 1920: With only an "experimental" license, College Station, Texas' station WTAW broadcast the first college football game of Texas University versus the Agricultural and Mechanical College of Texas.
- July 2, 1921 was the first boxing broadcast: Jack Dempsey versus Georges Carpentier.
- August 4, 1921 broadcast the first Davis Cup, Britain versus Australia, via Pittsburgh's KDKA. The next day, they did the first baseball game: Pirates (8 to 3) versus Phillies, with Harold Arlin at the mike.
- October 4, 1922: the World Series is broadcast on WJZ.
- January 1, 1923: the first regional Rose Bowl is broadcast by KHJ, Los Angeles, following by the first national broadcast by NBC in 1927.
- October 10, 1923: the World Series is broadcast, nationally.
- 1928: CBS affiliates got free sports programming in exchange for national sales promotion.
- 1935: NBC broadcast the entire Chicago Cubs season.
- 1937: "18 Weeks from the NY Hippodrome," a boxing series, became the first subsidized sporting event—Adams Hats becoming the first sponsor.
- 1939: Major League Baseball was broadcast on the radio, the World Series going for $400,000 (Zimbalist, 1994, p. 149).
- 1940: NFL championship game (Bears versus Redskins) broadcast, the Mutual Broadcast System paying $2,500 and Red Barber announcing.

If you keep reading about Red Barber in this book and maybe are learning about him for the first time—or, if you have been a longtime fan of his, let me include an example of his sportscasting from an October 5, 1947, baseball game in Yankee Stadium. Check his style:

Joe DiMaggio up, holding that club down at the end. The big fellow, Hatten, pitches . . . a curveball high outside for ball one. . . . Swung on, belted! It's a long one! Deep into left-center! Back goes Gionfriddo! Back, back, back, back, back, back! . . . He . . . makes a one-handed catch against the bull pen! Oh-ho, Doctor! (Heller, 2003)

It is worth noting how exponentially popular radio continues to be. In 1922, American households had fewer than 500,000 radio sets; in 1923, that statistic rose threefold, and in 1924, sales of sets reached some 2 million. During the Depression, 18 million sets were in use, that number increased to 56 million by the time we entered World War II (Smith, 2001). "Conceivably the one media that has had the greatest impact on sports and the audience is radio," Eric C. Covil (n.d.). "Perhaps no other form of the media, at this time, covers the different levels and varieties of athletics more than radio. Everything from high school basketball to professional auto racing fills the airwaves of many of the more than 13,000 radio stations in the U.S. and the newest creation, satellite radio."

Today, counting radios in our homes, cars, and portable devices, low estimates are about 600 million radios, each person in the United States having at least two (be sure to do Exercise 5.1). Consider the many terms associated with radio in the twenty-first century: wireless, mobile, digital, atomic, streamed, Web cast, podcast, and probably more by the time you read this sentence. Miller (2000) states that baseball broadcasters should have a sense of humor and make the broadcast entertaining. Miller also states that the responsibility is to the fans, first, to report clearly and vividly the action taking place. Can you think of a more accurate way of describing the role of sports broadcasters?

"Sports talk radio," which is mainly geared to men in that ideal socioeconomic demographic of ages twenty-five to fifty-four, began briefly with station KMVP in Denver. "What defines great sports talk radio?" asks Alan Eisenstock (2001, p. 259). "The answer is . . . *urgency.* You *have* to listen. You make an appointment to tune in and you are always reluctant to tune out." Zagacki and Grano (2005) find it therapeutic for fans. According to Arbitron, today, sports talk draws an audience of 41.8 million at least once a week. With some 150 national all-sports stations, the format accounts for advertising revenues of $2.2 billion, along with broadcast rights fees of $443 million (Miller, 2005). Led by Boston's WEEI-AM, the discussions can be characterized as "guy talk" (Dempsey et al., 2007). New York's WFAN became the first all-sports radio station, in 1987, with ESPN and Fox Sports radio currently leading the field. Some of the most popular programs include the following:

- *The Big Show,* on Boston's WEEI weekday afternoons 2-6 p.m., it has been popular since its debut in 1995. Glenn Ordway, a former Boston Celtics play-by-play announcer, facilitates its roundtable.
- *Gametime React,* hosted by J.T. the Brick, airs weeknights from Los Angeles 7-11 p.m. on Fox Sports Radio.
- *The Herd with Colin Cowherd,* hosted by Colin Cowherd, is on ESPN Monday through Friday 10 a.m.-1 p.m., with parts of it on podcast.
- *The Dan Patrick Show* has been syndicated by ESPN since 1999, offered weekdays 1-4 p.m.
- *The Jim Rome Show,* also known as "The Jungle," comes out of Los Angeles Monday thorugh Friday from 9 a.m.-noon for 2.5 million listeners at some 200 affiliate stations, as well as airing on its own Web site (www.jimrome.com).
- *Mike and the Mad Dog,* so named for co-hosts Mike Francesa and Chris "Mad Dog" Russo, airs starting at 3 p.m. Monday through Friday on New York's WFAN. Started in 1989, today it is simulcast on the YES Network and Albany's WROW.
- *Mike and Mike in the Morning,* hosted by Mike Golic and Mike Greenberg on ESPN Monday through Friday from 6-10 a.m. as well as simulcast on ESPN2. The highly rated drive-time sports-talk show, which draws 3 million listeners, has as its motto for the many ads: "What makes them different, makes them great." You can get some good insights into the program from Greenberg's 2006 autobiography *Why My Wife Thinks I'm an Idiot: The Life and Times of a Sportscaster Dad.*

- *The Sports Reporters* airs on ESPN at 10 a.m. Sunday mornings, replayed later, with a roundtable consisting of John Saunders and revolving guests such as Mitch Albom, Mike Lupica, Bob Ryan, Stephen A. Smith, Michael Wilbon, and others. When it began in 1988, Gary Thorne was host, followed by the late Dick Schaap. The best part, fans feel, is the ending section, called "Parting Shots," when panelists air their opinions on various sporting issues.

Going back to the notion of "guy talk" in sports radio, many followers of *Imus in the Morning* tuned in for just that combination of wide-ranging commentary. Yet, when Don Imus got his come-uppance in April, 2007, by referring to the Rutgers women's basketball team with the simultaneous sexist and racist term "nappy-headed hos," he was obviously giving more than just a sports report. In a series of events that escalated more than anyone might have imagined, the "equal-opportunity offender" provided a classic case of media-on-media, just as sport stories so often get moved to the front page. The good part was not only what topics came to the table but also that the nation got to see some extremely admirable young women athletes, along with their articulate, classy coach.

There is one major exception to testosterone talk shows: Nanci Donnellan (1996), a.k.a., *The Fabulous Sports Babe,* famous for telling callers to "Get a job, get a haircut, get a life." She reviews her background: "It's a mean business, I learned early on, but big deal. You know how this game is played when you're breaking in or you're an idiot. So I paid attention, learned how to read a room, and paid more dues than a lifelong member of the Shriners" (p. 90).

TELEVISION

As an announcer I know I shouldn't say this, but I've always felt there should be a second audio channel for sports telecasts. On the first channel, viewers could hear the play-by-play and color commentary of the announcers. The second channel, however, would broadcast only what the fans hear in the stadium. Viewers would have a choice of which one they want to listen to. Why? Because some of us just talk too damn much. And it's not just the talking. It's the analysis. Does every single play have to be analyzed and replayed and hashed over?

(Berman, 2005, pp. 203-204)

It might surprise you to learn that, according to the *Football Television Briefing Book* (1981), as early as 1938 the first sports telecast took place in Philadelphia, generally placed in the same year that television debuted at the 1939 World's Fair. Television is usually associated in the "Golden Age" of the medium, in the 1950s, because that is when it really took off, boxing being one of the most popular television programs. Because few people could afford their own sets, most of that early sports attention took place in bars. If you know someone who lived during that era, you might ask him or her if they ever watched the Friday Fights, a Gillette-sponsored institution.

Until the 1970s, television was mostly filled with children's programs, Westerns, comedies, and shows aimed at a wide audience. At that time, the television sportscaster had what Johnson (1971, pp. 192-193) called:

an odd job . . . neither art nor science, neither common labor nor honored profession . . . The sportscaster is easier to define by what he is not than by what he is. He is not quite a journalist, not quite a carnival barker, not quite an orator or interlocutor or master of ceremonies or trained seal. Yet he is a little of all of them.

Everything was about to change for the ratings leaders, CBS and NBC.

ABC, with nothing to lose, listened to its sports director, Roone P. Arledge, and before the end of the decade ABC became the network leader by broadcasting football.

To obtain more audience involvement, he attempted to capture the full ambience of the game setting. He used cranes, blimps,

and helicopters to obtain novel views of the stadium, the campus, and the town; hand-held cameras for close-up shots of
cheerleaders, pretty coeds, band members, eccentric spectators,
and nervous coaches; and rifle-type microphones to pick up the
roar of the crowd, the thud of a punt, or the crunch of a hard
tackle. (Rader, 2004, pp. 252-253)

He not only brought *The Wide World of Sports* to the screen in the
1960s, his real baby was *Monday Night Football* in 1970. Here, his
foresight even extended to include the role of sportscasters: "Since
time immemorial, there'd been two guys in the announcers' booth—
the play-by-play voice and the analyst, or x's and o's expert, who was
more often than not an ex-jock. I'll mention no names—it wasn't al-
together the fault of the announcers either—but was there any law
that said games had to be announced as though they were being
played in a cathedral?" (Arledge, 2003, p. 101). Recognizing this,
Roone Arledge is the one responsible for bringing us the person who
might be the most famous sportscaster in history: Howard Cosell.

A television rating, for your reference, measures the percentage of
a country's population of homes tuned to a particular broadcast, while
a share is the estimate of audience percentage from all television sets
in use during a give time period (Fuller, 1992, pp. 36-7); in the United
States, for example, a single ratings point, equaling one percent of the
106.7 million television households, is 1,067,000. It is upon ratings
and shares that advertisers decide where to put their sponsorship—
wanting to reach specific target markets. Needless to say, since sports
shows tend to attract men between the ages of eighteen and thirty-
five, the most sought-after group, you can now see why so much beer,
and so many cars and gizmo/gadgets are advertised during sports programming. According to Nielsen Media Research (nielsenmedia
.com), Super Bowls have accounted for four of the top-rated television programs of all time: *M*A*S*H* special (2/28/83), *Dallas*
(11/21/80), *Roots* (1/30/77), Super Bowl XVI (1982) and Super Bowl
XVII (1983), the 1994 Lillehammer Olympics, and Super Bowl XX
(1986), then parts 1 and 2 of *Gone With the Wind* in 1976 and Super
Bowl XII (1978).

Television works in reverse, too. Television has reshaped itself to accommodate "sportainment." Though technology, since the introduction of instant replay to more recent innovations such as SimulCam, has helped viewers better understand the action, at the same time, various rules of sports games have had to change so they can fit into time slots. As this is being written (7/16/2006), the start time for a New York Mets-Chicago Cubs game is pushed up so ESPN's ESPY Awards show can air in prime time.

"It's a quixotic relationship we have with television sportscasters," (Douglas S. Looney, 2000). "It can be more like family than anything else. That means we sometimes listen closely to them and other times not; that we get aggravated with their quirks and their phrases, Marv Albert repeatedly saying a basketball players score a hoop 'from downdown' but we forgive; that we take issue with them and can't imagine why they don't think like us; that we laugh at their ties and their haircuts."

Much has been written about television's framing and interpretive powers, about how the networks developed, about its role in rules and rulings, statistics and salaries, sweeps and scheduling, and, most of all, about our perception(s) of sports (Auletta, 1991; Bilby, 1986; Blumenthal and Goodenough, 1991; Boyer, 1988; Goldenson and Wolf, 1991; Gunther, 1994; Paley, 1979; Paper, 1987; Quinlan, 1979; Slide, 1991; Smith, 1990; Stark, 1997; Watson, 1998; Williams, 1989). The question posited here is the role of sportscasters in the interdependence between sports and television. In bemoaning a decline in "The Art of Sportswriting," Andrews (1987, p. 8) comments: "Television sports coverage seems perpetually at odds with itself. It spends a small fortune to bring you the game and then devotes much of its vast technical resources to distracting your attention from the game. When there is action on the field you are frequently getting instant replay of what is already past."

Traditionally, the three commercial networks have held the monopoly on the audience for sports and sportscasting. Many people would agree that, "ABC has traditionally been the master of milking sports coverage" (Robins, 1988, p. 74). Under the tutelage of Roone Arledge, ABC became the undisputed leader, with NBC anxiously hoping to join in on sports ratings. Yet Stephen Singer (1987, p. 5), a former editor for *Sport Magazine,* has rated CBS the best all-around network for sportscasters, especially citing Brent Musburger and John Madden. Not to be discounted, the success of twenty-four-hour sports on ESPN since 1979 has made major inroads into garnering the sports audience, introducing lesser-known sports and making networks evermore edgy about losing audiences to cable and other sources.

More than two decades ago, Roone Arledge was quoted as saying, "You must use the camera—and the microphone—to broadcast an image that approximates what the brain perceives, not merely what the eye sees. Only then can you create the illusion of reality" (cited in Talen, 1986, p. 50). The pictures in our heads of sports of television are a topic unto themselves.

Networks compete heavily for sports broadcasting rights, knowing they can make enormous amounts of money from advertisers, and also have access to audiences for future programs. Consider some of these contracts:

League	Network	Contract years	Fees	End of contract
MLB	Fox	6	$2.5 billion	2006
	ESPN	6	875 million	2005
NBA	ABC/ESPN	6	2.4 billion	2008
	AOL	6	2.2 billion	2008
NFL	ABC	8	4.4 billion	2006
	CBS	8	4 billion	2006
	Fox	8	4.4 billion	2006
	ESPN	8	4.8 billion	2006
NHL	ABC/ESPN	5	600 million	2004
NCAA (M)	CBS	11	6 billion	2013
NCAA (W)	ESPN	11	200 million	2013
NCAA BCS	ABC	8	930 million	2006

NASCAR	NBC/AOL	6	1.2 billion	2006
Olympics	NBC	13	3.5 billion	2008
PGA	ABC/ESPN, CBS/USA, NBC, Golf Channel	4	850 million	2006

SPORTS/TELEVISION

Sports television is just that: televised sports. These are the games that people play, and television is but a chronicler of the fleeting dramas involved, the successes and the failures. What they do on the fields and in the arenas is not Armageddon, and what we do in the production trucks is not brain surgery. And, yes, we do it in the final analysis for money, whatever ideals we choose to protect and promote along the way.

(Spence, 1988, p. 343)

We are not a nation of Couch Potatoes for nothing; we love our televisions. Nielsen research shows that our televisions are on an average of seven hours and ten minutes per day, and we have been told that we Americans clock in some 179 hours of sports annually. Television, in fact, has changed the face of sports. Drawing enormous audiences for some events, it can be just as lucrative in sponsorships for specific target groups, like golf. In return, advertising has brought with it arbitrary, mandatory time-outs, instant replays, stars and celebrities, infomercials replete with sports-related associations, extended playoffs, featured names on jerseys, changed the Bowl Championship Series, made halftime entertainment key, and more—to say nothing of network self-promotion throughout its sports programming.

What television has not done, however, is let us enjoy certain games the way we would like—explaining why we hardly see soccer in its entirety, or why baseball during the day is so limited, or why we have to pay for premium sporting events. "The best of sports television is extraordinary dramatic theater, brought from distant places, with the results in question, as athletes perform not only for the fans in the stands but also for the lens in the camera," Richard Sandomir (1991) has noted. "A televised game is an exercise in video adaptation and enhancement: it is tracked by a fleet of high-tech cameras, replayed in slow motion from multiple angles, diagrammed by an analyst with an electronic pencil, called by announcers receiving a stream of instructions in their earpieces and illustrated with dazzling graphics."

Televised sport is live; as such, it is "up close and personal" history unfolding in front of us. Cameras can direct our attention, or redirect it such that we can witness, circuslike, the entire excitement around the action. Garry Whannel (1992, p. 4) has noted:

> In that it chooses particular sports and gives us a particular view of them, television must inevitably affect the ways in which we see and understand sports. Moreover, the coverage is not simply concerned with sport; it inevitably also continually makes implicit and explicit statements, in words and pictures, about our sense of nation, of class, of the place of men and women, our relation to other nations, and so on.

Furthermore, television has made stars out of sportscasters. "Chris Berman, Curt Gowdy, Chris Schenkel, Bob Costas, Jim McKay, and Al Michaels represent the evolution of Grantland Rice and Red Smith from yesterday," writes Phil Schaaf (2004, p. 160). You might add others, of course.

Although there are enormous amount of televised sports available, it seems appropriate to highlight some of the key programs and sources for that programming. What follows are brief descriptions of ESPN, *MNF*, the Olympic Games, Pay-per-View (PPV), *Playmakers*, *Real Sports*, the Super Bowl, and TBS/TNT.

ESPN

Why was ESPN different? Its arrival and announcement addressed several issues which, at the time, were not considered feasible. What company would propose programming in a single narrow area of interest, i.e., sports? Who would do a service twenty-four hours a day when 'everyone knew' there was no television audience overnight? Perhaps the most significant question of all was, who would dare come to the cable industry with an idea that would be totally advertiser supported? (Rasmussen, 1983, pp. 16-17)

ESPN, which originally meant the Entertainment & Sports Programming Network, is based in Bristol, Connecticut, but it has tentacles worldwide. Based on the blind assumption that fans would watch and/or care about sports and sporting events 24/7, it began broadcasting on September 7, 1979, by means of an RCA Satcom 1 satellite that visionary/founder Bill Rasmussen rented for $35,000 a month. Rasmussen, who *USA Today* has called "the father of cable sports" and who *Sports Illustrated* has listed as one of the forty key persons in terms of altering and elevating sports, is currently chair of sportsat home.com.

His opening program nearly three decades ago, *SportsCenter,* today is reportedly viewed at least once each day by more than 4 million homes. "Featuring an engaging cast of smart-mouth, quipping, clever anchors like Chris Berman, Dan Patrick, and Keith Olbermann and managed behind the scenes by the brilliant John Walsh, [it has] become obligatory viewing for several generations of sports enthusiasts" (Bryant and Holt, 2006, p. 37). Personalities on the signature show have become celebrities in their own right—writing books, appearing on other sports shows, writing columns, and appearing in advertising other than is aired on ESPN. Olberman and Patrick (1997, pp. 11-27) have shared something of a glossary/explanation for their "sports speak" on the show, including terms like "A good craftsman never blames his tools" (for when a player breaks, throws, or slams a bat), "Check please" (the end of something). It's amazing to think that, on February 11, 2007, *SportCenter* aired its 30,000th episode.

Although at first there were worries about whether an audience existed, or whether there would be enough sports programming available, the model continues to grow. In 1984, ABC bought 85 percent of ESPN for $188 million, including another $14 million for the station's satellite broadcasting facilities, and then it was later sold to the Walt Disney Corporation as part of a $19 billion deal along with ABC; now, ESPN is the largest profit generator for the parent company—with an equity stake in nineteen foreign networks, ESPN .com—the most-visited Web site, ESPN sports bars, *ESPN The Magazine*—with a circulation of 1.38 and $252.1 million in advertising revenues, and the ESPN theme park attraction. ESPN2, which focuses on live-event coverage and is the decade's fastest growing cable channel, is now in 39 million households after launching in 10 million. ESPN Inc. includes the ESPN Family of Networks: ESPN, ESPN2, ESPN on ABC, ESPNEWS (24/7 highlights), ESPN Classic (documentaries and replays), ESPNU (college athletics), ESPN Deportes (Spanish-language), ESPNHD (high definition), ESPN2HD, ESPN Now, ESPN Plus, ESPN PPV, ESPN360, ESPN Radio, and ESPN Deportes Radio.

Essentially, ESPN is a marketing machine, with a wide range of business ventures such as ESPN.com, ESPN Original Entertainment, *ESPN The Magazine,* ESPN Deportes La Revista, ESPN Books, ESPN Zone, ESPY Awards, and ESPN Integration. Its key programs, listed alphabetically, include: *Around the Horn, Baseball Tonight, College GameDay* (football), *ESPN College Football Primetime, ESPN First Take* (replacing *Cold Pizza* as of May, 2007) *Friday Night Fights, Jim Rome Is Burning, Mike and Mike in the Morning, Monday Night Countdown, Monday Night Football* (MNF), *NBA Friday, NASCAR Countdown, NBA Shootaround, Outside the Lines, Pardon the Interruption, Saturday Primetime, College GameDay* (basketball), *SportsCenter, Sunday NFL Countdown,* and *Sunday Night Baseball*—many of which are listed throughout this book. *Pardon the Interruption* (PTI), which features Tony Kornheiser and Michael Wilbon discussing stories, sports, and "stuff," is an interesting example. Produced by ESPN Original Entertainment, the 5:30-6 p.m. program is filmed in Washington, DC, broadcast on both television and satellite radio, and is also available by podcast. Since its debut on October

22, 2001, the scripted segments have drawn a loyal following, and while it discusses popular culture it has, at the same time, become part of it.

ESPN has run, with ABC, an annual multisport, seasonal event called the "X" (for extreme) Games. The regular X is usually held in the summer in Los Angeles, the Winter X in Aspen/Snowmass, Colorado, but some competitions occur elsewhere and at different times (Duncan, 2004). Since it began in 2006, crazy contests range from skateboarding to motocross and more.

There have been a number of books written about the sports network. The corporation itself has operated a company called ESPN Books since 2004, which produces an annual almanac and has a wide range of authors. You might want to check out founding chair Stuart Evey's memoir from ESPN's twenty-fifth anniversary: *Creating an Empire: The No-Holds Barred Story of Power, Ego, Money, and Vision that Transformed a Culture* (2004). Others of interest are Bill Rasmussen's *Sports Junkies rejoice! The birth of ESPN* (1983), Michael Freeman's *ESPN: The Uncensored History* (2000)—"a balanced account of a megamedia company formerly mocked for its goofy programming and red ink" (p.18), Charles Hirshberg's *ESPN 25: 25 Mind-Bending, Eye-Popping, Culture Morphing Years of Highlights* (2004), Jay Lovinger's *The Gospel According to ESPN: The Saints, Saviors, and Sinners of Sports* (2003), Keith Olbermann and Dan Patrick's *The Big Show: Inside ESPN's SportsCenter* (1997), and Shelly Youngblut's *The Quotable ESPN* (1998). That last one has some funny slips and clips, such as:

- Billy Crystal, talking about Mickey Mantle: "He just was everything. If it was a hot, gorgeous day and I lived right on the beach, I'm inside watching the Yankees. I limp like him. I walk like him. At my Bar Mitzvah I had an Oklahoma accent. After my haftorah I wanted a beer. And I think I once told my parents, Play me or trade me."
- Roone Arledge on Howard Cosell: "He's the garlic that makes the stew work."

• Howard Cosell on Mike Tyson: "He's a common criminal who's getting what he deserves. He's finished, washed up, deserves to be, period. He's a thug."

But all is not laughs at ESPN; gender imbalance continues—men outnumber women by a 48:1 ratio (Tuggle, 1997; Adams and Tuggle, 2004, and Eggerton, 2005). It has a better record in terms of being gay-friendly (Ziegler, 2007), dating from its airing of the ground-breaking *Outside the Lines* special "The World of the Gay Athlete" in 1998.

The company continues to grow. In 1993, Keith Olbermann and Suzy Kolber started *SportsNite* on ESPN2 and in 1996 came ESPNEWS. The next year, ESPN bought the Classic Sports Network, renaming it ESPN Classic, and ESPNU followed in 2005. International expansion, thanks to satellites, has occurred in Asia, Africa, Latin America, and Europe. Employing some 129,000 people, by 2004 its annual revenue was reported to be $30.8 billion.

You may be familiar with many of ESPN's employees. From radio, you may know Colin Cowherd, Dan Davis, Mike Golic, Mike Greenberg, Neil Jackson, Mark Kestacher, Christine Lisi, Mark Madden, Al Morganti, Dan Patrick *(SportsCenter),* Bob Picozzi, Jay Reynolds, Stan Savran ("Stan, Guy, love the show"), Jason Smith, and John Stashower, for starters. From television, you may know Greg Anthony *(NBA Shootout),* Chris Berman, Bonnie Bernstein, Norman Chad *(World Series of Poker),* John Clayton ("The Professor"), Linda Cohn (the first female sports anchor), Beano Cook (college football historian), Josh Elliott *(Classic Now),* Brian Kenny, Tony Kornheiser, Tim Kurkjian *(Baseball Tonight),* Lon McEachern, Rachel Nichols ("breaking news"), and many more. In addition, sportswriters such as Pat Forde (ESPN.com), Chuck Hirshberg *(ESPN 25),* "Mort" Mortensen *(NFL Countdown),* Rob Neyer (baseball columnist), Buster Olney *(ESPN: The Magazine),* Len Pasquarelli (NFL), Jeremy Schaap *(Outside the Lines),* Bill Simmons ("The Sports Guy"), George Solomon (ESPN's first ombudsman), Jason Stark *(Baseball Tonight),* Michael Wilbon *(PTI),* and Gene Wojciechowski *(ESPN The Magazine)* are affiliated with the network.

Some other sports names you might know from ESPN, many whose extended profiles are included here: John Anderson, Mike Breen, Hubie Brown, Chris Connelly, Lee Corso, Jay Crawford, Rece Davis, Chris Fowler, Ron Franklin, Peter Gammons, Jay Harris, Kirk Herbstreit, Fred Hickman, Tom Jackson, Dana Jacobson, Brian Kenny, Suzy Kolber, Tony Kornheiser, Bob Ley, Steve Levy, Kenny Mayne, Sean McDonough, Jon Miller, Joe Morgan, Brent Musburger, Brad Nessler, Mike Patrick, Karl Ravech, Tony Reali, Jim Rome, John Saunders, Stuart Scott, Howie Schwab, Dan Shulman, Michele Tafoya, Joe Theisman, Mike Tirico, Dick Vitale, Michael Wilbon, and many more. For more ESPN personnel, past and present, see http://en .wikipedia.org/wiki/List_of_ESPN_personalities.

"By virtue of its omnipresence, its audience, its content, its credibility, its popularity, ESPN is the king of sports television," sportswriter Jim Shea (2000, p. 1) has noted. "It has become the most dominant force in the history of sports broadcasting, an interconnected colossus of multimedia synergy, which now routinely influences and alters the way sports are viewed, covered, and even played."

Monday Night Football (MNF)

In May 2005, the NFL and ESPN announced a $8.8 billion, eight-year (2006-2013) deal for broadcast of *Monday Night Football*. In replacing ABC, ESPN's contract is about twice what its sister company had been paying out for a prime-time show that some say may be past its prime. And the new deal is nearly twice the $600 million a year ESPN had been paying to carry games on Sunday night. ESPN also gets rights to wireless and Spanish-language telecasts.

In the early days of sports journalism, an evolution occurred that went beyond print media to the radio, where it discovered its real niche with television following with the success of ABC's gambit of *Monday Night Football* beginning September 21, 1970. Running so far behind the other networks it was jokingly called the Almost Broadcasting Company, ABC had nothing to lose by trying sports. Arledge's prescient memo about sports television still holds: "Heretofore, television has done a remarkable job of bringing the game to the viewer— now we are going to take the viewer to the game! We will utilize every production technique . . . to heighten the viewer's feeling of actually sitting in the stands and participating personally in the excitement and color. In short—*We are going to add show business to sports!*" (cited in Gunther and Carter, 1988, pp. 18-19).

MNF's immediate and immense popularity stunned producers and fans alike, creating a simultaneous revolution within the world of sport and the world of media. It has featured names still known to sports followers today—Howard Cosell, Frank Gifford, Don Meredith, Joe Namath, O.J. Simpson, Fran Tarkenton, Keith Jackson, Alex Karras, Fred Williamson, Al Michaels, Dan Dierdorf, Chris Berman, Boomer Esiason, and many others—including brief bits for Rush Limbaugh and Dennis Miller (Fuller, 2001). Lesley Visser, who had been a sportscaster with CBS, became *MNF*'s first female commentator, in 1996—setting the stage for other women, notably Melissa Stark and Lisa Guerrero.

"In the beginning, there was only magic," Gunther and Carter (1988, pp. 365-366) have outlined. There was Arledge, with the vision to transform a football game into a potent stew of drama, comedy, and soap opera; and Cosell, with the personal and talent to bring new viewers to the set. There was Gifford, with his jock expertise and sex appeal; and Meredith, with his country wit. There was [Chet] Forte, with his technical brilliance; and [Don] Ohlmeyer, with his ability to lead. There was also a company, ABC, that was willing to gamble, and an industry, sports television, ready to be awakened." Frank Gifford (1993, p. 9) adds his perspective: "In terms of broadcasting techniques, the early years of *MNF* resembled the early days of television. We made it up as we went along."

The program was not without its own controversies, particularly for Don Meredith. In 1973, it was clear that he was using marijuana while covering a Denver Broncos-Oakland Raiders game when he declared, "We're in Mile High City and I sure am," or that he had been drinking during a Buffalo Bills-Kansas City Chiefs game, but he really went over the line by referring to President Richard Nixon as "Tricky Dick." Howard Cosell drew criticism for a 1983 offhand referral to an African American (Alvin Garrett of the Washington Redskins) as a "little monkey"; although he insisted it was a word he also used for his grandchildren, responses of racism persisted.

Although *MNF* was the longest-running show in prime time except for *60 Minutes,* and although it predominated on ABC some 555 Monday nights with high ratings, and although the show can be seen in Canada (on TSN), in Europe (on NASN), and in Spanish, it made a move to ESPN in 2006. Walt Disney owns both networks, so ESPN has aired the show since August 14, 2006 (Oakland Raiders-Minnesota Vikings). New graphics were added, and a time-score box has been placed digitally in the lower center of the television screen, while the program still continues to be aired on national radio.

With Joe Theismann and Tony Kornheiser as sportscasters, the October 23, 2006, contest between the New York Giants and the Dallas Cowboys counted the largest audience in cable television history (16,028,000). Ron Jaworski, a former NFL quarterback, has recently been named to replace Theismann—making me wonder what Howard Cosell might say about *MNF*'s jockocracy heritage. Is it Monday yet?

The Olympic Games

The Olympics, a global multisport extravaganza that takes place in a different city every four years, alternately summer or winter every two years since 1992, brings together the best athletes in the world from participating countries. Gold (first place), silver (second), and bronze (third) medals are awarded to winners; the next games will take place in the summer of 2008 in Beijing, 2012 in London, winter of 2010 in Vancouver.

There has been a great deal of academic research on the Olympic Games (Baker, 2000; Barney, Wenn, and Martyn, 2002; Billings, 2007; Daddario, 1998; de Morgas Spa, Rivenburgh, and Larson, 1995; Dyreson, 1998; Findling, and Pelle, 1996; Fuller 1987a and b, 1990 b and c, 1996; Guttmann, 1992; Hoberman, 1986; Larson, and Park, 1993; Lenskyj, 2000; Mandell, 1987; Preuss, 2000; Roche, 2000; Senn, 1999; U.S. Olympic Committee, 1996; Wilson and Derse, 2001; Young and Wamsley, 2005). For more information, see www.olympic.org.

Pay-per-view (PPV)

Although it could be argued that most of our television comes pre-paid, the concept of pay-per-view (PPV) actually began during the late 1980s. Cable companies provided a phone-in number that automatically allows us to see programs of our choice. That choice, as it turns out, is usually sports-related—especially for boxing; in 2003, for example, the Lennox Lewis-Mike Tyson heavyweight fight rang up a record $106.8 million, which was jointly distributed by HBO and Showtime. Next, *Wrestlemania* brought in more than $28 million per show—such that PPV event revenues top $363 million annually.

Playmakers

Premiering on ESPN's Original Entertainment on August 26, 2003, *Playmakers* (based on Fuller, 2004a; see also Cummins, 2006) was an eleven-part series billing itself this way: "A gritty ensemble chronicling the behind-the-scenes and off-the-field lives of the players, families, coaches and owner of a fictional professional football team. This lightning-paced series takes you beyond Sunday's glory, 'good guy' endorsements, and super-jock celebrity." Following a huge promotional campaign, with its own Web page, the moniker challenged, "If all you see is the athlete, open your eyes," and trailers highlighted the main characters by their fictional names and football positions: middle linebacker Eric Olczyk (Jason Matthew Smith—*he hates the game*), running back Leon Taylor (Russell Hornsby—*he loves the game*), and running back Demetrius Harris (Omar Gooding—*he abuses the game*). Its goal was to mirror reality, and many of the topics were simply usurped from media headlines—the idea being to make the players real, beyond just playing football.

If the idea was to deal with "reality" relative to pro football, *Playmakers* might be said to have scored an instant touchdown, but one that worked more like a boomerang. True to its stated decision to be a gritty gridiron profile, those topics included everything ranging from drug use to domestic violence, injuries to criminal intent, hidden homophobia to open racism, and the politics inherent in team play, team ownership, coaching, and corporate controls. Some saw it as a male soap opera. Just to give you some sense of it, these were some of the episode titles: *Game Day, The Piss Man, The Choice, Halftime, Man in Motion, Talk Radio, Down and Distance, The Outing, Tenth of a Second,* and at the end we watch one of the players considering moving into sportscasting.

Ratings were good, but critical reactions were mixed, and *Playmakers* was rent with controversy both with media and chat groups. Here is a sampling:

- *Playmakers* is well-written and well-acted, but it is professional football as observed by Joan Didion rather than John Madden—*New York Times.*
- Just because the show deals with clichés doesn't make it unbelievable or unwatchable. *Playmakers* is superbly cast—*Houston Chronicle.*
- If pro football bores you, are you likely to find anything intriguing in *Playmakers?* Surprisingly, yes—*Washington Post.*
- If anything, *Playmakers* is too dark, so full of brooding hulks that there's no room left for the 'ain't we still havin' fun' approach of the inspired Mac Davis in *North Dallas Forty*—*Denver Post.*
- Intelligently scripted and convincingly acted, this series is akin to open heart surgery in its unsparing depictions of pay-for-play gladiators—*Dallas Morning News.*
- If nothing else, it's nice to see a drama about sports and know you're not going to end up sitting through a scene where a father and son tearfully play catch as the violins crescendo—*Salon.*
- What's interesting, ultimately, is that ESPN is actually trying to defuse its viewers' relentless hero worship—*LA Daily News.*
- If *Playmakers* is a hit, will the ESPN empire eventually resemble MTV, which pays lip service to music but is really just about youth marketing?—*Newark Star-Ledger.*
- Despite a strong cast and an interesting look, *Playmakers* is undermined by writing that's thoroughly condescending in both its predictability and in the way it assumes viewers are too dumb to get what's going on without it being drummed into their heads.

The result is not a total bust, but a major disappointment—*Chicago Sun-Times.*

- You find yourself thinking the series would be significantly better without the flow of self-analytical, cerebral monologues—*Boston Globe.*

- For the writers and producers behind *Playmakers,* the game has to be about getting better. In football terms, the series is starting its first season playing like an expansion team full of promise yet plagued by uncertainty and lack of experience—*Cleveland Plain Dealer.*

Nevertheless, yielding to pressure from NFL executives and players, an official announcement was made February 4, 2004, that *Playmakers* would be permanently cancelled after only its first season. Without mentioning the NFL by name, Mark Shapiro, ESPN executive VP of programming and production issued this statement: "Many considerations went into this decision, not the least of which was the reaction from a longtime and valued partner" (cited in Consoli, 2004). Although when it first came on advertisers scrambled to be part of *Playmakers,* and they were happy to participate in what was such a lucrative viewership, nevertheless there were problems. Who fumbled, you might wonder. Consider: ESPN paid the NFL $4.8 billion for rights to Sunday night games for eight seasons; it behooves the network to be pro- pro football!

At no point in *Playmakers'* history was the NFL even mentioned—and not in previews or promos, in ads, or in any episodes. Yet, you will recall, Disney is the parent company of both ESPN and ABC, with whom, along with the NFL, it reportedly has a mutually dependent relationship. The two parties (Disney and the NFL) constructed a $9.2-billion contract granting ESPN and ABC rights to broadcast games on Sunday and Monday nights. Never had either of those parties endorsed *Playmakers;* in fact, as the series sprang, various members and players of the NFL grew increasingly upset with it. In particular, some players called it "stereotypical garbage," complaining that its characters were flawed. Paul Tagliabue, NFL commissioner, let it be known that he was concerned about the show's one-dimensionality and potential for perpetuating racial stereotypes. So, although the episodes were well received by a high audience ratio, men and women alike, the series failed to appease its higher powers. Its cancellation also freed up a time slot in prime time for yet more sports.

But don't forget the economics of it all: The very week that ESPN canceled *Playmakers,* it also announced its release on a three-disc DVD set at a list price of $49.99—eleven episodes, with audio commentary by creator/producer John Eisendrath, behind-the-scenes featurettes, Dolby sound, and widescreen anamorphic format. *Playmakers* offers a classic case study: Factoring in content, profit motives, consumer appetites, network operations, public relations and political economy, it becomes increasingly difficult to determine where stories begin and fictionalizing finishes. Here, it makes us better understand those who claim that ESPN really stands for "Endlessly Self-Promoting Network." Maybe it is *all* fiction.

Real Sports

HBO's monthly magazine headliner, hosted by Bryant Gumbel since 1995, *Real Sports* takes the game into the media arena by means of exploring sports issues, controversies, and people. In operation since 1995, its main correspondents are James Brown (former basketball player and host of several HBO boxing telecasts), Mary Carillo (former tennis player, now tennis announcer), Frank Deford (prolific sports writer and commentator), Bernard Goldberg (sports writer/reporter), and Armen Keteyian (veteran sports journalist). Winner of fifteen sports Emmy awards, it has been honored by Northeastern University for "Excellence in Sports Journalism," "Outstanding Sports Journalism" for its investigative pieces, and a 2005 Sport Emmy Award for outstanding editing.

Super Bowl

"America's annual sports extravaganza" (Fuller, 1999c), this "Super Sunday" NFL championship contest has become the largest television event of the year, an unofficial national holiday, and our second-largest day of food consumption, after Thanksgiving. Since its inception in 1967, Super Bowl consistently has been a ratings leader, drawing audiences of 80 to 90 million Americans and a billion worldwide, with recent advertising rates of $2.6 million for thirty seconds. Its halftime shows are well-established in our popular culture, new technology has been introduced for its production (Mullen and Mazzocco, 2000), it has been blamed for inducing domestic violence (Fuller, 1992a; Goodman, 1998), and it quite naturally has drawn a good deal of academic attention (McAllister, 1996; O'Neill, 1991; Schwartz, 1998; Weiss and Day, 2002). For more, log on to www .superbowl.com.

TBS/TNT

Better known as Turner Sports, the network has a number of outstanding sportscasters, including Danny Ainge, Marv Albert, Charles Barkley, Hubie Brown, Mike Fratello, Kevin Harlan, Ernie Johnson, Cheryl Miller, Craig Sager, Kenny Smith, Dick Stockton, John Thompson, and Peter Vecsey.

As you might easily imagine, an entire book could be written about ancillary sport/media topics such as major networks (e.g., Fox Sports, Turner Broadcasting Systems, CNN/SI), team-owned networks (e.g., YES, Houston Astros, (Kansas City) Royals TV, Minnesota Twins' Victory Sports, Colorado Avalanche and Denver Nuggets), even "narrowcasting"—niche sports (e.g., bass fishing, rugby, luge). NASCAR, which can provide its own special story, is mostly dealt with in Chapter 4, as is the Super Bowl under in Chapter 3, and events such the World Cup, the Tour de France, even the X Games appear elsewhere.

CONTROVERSIES

Sportscasting has its own built-in history of dealing with controversy, which typically has resulted in dismissal of the offending sportscasters. The AskMen blog (www.askmen.com/sports/fitness_ top_ten/58_fitness_list.html) lists the "Top 10 Disastrous Announcer

Comments," (listed in reverse order as follows with my editorial additions):

10. *Boomer Esiason*'s "I think maybe Peyton Manning is this generation's Dan Marino"—referring to Marino, the man many people consider "the best NFL quarterback to *never* win a Super Bowl."

9. *Mike North*, confusing South Korean pitcher Jae Kuk Ryu's start for the Chicago Cubs: "Who was the Chinaman on the mound the other day? Whoever it was shouldn't wear a major League uniform every again. He was dreadful."

8. *Keith Hernandez*'s chauvinistic comment, during a New York Mets broadcast for SportsNet New York, upon seeing a woman in the San Diego Padres dugout: "Who is the girl in the dugout, with the long hair? What's going on here? You have got to be kidding me. Only player personnel in the dugout." He actually made it worse later, when he tried to apologize by saying how much he loved "you gals out there."

7. *Don Cherry*, a staple for *Hockey Night in Canada*, upon learning that the Winnipeg Jets had hired a man named Alpo Suhonen as coach in 1989, reacted with "Alpo? That's dog food isn't it?"

6. *Bryant Gumbel*, who you may know from his fifteen-year stint on *The Today Show* or Olympics coverage, made a gaffe on HBO's *Real Sports with Bryant Gumbel*, a monthly HBO sports newsmagazine that debuted on April 12, 1995, about former NFL commissioner Paul Tagliabue's holding player union president Gene Upshaw on a leash, but that was nothing compared to what he said on February 16, 2006, about the Winter Olympics: "So try not to laugh when someone says these are the world's greatest athletes, despite a paucity of blacks that makes the Winter Games look like a GOP convention." (The really amazing thing is an African American made what were misconstrued as racist comments, but it seems appropriate to include Gumbel's inclusion to the above statement): "Try not to point out that something's not really a sport if a pseudo-athlete waits in what's called a kiss-and-cry area, while some panel of subjective judges decides who won."

5. *Larry Krueger,* a radio talk show host of *Sportsphone 680,* in-
sulted Giants players and their manager Felipe Alou about
their losing streak with this ill-considered jibe on August 3,
2005: "San Francisco has too many brain-dead Caribbean hitters hacking at slop nightly."

4. *Al Campanis,* general manager of the Los Angeles Dodgers,
made this remark on Ted Koppel's *Nightline* exactly forty
years after Jackie Robinson's MLB debut (April 15, 1947):
"[Blacks] may not have some of the necessities to be, let's say,
a field manager, or, perhaps, a general manager." Yes, he was
fired two days later.

3. *Rush Limbaugh,* the radio talk show host who prides himself
on his conservative opinions, overstepped a line when he
made this racist appraisal of Donovan McNabb on *Sunday
NFL Countdown* in 2003: "Sorry to say this. I don't think he's
been that good from the get-go. I think what we've had here is
a little social concern in the NFL. The media has been very de-
sirous that a black quarterback do well. There is a little hope
invested in McNabb, and he got a lot of credit for the performance of this team that he didn't deserve." Before being asked
to leave, Limbaugh resigned.

2. *Jimmy "The Greek" Snyder,* an analyst on CBS's *The NFL Today,* insinuated about his abilities of prediction but was quite
direct about race, stating on a 1983 show, "During the slave
period, the slave owner would breed his big black with his big
woman so that he would have a big black kid—that's where it
all started." Fired immediately, his broadcasting career soon
lacked all probabilities.

1. *Howard Cosell*'s "little monkey" comment, cited earlier.

No doubt you know some other ill-chosen phrases that have gotten
sportscasters into trouble—or that should have. How about NFL analyst Tom Brookshier's 1983 assessment that the University of Louisville basketball team had "a collective I.Q. of 40"? Or *Chicago Sun-
Times* reporter Joe Cowley's calling Toronto, in 2004, "nothing but a
city in a third-world country"? *Dallas Morning News'* Tom Cow-
lishaw, who often appears on ESPN's *Around the Horn* talk show and
is a lead reporter for ESPN2's *NASCAR Now,* drew heat when he

deemed the Miami Heat "unworthy opponents" of the Dallas Maver-
icks in the 2006 NBA Finals—a prediction he later had to eat.

BEYOND BROADCASTING

Much of what appears on television shares a symbiotic relationship with other media. For example, just as we might log onto the
Internet to access scores, motion pictures appear as made-for-TV
specials—such as ESPN 2's *Four Minutes,* about runner Roger Bannister's breaking the time barrier on May 6, 1954. Or, think about the
network's own foray into the print media with *ESPN The Magazine,*
which debuted in 1998 with a circulation of 350,000 that soon doubled, never mind its top-traffic Web site (espn.com). In general, you
should be well aware that this notion of symbiosis refers to an interplay between broadcasters/sportscasters, sponsors/sportscasters, and
the events they are covering.

Technology

Today, we can access sporting events on our personal computers,
our cell phones, pagers, and on our iPods. We might wonder what will
become of the ballpark when broadband, wireless, and on-demand
media have evolved to where we never need to be without knowledge
of our favorite teams and players (Fuller, forthcoming). As audiences
become more fragmented and niche oriented, convergences between
media conglomerates and media venues allow for increasingly sophisticated means of marketing sports. When you consider the enormous growth of the billion-dollar online sports services industry, the
consumers, are important determinants of programming.

Collegiality and Competition

By the same token, collegiality between sportscasters both on and
off the air plays a critical role in both their and our understanding. For
example, Len Berman (2005, p. 191) raves about his relationship

with Bob "The Cooz" Cousy doing Celtics games, saying how he and the former player, then analyst, ". . . would talk about life as much as basketball. One thing he taught me: when you're all uptight and your blood pressure is racing, try to slow everything down. Brush your teeth slower. Pull up your pants more deliberately. Everything. It works, and I do it to this day."

Dick Enberg (2004, pp. 110-111) describes the synchronicity he shared with Don Drysdale:

> Although Drysdale and I had a special relationship away from the field, it was even better in the broadcast booth. Most baseball announcers do their scheduled innings alone, but we developed an open-mike system so that both of us could talk in the same inning. As the lead announcer, I called six innings, and Don called three, but we had to toggle switches on our mikes that allowed each of us to go on the air whenever we wanted. We knew that going one on one we'd never beat Vin Scully, the broadcasting poet of the Dodgers, but we thought the two of us together would be reasonably competitive for the Southern California audience.

Enberg also honors Bud Collins, who he replaced as play-by-play announcer at Wimbledon. "He never showed an ounce of resentment. Instead, he graciously assisted me to understand the sport and its subtleties . . . What a tremendous ally!" (p. 202).

Jon Miller (2000, p. 199), stated that his partner, Joe Morgan, helped him: "I've never known anyone who consistently offers as many good insights on a baseball telecast as Joe. When Joe is on the telecast, there's always a moment when you say, 'You know, that's a really good point' . . . The great thing about Joe is that he's just a totally natural, up-front person" (p. 202). Together, they have established what they call a camera angle "relationship shot" that they frequently use: "It's shot from a camera placed high above third base to show both the pitcher and a runner at first base. The point is not only to see them, but to see them reacting to each other's movements in base-stealing situations" (p. 206).

There is a National Sportscasters and Sportswriters Hall of Fame (NSSA), located in Salisbury, North Carolina. Formed in 1959, its first honorees were Lindsey Nelson and Red Smith. After you read this next media section, dedicated completely to the subject of sportscasters, you might want to make your own selections.

SPORTSCASTERS

Because we all need mentors, this section introduces you to subjects surrounding sportscasters in terms of their recognition, the issue of "jockocracy," sportscaster celebrityhood, sportscaster signature statements, sportscasters as newscasters, and sportscasters in the media. It closes with some incredible sportscaster profiles—ranging from pioneers to today's hottest representatives.

From his half-century of broadcasting, sportscaster great Red Barber (1970, p. 225) shared the fact that for many years he kept this stanza from Rudyard Kipling's *The Elephant Child* on his desk:

> I keep six honest serving men
> (They taught me all I knew):
> Their names are What and Why and When
> And How and Where and Who.

For sportscasters, these essentials of reporting are basic, almost taken for granted. Barber adds, "Without trying to top Kipling, let me name an additional six serving-men for the radio-television sports broadcaster to call upon in his play-by-play profession. They are preparation, evaluation, concentration, curiosity, impartiality, and, if such can be achieved, imperturbability." In addition to athletes and audiences, it should be noted that sportscasters have many other constituencies that they need to consider: producer(s)/director(s) of their programs, network owners, franchise owners, and corporate sponsors. If all goes according to plan, everyone wins.

"Members of the on-air television sports fraternity make up a mixed bag of types and talents," wrote William O. Johnson, Jr. back in 1971. "They are a cast of characters with almost nothing in common except the drive to appear frequently before millions of people and speak for high pay. There seems to be no approved method. And none *un*-approved, for that matter" (p. 195). Would you say much has changed?

"Ah, the voices of sports broadcasting. Some are high, some are low. Some are deep, some are soft. Some are tough, some are tender. Some are just, well, damn irritating. They are the voices that fill our weekends with sound and fury signifying nothing. Some do it better than others," (Norman Chad, 1990). He supplies some analyses: Keith Jackson sounds like "a steer auctioneer," Dick Enberg "a roomful of cotton balls," Bob Costas "the kid in the back of the room in seventh grade," Dick Stockton "the guy who organizes the senior class trip," John Madden "that big, friendly dog that slurps the water out of your toilet bowl," Pat Summerall "12-year-old Scotch," Greg Gumbel "like Bryant Gumbel," Chris Berman "like Fred Flintstone on amphetamines," Tim McCarver "half-and-half that's gone sour," and Al Michaels simply "sounds great."

Sportscaster Recognition

In 1978, the National Sportscasters and Sportswriters Association decided to elect people for an annual "Sportscaster of the Year" award for broadcasters making "major contributions to baseball." Named for sportswriter Ford C. Frick, who served as president of the National League from 1934 to 1951 and Baseball Commissioner from 1951 to 1965, in addition to being a ghostwriter for Babe Ruth in the 1920s, the winners' names are located on a plaque in the Baseball Hall of Fame at Cooperstown, New York. Chronologically, they include the following: Mel Allen and Red Barber (1978), Bob Elson (1979), Russ Hodges (1980), Ernie Harwell (1981), Vin Scully (1982), Jack Brickhouse (1983), Curt Gowdy (1984), Buck Canel (1985), Bob Prince (1986), Jack Buck (1987), Lindsey Nelson (1988), Harry Caray (1989), By Saam (1990), Joe Garagiola (1991), Milo Hamilton (1992), Chuck Thompson (1993), Bob Murphy (1994), Bob Wolff (1995), Herb Carneal (1996), Jimmy Dudley (1997), Jaime Jarrin (1998), Arch McDonald (1999), Marty Brennaman (2000), Felo Ramirez (2001), Harry Kalas (2002), Bob Uecker (2003), Lon Simmons

(2004), Jerry Coleman (2005), Gene Elston (2006), and Denny Matthews (2007). Its 20-member electorate, comprised of living Frick winners and broadcast historians/columnists, currently includes Frick honorees Marty Brennaman, Herb Carneal, Joe Garagiola, Curt Gowdy, Ernie Harwell, Jaime Jarrin, Milo Hamilton, Harry Kalas, Bob Murphy, Felo Ramirez, Vin Scully, Chuck Thompson, Bob Uecker and Bob Wolff, and, historians/columnists Bob Costas (NBC), Barry Horn *(Dallas Morning News),* Stan Isaacs (formerly of *New York Newsday*), historians Ted Patterson and Curt Smith, and Larry Stewart *(Los Angeles Times).*

As you will note under individual sportscaster's profiles, there are a number of other awards and recognitions, ranging from local Halls of Fame to sport-specific prizes. Many of the sportscasters themselves are immortalized in various books (Albert, 1993; Allen, 1959, 1964; Barber, 1947, 1970, 1997; Bender, 1994; Berkow, 1986; Berman, 2005; Borelli, 2005; Bradshaw, 2001, 2002; Brickhouse, 1986, 1996; Buck, 1997, 2003; Cannon, 1978; Caray, 1989, 2003; Castiglione, 2006; Coleman, 1973, 1982, 2000; Cope, 2002; Cosell, 1973, 1974, 1985, 1991; Costas, 1998, 2001; Cousy, 1958; Deford, 2000; Drysdale, 1990; Dunphy, 1988; Edwards, 1993; Eisenstock, 2001; Elston, 2005; Enberg, 2004; Feherty, 2003; Garagiola, 1990; Garner, 1999, 2000; Gifford, 1976, 1993; Glickman, 1996; Gowdy, 1966, 1993; Graham, 1981, 2003; Greenberg, 2006; Green, 1997; Greenwald, 1997; Hamilton, 2006; Harmon, 1998; Harwell, 1985, 1991, 2001, 2002, 2004; Hearn, 2004; Hodges, 1952, 1963; Hubbell, 1975; Hughes and Miles, 2005; Jackson, 1987; Johnston, 2005; Keegan, 2002; Kiner, 1987; Kornheiser, 2003; LaRussa, 2003; Lawler, 2003; Levine, 1993; Lupica, 1988; Madden, 1984, 1988, 1996; Matthews, 1999, 2006; McCarver, 1987; McKay, 1973, 1998; Miller, 1998; Nelson, 1966, 1985; Olbermann and Patrick, 1997; Oppenheim, 1994; Packer, 1986, 1999; Petterchak, 1996; Peyer, 1997; Rashad, 1988; Remy, 2004; Reynolds, 2005; Rice, 1954; Russo, 2006; Schaap, 2001; Schemmel, 1996; Sherrod, 1988; Smith, 1978, 1992, 1995, 1998, 2005; Stern, 1949; Stone, 1999; Storm, 2002; Stram, 1986; Summerall, 2006; Thompson, 1996; Thornley, 1991; Uecker, 1982; Vitale, 1988, 2003; Whitaker, 1998; Wolf, 1983, 2000; Wolfe, 1998; Wolff, 1992); see also Appendix 2

Jockocracy

Generally speaking, these alleged analysts and colormen serve a limited role—and they rarely proved themselves capable of bridging the gap between entertainment and journalism. The bottom line: they are not communicators.

> Put an ex-jock in the booth, and their cliche-ridden presentation of a game is the least of their sins. As a result of their lack of training, most of them are blessedly lost when trying to establish a story line for a telecast—i.e., detecting trends, keying on the personality and experiences of a player as they relate to his performance on the field, knowing his strengths and weaknesses, recalling the flow of events from earlier in the game as a series of plays rather than as a contest, and often they are ignorant of the human perspective. (Cosell, 1985, p. 134)

In 1985, sportscaster Howard Cosell introduced the term "jockocracy," decrying the use of former professional athletes in the broadcasting booth (Fuller, 2005a); in particular, Cosell was angry that, despite the fact that they had no formal training in sports journalism, they formed a fraternity of highly-paid, self-appointed "experts." The media went wild at his perception. While the argument can be made that some of these ex-jocks have performed well, especially in terms of their popularity, the press box paradigm shift has manifested itself into a number of iterations even the late, brilliant Cosell could not have foreseen.

Journalism purists lament of sports broadcasting becoming "jockocrappy" (Moynihan, 2003). For television producers, on the other hand, the process of employing "ex-"s has been so successful in sports that they have also tried to incorporate comedians as commentators (e.g., Fuller, 2001). "Howard Cosell wasn't trying to be ironic when he condemned the 'jockocracy' that crept into network broadcasts of sporting events," Bill Peterson wrote (2000):

> Trained as an attorney, Cosell nonetheless took journalism almost as seriously as his own celebrity. As long as news gather-

ing professionals made the commitment to learn journalism and practice it with competence that comes through experience, Cosell expressed outrage that former athletes started ahead of them at the top of the profession. The debate really boils down to taste, because sports broadcasts aren't, strictly speaking, journalistic venues. Former athletes bring to the booth deep firsthand knowledge of the games. Good reporters bring every bit as much knowledge, though it's of the third-person strain. As the game is broadcast, though, viewers really want to understand important strategic points that are more readily identified by former players and coaches, who have the right kind of knowledge for that task. (p. 1)

Feminists have preempted the term to mean patriarchy in particular, convoluting it to terms like "phallocracy," "penocracy," and/or "cockocracy," considering its role vis-à-vis subjects like Title IX, sexual harassment, or women sportscasters. In October 2002, commentator/self-appointed curmudgeon Andy Rooney of *60 Minutes* set off a firestorm of controversy when he said female sports broadcasters sidelined reporters and had no business covering football games.

The jockocracy issue is not a new one. Pretelevision days' Waldo Abbot (1941, p. 62) stated: "Undoubtedly a good background knowledge of sports is essential; but the knowledge of how to dramatize the voice, to pick vivid, descriptive words quickly, to keep on giving information in the midst of excitement, and to inject the thrill of the game without hesitation into the microphone are more essential than previous participation in the sport." In 1932, Jack Graney became the first ex-athlete to occupy the broadcast booth, becoming the "Voice of the Indians." Many of television's color commentators are ex-jocks who, according to Klatell and Marcus (1988, p. 17), "have taught us several valuable lessons: it isn't nearly as easy as it looks; being good at an activity like sports is not the same as being good at understanding or explaining it; mediocrity is so commonplace anyone with a little spark or originality will shine through."

Colleges and universities have been forced to reflect on their actions relative to jockocracy, many of them needing to come to terms with privileged academic, social, and cultural separations of their athletes (Sperber, 2007; Bowen et al., 2003.) The concept is even blamed for events at Columbine in 1999, the Colorado high school where dominant athletes were the targets of student snipers. Katz and Jhally (1999) have written: "The lessons from Columbine High—a typical suburban 'jockocracy,' where the dominant male athletes did not hide their disdain for those who did not fit in—are pretty clear. The 17- and 18-year-old shooters, tired of being ridiculed or marginalized, weren't big and strong and so they used the great equalizer: weapons." Perhaps we need to reassess sports star celebrities ("the gods and goddesses of athleticism"), remembering Cosell's admonition that, "Rule Number One of the 'Jockocracy' is that pro-athletes and politics never mix." Too many sports stars have become popular superstars, legends, gods/goddesses of athleticism, and/or icons; David Laurell (2003) says they make up "jockocracy's Mount Rushmore." Still, the jock-as-role-model has a long way to go.

"The viewing public is different that it was," declares writer/sportsman Alan Williams (n.d.), who urges us to consider Cosell when we wonder about the future of televised sports: "We're more informed. If we want to know how the Cowboys do on third down conversions in the red zones, all we have to do is look it up on the Internet. Better still, some geek in the truck will punch up the graphic as we watch. We're smart enough to figure out what it means." Calling for real *sports journalists,* who should be "erudite, honest, and fearless," not sports personalities and not people who have played the game, he gleefully declares that, "Somewhere, Cosell is laughing."

Cosell's rant against television networks' providing broadcasting jobs for former pro athletes with little or no training also applies to the sports arena, according to Bob Barcelona (2004), who sees its detrimental role in recreational sports management. Hubert Mizell (2003) also has tackled retiring athletes who become "network yaps," deciding that, "A majority of jock announcers strain to remain too cozy with guys still wearing NFL uniforms, as well as coaches. Trying to keep the high-fives going and avoid sneers. All of which means TV audiences are frequently and generously served commentary that is more velvet-gloved than bare-knuckled." (A *TV Guide* poll taken during Cosell's tenure named him concurrently the most liked and the most disliked sportscaster!)

In what is perhaps the ultimate irony, Cosell's pontificating prescience about what audiences deserve has come nearly full circle, as technology and ever-growing information resources encourage us to be more proactive sports consumers. Today, while we bemoan jockocracies in a number of arenas, ranging from recreational to ecopolitical examples, it behooves us to (re)consider the evolution of a sports term diffused into global rhetoric. Taken to yet a larger level, it behooves all of us to question hegemonic sexism, racism, religious intolerance, and any number of other areas where a particular population feels privileged.

Sportscaster Celebrityhood

> As might be anticipated, Big-Sports-Big TV was to create a new celebrity class—the big-time television sportscaster. Many names could be found on a list of sportscaster celebrities of the industrial age, including Curt Gowdy, Jim McKay, John Madden, Pat Summerall, Al Michaels, Dick Stockton, Keith Jackson, Don Meredith, Frank Gifford, Brent Musburger, and Dick Vitale— many of whom survived or even thrived in the information age—but the archetype sportscaster of the industrial age was Howard Cosell. Howard Cosell was a sportscasting-lightening rod: for many years he was simultaneously voted the 'most loved' and 'most hated' sportscaster in America. (Bryant and Holt, 2006, pp. 35-36)

In the 1950s, Mel Allen was so popular that he was spoofed in the comic book *Mad,* along with Leo Durocher and Yogi Berra. Illustrator Jack Davis caricatured them in a baseball story called "Hex!"

Dating from the days of radio, Red Barber was such a favorite sportscaster, being an on-air personality for almost sixty-three years, that people always felt free to approach him; in fact, reports his friend, NPR journalist Bob Edwards (1993, p. 14), "It was difficult for Red to have a peaceful meal in a public place. He was asked for autographs, introduced to fellow diners, stared at, pointed and whispered about. Radio celebrities once ranked with movie stars, and Red Barber was one of radio's biggest stars."

The nagging question is: did Howard Cosell create Muhammad Ali, or vice versa? Who needed the other more? (see Kindred, 2006). Jim Spence (1988, p. 10) had this theory about criticism of Cosell: "To be brutally frank, a lot of Americans looked at him, not a handsome man, and listened to that gratingly irritating voice, and perceived in both demeanor and tone a haughty manner, and decided he was first and foremost a Jewish guy from New York who supported blacks." Whatever the case, the phenomenon of the sportscaster as celebrity is upon us. Klatell and Marcus (1988, pp. 15-16) state:

> The "star" announcers and commentators—the Maddens, Giffords, Musburgers, Michaels, and Cosells of the industry—are so removed in salary, visibility, and status from the humble local announcers or nightly sportscasters that they hardly seem employed in the same business.
>
> In fact, a case can be made that they are not employed in the same business. The million-dollar salaries and incessant promotional campaigns mounted by their employers place them at a level equal to or higher than that of the athletes they are covering. In some cases, the television announcers, their associated personnel and vans full of high-tech equipment, have overwhelmed the event and its erstwhile participants.

On February 2, 1950, Phil Rizzuto was the very first mystery guest on the long-running 1950-1967 game show *What's My Line?* In 1999, Vin Scully was in the movie *For Love of the Game,* while Chris Berman has appeared as himself in *Necessary Roughness* (1991), *The Program* (1993), *Little Big League* (1994), *Eddie, Kingpin,* and *My Oh My!* in 1996, *Even Stevens* (2000), a remake of *The Longest Yard* (2005), as well as being in a 1995 Hootie and the Blowfish video and a number of television episodes. Howard Cosell has starred as himself in a number of movies, including *Bananas* (1971), *Two-Minute Warning* (1976), *Fighting Back: The Story of Rocky Bleier* (1980), *Broadway Danny Rose* (1984), *Johnny Be Good* (1988), *The Life and*

Times of Howard Cosell (1991), *Muhammad Ali: The Whole Story* (1996), and *When We Were Kings* (1996). Additionally, he had hosting spots for *The Tonight Show Starring Johnny Carson* (1972-1985), *Battle of the Network Stars* (1976-1988), *Saturday Night Live* (1975), roasts for Frank Sinatra, O.J. Simpson, Dean Martin, Bette Davis, Hugh Hefner, and appearances on programs like *The Flip Wilson Show, Rowan & Martin's Laugh-In,* and of course a number of sports-related shows. Of all sportscasters, Cosell is probably the most lampooned in popular culture: His name was often cited in the 1970's show *Match Game,* and *Sesame Street*'s "Showered Rosell" character was named for him, as was the video game *Crash Tag Team Racing*'s "Chick Gizzard Lips" and the *Beetlejuice* cartoon guy "Howard Grossnell." Nick of the reporting team Nick & Chip on *Codename: Kids Next Door* mimicked him when on air, as did an Asian character in the 1985 film *Better Off Dead* who supposedly learned English from Cosell's sportscasts.

Claiming he doesn't consider himself a "celeb," Len Berman (2005, p. 143) recounts a funny story about returning to his old elementary school in Queens for a "Principal for a Day" program; when the kids wrote to thank him, one wrote about how cool it was for someone "sort of famous" to have come for a visit. "So that's it," he has decided: "I'm sort of famous." By contrast, he recalls working as "color commentator alongside Johnny Most, the legendary voice of the Boston Celtics. Truth is, Johnny didn't need a color man. He was the entire show" (p. 189). Phil Rizzuto is mentioned by Adam Sandler in *Billy Madison* (1995), when he tries to write it in cursive but has problem with the z's; Rizzuto is on a *Seinfeld* episode in a key chain that yells "Holy Cow!"; and as "Scooter," the main character in Mick Foley's 2005 novel of that title. You will read many more examples in the sportscaster profiles.

Sportscaster Signature Statements

Many sportscasters' comments are associated with them. "An individual home run call allows an announcer to put his own stamp on the game at the moment of greatest impact, (Ken Levine, 1992, p. 24). "Listeners look forward to the call because they look forward to the event, and a good one can really enhance the action while showing the announcer off in the best possible light. The only problem is, it's hard to invent a classic, original home run call. The good ones, it appears, have been taken." He cites Mel Allen's "Going, going, gone!" of "Ballantine blast"; Harry Caray's "It might be, it could be, it *is* a home run!"; John Rooney's "It's a goner!"; Rosey Rowswell's "Raise the window, Aunt Minnie!" Lon Simmons' "You can tell it good-bye!"; Larry Beil's "Aloha means goodbye"; Milo Hamilton's "It's gone! Holy Toledo!"; Keith Jackson's "Whoa, Nellie!" Bob Prince's "Kiss it goodbye!" Van Miller's "Fandemonium"; or Dave Niehaus' "It will fly away!"

Harry Kalas is associated with, "Swing . . . and a long drive, watch this baby, way outta here!" Then too, Mel Allen is also known for his, "How about that?" Marv Albert is known for "Kick save and a beauty"; Russ Hodges for "Bye-bye, baby"; Ernie Harwell for "Long Gone!"; Howard Cosell for, "He . . . could . . . go . . . all . . . the . . . way!"

Jon Miller (2000, p. 78), voice of the San Francisco Giants and host of *ESPN Sunday Night Baseball,* would add to this list Russ Hodge's distinctive call: "Tell it bye-bye baby." Miller, a baseball "purist," states that the best games are played between rivals. Miller's own moment of celebrity included a brief skit on *The Late Show with David Letterman* relative to Cal Ripken's breaking Lou Gehrig's record.

Other broadcasters are associated with statements they have made. Heywood Hale Broun, a CBS correspondent for some two decades, is recalled for saying, "I think we've taken the fun out of sport by insist-ing that everybody must be a champion or a failure. Sports do not build character. They reveal it." Johnny Most's "Havlicek stole the ball," screamed when the Celtics beat the Philadelphia 76ers by a sin-gle point in 1965, became his trademark, and Al Michaels will long be remembered for "Do you believe in miracles? Yes!" when he was announcing the U.S. hockey team's victory in the 1980 Lake Placid Olympics. Perhaps you can think of other examples.

Sportscasters As Newscasters

During the 1972 Munich Olympic Games, sportscaster Jim McKay ended up reporting on the massacre of the Israeli Olympic team by

Palestinian Arab terrorists; the anchor declared that this event began an "end to innocence in sports" in ABC's 2002 documentary *Our Greatest Hopes, Our Worst Fears: The Tragedy of the Munich Games.*

Merle Harmon drew plenty of memorable assignments during his forty-five years in sports broadcasting, but the one on the night of August 8, 1974, was unique. He went into the booth to call a World Football League game and became the only sports announcer in history to introduce the President of the United States for a speech on national television. With the start of the game on hold, the camera moved to the White House Oval Office where a grim Richard Nixon informed the nation that he was resigning the next day. "After that, our game was pretty anti-climatic," Harmon said. Phil Rizzuto, an unabashed Yankee supporter, had to break into one of its broadcasts in 1978 to announce the death of Pope Paul VI, adding, "Well, that kind of puts a damper on even a Yankees win."

No one tuned into *MNF* on December 8, 1980, could forget Howard Cosell's announcement that John Lennon had been murdered. Or, Al Michaels' presiding during the October 17, 1989, San Francisco-Oakland World Series third game when there was an earthquake. Warner Wolf saw the events of September 11, 2001, unfolding from his Manhattan home, and reported them directly to listeners of the *Imus in the Morning* show. More and more, our sportscasters are required to be able to ad-lib about more than just the sporting event at hand.

"In many instances," Klatell and Marcus (1998, p. 16) remind us, "The broadcast booth, rather than the action on the field, has become the center of the telecast, with multiple on-air personnel orchestrating a combination of entertainment, network promotion, and commentary for the benefit of non-sports fans and their impact on ratings." Not all analyses of fellow sportscasters have been positive. Phil Schaap (2001, p. 389), at first lauding Howard Cosell for being the first to ask "intelligent questions, probing for significant stories," accuses him of bringing "journalism to sports on television, and then destroying journalism in sports on television." The problem, Schaap states, began when "Cosell decided that he was more important than the story, that the questions he asked were more meaningful than the answers he elicited. He stopped probing and began promoting—self-promoting. He brought the cult of the individual to sports journalism" (p. 390).

Sportscasters in the Media

The cult cable hit *Sports Writers on Television* is an example of what we might call "media on media." Produced by SportsChannel and syndicated across the country, it has been hosted by Bill Jauss, Bill Gleason, Ben Bentley, Lester Munson, and Rick Telander, Bill Veeck and Billy Corgan. The program was part of the 1994 film *Hoop Dreams.* The sportswriters themselves have been spoofed on *Saturday Night Live* as "Da Bears."

Working in a few movies and television shows as "a radio play-by-play announcer, a nebulous voice to be heard the background," Dick Enberg (2004, p. 171) described how that process worked: "The audience might hear me in the third inning of a baseball game as a burglary took place, then a couple of innings later when the crime had been detected. It was a means for a scriptwriter to show the passage of time." Later in his broadcasting career, he appeared in the Disney film *Gus,* Warren Beatty's *Heaven Can Wait* (1978), *Mr. 3000* (2004), and he has hosted a few game shows, including ESPN's *Sports Challenge.* Mel Allen had a cameo in the movie *The Naked Gun;* Phil Schaap has appeared as an on-screen sportscaster with James Caan in *The Gambler* (1974), and with Burt Reynolds in *Semi-Tough* (1977); Merle Harmon was an NCAA finals anchor in *Glory Road* (2006),

In addition to hosting the 2005 television series *Tennis Insiders,* Bud Collins has starred as himself in the "Psych" episode of *Spellingg Bee* (2006), *Anything to Win—Rosie Ruiz and the Boston Marathon Scandal* (2006), *ESPN SportsCentury* (sixteen episodes, 2000-2004), *The Curse of the Bambino* (2003), E! True Hollywood Story—Anna Kournikova (2003), and *She Got Game* (2003). Bob Costas appeared as himself in BASEketball (1998) and *Pootie Tang* (2001), and in 2006 he was the voice of the animated character Bob Cutlass, a race announcer, in *Cars.* Monte Moore appeared as himself in *Rebels of Oakland: The A's, the Raiders, the '70s* (2003).

Gayle Gardner has appeared as herself in the 1989 television series *The More You Know,* Johnny Most was a contestant on the *$64,000*

Question game show, and Jim Lampley, joined by Larry Merchant and Max Kellerman did the play-by-play for Sylvester Stallone's 2006 comeback/comeuppance film *Rocky Balboa.*

SPORTSCASTER PROFILES

As you might imagine, collecting names of sportscasters who should be profiled for their contributions to both sports and the media has been a tedious and tenuous process. Although it is tricky to put together such an extensive list, knowing that some readers may find enormous errors in submission and/or omission, this alphabetical listing of more than 200 sportscasters is based on input from family, friends, students, and colleagues, Curt Smith (1995, 1998), and of course the Internet. It is only meant to get you started; for more, you might consult www.sportsansofamerica.com or http://en.wikipedia .org/wiki/Category:American_sports_announcers.

One of the things that will strike you is the number of father-son sportscaster legacies, such as the Alberts, Brennamans, Bucks, Carays, Hammonds, Packers, and Rosens, as well as brothers who have become sportscasters, like the Golics or the Gumbels.

Kenny Albert (1968-): It may not be fair to begin by saying he is Marv Albert's son, because he has developed a strong reputation for doing play-by-play for Fox in a range including MLB, NFL, NHL, as well as ice hockey for the NBC Olympics and New York Rangers and college basketball for ESPN.

Marv Albert: "The Voice of Basketball" did the New York Knicks for three decades ("Yesssss!") before becoming the lead play-by-play man for the New Jersey Nets. He endured some notoriety in 1997 for felony charges, but NBA fans are glad he is still broadcasting. Learn more from his 1993 autobiography *I'd Love to but I Have a Game: 27 Years Without a Life.* Bryan Curtis (2007) has called the forty-year veteran of the broadcasting booth "the finest sports announcer of his generation . . . Like Howard Cosell before him, Albert is the only announcer about whom you could say you would watch a game merely to hear the announcing."

Mel Allen (1913-1996): the "Voice of the Yankees" was so much an institution in the 1940s and 1950s that his "How About That!" became a household term. After calling more World Series and All-Star Games than any other sportscaster, in addition to a number of college football bowl games, he did voiceover narrations for Fox Movietone newsreels and hosted *This Week in Baseball, Truth or Consequences,* and NBC's *Monitor* on radio. Most memorably, in 1980 he called Yankee outfielder Reggie Jackson's 400th home run, then Yankee pitcher Dave Righetti's no-hitter on July 4, 1983. Understandably, Allen was one of the first two winners, with Red Barber, of the Baseball Hall of Fame's Ford C. Frick award in 1978 (which said, "Throughout his career, he was even more popular than many of the outstanding players he covered"), and in 1988 he was inducted into the Radio Hall of Fame. Read his autobiographies *It Takes Heart* (1959) and *You Can't Beat the Hours* (1964), along with the section about him in Curt Smith's 1995 *The Storytellers: From Mel Allen to Bob Costas: 60 Years of Baseball Tales from the Broadcast Booth* and in Stephen Borelli's *How about That! The Life of Mel Allen* (2005).

Joe Angel: Colombia-born "Voice of the (Baltimore) Orioles," along with Jim Hunter, Fred Manfra, Buck Martinez, and Jim Palmer, his call for home runs might be "Adios!" or "Hasta la vista!"

Greg Anthony: a first-round draft selection in 1991 by the New York Knicks, after the NBA he became an analyst for ABC and ESPN.

Richie Ashburn (1927-1997): outfielder, then broadcaster for the Philadelphia Phillies, considered one of the city's most beloved sports figures (Fuller, 1997b).

Red Barber (1908-1992): a baseball sportscaster icon who did play-by-play for four decades (Cincinnati Reds, 1934-38, Brooklyn Dodgers, 1939-1953, New York Yankees, 1954-1966), along with college and professional football, Barber can claim having the longest sportscasting career in American history. With a pleasant, popular style, he is associated with several signature catchphrases, including "They're tearin' up the pea patch"—a team on a winning streak; "The bases are F.O.B. (full of Brooklyns)"—Dodgers had loaded the bases; "Can of corn"—a soft, easily caught fly ball; "Rhubarb"—an on-field dispute; "Sittin' in the catbird seat"—great performance; "Sittin' in the tall cotton"—success. When, on Opening Day 1934, he broadcast his first play-by-play for a major league game, the Reds losing to the Chicago Cubs 6-0, it was the first major league game he had ever seen in person. Barber's call about Joe DiMaggio's at-bat in the 1947 World Series is often cited. Determined to be fair, he respected Jackie Robinson, despite his Southern background, and he aimed to adopt a nonbiased reportorial speaking style. He was recipient, with Mel Allen, of the first Ford C. Frick award from the Baseball Hall of Fame, in 1978; the next year he received a Distinguished Alumni Award from the University of Florida, was given a Gold Award by the Florida Association of Broadcasters, and was inducted into the Florida Sports Hall of Fame. In 1995, Barber was inducted into the Radio Hall of Fame. Old-timers will appreciate his books *When all Hell Broke Loose in Baseball* (1947), *The Broadcasters* (1970), *Rhubarb in the Catbird Seat* (1997), as well as Bob Edwards' *Fridays with Red: A Radio Friendship* (1993). In his last interview, on Bob Costas' *Coast to Coast,* Barber provided an incredible insight: "When I began I think there were 3 commercials for 9 innings. So it meant you were on the air all afternoon. You had opportunity. You had room on the air to tell stories. Now, as you well know, you gotta hustle at the end of every third out. You're not allowed any talking time between innings. You're not allowed any feature time. If you're doing television today, you don't have an opportunity to tell a feature story. You don't have an opportunity really to be much of a personality" (cited in Edwards, 1993, p. 74).

Bud Blattner: veteran broadcaster, inducted into the U.S. Table Tennis Hall of Fame.

Johnny Bench: former player for the Cincinnati Reds, considered one of the greatest catchers in MLB history, in retirement he became a broadcaster, golfer, and the only professional baseball player to become a professional bowler. In 1972, he hosted a television show called *M.V.P.,* and later starred with Tommy Lasorda in *The Baseball Bunch.*

Chris Berman: anchor of *SportsCenter, Monday Night Countdown, Sunday NFL Countdown, Baseball Tonight,* U.S. Open golf, and other programming for ESPN, where he has been since it started in 1979. He has been honored by the National Sportscasters and Sportswriters Association and the American Sportscasters Association. Nicknamed "The Swami," he has long been a fan favorite—

who often imitate his "Back, back, backbackbackbackback . . . gone!" a multiple Emmy-award winner.

Len Berman: another multiple Emmy-award winner, Len Berman has been anchoring on WNBC since 1985. He may be best known for his monthly *Spanning the World* segment, which is also the title of his 2005 book.

Bonnie Bernstein: As it says on her Web site (www.bonniebernstein .com), "Bonnie Bernstein is one of the most recognizable and highly respected journalists in her field." Currently covering ESPN's *Sunday Night Baseball,* college football on ABC, and the NFL for CBS/Westwood One Radio, she was the first female weekday sports anchor for the Reno, Nevada, NBC affiliate. Bernstein made the record books when, for the Super Bowl in 2004, she served as both network radio and television correspondent for the same broadcast. In 2006, she started the consulting firm Velvet Hammer Media "for aspiring and working journalists and media training for corporate executives."

Terry Bowden: is a college football coach turned analyst/commentator on Westwood One Radio, he does the NCAA game of the week and hosts *The Terry Bowden Show.*

Terry Bradshaw: after playing as a four-time Super Bowl-winning quarterback with the Pittsburgh Steelers, he became a football analyst, and currently co-hosts FOX's *NFL Sunday.* He has recorded six albums of country/Western and gospel music, has been in the movies *Hooper* (1978), *Cannonball Run* (1981), *The Adventures of Brisco County* (1994), the voice of Broken Arm Bot in *Robots* (2005), and *Failure to Launch* (2006), and co-written *It's only a Game* (2001) and *Keep it Simple* (2002).

Bob Brenly: a MLB catcher and manager, he is now a Chicago Cubs broadcaster.

Marty Brennaman: radio voice of the Cincinnati Reds, he is associated with, "This one belongs to the Reds."

Thom Brennaman: son of sportscaster Marty Brennaman, with whom he did play-by-play for the Cincinnati Reds, he became the first television voice for the Arizona Diamondbacks, was voice of the Cotton Bowl on Fox from 2000 to 2006, and did the 2007 Fiesta Bowl.

Jack Brickhouse (1916-1998): "Hey, Heeeey!" enthusiastic announcer of Chicago Cubs games, Brickhouse broadcast his 5,000th baseball game on August 5, 1979. Recipient of the Ford C. Frick award from the Baseball Hall of Fame in 1983, he wrote two autobiographies—*Thanks for Listening* (1986) and *A Voice for all Seasons* (1996), the latter the same subtitle as Janice A. Petterchak's 1996 *Jack Brickhouse: A Voice for all Seasons.*

Tom Brookshier: football player and coach, unfortunately associated with a disparaging comment about University of Louisville basketball players' collective IQs.

James Brown: "J.B." is best known as host of FOX's *NFL Sunday* as well as *America's Black Forum.*

Jack "The Almighty" Buck (1924-2002): St. Louis Cardinals (1954-2001), CBS radio voice for *Monday Night Football* (1978-96), World Series, and Super Bowl broadcaster, his two autobiographies (1997, 2003) describe an invaluable fourteen-year partnership with Harry Caray. His famous humor and "That's a winner" commentary helped him win the Ford Frick award in 1987 and the Pete Rozelle award in 1996. Check out his books *That's a Winner!* (1997) and *Forever a Winner* (2003), as well as La Russa et al.'s 2003 *Jack Buck: Forever a Winner.*

Joe Buck: son of sportscaster Jack Buck, he has won many Emmys for his work on Fox Sports. Hired at age twenty-five in 1994, the youngest sportscaster to do NFL on network television, two years later he teamed with Tim McCarver; he led Fox's play-by-play for MLB—again setting a record as the youngest announcer for a World Series. September 8, 1998, he called Mark McGwire's 62nd homer breaking Roger Maris' record. His phrase "We'll see you tomorrow night" is in honor of his father, who had used it for Kirby Puckett's winning homer in the 1991 World Series, and some of his own calls have become memorable: "Down the left field line—is it enough? GONE!!!!! There it is, sixty-two! Touch first, Mark. You are the new single-season home run king!"; "Floater . . . center field. The Diamondbacks are World Champions!"; "Red Sox fans have longed to hear it: The Boston Red Sox are World Champions"; and "For the first time since 1982, St. Louis has a World Series winner!"

Buck Canel (1906-1980): an Argentinean-American Spanish-language MLB sportscaster, he won the 1985 Ford C. Frick award.

His trademark line was "Don't go away, this game is really getting interesting."

Harry Caray (1914-1998): famous for "Holy Cow!," "It might be . . . it could be . . . it is!," and a fun seventh-inning stretch routine, he did both radio and television for MLB, from the St. Louis Cardinals to the Chicago Cubs, with the Oakland Athletics and Chicago White Sox in between. Son Skip Caray and grandson Chip Caray have also become baseball broadcasters. Presented the Ford C. Frick award in 1989, his memory lives on in three Harry Caray restaurants. You might want to check out his autobiography, *Holy Cow!* (1989), where he shares tidbits about his beginnings: "Now you have to understand a few things here. I didn't know anything about broadcasting. Nothing. I had never in my life seen a radio studio. Or even a microphone. But I was not about to let any of that stand in my way" (p.40). There are also some great remembrances of him: Rich Wolfe's 1998 *I Remember Harry Caray* or *Where's Harry? Steve Stone Remembers his Years with Harry Caray* (1999).

Mary Carillo: her tennis experience has helped her cover the sport for the USA Network, CBS Sports, and ESPN. She also appears on *Real Sports with Bryant Gumbel.* "She may be the best female broadcaster extant, better than most men," according to Marty Glickman (1996, p. 186). "There isn't a moment's hesitation or lack of confidence in her commentary. Clarity, knowledge, and believability are inherent in everything she says. She exudes class. I love that." Calling Carillo "a cross between Ava Gardner and Henny Youngman," Sally Jenkins (1999, pp. 81-82) points out, "What separates her from both her male and female colleagues is a natural gift for words. An Agassi passing shot is 'sincere,' an unforced error by John McEnroe 'unpardonable.' She is one of the best reporters on her sport, and she brings players to life as characters."

Herb Carneal (1923-2007): "Voice of the (Minnesota) Twins," he won the 2004 Frick award.

Joe Castiglione: a radio announcer for the Boston Red Sox, most recently with Dave O'Brien, he co-authored *Broadcast Rites and Sites: I Saw it on the Radio with the Boston Red Sox* (2006).

Tom Cheek (1939-2005) announcer of Toronto Blue Jays games on radio from 1977 to 2004, his best-known call comes from the 1993 World Series: "Touch 'em all, Joe! You'll never hit a bigger home run in your life!"

Don Cherry: hockey commentator for CBC, he co-hosts the *Coach's Corner,* with Ron MacLean, on *Hockey Night in Canada.* Calling his audience "All you kids out there . . ., " he is a Canadian icon. Labeled "part Rush Limbaugh and part Dick Vitale" by Leigh Montville (1993), he has a chain of sports bars/restaurants bearing the Don Cherry name.

Gil Clancy: a former trainer, working with the likes of boxers Muhammad Ali, Joe Frazier, George Foreman, Oscar de la Hoya, and Emile Griffith, he has been a stand-out boxing commentator and is a member of the International Boxing Hall of Fame.

Eric Clemons: play-by-play sports anchor and director of WVOE in New Orleans 1998-2005, he moved from Chicago to Mobile to Boston before getting there.

Linda Cohn: now with ESPN's SportsCenter, she was, in 1987, the first full-time female sports anchor.

Jerry Coleman: "Ohhhh, Doctor" and "You can hang a star on that baby" voice of the San Diego Padres for some three decades, he has a number of other famous phrases, such as "There's a deep fly ball . . . Winfield goes back, back . . . his head hits the wall . . . it's rolling towards second base," "Montreal leads Atlanta by three, 5-1," "There's two heads to every coin," "That noise in my earphones knocked my nose off and I had to pick it up and find it," and "At the end, excitement maintained its hysteria."

Ken Coleman (1925-2003): thirty-four-year sportscaster practitioner and author, the "Voice of the (Boston) Red Sox" was a founding father of theRed Sox booster club and was inducted to the Boston Red Sox Hall of Fame in 2000. Here are some of his classic comments: "Fly ball, left field . . . Yastrzemski is going hard . . . way back . . . way back . . . and he dives and makes a tremendous catch! One of the greatest catches I've ever seen!" and "STRIKE THREE! Roger Clemens has broken the Major League record for strikeouts in one game! He now has 20!" Coleman's 1973 book *So You Want to be a Sportscaster: The Techniques and Skills of Sports Announcing by one of the Country's Most Experienced Broadcasters* still has value today, as do his autobiographies *Diary of a Sportscaster* (1982) and *Talking on Air: A Broadcaster's Life in Sports* (2000).

Cris Collingsworth: with a law degree from the University of Cincinnati, the former wide receiver has hosted WLW-Cincinnati's

Sports Talk on radio and most recently has co-hosted, with Bob Costas, HBO's *Inside the NFL* and been a studio analyst for *NBC's Sunday Night Football.*

Bud Collins: a sportswriter for the *Boston Herald* and the *Boston Globe* before moving to public television to do tennis commentary, he is so associated with the sport that he was elected, in 1994, to the International Tennis Hall of Fame.

Myron Cope: a radio color commentator for the Pittsburgh Steelers from the 1960 until retirement in 2005, many of his catchphrases are included in his 2002 autobiography, *Double Yoi! A Revealing Memoir by the Broadcaster/Writer.* In addition to expressions like "Okel Dokel!" and the "Double Yoi" of his book title, he had nicknames for the players and teams but he is most associated for introducing "The Terrible Towel"—encouraging fans to wave yellow towels during games. He was inducted into the Radio Hall of Fame in 2005.

Howard Cosell (1918-1995): simultaneously the most loved and hated, respected and repulsive sportscaster of all time, Cosell prided himself on "tell(ing) it like it is." From his perspective, the role of the sportscaster was first and foremost as a journalist, obliging one to speak the truth no matter if it conflicted with the reigning sports establishment. His law degree and extensive vocabulary made him stand out in the broadcasting booth—giving criticism and getting it in return. After representing Little League in 1953, he was asked to host a show on New York's WABC and soon made the switch to sportscasting. He had a radio show called *Speaking of Sports,* served as sports anchor from 1961 to 1974, and really made a name for himself covering the controversial boxer Cassius Clay (Muhammad Ali). It was at this time that he came up with his classic line: "I'm just telling it like it is." In 1973, at the Joe Frazier-George Foreman fight in Jamaica, he uttered what some sports historians consider to be one of the most famous call: "Down Goes Frazier! Down Goes Frazier! Down Goes Frazier!" As a sportscaster, Cosell developed his own special style, bringing deep analysis and contextualization to new levels and doing it all with an emphasis on proper language skills. It has been reported, however, that some audiences would tune in to *Monday Night Football*— which he joined in 1970 with ex-football players Frank Gifford and Don Meredith, just so they could destroy their television sets when Cosell was on the screen. He made no effort to conceal what he considered superiority to athletes-turned-commentators; (see the discussion of what he termed "jockocracy" elsewhere in this chapter). Prolific, Cosell covered various Olympic Games (playing a key role for ABC during 1972 attacks on the Israeli athletes in Munich) and World Series, along with hosting his own television talk show, *Speaking of Everything;* when he left the NFL, in 1984, he declared it "had become a stagnant bore." He also managed to write a number of books: *Like It Is* (1974), plus several collaborations (*Cosell*, 1973; *I Never Played the Game*, 1985; and *What's Wrong with Sports* (1991). Just before his death, Cosell was honored by ESPN with the Arthur Ashe Award for Courage. Although he states that, "Cosell was the first sportscaster who really said something," Len Berman (2005, p. 63)'s personal experience with him was overwhelmed by Howard's bragging about how he was, despite criticisms, Number One. "He is a man of strong stands and extreme confidence, one who would correct the grammar of Ernest Hemingway, criticize the thought process of Albert Einstein, appoint himself the social conscience of Mahatma Gandhi," observed William O. Johnson, Jr. (1971, p. 198). "Yes, Howard Cosell can seem overblown and overbearing, but there is about him an intelligence, an integrity and a persistence of personal conviction that is as fascinating as it is admirable." "He had neither a pleasant voice nor a pleasant face, but he worked hard, never flinched from asking tough questions, and utilized his prodigious memory and prodigious vocabulary to great advantage," Jon Enriquez (2002, p. 205) has written. "He was intelligent, insightful, and provocative, utterly unlike the smooth, portentous commentators working NFL games on other networks . . . Cosell's sesquipedalian, provocative persona contrasted nicely with (Don) Meredith's folksy, regular-guy style. Keith Jackson, a veteran of ABC's college football crew, provided play-by-play, but the main focus was the by-play between Cosell and Meredith." In Cosell's own words, "We make sports entertaining." An obituary by Tony Kornheiser in the *Washington Post* (April 24, 1995) declared, "Cosell was The Key Figure in bringing sports upstairs out of the furnished basement and into the family room. It was Cosell, through *Monday Night Football*, who took sports from lazy weekend afternoons into the white light of prime time, and in so doing fastened sports on the cultural map forever."

Bob Costas began with NBC in the 1980—jokingly referred to as "Sportboy" by David Letterman; since then, he has won many National Sportscaster of the Year awards and Emmys. He has hosted NFL, NBA, and MLB, teaming with Bob Trumpy for football, Isiah Thomas and Doug Collins for basketball, Tony Kubek, Joe Morgan and Bob Uecker for baseball. Associated with the expression "Do you believe it?!" he has covered NBC Olympics for Barcelona 1992, Atlanta 1996, Sydney 2000, Salt Lake City 2002, Athens 2004, and Turin 2006; he has hosted *Later with Bob Costas* (NBC, 1988-1994), *Costas Coast to Coast* (radio, 1986-1996), and HBO's *On the Record with Bob Costas* (2001) was co-host of *Inside the NFL* (2002), and *Costas Now* (2005). Called "a fan's fan" by sportswriter Richard Sandomir (1995), a case made clear in his 2001 book *Fair Ball,* this is what PBS interviewer Charlie Rose contributed about Costas: "He is as good a pure broadcaster as I've ever seen. He understands the medium, cares about his performance, and has a great combination of brains, spontaneity and a sense of humor. He has a marvelous connection between his brain and his mouth. With Bob, you can go in so many directions. You can tease, and he takes and plays with it."

Bob Cousy: MVP basketball player at Holy Cross, Boston Celtic legend, Naismith Memorial Basketball Hall of Fame member, he is known as "The Cooz," or "Houdini of the Hardwood." He was chosen one of the "100 greatest athletes of the twentieth century," as well as one of the best basketball commentators. Cousy's philosophy is clear in his 1963 autobiography *Basketball Is My Life,* "Do your best when no one is looking. If you do that, then you can be successful in anything that you put your mind to."

Irv Cross: a former football player and coach, then NFL analyst and commentator; when CBS Sports hired him, in 1971, he was the first black sports analyst on national television. Today, he is director of athletics at Macalester College in St. Paul.

Randy Cross: after being an NFL offensive lineman, he is now a sportscaster specializing in football analysis.

Bill Curry: a former football player and coach who has played under some of the best coaches (Bobby Dodd, Vince Lombardi, and Don

Shula), he juggles analysis at ESPN with heading a leadership program at Baylor School.

Howard David: radio play-by-play for a range of teams, including the New Jersey Nets, Milwaukee Bucks, Boston Celtics, New York Jets, and Miami Dolphins, along with Sunday Night Football, Princeton University basketball and football, and World Series of Poker.

Dizzy Dean (1910-1974): "The first modern TV sportscaster—the personality who launched television toward its rendezvous with billion-dollar league contracts and ultra-tech saturation coverage of media megagames—was Dizzy Dean," according to Ron Powers (1984, p. 65). Famous for fracturing the English language with expressions such as, "The runner slud into third," or "He swang at the ball," Dean was a pitcher for the St. Louis Cardinals, the Chicago Cubs, and the St. Louis Browns before coming to the broadcast booth. William O. Johnson (1971, p. 194) has written: "Dizzy's technique for describing a game, of course, was to be as ungrammatical as he could, to butcher the language at every turn, to toss in frequent bursts of 'The Wabash Cannonball,' and to discourse at length on the marvels of eating good sow belly and black-eyed peas. Occasionally, he might casually mention the score of the game." One of Dizzy's major bloopers came while he was announcing for CBS and said, "I don't know how our folks come off calling this the *Game of the Week*. There's a much better game—Dodgers and Giants—over on NBC." Check out Curt Smith's *America's Dizzy Dean* (1978).

Dan Dierdorf: after playing thirteen NFL seasons, he has been a blow-by-blow announcer for ABC Sports boxing and began working for *MNF* in 1987. A three-time Emmy nominee, he has worked on radio in St. Louis and was a finalist for the Football Hall of Fame. "Linemen are the only players who really analyze the entire field," he shared with Joseph Schuster (1989, pp. 18-19). "I will always believe that the *game* is the most important thing happening on a Monday night. My role is not to dominate with my voice; it is to add pieces that help people better understand."

Mike Ditka: "Iron Mike" coached the Chicago Bears for eleven years and is the only one in the team's seventy-five-year history to have won an NFL championship as a player and as a head coach. He began broadcasting with NBC in 1992 as an analyst on *NFL Live* briefly co-hosting with four-time Super Bowl winner Joe Montana, and currently is a commentator for ESPN.

John Dockery: drafted by the New York Jets during his Harvard years, he retired at age thirty-two to become what he called a "three-headed monster"—analyst/reporter/entertainer for first CBS, then NBC, and today he is a sideline reporter for *MNF.*

Jerry Doggett (1917-1997) broadcast Brooklyn and Los Angeles Dodgers baseball games from 1956 to 1987.

Don Drysdale (1936-1993): a pitcher with the Brooklyn/Los Angeles Dodgers, "Big D" won the Cy Young award and in 1984 was inducted into the Baseball Hall of Fame. Mostly known for broadcasting the Dodgers (1988 until he died), he also did baseball telecasts, Superstars, *Wide World of Sports,* and hosted *Radio Baseball Cards.* His 1990 autobiography is titled *Once a Bum, Always a Dodger: My Life in Baseball from Brooklyn to Los Angeles.*

Jimmy Dudley (1909-1999): a Cleveland favorite, he has been the voice of the Browns, then the Indians, known for "So long and good luck, ya' heah!" In 1997, he won the Ford C. Frick award.

Don Dunphy (1908-1998): a preeminent boxing announcer on both radio and television, Dunphy did blow-by-blow reports for more than 2,000 matches in his long career—including calling Joe Louis-Billy Conn (1941), Muhammad Ali-George Foreman in Zaire (1974), and the movie *Raging Bull* (1980). You can learn more from his 1988 autobiography, *Don Dunphy at Ringside,* where he recounts his key post Louis-Conn fights: Marciano-Walcott (9/23/52), Ali-Spinks (2/15/78), Graziano-Arnold (3/9/45), Leonard-Hearns (9/16/81), Basilo-Robinson ((9/28/57), Zale-Graziano (9/27/46), and two Ali-Frasier contests. "Before TV, the sports announcer was the bridge between the sports event and the folks gathered around their radios at home," he recalls (Dunphy, 1988, p. 107). "When I was announcing, I always considered myself to be the eyes of the audience, and I am sure that Ted Husing, Bill Stern, Sam Traub, and the other premier sports voices of that era felt the same way" (p.107).

Bob Elson (1904-1981): known as "The Old Commander" from his Navy days and "Voice of the White Sox" from his Chicago days, his easygoing manner won him the Ford C. Frick award in 1979—which recounted his broadcasting "more than 5,000 baseball games in an unprecedented five different decades (1930-1970) with the Chicago Cubs, Chicago White Sox and Oakland Athletics."

Gene Elston: "Voice of the Houston Astros" from 1962-1986, he authored *The Wide World of Sports* in 2005.

Mike Emrick/"Doc": doing play-by-play since 1973, counts as one of the most famous announcers in professional ice hockey. As the voice of the Philadelphia Flyers (1988-1993), he has worked for practically all the networks. According to fellow sportscaster Marty Glickman (1996, p. 187), "Mike is the best hockey announcer on the air. Smooth and quick, he has the feel of the game."

Dick Enberg: considered one of the most respected play-by-play American announcers, his "Oh, my!" has graced our airwaves for more than forty years. Ending early coverage of the California Angels on radio with "And the halo shines tonight," Enberg easily moved on from MLB to cover NFL, NBA, the U.S. Open, The Masters, and PGA Championship golf, college basketball and football, Wimbledon, French Open and Australian Open tennis, boxing, the Breeders' Cup, Super Bowls, and Olympic Games. Host of *Sports Challenge* and co-producer of the Emmy Award-winning sports-history series *The Way It Was* in the 1970s, he served some twenty-five years with NBC and joined CBS in 2000. Enberg also is lead commentator for ESPN2 tennis, Thursday-night NFL games on Westwood One radio, and narrator for Fox Sports Net's *In Focus.* Our first sportscaster to visit the People's Republic of China, in 1973, he has been appropriately awarded Emmys (including one for Lifetime Achievement) and honored as National Sportscaster of the Year, Pro Football Hall of Fame's Pete Rozelle award, the NBA's Curt Gowdy award, and a star on the Hollywood Walk of Fame. You can find his 2004 book *Oh My!* cited frequently throughout this book; the veteran who has been called the most versatile sportscaster in the country discusses his signature explanation: "Those two words have become my great friends as a broadcaster, describing the total range of athletic emotions—from deep despair to triumphant exultation. At the very least, they serve to call back the television spectator who may have wandered off to the refrigerator. I've always tried to use it as an exclamation point, a signal that the play was unique or spectacular enough to warrant the viewer's return to the TV set" (pp. 29-30).

Julius Erving: "Dr. J." made the natural transition from MVP in the ABA to being a color commentator in the NBA. Inducted into the Basketball Hall of Fame, his signature "Tomahawk" dunk earned him the number10 slot on *SLAM* Magazine's Top 75 NBA Players of All Time.

David Feherty: a European Tour and PGA Tour golfer, the Northern Ireland native has a column in *Golf* magazine and co-announces, with Gary McCord, the Tiger Woods PGA Tour series. He is the author of the amusing 2003 book *Somewhere in Ireland, a Village is Missing an Idiot,* offering this advice: "Any professional athlete who attempts to jump from competition to commentary is liable to land gumshield-first into a number of problems, not the least of which is the ethical dilemma of what to say and how to act whenever one of his buddies appears on the screen in front of him" (p. 133).

Roy Firestone: known for his interviews on *SportsLook* and *Up Close Prime Time,* as well as appearing in the movie *Jerry Maguire* (1997), the media-oriented announcer currently hosts HDNet's *Face to Face with Roy Firestone* and AOL's *Time Out with Roy Firestone.*

Peggy Fleming: winner of a 1968 Olympic gold medal, she has since commentated on figure skating for ABC Sports for more than twenty years.

Lanny Frattare: "Voice of the Pittsburgh Pirates" since 1976, his signature call is "Go, ball, get outta here!"

Joe Garagiola: beginning as a catcher in MLB, he may be best known for his affiliation with NBC—teaming with Bob Wolff to broadcast baseball, co-anchoring *The Today Show,* and hosting various game shows. Author of *Baseball is a Funny Game* (1990), he can be seen hosting the Westminster Kennel Club Dog Show.

Gayle Gardner: a broadcaster for both NBC Sports and ESPN, she has said, "In the end, I think you really only get as far as you're allowed to get" (cited in *Sports Illustrated,* June 17, 1991, p. 87).

Joe Gibbs: a Hall of Fame football coach of the Washington Redskins, as well as a NASCAR Championship team owner, he has served on *NFL Live.*

Frank Gifford: after playing for the New York Giants, he made an easy transition to the broadcast booth; best known for announcing

MNF in the early days with Howard Cosell and Don Meredith—although in some circles he is better known as the husband of Kathie Lee Gifford. The six-time Emmy-winner of the Pete Rozelle Award, he wrote *Gifford on Courage* (1976) and *The Whole Ten Yards* (1993).

Earl Gillespie (1922-2003): "Voice of the Milwaukee Braves."

Jerry Glanville: a football coach and analyst on HBO's *Inside the NFL,* CBS's *The NFL Today,* and FOX's NFL coverage, he is known for singing "On the Road Again."

Marty Glickman: a sprinter in the 1936 Berlin Olympics who claimed to witness anti-Semitism there in his 1996 autobiography *Fastest Kid on the Block,* he had a sportscasting career spanning nine presidents. Starting with Paramount News sports newsreels, he was a New York favorite for the Knicks, Giants, and Rangers. "In fifty-five years of broadcasting, I covered everything from marble-shooting to NFL championships; from Little League baseball to the NCAA Final Four of basketball; from water polo in Moscow to the Millrose Games," he reminisces (1996, pp. 5-6). "I broadcast on radio, network television, cable television, public address systems, and newsreels, and called horse races. On closed-circuit radio I described the Ringling Brothers Barnum and Bailey three-ring circus to four hundred blind people. It was the most difficult broadcast I ever did." Further, Maury Allen (1971, p. 137) credits Glickman with the phrase "Good—like Nedick's," made popular by New York City kids.

Bob Golic: Notre Dame football and the NFL made him the ideal analyst for CNN's *NFL Preview.* Bob's brother, Mike Golic, another NFL former player, is co-host of ESPN radio's *Mike and Mike in the Morning.*

Curt Gowdy (1919-2006): beloved "Voice of the (Boston) Red Sox" (as well as, at times, the Super Bowl, the World Series, and NCAA basketball), he worked with NBC Sports in the 1960s and 1970s and was the first sportscaster recipient of the George Foster Peabody Award for broadcast excellence. Gowdy was like a "walking history" of some of our key sports stories, including, in the 1940s, Bud Wilkinson's early attempts to make Oklahoma a college football power, and Hank Iba's Oklahoma A&M basketball squads, the New York Yankee renaissance, Ted Williams' home run during his final at-bat on September 28, 1960, the first Super Bowl (1967), the infamous 1968 *Heidi* episode (discussed in Chapter 2), Franco Harris' "Immaculate Reception" (1972), and Hank Aaron's record-setting 715th home run in 1974. Elected to the National Sportswriters and Sportscasters Hall of Fame, he has been recognized with the Ford C. Frick and Pete Rozelle awards, as well as a Lifetime Achievement Emmy. Gowdy was president of the Basketball Hall of Fame for many years, monitoring its annual Curt Gowdy Award for outstanding basketball writers and broadcasters; he authored *Cowboy at the Mike* (1966) and *Seasons to Remember: The way it was in American Sports, 1945-1960* (1993); Gowdy quite naturally also has been inducted into the Boston Red Sox Hall of Fame.

Jim Gray: known for a deadpan style in interviews, he works with the Westwood One Radio Network and ESPN. People still talk about his 1999 interview with Pete Rose, when he aggressively asked, "Pete, now let me ask you. It seems as though there is an opening, the American public is very forgiving. Are you willing to show contrition, admit that you bet on baseball and make some sort of apology to that effect?" Despite the denial, in another five years Rose admitted he had gambled.

Tim Green: he has worked the NFL to NPR, (hosting *A Current Affair)* and been a color commentator on Fox; he has written a number of novels and the 1997 autobiography *The Dark Side of the Game: My Life in the NFL.*

Hank Greenwald: San Francisco Giants broadcaster on KNBR, he is the author of *This Copyrighted Broadcast* (1997).

Lisa Guerrero (Coles): a cheerleader, actress, and model, she became a respected sportscaster for Fox on *Overtime, Fox Extra Innings,* Toughman competitions, and *The Best Damn Sports Show Period,* then ABC's *Monday Night Football* television—until replaced by Michele Tafoya. She was in *Batman Returns* and *Love Potion No. 9* in 1992, *Fire Down Below* (1997), *Today You Die* (2005), and was executive producer of *A Plumm Summer* (2007).

Bryant Gumbel: known as host of NBC's *Today Show* from 1981 to 1996, his real love has been sports. After a San Diego Chargers versus Miami Dolphins matchup in 1982, he famously declared, "If you didn't like this football game then you didn't like football!" Gumbel has hosted, since 1995, HBO's emmy-winning *Real Sports with Bryant Gumbel.*

Greg Gumbel: Bryant's older brother, now a play-by-play announcer at CBS with Dan Dierdorf, Gumbel has worked with a number of sportscasters, including Terry Bradshaw, John Madden, Joe Morgan, Bill Walton, Mike Ditka, Cris Collingsworth, Joe Gibbs, Phil Simms, and more. A motivational speaker, he has hosted and done play-by-play for five Super Bowls.

Pat Haden: a quarterback for the Los Angeles Rams (1976-1981), after USC and Loyola Law School, this Rhodes Scholar sportscaster practices law but found time to do the 2007 Orange Bowl.

Halsey Hall (1898-1977): a Minneapolis-St. Paul announcer for more than a half-century, he can claim using "Holy cow!" for homers way before Harry Caray—as noted in Stew Thornley's *Holy Cow! The Life and Times of Halsey Hall* (1991).

Milo Hamilton: according to the Radio Hall of Fame, "Hamilton has witnessed nine no-hitters, Ernie Banks' five grand slams in a season, Roger Maris' 61st home run in 1961 and Hamilton was behind the microphone for Hank Aaron's historic 715th home run in April 1974. Hamilton's call of that Aaron blast is one of the most memorable sports moments of the 20th century." Beginning with the Atlanta Braves in 1966, he has been with the Houston Astros since 1985 and is co-author of *Making Airwaves: 60 Yyears at Milo's Microphone* (2006).

Tom Hammond: he has been a staple for NBC sports, with Bob Costas and Dan Hicks, along with announcing Southeastern Conference men's college basketball. For the Olympic Games, he has covered track and field, figure skating, and ice dancing. His son, David Hammond, is a radio basketball and football commentator for Syracuse University and does play-by-play for the AFL on NBC.

Kevin Harlan: growing up in Green Bay, son of Packers' head coach Bob Harlan, he broadcasts NFL and college basketball for CBS, NBA on TNT, co-hosts "Crunch Time" on Kansas City radio, and is the voice of Westwood One Radio's Final Four coverage. With all this activity, he has come up with several memorable lines, such as "Right between the eyes!" "He just sucked the gravity right out of the building!!" "He's a flamethrower!!!" and "Oh baby, what a play!"

Merle Harmon: self-described on his Web site (http://merleharmon .com) as a motivational keynote speaker, humorist, and sports expert, he has served as the voice of MLB teams, called the New York Jets for nine seasons, and has announced Winter Olympics and World Games. *Merle Harmon Stories* was published in 1998.

Ken Harrelson: "Yes" announcer for the Chicago White Sox on WGN-TV, he has said, "Baseball is the only sport I know that when you are on offense the other team controls the ball."

Ernie Harwell: the first active announcer honored with the Ford Frick award, he's best known as the "Voice of the (Detroit) Tigers." "When radio began in the mid-1920s, voice was everything," he wrote (cited in Keegan, 2002, p. 32). "That's not true anymore. The voice on radio—and its big brother, TV—is secondary to content. I think the modern way is better, but I miss some of the great voices of the past." He is the author of *Tuned to Baseball* (1985), *Ernie Harwell's Diamond Gems* (1991), *Stories from My Life in Baseball* (2001), *The Babe Signed My Shoe* (2002), and *Life After Baseball* (2004), and is the subject of Tom Keegan's *Ernie Harwell* (2002) and Tom Stanton's *The Final Season: Fathers, Sons, and One Last Season in a Classic American Ballpark* (2002). Paul Carey, Harwell's broadcast partner, marvels at his edge as a broadcaster: "He has a great ability to remember verbatim what somebody tells him on the field and then bring it up on the air . . . He remembered every word. He has a great capability for that, plus one other—he had good relationships with players, who would often tell him things they wouldn't tell other media" (cited in Keegan, 2002, p. 227).

Chick Hearn (1916-2002): NBA announcer for the Los Angeles Lakers, he is fondly remembered for inventing phrases such as "slam dunk," "no harm," and "no foul." Inducted into Basketball Hall of Fame in 1991 the American Sportscaster Hall of Fame in 1995, here are some other "Chick-isms": "Air-mail Special!," "You could call it with Braille," "They couldn't beat the Sisters of Mercy," "Dribble-drive," "I'll bet you an ice-cream," "He's got ice-water in his veins," "He has two chances, slim and none, and slim just left the building," "If that goes in, I'm walking home," "There are lots of referees in the building, only three getting paid," "Tattoo dribble," "This game's in the refrigerator: the door is closed, the lights are out, the eggs are cooling, the butter's getting hard, and the Jell-O's jigglin'!" and many more. Check out the posthumous *Chick: His Unpublished Memoirs and the Memories of Those who Loved Him.*

Tom Heinsohn: he played for the Boston Celtics, coached them, and then the Basketball Hall of Famer was their color commentator for *Fox Sports New England.*

Dan Hicks: an NBC sportscaster since 1992, he has used some quotable calls, such as "A remarkable week by a remarkable player on a remarkable golf course" (Tiger Woods), "And Scott survives! The youngest champion in the history of The Players Championship (Adam Scott), or "Ian Thorpe has a new world record, and this time it's for Olympic gold!" He is married to fellow sportscaster Hannah Storm.

Russ Hodges: "Voice of the Giants" (first in New York, then San Francisco) from 1949-1970, he is mostly remembered for his signature "Bye-bye, baby." Jon Miller (1998, p. 76) tells about Hodges' influence on him: "To me, Russ was the consummate broadcaster. His voice was not a classic, but it was rich and distinctive. He gave listeners a great picture of the game through the radio, and when things got exciting, Russ had this knack for getting excited, but in a very controlled way."

Mark Holtz (1945-1997): broadcaster for the Texas Rangers whose signature phrase was "Hello Win Column."

Pat Hughes: play-by-play announcer for the Chicago Cubs since 1996 on WGN radio as well as Marquette University basketball, he has received Illinois and Wisconsin Sportscaster of the Year awards. Have you heard him call, "This ball's got a chance . . . GONE!"?

Jim Hunter: after anchoring CBS' Sports Central USA for a long time, now he is with the Baltimore Orioles broadcasting both radio and television.

Ted Husing (1901-1962): a pioneer sportscaster schooled by broadcaster Major J. Andrew White, he spoke so fast he was called "Mile-a-Minute Husing." Associated with CBS and college football, where his play-by-play set a standard for identifying players and interviewing players and coaches, he additionally covered a range of sports such as boxing, horse racing, track and field, regattas, seven World Series, tennis, golf, four Olympic Games, and the

Indianapolis 500. You can learn more firsthand on his Web site, www.tedhusing.net.

Keith Jackson: instrumental in launching *MNF,* he called so many games from 1966 to 2006 that he has earned the nickname "Mister College Football." He has played himself in some sports documentaries, a sportscaster in *The Fortune Cookie* (1966) and *Summer of Sam* (1999).

Tom Jackson: a linebacker for the Denver Broncos, he made an ideal NFL analyst for ESPN when he teamed with Chris Berman. Host of "Jacked Up!" on *Monday Night Countdown,* he has had controversies, such as claiming the New England Patriots didn't like their coach, Bill Belichick, asking Michael Irvin if he was retarded, and difficulty with Rush Limbaugh's social commentary on *NFL Countdown.* His 1987 *Blitz: An Autobiography* is very telling.

Jaime Jarrin: the Ecuadorian-born, Spanish language voice of the Los Angeles Dodgers was presented the Ford C. Frick award in 1998.

Ron Jaworski: the "Polish Rifle" played for the Philadelphia Eagles before being an NFL analyst on ESPN, and he is also team president of the Philadelphia Soul of the Arena Football League, which is owned by Jon Bon Jovi, along with a number of entrepreneurial ventures.

Ernie Johnson: known as baseball's television "paterfamilias," he broadcasts for both TNT and TBS. Following in the footsteps of his father, Ernie Johnson Sr., an MLB pitcher and Braves play-by-play announcer, he called Atlanta Braves games.

Daryl Johnston: "Moose," who was a Dallas Cowboys fullback from 1989 to 1999, reports *The NFL on FOX* with Dick Stockton. He is the author of *Watching Football: Discovering the Game Within the Game* (2005).

Charlie Jones: longtime NFL voice and Emmy Award-winning sportscaster for NBC and ABC, he participated in these historic firsts: Super Bowl, AFL title game, NBC's *SportsWorld,* World Cup gymnastics, Senior "Skins" golf, and a multination athletic event in China.

Jim Kaat: former pitcher, then MSG play-by-play broadcaster, he teamed variously with Dick Stockton, Greg Gumbel, Ken Singleton, Tim McCarver, Josh Lewin, and Brent Musburger; he won an Emmy for on-air achievement in 2006.

Harry Kalas: "It's outa' here!" marks this play-by-play announcer for the Philadelphia Phillies. Beginning his career calling minor league games for the Hawaii Islanders while in the U.S. Army stationed in Hawaii, he moved on to the Houston Astros, then the Phillies. Of all his calls, he is most associated with Mike Schmidt's hit for his 500th career home run: "Swing and a long drive, there it is, number 500! The career 500th home run for Michael Jack Schmidt!" Or, maybe it was when Tug McGraw struck out Willie Wilson in the 1980 World Series (Phillies versus Kansas City Royals): "65,000 on their feet here at Veterans Stadium, the Tugger needs one more!" Then again, during Game 6 of the 1993 National League Championship Series (Phillies versus Atlanta Braves): "Swing and a miss!!! Struck him out! The Phillies . . . are the '93 . . . National League Champions!!!"

Len Kasper: after announcing for the Milwaukee Brewers and the Florida Marlins, he now does play-by-play for the Chicago Cubs, often employing "And it's gone" or "And it will get out."

George Kell: Arkansas born (and still residing there), he was a baseball player elected to its Hall of Fame in 1983 who worked with CBS' *Game of the Week.*

Ralph Kiner: accomplishing 369-career homers, he began his broadcasting career at Chicago's Comiskey Park in 1961. Many of his homers landed in a spot at Forbes Field that has since become known as "Kiner's Korner"—which is the title of his 1987 book. Beginning in 1961, Kiner went into the broadcast booth for the Chicago White Sox, later joining Lindsey Nelson and Bob Murphy for the New York Mets. Even though he messed up names, such as calling Dwight Gooden "Greg Goossen," or Darryl Strawberry "Darryl Throneberry," he was beloved by fans and was inducted into the Baseball Hall of Fame in 1975, and the New York Mets Hall of Fame in 1984. The Mets honored him with "Ralph Kiner Night" July 14, 2007 at Shea Stadium.

Tony Kornheiser: a sportswriter/columnist for *The Washington Post,* host of his own radio program *The Tony Kornheiser Show,* he has done *Pardon the Interruption* on ESPN as well as being a color analyst for *MNF* with Mike Tirico and Joe Theismann. Calling him a "Prime-time wisenheimer," Bryan Curtis (2006) declares Kornheiser "an unlikely TV star, a cynic with a face fit for radio. He might also be the best addition to *Monday Night Football* since Howard Cosell." Reportedly, the CBS sitcom *Listen Up* was based on Kornheiser's columns; see his 2003 book *I'm Back for More Cash: A Tony Kornheiser ollection (Because You Can't Take Two Hundred Newspapers into the Bathroom)*.

Andrea Kremer: a sideline reporter for NBC's Sunday Night Football, previously with ESPN's SportsCenter, the University of Pennsylvania grad has reported on football across the country.

Tony Kubek: a Yankee from 1957 to 1965, he became a color commentator for NBC's *Saturday Game of the Week* for twenty-four years, teaming unflinchingly with Jim Simpson, Curt Gowdy, Joe Garagiola, and Bob Costas. He also did more than a dozen World Series, the Toronto Blue Jays on The Sports Network, the Yankees on MSG, and other events.

Jim Lampley: maybe best known as the voice of HBO boxing, this sportscaster is also involved in several businesses. His breakthrough, hosting halftime for MNF, showed his flexibility such that he has covered a range from baseball to racing to thirteen Olympic Games. Jim Rome has called him, "the smartest guy in the Jungle." He appears as himself in the Will Ferrell 2007 comedy *Blades of Glory*.

Jerry Lawler: "The King" has moved from the wrestling ring to the broadcast booth, serving as color commentator for *WWE Raw*. His many antics are outlined in *It's Good to be King . . . Sometimes* (2003).

Cawood Ledford (1926-2001): University of Kentucky basketball and football play-by-play announcer, he also did NCAA Men's Final Four on radio, as well as many Kentucky Derbys.

Ken Levine: after writing and producing, with partner David Isaacs, for television's *MASH* and *Cheers,* he decided to try sportscasting. His 1993 book *It's Gone!. . .No, Wait a Minute. . .: Talking My Way into the Big Leagues at 40* details how he spent the 1991 season doing play-by-play for the Baltimore Orioles. Now announcing for the Seattle Mariners, he offers this tip: "I try to get out to the park at least 3 hours before the first pitch. That gives me plenty of time of 'schmooze.' The best tidbits come from sitting around the clubhouse and wandering around the batting cage. Plus, I still get a major rush stepping out onto a major league playing field" (1993, p. 85).

Vince Lloyd (1949-1987): "Voice of the Chicago Cubs." Chicago sportswriter Tim Cronin praised him: "He always had excitement in his voice. There always was passion, not so much for the outcome of the game, as for his love of the event being broadcast"; he called him "The Pro's Pro"—a man with a God-given baritone voice.

Verne Lundquist: a CBS Sports caller of college football and basketball, along with The Masters and PGA Championship golf tournaments, he was the Voice of America's Team in the 1970s. Also, add NFL Films and regional NFL games. Fans recall his compassion for Jackie Smith of the Dallas Cowboys, who dropped a touchdown pass in Super Bowl XIII versus the Pittsburgh Steelers": "Bless his heart, he's got to be the sickest man in America!" Or, Tiger Woods' birdie in the 2005 Masters: "Oh wow! In your life have you seen anything like that?" He was elected to the National Sportscasters and Sportswriters Association Hall of Fame in 2007.

John Madden: "Gesticulate, or Telestrate: Madden is best at what he does," Curt Smith (1998, p. 17) has declared. An NFL player, coach, and Pro Football Hall-of-Famer, he has been a color commentator since 1979—many fans' favorite and one of the highest paid sportscasters in the business. He has been doing NBC's Sunday night NFL games since 2006, the same year he became the first sportscaster for all the "Big Four" networks, and still manages to do a fifteen-minute syndicated radio chat each weekday morning at 8:15 a.m. out of KCBS-AM in San Francisco. He has developed his own style, replete with what have become known as "Maddenisms"—simple comments like: "You can't win a game if you don't score any points," or "If the quarterback completes a pass in the endzone, it's a touchdown." Madden played himself in *Little Giants* (1994), and his voice predominates on the Madden NFL series of football video games. He has been "one of the most important announcers in the history of television," according to Phil Schaaf (2004, p. 160). "When he retires, he will be remembered more for his announcing than coaching, an improbability when he was hoisted onto his players' shoulders after winning the Super Bowl."

Paul Maguire: a former football player for both the Buffalo Bills and the San Diego Chargers, he began as an NBC analyst in 1971. Following many years with Sunday Night Football, he now does college football for ABC, as well as *NFL Live.*

Mark Malone: the nation's most recruited quarterback in 1975, he went from the Pittsburgh Steelers to the broadcast booth—WPXI-TV Pittsburgh, then ESPN, and sports director at WBBM-TV Chicago since 2004.

Dan Marino: a Hall of Fame quarterback for the Miami Dolphins, the restaurant owner is a commentator for both CBS's *The NFL Today* show and HBO's *Inside the NFL.*

Ned Martin (1923-2002): Red Sox play-by-play announcer from 1961 to 1992—including Carl Yastrzemski's entire career, and this memorable moment from July 24, 1979: "Long drive, right field . . . way back . . . near the wall . . . and there it is! Home run number 400, Carl Yastrzemski! Now . . . listen and watch!" Although associated with his signet "Mercy!" longtime fans still remember his call on WHDH radio during the Red Sox's "Impossible Dream" season of 1967 at Fenway Park: "The pitch is looped toward shortstop. Petrocelli's back. He's got it! The Red Sox win! And there's pandemonium on the field. Listen!" Or, Carlton Fisk's 12th inning game-winning in 1975: "The 1-0 delivery to Fisk. He swings . . . long drive, left field . . . if it stays fair, it's gone . . . HOME RUN! The Red Sox win! And the series is tied, three games apiece!" Also from Fenway, on April 29, 1986: "A new record! Clemens has set a major league record for strikeouts in a game . . . 20!" Partnering with Curt Gowdy, Art Gleason, Mel Parnell, Ken Coleman, Johnny Pesky, John McClain, Dave Martin, Jim Woods, Ken Harrelson, Bob Montgomery, and Jerry Remy during thirty-one seasons with the Sox, it has been speculated that Martin may have seen more of their games (5,000+) in person than anyone else. He was inducted into the Boston Red Sox Hall of Fame in 2000.

Denny Matthews: The "Voice of the Kansas City Royals," having seen more of their games than anybody, he was named the Ford C. Frick award winner in 2007. He is the co-author of *Play by Play: 25 Years of Royals on Radio* (1999) and *Tales from the Royals Dugout* (2006).

Bill McAtee: host of USA's golf and tennis, he has also done boxing, figure skating, and many other sports.

Tim McCarver: declared in 1986, and still true today as, "the very *best* at what he does," he was a catcher for the St. Louis Cardinals whose tiebreaking home run in the 10th inning won Game 5 of the 1964 World Series. Paired first as a color commentator with Richie Ashburn and Harry Kalas, then Al Michaels and Jim Palmer at NBC and ABC, he is currently paired with Joe Buck for Fox Sports. McCarver has won three Emmys for *Sports Event* analyst. Although on the one hand he has been criticized for ideas or name gaffes, other fans like the way he goes with an idea. His timing has been lucky: San Diego Padre Steve Garvey's game-winning home run in the 1984 National League Championship Series, the sixth game of the 1985 World Series between the Kansas City Royals and St. Louis Cardinals—the Royals' dramatic come-from-behind victory, the 16-inning sixth game of the 1986 National League Championship Series that he called with Keith Jackson (between the New York Mets and Houston Astros), the 1987 Minnesota Twins' beating the St. Louis Cardinals in seven games in the World Series, the LA Dodgers beating the New York Mets in the 1988 NLCS, the 1991 World Series (Minnesota Twins versus Atlanta), Atlanta Braves' Francisco Cabrera's game-winning hit, Joe Carter's game-winning homer in the 1993 World Series, return of the New York Yankees to win the 1996 World Series, Mark McGwire's record-hitting home run in 1998, David Cone's perfect game for the New York Yankees in 1999, the Arizona Diamondbacks' comeback victory in the 2001 World Series, the Anaheim Angels' win of the 2001 World Series, the 2003 American League Championship Series between the New York Yankees and the Boston Red Sox, the Florida Marlins beating the New York Yankees in the World Series, the Boston Red Sox winning the pennant in 2004 and ending the "Curse of the Bambino." McCarver set a record in 2003 by broadcasting his thirteenth World Series. "Tim McCarver likes to talk," baseball historian Roger Angell (1999, p. 28) has noted. "He laughs and enjoys himself at ballgames. He makes jokes—puns, even. He uses fancy words. He's excitable—he gets carried away by the baseball. He's always going on and on about some little thing. He thinks he knows how the game should be played."

Tim McCormick: a 1984 NBA draft inflicted with injuries in his eight-year stint, he found his next niche covering basketball, today for FSN Detroit and running the Top 100 Basketball Camp for high school basketball players.

Arch McDonald (1901-1960): "Voice of the (Washington) Senators" from 1934 to 1956.

Sean McDonough: a "mikeman" at age twenty-six for the Red Sox, his 1993 infamous: "The Phillies have taken the lead *by a field goal,* 10-7" at least got him some attention. The year before, he gave this emotional call relative to Atlanta's Angel Cabrera's game-winning hit against the Pittsburgh Pirates: "Line-drive and a base-hit!!! Justice will score the tying run, Bream to the plate . . . and he's safe, safe at the plate!!! The Braves go to the World Series!" Although he has worked for CBS Sports, ABC, and ESPN, doing a range of events, he has mainly been known for broadcasting Boston Red Sox games on WSBK-TV (Channel 38)—until being replaced by NESN announcer Don Orsillo in 2005. When interviewed by one of my students at Worcester State College, his advice to aspiring sportscasters was to "Be patient and be realistic." Sean's father, legendary *Boston Globe* sportswriter Will McDonough, counts as another local icon.

John McEnroe: considered one of the best-ever tennis players, having won seven Grand Slam singles titles, he is, like Chris Evert, Mary Carillo, and Martina Navratilova for women's tennis, an ideal commentator for events like the U.S. Open.

Al McGuire (1928-2001): considered one of the profession's most articulate and colorful commentators, he played, coached, and broadcast basketball and was inducted into the Basketball Hall of Fame in 1992.

Jim McKay: making his mark with ABC's *Wide World of Sports* from 1961 to 1998, he is most associated with introducing the phrase "The thrill of victory, the agony of defeat." Be sure to read his 1973 autobiography *My Wide World* to see why he has won two Emmys and the George Polk award for sports journalism relative to the 1972 Munich Olympics and has been inducted into the U.S. Olympic Hall of Fame. In 1998, he updated the book, stating in the Preface how much more he has done than the Olympics: "I have covered golf in Scotland, tennis at Wimbledon, cliff diving in Acapulco, barrel jumping in the Catskills, lumber-jacking in Wisconsin, the Triple Crown of horse racing (Kentucky Derby, Preakness, and Belmont), stock car racing in South Carolina, ski racing

in St. Moritz, speed skating in Lake Placid, waterskiing in Australia, baseball in Japan, the Indy 500, gymnastics in China and roller
skating in Madrid" (p. i.). Considering McKay "the quintessential
good guy," Douglas S. Looney (2000) claims, "There's never been
anybody better. It seems improbable there ever will be. Everything
about him bespeaks class, eloquence, and professionalism." Jim
McKay's son, Sean McManus, is president of CBS' sports and
news divisions.

Larry Merchant: at heart a sports columnist (for *The Philadelphia
Daily News* and *The New York Post*), he has evolved into a boxing
commentator for *World Championship Boxing, Boxing After Dark,*
and various HBO pay-per-view telecasts.

Don Meredith: "Dandy Don," a quarterback for the Dallas Cowboys
from 1960-1968, he became a color commentator on *MNF* in
1970. His signature singing at the end of each game of "Turn out
the lights, the party's over" is an example of why he has been so
popular.

George Michael: no—not the singer, but the sportscaster with a long-
running show: *The George Michael Sports Machine* (1980-2007).

Al Michaels: after growing up a block from Ebbets Field, he worked
for NBC Sports from 1977 to 2006, then joined ABC Sports. Best
known for "Do you believe in miracles? Yes!"—from his "Miracle
on Ice" broadcast at the 1980 Winter Olympics. In addition to
many awards, he has been selected "Sportscaster of the Year" from
both the American Sportscasters Association and the *Washington
Journalism Review,* and has his own star on the Hollywood Walk of
Fame. Among television's most respected sports journalists, Michaels has hosted the five major American pro sports championships (Super Bowl, World Series, NBA Championships, Stanley
Cup Finals, and WBA), as well as all three Triple Crown races and
the Indianapolis 500. Lead announcer for the Cincinnati Reds, he
made this call for his team: "1 and 2: the wind and the pitch to
Bench; change up hit in the air to deep right field, back goes
Clemente at the fence . . . she's gone! Johnny Bench, who hits almost every home run to left field hits one to right. The game is
tied." You may know him best doing play-by-play for *MNF,* starting with Dan Dierdorf and Frank Gifford; after two decades on that
show, three with ABC/ESPN, in 2006 he joined John Madden at
NBC on Sunday night football. Two of Michaels' more famous

broadcasts were of the 1980 Lake Placid Olympics ice hockey match between the United States and the Soviet Union, and the attempted third game of the 1989 World Series, when he was in the booth with Tim McCarver and Jim Palmer, prior to the Loma Prieta earthquake.

Matt Millen: sometimes referred to as "Little Madden" from his days as a football commentator on radio and television, he is president and CEO of the Detroit Lions.

Johnny Miller: after twenty-five PGA Tour wins and induction into the World Golf Hall of Fame it was natural that he should become a golf commentator; as with Nick Faldo, the fans have adored his perspectives and presentations.

Jon Miller: "Voice of the (Baltimore) Orioles," then the San Francisco Giants, he has called nine World Series on ESPN Radio and since 1997 has been their primary play-by-play voice. Check out this call from 1983, his first year in Baltimore: "Everybody else is in muted silence. The pitch! Line drive! Ripken catches it at shortstop! And the Orioles are champions of the world!" But he is better known for this, from a 2003 game between the Giants and Arizona Diamondbacks: "That was the worst base-running in the history of the game!" He co-wrote the 1998 book *Confessions of a Baseball Purist: What's Right—and Wrong—with Baseball, As Seen from the Best Seat in the House.* "Baseball entertains you and you care about it," he has famously said. He claims he didn't know he was a baseball "purist" until acting commissioner Bud Selig gave him the moniker on national television in 1993. Ken Coleman (1982, p. 107) has called Miller "a broadcaster's broadcaster. He's into studying how to use his voice the way an actor studies how to act."

Van Miller: when he retired in 2003, his thirty-seven years with the Buffalo Bills made him the longest-tenured commentator with a single team.

Monte Moore: a Midwesterner who moved when Chuck Finley's Kansas City A's became the Oakland A's in 1968, he stayed on as their radio voice through the 1977 season, its television voice until 1980.

Ted Moore: a "Voice of the (Pittsburgh) Packers."

Joe Morgan: legendary MLB second baseman, especially with the Cincinnati Reds—for whom he was responsible for scoring the winning run in Game 7 of the 1975 World Series, the ESPN color commentator was inducted into the Baseball Hall of Fame in 1990. As a baseball broadcaster, he has won a CableACE (1990) and Emmys in 1998 and 2005. Today, he is teamed with Jon Miller on ESPN's *Sunday Night Baseball.*

Johnny Most (1923-1993): gravelly radio voice of the Boston Celtics from 1953 to 1990, his "Havlicek stole the ball!" remains in basketball broadcasting lore. An unabashed "homer," he once described Los Angeles Lakers' Kurt Rambis as "something that had crawled out of a sewer," called Magic Johnson "Crybaby Johnson," and nicknamed Washington Bullets' Rick Mahorn and Jeff Ruland as "McFilthy" and "McNasty," respectively. Posthumously, Most was awarded the Curt Gowdy Media award by the Basketball Hall of Fame. Jon Miller (1998, p. 199) calls his partner "*the* premier basketball analyst." You will enjoy Mike Carey and Jamie Most's *High Above Courtside: The Lost Memoirs of Johnny Most* (2003).

Anthony Munoz: considered one of the best offensive linemen from his days with the Cincinnati Bengals, the Pro Football Hall of Famer has worked at TNT, CBS, and Fox.

Bob Murphy (1925-2004): an "Original Voice of the Mets," was known for his "Happy Recap" and cheery disposition. In a remembrance on the Mets Homepage dated August 4, 2004, sportswriter Richard Sandomir wrote: "Murphy was part of a generation of announcers—along with Vin Scully, Ernie Harwell, Harry Caray and Jack Buck—who built their reputations in radio and whose voices became intimately linked to their teams." Recipient of the 1994 Ford C. Frick award, his voice evoked summer.

Brent Musburger: one of the most recognizable sportscasters, he studied at Northwestern's Medill School of Journalism and started as a sportswriter before coming to CBS Sports in 1973—going from play-by-play to hosting *The NFL Today* and currently calling ABC Sports' college football. He also covered basketball, tennis, Masters golf, The World's Strongest Man contests, baseball, the Tour De France, World Cup, NASCAR, and more. "You're looking LIVE at . . ." became part of his folksy style. In 1979, he starred as himself in *Rocky II* and *The Main Event,* later in *The Waterboy* (1998), and *Mickey* (2004). His brother, Todd Musburger, is a sports agent.

Jim Nantz: with CBS Sports *Television* since 1985, the versatile play-by-player has done NFL (he hosted NFL Today from 1998-2003), NBA, college football and basketball, the Masters and PGA Championship golf tournaments, the U.S. Open, Olympic Games, NCAA Final Four, Super Bowl, and more. His familiar greeting of, "Hello, friends!" has endeared him to many fans.

Lindsey Nelson (1919-1995): The "Voice of the New York Mets," his depth and breadth made him a beloved sportscaster. "Literate, personable, articulate. . . ." (Maury Allen, 1971, p. 1). Beginning with radio on the Liberty Broadcasting System, he started by doing recreations before moving to NBC baseball in 1957. He called Notre Dame "Fighting Irish" football, and did Mutual's Monday Night NFL radio broadcasts from 1974 to 1977, continuing on television for CBS. Co-author of *Backstage at the Mets* (1966), his famous self-introduction is also the title of his 1985 autobiography: *Hello Everybody, I'm Lindsey Nelson.* It provides this insightful anecdote: in 1939—"before the era of analysts and color men," he first heard that a Tennessee-Alabama game would be broadcast by Bill Stern of NBC, then by Ted Husing of CBS, and realized why broadcasters worked alone. "If he monopolized the microphone, the announcer was not building future competition for his job. The top play-by-play men of that day intended to remain the top play-by-play men. And they didn't want any pretenders to the throne throwing their names around on the air for the audience to know and perhaps love. It was a sound practice for survival" (p. 52). Nelson reviews his twenty-five years in MLB broadcasting, thirty-three in football, along with his military stint during Word War II in North Africa and Europe, traveling nonstop and meeting the likes of Ernie Pyle, Bob Hope, Dwight Eisenhower, Winston Churchill, George Patton, Andy Rooney, and so many athletes, coaches, and fellow sportscasters. He has been inducted into the National Sportscasters and Sportswriters Hall of Fame, the New York Mets Hall of Fame, the American Sportscasters Association Hall of Fame, and has won the Ford C. Frick award, the Pete Rozelle Radio-Television award, and an Emmy Award for Life Achievement.

David Niehaus: the "Voice of the (Seattle) Mariners," his sense of humor comes out in calls like, "Get out the rye bread and mustard, Grandma, it's 'grand salami time'!"

Keith Olbermann: host of MSNBC's *Countdown with Keith Olber-mann,* as well as ESPN radio's *The Dan Patrick Show,* he co-hosts NBC's *Football Night in America* with Bob Costas. He helped to launch ESPN Radio and ESPN2, and he co-authored, with Dan Patrick, *The Big Show: Inside ESPN's SportsCenter* (1997).

Merlin Olsen: a Hall of Fame defensive lineman for the Los Angeles Rams who never missed a game in his fifteen-year NFL career, making the Pro Bowl in all but his final year, he was a color commentator with Dick Enberg on NBC throughout the 1980s. You may recognize him from *Little House on the Prairie, Father Murphy,* or *Aaron's Way* on television, or in the movie *The Unde-feated* (1969), and he is cited in *Anchorman: The Legend of Ron Burgundy* (2004). He was named in the 1999 *Sporting News'* list as one of the 100 Greatest Football Players.

Don Orsillo: play-by-play announcer for the Boston Red Sox games on NESN since 2001, he works with former Red Sox second base-man Jerry Remy. He had quite an initiation, as his first game was a no-hitter by pitcher Hideo Nomo, and he later called Cal Ripken's last game.

Billy Packer: a college basketball color commentator, since 1974 he has covered every NCAA Men's Division I Basketball Champion-ship, including the Final Four. Co-author of *Hoops: Confessions of a College Basketball Analyst* (1986), he shares, "For me, basket-ball and broadcasting made a natural combination. Being a color man is just an extension of playing, coaching, recruiting, and liv-ing basketball" (p. 37). Packer also wrote *Why We Win* (1999)—in-terviews with coaches Red Auerbach, John Wooden, Ara Par-seghian, Anson Dorrance, Bobby Knight, Joe Gibbs, Pat Head Summitt, Chuck Noll, Tommy Lasorda, Mike Krzyzewski, Sparky Anderson, Dan Gable, Bill Walsh, Lenny Wilkens, Joe Paterno, and Dean Smith. He has two sons in the business: Mark Packer is on WFNZ, the all-sports radio station in Charlotte, North Carolina and Brandt Packer produces golf telecasts for ABC Sports.

Ron Pitts: coming from a football family, playing himself for the Buf-falo Bills and Green Bay Packers, he covers the NFL on Fox Sports.

Bob Prince (1916-1985): "The Gunner" served as "Voice of the (Pittsburgh) Pirates" from 1948 to 1975. His broadcast lingo, known as "Gunnerisms," include such terms as "Radio ball" for a fastball so fast it "could be heard but not seen," a "Soup cooler" was a pitch delivered high and inside, a "Hoover" a double play that would "clean up" the bases, "Bloop and a blast" a base hit and a home run, usually late in the game, "A bug loose on the rug" a ground ball scooting on Astroturf between all fielders on the defensive team, and a "Tweener" was a hit to the outfield wall between left field and center field or between right field and center field. He also popularized "the green weenie" good luck charm. He ended broadcasts with, "Good night, Mary Edgerley, wherever you are," a parody of Jimmy Durante's routine. Prince was posthumously awarded the Ford C. Frick award in 1986.

Mel Proctor: sportscaster for the Baltimore Orioles, Washington Nationals, San Diego Padres, and Los Angeles Clippers, he has done lots of practical jokes on the air.

Felo Ramírez: "The Pride of Bayamo," he is a Cuban-born, Spanish language radio voice of the Florida Marlins.

Jay Randolph: son of U.S. Senator William Jennings Randolph, he moved from being an amateur golfer to sports announcing for the Dallas Cowboys, SMU football, NBC pro and college football, golf, basketball, three Olympics and, most recently, the St. Louis Cardinals.

Ahmad Rashad: a wide receiver who became an Emmy award-winning sportscaster, he had everyone talking when he proposed to Phylicia (of *The Cosby Show*) during a pregame Thanksgiving Day show on November 28, 1985. As he recounts in *Rashad: Vikes, Mikes and Something on the Backside* (1988), he encountered difficulties when he changed his name (Bobby Moore) upon adopting the religion of Islam.

Ronald Reagan (1911-2004): yes, our fortieth president, known as "Dutch," was a sportscaster who recreated 1930s Cubs and White Sox games on station WHO in Des Moines. As Libby Hughes' 2005 book reveals *(From Sports to Movies to Politics)*. "I was doing the games by telegraphic report . . . the headphones on, getting the Morse Code from the ball park," Reagan (cited in Smith, 1995, p. 26) recalls. "He typed out the play. And the paper would come through to me saying something like, 'SIC.' That means strike one on the corner. But you're not going to sell Wheaties yelling 'SIC!' So I would say, 'So-and-so comes out of the windup, here comes the pitch . . . and it's a called strike breaking over the outside corner to a batter that likes the ball a little higher.'"

Beasley Reece: although he started off studying music, he had an NFL career from 1976 to 1984 before becoming a color commentator for NBC and CBS.

Pee Wee Reese (1918-1999): a player for the Brooklyn and Los Angeles Dodgers, he later moved to the broadcasting booth, with Dizzy Dean from 1960-1965 on CBS, then with Curt Gowdy from 1966-1968 on NBC. He was inducted into the Baseball Hall of Fame in 1984.

Jerry Remy: after being a MLB second baseman, it is only appropriate that he is now a color commentator for NESN Red Sox broadcasts, usually with play-by-play announcer Don Orsillo. Nicknamed "Rem Dawg," he was inducted into the Boston Red Sox Hall of Fame in 2006. He has a Web site called The Remy Report and is co-author of *Watching Baseball: Discovering the Game within the Game* (2004).

Phil Rizzuto: "The Scooter" helped win nine World Series as a Yankee shortstop, then turned to sports announcing with his famous "Unbelievable!" or "Did you see that?." Teaming with Mel Allen, Red Barber, Joe Garagiola, Jerry Coleman, and many others, his October 1, 1961, call of Roger Maris' record-setting home run stands out: "Here's the windup, fastball, hit deep to right, this could be it! Way back there! Holy cow, he did it! Sixty-one for Maris! And look at the fight for that ball out there! Holy cow, what a shot! Another standing ovation for Maris, and they're still fighting for that ball out there, climbing over each other's backs. One of the greatest sights I've ever seen here at Yankee Stadium!" He also had some slipups, such as, "Bouncer to third, they'll never get him! No, why don't I just shut up!" or "All right! Stay fair! No, it won't stay fair. Good thing it didn't stay fair, or I think he would've caught it!" The subject of Peyer and Seely's *O Holy Cow!: The Selected Verse of Phil Rizzuto* (1997), the player/sportscaster who used "WW" in his scorecard for "Wasn't Watching" is in the Baseball Hall of Fame.

Robin Roberts: beginning as a sports anchor and reporter, she became an ESPN sportscaster in 1990 and now is co-anchor of ABC's *Good Morning America.*

Ted Robinson: after working for the San Francisco Giants, Minnesota Twins, and the New York Mets, along with doing play-by-play for many other teams and several Olympics, today he is seen on NBC doing the French Open and Wimbledon—a natural step after covering tennis for the USA Network for nearly two decades.

John Rooney: best known as a broadcaster for the St. Louis Cardinals, he worked for CBS Radio from 1984 to 2003, he has been inducted into the Missouri Sports Hall of Fame.

Sam Rosen: the Germany-born play-by-play announcer for New York Rangers has partnered with Phil Esposito, John Davidson, Joe Micheletti, Tim Ryan, and Dick Stockton. His son, Mattew Rosen, is pregame radio host of the Phoenix Coyotes.

Bill Russell: five-time NBA MVP considered one of the best-ever defensive players, twelve-time All-Star for the Boston Celtics, Gold Medal winner at the 1956 Melbourne as captain of the U.S. national basketball team, he has seen the game from both sides. Although his broadcasting career was brief, doing ABC's *NBA Game of the Week* and analysis on WTBS, he brought great insight to the job.

Byrum Saam (1914-2000): "Voice of Philadelphia baseball" for forty years, having announced more than 8,000 games for the Phillies and Athletics, he received the Ford C. Frick award in 1990. Known for his catchphrase, "Rolling along," it was said that also described his temperament.

Billy Sample: a former professional baseball player turned sportscaster, he has some valuable thoughts on making that transition, shared with sports historian Curt Smith on April 19, 2006, Readers can go to the National Baseball Hall of Fame Web site (www .baseballhalloffame.org).

Ron Santo: a former Chicago Cubs and White Sox player, he has become a local favorite as radio color commentator. From his position on the board of the Juvenile Diabetes Foundation, his annually sponsored Ron Santo Walk for the Cure has raised more than $63 million for diabetes research since its inception.

Jerry Schemmel: as a survivor of a crash-landed plane in 1989, he described the experience in *Chosen to Live: The Inspiring Story of Flight 232 Survivor Jerry Schemmel* (1996); he has been a radio announcer for the Denver Nuggets since 1992.

Chris Schenkel (1923-2005): a play-by-play sportscaster on both radio and television, he set a standard for quantity and quality of sports journalism. After calling the nation's first football game on television (Harvard versus Army, in 1947), he was hired by the DuMont network to do New York Giants football, which he continued doing on CBS, along with other sporting events such as boxing, horse racing, and golf. When he joined ABC in 1965, he called college football, MLB, NBA, golf and tennis tournaments, boxing and bowling, car racing, Olympic Games, and more. Schenkel's smooth voice and level deliveries earned him the title "National Sportscaster of the Year" four times, along with a lifetime achievement Emmy, the Pete Rozelle Radio-Television award, and the Jim Thorpe Lifetime Achievement award.

Ray Scott (1920-1998): broadcasting on radio in the late 1930s, then moving to the DuMont Television Network in the 1950s, he became best known as the "Voice of the (Green Bay) Packers." Twice named National Sportscaster of the Year, in 2000 he was posthumously awarded the Pete Rozelle Radio-Television award.

Vin Scully: entering Ebbets Field under the tutelage of Red Barber at age twenty-two, he has been best known as the play-by-play voice of the Brooklyn and Los Angeles Dodgers (1958-2007), the longest of any broadcaster with a single club in professional sports history. Would-be sportscasters can learn a lot from him: he always used good grammar, and he has been able to combine reality with description such that fans associate him with the phrase, "I saw it on radio." Here is an example of what he succinctly said at the 1955 World Series: "Ladies and gentlemen, the Brooklyn Dodgers are the champions of the world." During the 1986 World Series, he reported: "If one picture is worth a thousand words, you have seen about a million words, but more than that, you have seen an absolutely bizarre finish to Game 6 of the 1986 World Series. The Mets are not only alive, they are well, and they will play the Red Sox in Game 7 tomorrow!" In 1988's World Series, when the Dodgers surprisingly beat the Oakland A's, he announced, "In a year that has been so improbable, the impossible has happened!" In 1965, for Sandy Koufax's perfect game, he narrated: "Two and two to Harvey Kuenn, one strike away. Sandy into his windup, here's the pitch: swung on and missed, a perfect game! On the scoreboard in right field it is 9:46 p.m. in the City of the Angels, Los Angeles,

California, and a crowd of twenty-nine thousand one-hundred thirty nine just sitting in to see the only pitcher in baseball history to hurl four no-hit, no-run games. He has done it four straight years, and now he caps it: on his fourth no-hitter he made it a perfect game. And Sandy Koufax, whose name will always remind you of strikeouts, did it with a flourish: he struck out the last six consecutive batters—so when he wrote his name in capital letters in the record books, that K stands out even more than the O-U-F-A-X." For his final MLB game for NBC, in 1989, San Francisco Giants versus the Chicago Cubs, he said, just prior to Will Clark's winning hit: "In every big series there comes a time when it becomes difficult to breathe, difficult to swallow. This is that moment." On CBS in 2004, when LA's Steve Finley came to bat in the ninth inning, he declared, "High fly ball into deep right field! Wherever it goes, the Dodgers have won . . . and it's a grand slam home run!" In addition to winning the Ford Frick award in 1982, in 1995 he was named California Sportscaster of the Year, received the Life Achievement Emmy Award for sportscasting, and was inducted into the Radio Hall of Fame, and was named Broadcaster of the Century in 2000 by the American Sportscasters Association. The Dodgers have announced that Scully has his contract through the 2008 season, earning about $3 million each year.

Lon Simmons: a legendary Bay Area broadcaster of both baseball ("You can tell it goodbye!") and football, especially associated with the San Francisco Giants, he received the 2004 Ford C. Frick award.

Phil Simms: playing quarterback for the New York Giants, including being Pro Bowl MVP, has helped him in his role as a sportscaster for CBS. He started with Dick Enberg and Paul Maguire on NBC covering of Super Bowls, then worked with Greg Gumbel, now Jim Nantz. His native Kentucky comes through in his speech and, although some fans accuse him of being too aggressive, he is mostly admired.

Ken Singleton: beginning in 1970 he played with the New York Mets, he currently is a commentator for Yankee games on YES.

Dewayne Staats: radio "Voice of the (Chicago) Cubs, he current is a play-by-play commentator for the Tampa Bay Devil Rays—having broadcast more than 4,000 major league games.

Melissa Stark: after anchoring at MSNBC and serving as a sideline reporter for MNF, she covered 2006 Torino Olympics.

Bob Starr (1933-1998): the 1980s "Voice of the (Anaheim) Angels," he replaced Ken Coleman as lead announcer for the Red Sox in 1989.

John Sterling: having announced New York Yankees since 1989, all games, in addition to pre- and postseason without missing a single one, he quite naturally is a local legend. Over the years he has partnered with Charley Steiner, Michael Kay, Joe Angel, and Jay Johnstone, and today he works with Suzyn Waldman. Known for announcing, "Ball-game over! Yankees win! Theeeeeee Yankees win!!" he has given the team some special nicknames: Jason Giambi is "The giambino," Alex Rodriguez—"Alexander the Great," Johnny Damon—"positively Damonic," Hideki Matsui is "A thrilla by Godzilla," Jorge Posada—"Jorgie Juiced One," Derek Jeter is "El Capitan!," and Bobby Abreu is "El Comedulce!"

Bill Stern (1907-1971): announcer of the nation's first remote sports broadcast and the first telecast of a MLB game, he was at the center of the debate about who invented the curveball—Candy Cummings or Fred Goldsmith (Stern chose the latter). You can read about it in his 1949 book *Bill Stern's Favorite Baseball Stories.* He was inducted into the Radio Hall of Fame in 1988. Don Dunphy (1988, p. 121) called him "the most dynamic sports announcer of his day."

Jackie Stewart: Sir John Young Stewart, better known to racing fans as "The Flying Scot," competed in Formula One from 1965 to 1973, winning three world titles, before broadcasting NASCAR and the Indianapolis 500.

Dick Stockton: a sportscaster since 1965, he became the Boston Red Sox's lead play-by-player. Calling Carlton Fisk's game-winning home run in Game 6 of the 1975 World Series, he hollered the famous phrase, "There it goes, a long drive. If it stays fair . . . Home run!" The talented Stockton has covered NFL, NBA, MLB, the Pan Am Games, the Olympic Games, and local broadcasts of the Oakland Athletics and the San Antonio Spurs. He is married to fellow sportscaster Lesley Visser.

Hannah Storm: currently co-host of CBS' *The Early Show,* she started sportscasting by hosting the Houston Rockets halftime and postgame shows on television, moved to *CNN Sports Tonight*, then NBC—where she did Olympic Games, NBA, and WNBA, NFL, MLB, figure skating, and more. She broke sports history by being the first woman to host baseball games (1994 to 2000), then NBA games (1997 to 2002) for NBC, and she also did NBA for TNT. The mother of three daughters, she is the co-author of a 2002 book called *Go Girl: Raising Healthy, Confident, and Successful Girls Through Sports.*

Hank Stram (1923-2005): a fourteen-year championship-winning coach of the Kansas City Chiefs, he became an NFL color commentator on CBS in 1978 for some two decades. It was a difficult transition, but he approached it this way, as reported in his 1986 book *They're Playing My Game*: "To improve my broadcasting performance, I applied some old techniques. I recorded my reporting faithfully and replayed it on a tape machine I kept in my car. I would listen to my broadcast and wince when I made a mistake or spoke too fast. Slowly I learned my lessons and corrected myself" (p. 22).

Pat Summerall: after playing football for the Detroit Lions, Chicago Cardinals, and New York Giants, he became one of our best-known sportscasters—at CBS, Fox, and, ESPN. Teamed variously with John Madden (they were called the "Bert and Ernie of Football"), Tom Brookshier, Jack Buck, and Brian Baldinger, he was inducted into the American Sportscasters Association Hall of Fame in 1999. He still does voiceovers for CBS Masters broadcasts, as well as commentary for the Golden Tee golf video game. His incredible life story is revealed in *Summerall: On and Off the Air* (2006).

Joe Theismann: a football quarterback and football announcer for ESPN (*Sunday Night Football* 1988 to 2005, then *MNF*) before being fired in 2007, he hosted the first season of the *American Gladiator.*

Chuck Thompson (1912-2005): known for *Ain't the Beer Cold!*, the title of his 1996 memoirs, he arrived in Baltimore in 1949 to broadcast the Orioles and never left. He offers this advice: "Everybody who ever listened to a baseball broadcast will always have the same complaint and 95 percent of the time the complaints are justified. Because people tune in and out, they say they don't hear the score enough. You simply can't give the score too often. That's why the late Red Barber had an egg-timer in the booth, to remind him that he should give the score at least every three minutes" (p. 48.)

Mike Tirico: the first recipient of Syracuse University's Bob Costas Scholarship for exceptional broadcast journalism, he soon became lead broadcaster on MNF as well as doing varied programming for ESPN/ABC.

Al Trautwig: a color commentator for MSG, NBC, and Versus, doing pre- and postanalysis for the New York Knicks and New York Rangers, he has anchored the Tour de France since 2004, the Olympic Games, and the Arena Football League. An original host for Classic Sports Network in 1996, he now has *Al Trautwig's MSG Vault.* He had a cameo in *Cool Runnings* (1993) announcing the bobsled competition, and was elected New York Sportscaster of the Year in 2000.

Bob Trumpy: a four-time All Pro playing tight end for the Cincinnati Bengals who turned to radio (WLW Cincinnati's *Sports Talk*), then NBC with Dick Enberg to call Super Bowls XXVII and XXVIII. Today, he is an analyst for CBS Radio Sports/Westwood One on *Sunday Night Football.*

Jerry Trupiano: after years of doing play-by-play for the Boston Red Sox since 1993, including calling their 2004 World Series-winning game ("Waaay Back!"), his next moves are, at this time, unannounced.

Ty Tyson (1888-1968): starting out at WWJ in 1924, where he called the first University of Michigan football game on radio, he later called the first Detroit Tigers contest.

Bob Uecker: self-proclaimed as "Mr. Baseball"; having played for the Milwaukee and Atlanta Braves, he has done radio play-by-play for the Milwaukee Brewers from 1970 to today. One of television's first color commentators, on ABC's *Monday Night Baseball,* he also has hosted *Bob Uecker's Wacky World of Sports* and *Bob Uecker's War of the Stars.* His signature "Get up, get up, get outta here!" is imprinted on the Miller Park mascot. Inducted into the Radio Hall of Fame in 2001 and recipient of the Ford C. Frick award in 2003, his 1982 autobiography is titled *Catcher in the Wry.*

Dave Van Horne: after spending his first thirty-two years as "Voice of the (Montreal) Expos" when they began in 1969, since 2000 he has been the lead radio play-by-play voice of the Florida Marlins. He has called ten no-hitters, including two perfect games.

Lesley Visser: the only sportscaster to do network broadcast of the Final Four, NBA Finals, Triple Crown, MNF, the Olympic Games, the Super Bowl, the World Figure Skating Championships, and the U.S. Open of tennis, she also was the first—and, to this day, the only woman to handle the Super Bowl Trophy Presentation. Beginning as a sportswriter for the *Boston Globe,* covering the New England Patriots, she was the first female to crush their threat of "No Women or Children Allowed in the Press Box." Then, joining CBS Sports in 1984 on *The NFL Today,* with Greg Gumbel and Terry Bradshaw, she made her mark. Ten years later, she was also the first woman on MNF, in 1995 the first female to sideline report a Super Bowl. At CBS since 2000, covering the NFL and college basketball, she was the first woman sportscaster to carry the Olympic Torch (see www.lesleyvisser.com), appropriately honored for being a "pioneer and standard-bearer." In 2006, she was the first woman to receive the Pete Rozelle Radio-Television award.

Dick Vitale: "Dickie V," or "Mr. College Basketball," is undoubtedly the most outlandish of all sportscasters. An NBA coach for the Detroit Pistons, he joined ESPN when it started, calling its first college basketball game in 1979. A color commentator, he has added more than 1,000 games since then—with play-by-players Brad Nessler, Dan Shulman, or Mike Patrick. While Duke University is an unabashed favorite, and he has been called "Duke Vitale," he covers all the biggest games with unbounded energy. Vitale has coined terms like "Diaper Dandy" for an outstanding freshman, "Maalox Masher" for a close game, and "dipsy-doo dunkeroo slam-jam-bam, baby!" for an exciting slam dunk. But most of all, his signature sentence ending is "baby!" His name and voice are on the Sega Genesis game *Dick Vitale's Awesome Baby!,* and he is the co-author of *Vitale:Just Your Average Bald, One-eyed Basketball Wacko who Beat the Ziggy and Became a PTP'er* (1988), where he comes clean: "One thing you can say for me as a broadcaster: I've never held back with my opinions. I've never steered clear of controversy. I say what I think, and I don't care about the consequences; I'll face those when they come. And they come—do they every come!"(p.18). He also has co-authored *Holding Court: Reflections on the Game I Love* (1995) and *Dick Vitale's Living*

Dream: Reflections on 25 Years Sitting in the Best Seat in the House (2003). Brian Lowry (2006, p. 1) has declared: "The decline in the booth is largely attributable to a pair of former coaches, football's John Madden and college basketball's Dick Vitale, whose zeal, amusing at first, degenerated into self-parody ages ago. Vitale, particularly, has become so annoying that listening to him is a chore, as he increasingly talks about everything *but* the game he's called." Following is a description of Dick Vitale by Norman Chad (1990):

> Imagine you're strapped to the barrel of a big gun that fires 250 rounds of ammunition per minute and then you hear 18,000 bowling balls rapidly coming at you and then a volcano erupts less than 100 feet away and then you are hauled into a VW Beetle in which a big-band orchestra and Z.Z. Top are jamming in the back seat and then you are dragged through an automotive plant's assembly line.

Murray Walker: a Formula 1 motorsport commentator born in Birmingham, England, he has a distinctive delivery style, making comments known "Walkerisms" or "Murrayisms" such as" "It's raining and the track is wet," "And what a bitter pill that must be to swallow," "Spin! Spin! Spin!"; "Fire! Fire! Fire!"; "Either that car is stationary, or it's on the move," "There's nothing wrong with that car except that it's on fire," "Excuse me while I interrupt myself . . .," or "With half the race gone, there's half the race still to go." The recipient of honorary doctorates from Bournemouth and Middlesex Universities, BBC's voice of the Grand Prix is also a Sky Sports' commentator.

Bill Walton: a legendary basketball player, he overcame stuttering to become an NBA color commentator for NBC from 1990 to 2002, then ABC/ESPN. He has some amusing catchphrases, such as "That's a terrible call! Terrible," "He couldn't even inbound the ball!"; "This is a game of men playing for the ultimate prize," or the exaggerated "worst pass in the history of Western civilization!"

Pam Ward: an ESPN on-air personality, she has been doing play-by-play for NCAA football games since 2001.

Pete Weber: the play-by-play voice of the NHL's Nashville Predators since 1998, he has also called the Los Angeles Kings and the Buffalo Bills. His quirky phrases include calling Indianapolis' anti-quated Bush Stadium "The Reverse Oz Effect," "It's Mary Kay time here in Nashville," or promoting *The Best Damn Sports Show Period* as "B.D.S.S.P."

Jack Whitaker: host of *CBS Sports Spectacular* since 1961, he is mostly associated with his coverage of golf and horse racing. The award-winning sportscaster was inducted into the American Sports-casters Association in 1997, the National Sportscasters and Sports-writers Hall of Fame in 2001, and Saint Joseph's University Ath-letic Hall of Fame in 2005. In *Preferred Lies and Other Tales: Skimming the Cream of a Life in Sports* (1998, p. 100), he declares the Masters to be "very likely the best sporting event in the world."

Ken Wilson: "Oh Baby!" hockey announcer for the St. Louis Blues on Fox Sports, he was the first announcer for the Seattle Mariners, with Dave Niehaus (1977-1982), did play-by-play for the Cin-cinnati Reds, and called Pete Rose's record-breaking hit in 1985. In 2004, NHL, when he moved to Honolulu, he opened Mama's Is-land Pizza and began doing play-by-play for the Hawaii winter baseball league in 2006.

Warner Wolf: "My philosophy on sportscasting isn't too complicated. In fact, it's common sense. You have to be informative, you can't be silly, but you can be entertaining. I have always felt that televi-sion is an entertainment medium and sportscasting is part of that," he wrote in *Let's Go to the Videotape!* (2000, p. 1). After stints on Monday Night Baseball, football, and the Olympics, he served as a sports anchor on *Imus in the Morning* when Mike Breen needed a sub until 2004. His first book, *Gimme a Break!* (1983) is another signature call.

Bob Wolff: with more than six decades doing sports on television, he was the voice of the Washington Senators from 1947 to 1960. "One problem I had in TV's early days was that I had to sell the product," Wolff reminisced (cited in Smith, 1995, p. 247). "This is before taped commercials; everything was live. Once, I got cigar-smoking lessons. Talk about a crisis. 'Don't do it like Mel Allen,' they began. 'He puts it in the front of his mouth. Put it on the side.' One night, I'm working that cigar and put it in the ashtray. 'Stop!' this guy orders. 'What happened?' I said. He say, 'Cigarettes, you put into the ashtray. Cigars, you keep in your mouth.' Finally, I get the technique right, and it helped my career. In the '60s I became

Voice of Madison Square Garden. The reason I got the job is the cigar sponsor, and others said to the Garden, 'You got to hire this guy. He can sell anything—not well, but he tries.'" Wolff's sense of humor comes through in his 1992 book *It's Not Who Won or Lost the Game: It's How You Sold the Beer.*

Dave Zinkoff (1910-1985): according to the Philadelphia Jewish Sports Hall of Fame (www.pjshf.com), "The Zink" was one of the most famous voices in the history of professional basketball. Voice of the Philadelphia Warriors, then the Philadelphia 76ers, he traveled with the Harlem Globetrotters and coined some funny phrases like "Dipper Dunk" and "Gola Goal."

The main point is that there are a lot of good sports stories to tell, and to telecast, and a lot of good people to tell them.

Chapter 6

Sociocultural Perspectives on Sports and Sportscasting

We hear it frequently: sports is a microcosm of the world around it. Social issues, financial issues, drugs, sexual and gender issues, high-finance and business issues—all sorts of topics more complex than 'ball meeting ball' or 'ball dropping through net' that show up every day.

(Hammel cited in Aamidor, 2003, p. 1)

THE PERVASIVENESS AND SALIENCE OF SPORTS

Echoing the sports-as-microcosm concept, Richard O. Davies (1994, p. vii) remarks, "Sports in recent decades have lost whatever innocence they might have once enjoyed and moved into the mainstream of national life. At times they have mirrored national trends and issues, at other times they have forced national policymakers to act." The sheer pervasiveness and salience of sports needs to be noted here, both in terms of their use of our time and of our money. "At times sport can be trivial and unimportant, at other a symbolically significant cultural form that is an indicator of wider social and cultural forces in society," (Raymond Boyle, 2006, p. 13).

From a wider perspective, our bent toward Western ethnocentrism must also be considered—coloring not only the nature and composition of games by sportscasters, but also of audience-receiver perceptions. Sportswriter Mark Starr (2006, p. 50) sets up the subjects of this chapter:

Sportscasters/Sportscasting

We have seen sports become increasingly central to the American experience. It is a prism, perhaps even *the* prism, through which we consider the most complex issues of our times: race (the black-power salute at the '68 Olympics, the dearth of Black NFL quarterbacks and coaches, un-hip-hop NBA dress codes) or gender (Title IX, Billie Jean King versus Bobby Riggs, the '99 Women's World Cup).

The Sociology of Sport

Sports broadcasting is a reflection of the culture in which it exists. As radio and then television began to develop, sports broadcasting was still very primitive, not only technologically, but also in terms of presentation and format. Now, decades later, sports broadcasting has adapted to the hurry-up, instant-gratification culture of modern times, which has produced such recent advances as the Internet and digital technology. Where once sports broadcasting seemed somewhat restrained and genteel, it now delivers its omnipresent message with an 'in your face' attitude. (Schultz, 2002, p. xv)

In 1965, Gerald S. Kenyon and John W. Loy's article, "Toward a sociology of sport" appeared in the *Journal of Health, Physical Education and Recreation;* since that seminal piece, a great deal of research has focused on sports sociology (Andrews, 2006; Andrews and Jackson, 2001; Bale, 1994; Berri, Schmidt, and Brook, 2006; Birrell and McDonald, 2000; Cashmore, 2005; Coakley, 2003; Coakley and Dunning, 2000; Davies, 1994; Dunning, 1999; Egendorf, 1999; Eitzen, 1999, 2004; Fuller, 2006a; Gerdy, 2002; Giulianotti, Bonney, and Hepwarth, 1994; Grafton and Jones, 2003; Gruneau, 1999; Horne, Tomlinson, and Whannel, 1999; Hughson, Inglis, and Free, 2004; Ingham and Loy, 1993; Jarvie, 2006; Jarvie and Maguire, 1994; Jones and Armour, 2000; Kew, 1997; Lapchick, 1996; Leonard, 1993; MacClancy, 1996; Magire, 2005; Mandelbaum, 2004; McPherson and Loy, 1989; Miller, 2001; Perrin, 2000; Rail, 1998; Rowe, 1995, 1999; Simon, 1991; Sugden, 2002; vanBottenburg, 2001; Wiggins, 1995; Wise, 1994; Zang, 2004).

"Sport, a seemingly trivial pursuit, is important" (D. Stanley Eitzen, 1999, p. 2). Eitzen follows up by pointing out how sport mirrors both the human experience and society, and that it is compelling—combining spectacle with drama, excellence, and clarity, and draws on our desire to identify with something greater than ourselves. This chapter deals with athletes as role models and then looks at a number of issues that are of critical importance to sports, sportscasters, and sportscasting. "Like most kids, I had gotten interested in sports because of the joy of the game," (Len Berman, 2005, p. 81). "But as a professional I have found myself spending more time reporting on drugs, lockouts, and court proceedings."

Even subjects relative to sports themselves are sometimes tricky. "Baseball is damaged when ex-players, especially those who are still in the game as coaches, scouts, or broadcasters, deride the present-day players," bemoans Jon Miller (2000, p. 50). In general, Miller moves away from controversial topics—making it clear, for example, that he prefers not to discuss whether baseballs are "juiced." Fans, Miller states, are only interested in one thing: the game.

In light of sports scandals such as the Len Bias and Ben Johnson drug cases, SMU's football probation, Pete Rose's gambling, Kobe Bryant's alleged rape charge, the Duke University lacrosse false accusations of rape, or any number of news stories, the issue of athletes, or athletes as role models/heroes becomes an anxious topic for sportscasters (Fuller, 1989, 1990, 1991; Graham, 1987). Snyder and Spreitzer (1983, p. 218) remind us that, "The sports announcer has three constituencies to please in addition to the listener or viewer—the owner of the sports franchise, the corporate sponsors who buy the advertising time, and the owner of the television or radio station." "Sportscasting is my profession, but I think I recognize the proper place of sports in society," Len Berman (2005, p. 235) has noted. "Sports is a diversion—a terrific diversion, yes, but still just a diversion. As much as I get immersed in the drama and the excitement of a pennant race or a locker room soap opera, I try to keep things in perspective."

The Language of Sport

> Spiced with metaphors from everyday life, the language of sport ranges from talk about playing hardball to sticky wickets to cheap shots. Routinely, whether in our homes, offices, or in boardrooms, we talk about offensive and defensive tactics, game plans, Monday morning quarterbacking, being team players, playing tough and playing fair. If we can't talk the talk, we are denied access to "level playing fields." (Fuller, 2006, p. 7)

Although we may not be aware of it, the language of sports surrounds our daily lives, whether at actual sporting venues, via the media, and/or in conversations and commentaries by the people around us. Sensitive to the many sociological implications of sports rhetoric, Segrave, McDowell, and King (2006, pp. 31-32) have delineated several areas where it might be identified: "Among the many linguistic conventions contributing to the cultural devaluation of women in sports may be included masculine generics, gender marking, naming practices, descriptive linguistics, the metaphorical language of sport, the language of sport in cultural discourses, and subcultural language." Consider, for example, how women's athletic teams are often associated with sexist names like Bell(ettes), how players are referred to as "girl," "gal," "lady," or by their first names when sportscasters call their counterparts by full or last names. Even team mascots, logos, and names might be sexist, with names like the "Lady Bucks"—that don't even make sense.

There is an increasing interest in the language of sports (Adler, 1992; Beard, 1998; Considine, 1982; Crouser, 1983; Fuller, 1999, 2006; Hafner, 1989; Oriard, 1991). "People who talk about sports—particularly sports reporters and commentators in the media—have an important opportunity to expand upon the considerable progress that has already been made," writes Nancy Huppertz (2002, p. 1, Women's Sports Foundation Web site). She suggests the following for equitable language usage:

1. *Avoid using male terms as generic.* They are not. Use alternatives. Examples:

WRONG: Man-to-man defense.
BETTER: One-on-one, One-to-one, Player-to-player
WRONG: She's guarding her man.
BETTER: She's guarding her woman or player.

2. *Use masculine tags for teams and tournaments in the same way that feminine tags are used.* Examples: "Bearcats and Lady Bearcats" versus "Bearcat men and Bearcat women," or "The Final Four and the Women's Final Four" versus "The Men's Final Four and the Women's Final Four."

3. *Avoid using so-called generic pronouns.* Use male terms when talking about females and male terms when talking about males. Use inclusive construction when talking about both. Example: "Every player has his ankles taped" versus "All the players have their ankles taped," or "Every athlete at the university is required to keep his grades up" versus "Every athlete at the university is required to keep her or his grades up."

4. *Use parallel terms for male and female leagues in the same sport.* Example: NBA and WNBA, MNBA and WMBA, PGA and LPGA, GPGA and LPGA (p. 2).

Because he was "Convinced that sports are out of whack in the American society," Howard Cosell (1985, p. 13) used the following explanation for his interest in writing about the topic, developing his thesis this way: "That the emphasis placed upon sports distorts the real values of life and often produces mass behavior patterns that are downright frightening; and that the frequently touted uplifting benefits of sports have become a murky blue in the morass of hypocrisy and contradiction that I call the Sports Syndrome." Once a sportscaster masters the rules of "sportsugese," with his/her own personal style, she or he has truly arrived.

Sports and Religion

Some scholars are interested in the interplay between sport and religion (Higgs, 1995; Kugelmass, 2007; Levine, 1993; Prebish, 1993; Price, 2001; Riess, 1998)—a seemingly odd relationship, when you consider the physical versus the other-worldly. The nagging question becomes: Are sports a religion? Or is religion a sport? Phil Patton

(1984, p. 113) has talked about the ritual that became what he called the "Church of Monday Night Football." If you wonder how religion might impact sports journalists, consider the case of Rany Jazayerli. Jazayerli writes for *Baseball Prospectus;* in his "Appeal for Tolerance" (to ESPN's Page 2 after 9/11), as a Muslim, he hoped his fellow Americans would respect his religion.

Sports in Popular Culture

> Informed and underpinned by the seemingly relentless commercialization of popular cultural activity, sport has found itself at the intersection of new media technologies allowing greater exploitation of image rights and a massively expanded, highly competitive print and broadcast media sector keen to secure differing forms of sports content as they chase readers, viewers and listeners in a complex media marketplace. (Boyle, 2006, p. 27)

It certainly cannot surprise you that sport is deeply embedded in our popular culture. In fact, the Popular Culture Association has had a thriving Sports Division for many decades, and much outstanding scholarship has emerged from that research. For starters, movies have featured sports since their inception, and as early as 1934's *Dizzy and Daffy* there was a running gag about a stuttering sportscaster. Although there are numerous examples of sports and sportscasting in a range of media, the sitcom *Good Sports,* which starred Farrah Fawcett and Ryan O'Neal as anchors for a cable sports network, ran with decent ratings during the 1991 television season.

But undoubtedly the most successful television program in this area has been *Arli$$,* an HBO sitcom with Robert Wuhl as a sports agent, Sandra Oh as his personal assistant, and a number of notable sports personalities making appearances, often as themselves, during its 1996-2002 run. Bob Costas holds the top award for being in five episodes, and Wuhl was on World Championship Wrestling's *Monday Nitro* as a guest announcer. The 1996 movie *Jerry Maguire,* is famous for the line "Show me the money!" a slogan that is still repeated today, yet one more reminder of how sports talk infiltrates our society.

ROLE MODELING/HEROES

"Good sport" is a term given to the competitor exhibiting valued social behaviors while engaged in a sporting contest. Thought to be aware of the sociocultural values of fairness, civil courtesy, and ethical behavior. . . . Adhering to social values and ethical standards of conduct the "good Sport" is said to display good sportsmanship, a term difficult to objectify. It is a relative term, since ethical values in sport vary according to the type of sporting contest, the place, the time era of the event, and the orientation of the competitors. (Mawson, 2006, p. 19)

It is appropriate to introduce the term "appropriate" as, all too often, sports role models are covered by the media if they seem appropriate. For example, when women athletes participate in what are considered "gender-appropriate" sports such as figure skating, swimming, gymnastics, and tennis, they receive more attention than when they play sports such as rugby, field hockey, even softball (Vincent, 2005). Although they generally receive less coverage than their Caucasian counterparts, when female African-American athletes participate in what are considered "race-appropriate" sports such as track and field and basketball, they receive more attention than when they play sports associated with the socially elite such as golf or horseback riding.

Consider the case of Sheryl Swoopes, who plays basketball for the Houston Comets in the Women's National Basketball Association (WNBA). Winner of three Olympic gold medals, and a three-time WNBA MVP referred to as the "female Michael Jordan," she was a media darling (Burris, 2006). When pregnant with her son, she appeared on numerous sports magazine covers; later, when she publicly "came out" with fellow player Alisa Scott, she was noticeably missing in the media. The most recent news about Swoopes, in fact, has been her bankruptcy.

Sports and Identity

This section on sports modeling/heroes deals with sports and identity, sports celebrityhood, and sports mentors.

"Media representations of sports contribute to the contested process of identity construction in American culture," (Aaron Baker 1997, p. xviii). "These analyses taken as a whole demonstrate that, although professional sports may often reproduce the conservative values of the corporate interests that own and represent them, there are also important examples of athletic texts that define identities outside the bounds established by dominant practice."

The literature on sports identity is wide-ranging, including Bass, 2005; Baker and Boyd, 1997; Falk, 2005; Hargreaves, 2001; Markula and Pringle, 2006; and Perinbanayagam, 2007. Also related are books on sport physicalities (Choi, 2000; Cole, Loy, and Messner, 1993; Guttman, 1996; Howe, 2003; Horrell, 1968; Lenskyj, 1994; Picart, 2006; Real, 1999; Weitz, 2002; Young, 2007) and sport psychology (Anshel, 1994; Butler, 1996; Cox, 1990; Diamant, 1991; Goldstein, 1983; Grout, Perrin, and Woodward, 2006; Horn, 1992; Kremer and Scully, 1994; Mechikoff, 1987; Murphy, 1995; Roberts, Spink, and Pemberton, 1986; Russell, 1993; Sheikh and Korn, 1994; Singer, Hausenblas, and Janelle, 2001;Stein and Hollwitz, 1994; Todhunter, 2000; Van Raalte and Brewer, 1996; Wann, 2001; Zimmerman and Reavill, 1998). In terms of sportscasting, we need to be acutely aware of the culture surrounding both athletes and spokespersons for them.

Celebrityhood

In an effort to better understand where sports and its stars fit into the wider socio-economic sphere, it behooves us to acknowledge and analyze how some athletes, and sportscasters, can become celebrities such that they go from the sports pages to the front pages (based on Fuller, 2006c). There is a growing literature on the topic (Andrews, 2001; Andrews and Jackson, 2001; Baker and Boyd, 1997; Burstyn, 1999; Davis, 1997; Fuller, 1992b, 2006c; Grout, Perrin, and Woodward, 2006; Hargreaves, 2001; Klein, 2000; Lapchick et al., 2006;

McKay, Messner, and Sabo, 2000; Mertzman, 1999; Messner and Sabo, 1990; Nelson, 1994; Smart, 2005; Tudor, 1997; Whannel, 2002), and an encouragement for you to consider it.

Although all too often news stories about sports celebrities tend to be negative, there certainly are exceptions. As a longtime AIDS researcher, I just happened to be in China during the summer of 2005 when Yao Ming, the famous 7-foot 6-inch NBA center for the Houston Rockets had his photo taken, wiping tears of a Chinese AIDS orphan in Beijing. For a country in denial about the disease, probable for implosion once the pandemic arrives there, (yet at the same time described as the world's "most likely to agree to unprotected sex with a new partner"), that photographic scene was momentous.

The subject of sport celebrityhood is an emerging interest in sports studies. While there are a number of books about individual stars, only recently have scholars considered the phenomenon (Smart, 2005; Whannel, 2002). Usually, we are treated to stories of triumph of the underdog, tragedy befalling heroes, pushy parents, addictions, and various value lessons, but this case study deals with an international icon using sports to help his country and his fans.

In premodern China, physical culture was often associated with military training; later, formal gymnastics were introduced as part of a general regimen, and basketball was introduced there in 1896 as part of a missionary plan of the YMCA. Now consider this: China has as many basketball fans (270 million) as the entire population of the United States; a game might draw 1 million viewers here, while some 30 million fans will be watching in China. Imagine how much a single athlete could ignite a country.

Born in 1980, the result of what has been called a "genetic conspiracy," as it is alleged that the government encourageed his 6-foot 2-inch basketball-playing mother and 6-foot 10-inch basketball-playing father to marry—Yao Ming's story is part of Chairman Mao Zedong's master plan to put genetically gifted young athletes into the nation's Communist sports machine. China's "one-child" policy made his birth special in many ways. Weighing in at 11.2 pounds, 23 inches, at birth, the infant Yao (Yao being the family name) was about twice the size of an average Chinese newborn. From the start, then, he was unique—actually, if truth be told, a freak. By the age of nine, he was told to start basketball training, five afternoons a week and on Saturdays. He hated the sport, but was obedient, in his words, "purely for my parents, because I respect them so much." By age thirteen, at 6 feet 7 inches, he was enrolled full time at the Shanghai Sports Technology Institute, with coaches and scientists working with him round the clock to turn him into a star. It did not take too long for Nike to take note, and soon he was allowed to travel outside the country, participating first in Nike's junior basketball camp in Paris and then being granted freedom to tour the United States in 1998. But the best break came with the introduction of capitalism into China under the leadership of Deng Xiaoping, and by 2002 Yao was allowed to enter the NBA draft—with Beijing announcing that he would be required to return over 50 percent of his earnings to the central government.

After a number of hassles, twenty-one-year old, 296-pound Yao became eligible for the NBA draft, and he was the first pick of the Houston Rockets—with a five-year contract worth $76 million. A telling documentary called *The Year of the Yao* (produced and directed by James D. Stern) is a classic case of cross-cultural communication. Picture this modest, shy young man encountering the brash basketball players we are used to seeing in the U.S. media. A journalist (Bonjean, 2005) gives this good example: "When a teammate is shown in his Mercedes-Benz sports car, Yao is shown thanking his parents for the wealth they had given him—only he was talking about spiritual wealth." Although he topped a Celebrity List released by Forbes China, earning 150 million yuan ($18.1 million), and he has gained international popularity, his humility is what is most revered. He has made it into textbooks as a hero and role model, he is an idol of Chinese teenagers, and posters and T-shirts with his image are sought after, but Yao Ming remains respectful, patriotic, and familial.

Encouraged by former Los Angeles Lakers star Magic Johnson (Fuller, 1994b), he participated in a campaign to encourage people to not discriminate against People Living With AIDS (PLWAs). In a thirty-second PSA, the two basketball stars play one-on-one ball, pushing one another, exchanging high fives. Magic says, "I have been living with HIV since 1991," and then Yao is shown teaching him how to use chopsticks before stating, in Mandarin, "Hugging, shaking hands or eating together will not transmit HIV. Don't be afraid.

Don't discriminate. Please show you care for people living with HIV/ AIDS and learn more about HIV/AIDS prevention."

China Daily, the only national English-language newspaper, with a circulation of more than 200,000, featured an incredible front page photo of Yao Ming wiping the tears of an AIDS orphan in Beijing on July 18, 2005, when he was there as part of the NBA's "Basketball without Borders" outreach event. It made an invaluable impression. In China, the impact was immense. For a country still so ignorant about the causes, never mind the caring for HIV/AIDS, Yao's photo truly speaks 1,000 words.

Sports Mentors

Sportscasters themselves are quite open about their own mentors in the field. Russ Hodges was the first broadcaster Jon Miller (2000, p. 76) ever heard, and he obviously made quite an impression: "To me, Russ was the consummate broadcaster. His voice was not a classic, but it was rich and distinctive. He gave listeners a great picture of the game through the radio . . ." He also found Vin Scully's style extraordinary, stating that Scully's command of the language and ability to create images was "beyond compare" (Miller, 2000, p. 87).

Johnny Most (cited in Carey, 2003, p. 15) reports that his broadcasting style was influenced by what he terms "four legends": Ted Husing, Bill Stern, Mel Allen, and particularly Marty Glickman. He elaborates: "Husing had a great vocabulary and a gift for painting vivid pictures with his phrase" (p. 16), while Stern was like Howard Cosell—brash, loud, cocky, know-it-all, controversial. He liked the way his idol Mel Allen referred to a home run as a "Ballantine Blast," how he called Joe DiMaggio "Joltin' Joe, Phil Rizzuto "The Little Scooter," Mickey Mantle "The Mick." From Marty Glickman, a fellow Jewish broadcaster who also recognized anti-Semitism in the sporting arena, he learned that, "To be an effective play-by-play man, you had to be hard-hitting, expressive, quick, accurate but concise" (p. 17).

For female sportscasters today, trailblazers like Phyllis George, Gayle Gardner, Leslie Visser, Suzy Kolber, Billie Jean King, Donna de Varona, Robin Roberts, Suzyn Waldman, Andrea Kirby, Jane Chastain, Jeannie Morris, Leandra Reilly, Gayle Sierens, and others are often cited as mentors. You have encountered many more names here, such as Linda Cohn, Hannah Storm, Mary Carillo, Melissa Stark, Sally Jenkins, Bonnie Bernstein, and too many to repeat who form something of a second wave of role models. Most of these female sportscasters can also recite the famous locker room legends—or at least they should be aware of these histories.

Stuart Scott was the first black male anchor on ESPN's *Sports Center,* the Gumbel brothers' successes in the field, Robin Roberts' expertise in both sportscasting and newscasting, and many other African Americans have made contributions.

SOCIOLOGICAL ISSUES RELATIVE TO SPORTSCASTING

There are a surprising number of controversial issues surrounding sports. This section deals with discrimination (Putnam, 1999; Simon, 1991; Coakley, 2003; Yiannakis and Melnick, 2001), and racial, gender, and gender-orientation sports issues. Regarding discrimination, the issues run the gamut from what was *not* said a half-century ago when Jackie Robinson entered baseball's major league to what Isaiah Thomas *said* about basketball's white Larry Bird. Women sportscasters, a rare breed, typically emerge via the former-athlete route, notable exceptions being Phyllis George, Becky Dixon, and Gayle Gardner. Drugs and doping, gambling, and sports violence are also included in this section—all topics that sportscasters need to know and understand in their profession.

Gender

One of the recent successes of the feminist agenda has been to show that organized sport serves as a powerful cultural arena for constructing and perpetuating the ideology and practice of male privilege and dominance, sport assuming a profound role in the production and maintenance of male hegemony, contributing to historical patterns of male empowerment and female disadvantage. Women's sport is often trivialized and marginalized, and female athletes themselves frequently stereotyped as feminized women rather than competitive athletes. (Segrave, McDowell, and King, 2006, p. 31)

Far too many sportscasters are guilty of perpetuating the notion that we still think of sports as being in the masculine domain. We are, after all, a patriarchal society—nowhere more evident than in sports (Davis, 1997; Fuller, 1999c, Messner, 2005). Sexist broadcast commentary, reflecting wider societal attitudes, persists (Duncan and Messner, 2000; Eastman and Billings, 2000, 2004). In 1996, Mary Jo Kane, director of the Tucker Center for Research on Girls and Women in Sport at the University of Minnesota, set up a classification of issues, including "hierarchy of name," "asymmetrical gender marking," "trivialization and sexualization," "ambivalence," etc. Segrave, McDowell, and King (2006, pp. 31-37), discuss the many linguistic conventions that contribute to a cultural devaluation of women in sports: masculine generics, gender marking, naming practices, descriptive linguistics, the metaphorical language of sport, the language of sport in cultural discourses, and subcultural language.

"Gender equity is an atmosphere and a reality where fair distribution of overall athletic opportunity and resources, proportionate to enrollment, are available to women and men and where no student-athlete, coach, or athletic administrator is discriminated against in any way in the athletic program on basis of gender," (NACWAA, 1992). "That is to say, an athletics program is gender equitable when the men's sports program would be pleased to accept as its own, the overall participation, opportunities, and resources currently allocated to the women's sports program and vice versa." Since 1977, Carpenter and Acosta (2006) have been monitoring NCAA member schools offering women's athletics; their most recent Executive Summary finds both good news "the highest ever participation by women in our nation's intercollegiate athletics programs," along with the bad: "The data also continue to show a depressed representation of women as head coaches and as head administrators of their programs. Indeed, 2006 represents the lowest ever ratio of female coaches for women's teams."

News per se includes scant coverage of women's sports, according to Messner, Duncan, and Cooky (2003). Their study of television news on major networks and ESPN's *Sports Center* found it generally "missing in action"; if it did appear, women's sports news tended to be humorous or based on "sexual objectification" (p. 42). "Sports commentary remains a world dominated by men, who serve up a staple of images and commentary that reinforces the idea that sports are a man's world (indeed a *heterosexual* man's world," (p. 49) they conclude.

Sex discrimination in sports has been broadly researched (Birrell and Cole, 1994; Brackenridge, 2001; Chambers, 1996; Choi, 2000; Coventry, 2004; Crosset, 1995; Gavora, 2002; Gogol, 2002; Hemphill and Symons, 2002; Heywood and Dworkin, 2003; Hnida, 2006; Lenskyj, 2003; Messner, 2002; Messner, Sabo, and McKay, 2000; Nelson, 1991; Pemberton and de Varona, 2002;.Robinson, 2002; Salter, 1996; Simon, 2005; Scranton and Flintoff, 2002; Shipnuck, 2006; Steiner, 1995; Suggs, 2006; Turco, 1999; White and Young, 2006; Wushanley, 2004; Zimmerman and Reavill, 1999). On the one hand, we applaud the fact that more women than ever are involved in sports media, and that organizations like the Association of Women in Sport Media (AWSM), Female Athletic Media Executives (FAME), and Women in Sports Events (WISE) continue to increase their memberships. Nevertheless, their numbers are still small; in 2000, Rudy Martzke reported that only 20 percent, or 81 of 416 sportscasters on national network and cable television, were female.

Worse, many of these women are encountering the famous "glass ceiling," along with continued sexual harassment and objectification (Brackenridge and Fasting, 2002; Kirby, Greaves, and Hankivsky, 2000; Volkwein-Caplan and Sankaran, 2001). Clearly, the "old boy's network" is tough to crack, particularly in what has been long considered a man's domain of sport. Michael A. Messner (2002, p. 126) reminds us that, "Examining the ways that the televised sports manhood formula cuts across sports programming and the accompanying commercials provides important clues to the ways that ideologies of hegemonic masculinity are both promoted by, and in terms serve to support and stabilize, the collection of interrelated institutions that make up the sport-media-commercial complex."

The sports-media complex is a world powered mostly by white men. Even though *Sports Illustrated*'s infamous swimsuit issue dates to the 1960s, many of its issues relative to sexism, homophobia, racism, and ageism still remain (Davis, 1997); today, in fact, besides being the largest revenue-producing single edition in the magazine business—gaining more than $1 billion in advertising in 2004, it has been elevated to having an accompanying "making-of" documentary that continues to draw high ratings. Fran Harris (2001, p. 66), who played on the Houston Comets championship team in 1997 and became an NCAA basketball announcer after retiring, offers, "As a broadcaster, not only do I have to compete with other women who are in pursuit of the next best microphone gig but I've also gotta get my hustle on against guys who know the guys, who know the guys whose Daddy owns the company. You see, there's no Title IX in sportscasting."

Title IX

> No person in the United States shall, on the basis of sex, be excluded from participation in, be denied the benefits of, or be subjected to discrimination under any education program or activity receiving Federal financial assistance. (Title IX of the Education Amendments of 1972)

These thirty-seven words have had a profound effect on how we approach issues in education, albeit sometimes considered controversial (Blumenthal, 2005; Carpenter and Acosta, 2004; Gavora, 2002; Kane, 1996; Porto, 2003; Simon, 2005; Suggs, 2006). At the least, it has encouraged female participation in sports at many levels, including in the broadcast booth. "In the main, it has been extraordinarily but not completely successful: It has created opportunities for thousands of female athletes, and it has forced the American public to recognize the value of women's sports, but women's teams still lack the deep cultural significance that athletics departments ascribe to men's sports," Welch Suggs (2006, p. 188). In 2005, Street and Smith's *SportsBusiness Journal* released its list of the twenty most influential women in the sports business (www.sportsbusinessjournal.com):

1. Lesa France Kennedy, President, International Speedway Corp.
2. Dawn Hudson, President and CEO, Pepsico North America

3. Nancy Monsarrat, Director of U.S. Advertising, Nike
4. Stephanie Tolleson, Senior Corporate VP, IMG
5. Heidi Ueberroth, Exec. VP/Global Media Properties & Marketing Partnerships, NBA
6. Lee Ann Daly, Executive VP, Marketing, ESPN
7. Jeanie Buss, Executive VP, Los Angeles Lakers
8. Jamie McCourt, Vice Chairman, Los Angeles Dodgers
9. Cathy Bessant, CMO, Bank of America
10. Amy Trask, Chief Executive, Oakland Raiders
11. Cindy Alston, VP of Communications and Equity Development, Gatorade
12. Jennifer Shaw, Senior VP, GM Mediaworks
13. Bea Perez, VP of Sports Marketing, Coca-Cola North America
14. Val Ackerman, President, USA Basketball
15. Lisa Murray, Executive VP and CMO, Octagon
16. Donna Orender, President, WNBA
17. Pam Gardner, President of Business Operations, Houston Astros
18. Christine Driessen, CFO, ESPN
19. Linda Bruno, Commissioner, Atlantic 10
20. Donna Lopiano, CEO, Women's Sports Foundation

Ordman and Zillman (1994) analyzed men's basketball and women's gymnastics to assess whether sports reporters' perceived competence is gender dependent; in magazine and radio formats, females rated less competent in both instances. In 2000, Eastman and Billings compared sportscasting in print (*The New York Times* and *USA Today*) and on television (ESPN's *SportsCenter* and CNN's *Sports Tonight*), revealing enormous favoritism toward male athletes and men's sports—a gender bias that occurred even at times when women's sporting events were newsworthy. Four years later, they analyzed 1,156 descriptors in sportscasters' commentary in sixty-six men's and women's college basketball games' telecasts; they found stereotypical referrals to black players as naturally athletic, quick, and powerful, along with more emphasis on the white female players (Eastman and Billings, 2004).

Mitrook and Dorr (2001, p. 17) analyzed women broadcasters in the media; they were viewed as less credible than their male counterparts and, "While both the male and female participants revealed a tendency to rate the female broadcaster lower than the male broadcaster, the male participants exhibited a distinct pattern of rating the female broadcaster consistently lower than the female participants did." Female sportscaster credibility as studied by Janielle L. Mahan (2004) found that, "Attractiveness is positively correlated with competence and expertness, dynamism, and trustworthiness, except when a sportscaster is highly attractive."

Focusing on announcer comments during the 2002 NCAA Division 1 women's basketball championship game, James R. Hallmark (2006) has identified three preferred readings in ESPN's broadcast: (1) Connecticut's invincibility, (2) women's basketball is for real, and (3) damsel in distress. He includes a valuable literature review, identifying "common barriers to gender equity in media coverage," including the following:

- "Marking" women's broadcasts, such as saying it is the "women's final four" without comparably designating the men's game.
- Demeaning the contribution of women athletes by downplaying their athleticism.
- Focusing on women athletes' physically attributes (e.g., beautiful hair, legs, smiles, etc.) and/or their personal lives (e.g., children, husbands, etc.) in some cases, women athletes are treated as sex objects.
- Devoting less broadcast time to women's sporting events, particularly women's team sports.
- Using less sophisticated production techniques for women's broadcasts. (pp. 160-161)

Alison Trumbull (2003, p. 27) has taken a sociolinguistic approach to the study of sportscasting, analyzing the intonatial and syntactic qualities of Pam Ward, a pioneering play-by-play announcer for ESPN. In analyzing whether a woman's measure of success in a male profession is an indicator of gender equality, or whether it is an adaptation to a male genre, she cites this example of "turn-taking":

What is on screen	Who speaks
Players get into position	Analyst ends turn or play-by-play begins
Play begins	Play-by-play announcer
Touchdown scored	Play-by-play announcer
Celebration	No one
Celebrations, fans, coaches, players	Analyst
Setting up for kick	Analysts ends turn or play-by-play begins
Kick	Play-by-play announcer
Celebration	Play-by-play announcer
Replay	Play-by-play announcer
Commercial	No one

Although she recognizes the difficulty of drawing wide generalizations from two college football games aired on ESPN2, Trumbull concludes that, "The nature of each sportscaster's talk appears to be due to the combination of the requirements of the job, individual personalities, and influences of the sportscaster partner. This apparent similarity in use across genders raises the question of whether successful use of a traditionally male register is truly a transformation of the register, or simply one woman's consenting to talk like a man."

"The only thing that really bugs me about television's coverage is those damn women they have down on the sidelines who don't know what the hell they're talking about," curmudgeon Andy Rooney famously proclaimed on the MSG Network's *The Boomer Esiason Show* in 2002. If that wasn't bad enough, he added, "I mean, I'm not a sexist person, but a woman has no business being down there trying to make some comment about a football game." It was a shot heard round the media/sporting world. Typically, most of the female sportscasters didn't deign to comment, but many male sports-talk radio hosts had a field day with the assault.

In this chapter, the study of gender and sports includes both men and women (Burstyn, 1999; Davis, 1997; McKay, Messner, and Sabo, 2000; Messner, 1992; Messner and Sabo, 1990; Nelson, 1994; Pronger, 1990; Tuana, 2002; Whannel, 2002; Baughman, 1995; Betancourt, 2001; Birrell and Cole, 1994; Blue, 1987; Brackenridge, 2001;

Cahn, 1994; Carpenter and Acosta, 2004, 2006; Chambers, 1995; Choi, 2000; Clarke and Humberstone, 1997; Cohen, 1993; Costa and Guthrie, 1994; Creedon, 1994a; Crosset, 1995; Daddario, 1998; Festle, 1996; Fornoff, 1993; Fuller, 2006; Gavora, 2002; Greenberg, 1997; Guttman, 1991; Hall, 1996; Hargreaves, 1994; Hartman-Tews and Pfister, 2003; Heywood, 2000; Ireland, 2002; Lenskyj, 1986, 2003; Longman, 2000; Lowe, 1998; Mangan and Park, 1987; Markula, 2005; McKay, Messner, and Sabo, 2000; Messner and Sabo, 1990; Nelson, 1991, 1994; Pemberton, 2002; Ryan, 1995; Salter, 1996; Sandoz, 1997; Sandoz and Winans, 1999; Simon, 2005; Smith, 1998; Stanley, 1996; Stauffer and Cylkowski, 1994; Suggs, 2006; Theberge, 1981, 2000; Turco, 1999; Wushanley, 2004). Specifically, it also refers to female athletes (Chastain, 2004; Drinkwater, 2000; Hamm, 2000; Kirby, Greaves, and Hankinsky, 2001; Lawler, 2002; Littman, 2000; Mangan, 1987; Oglesby, Greenberg, Hall, Hill, Johnston, and Easterby, 1999).

Historically, although it did not begin until the mid-twentieth century, women began broke barriers and set some important records. The year 1950 stands out: this is when Althea Gibson became the first African American to win the U.S. National Tennis Championship, Florence Chadwick was the first woman to swim both ways across the English Channel, and the Ladies Professional Golf Association (LPGA) was granted its charter. Soon, women were competing in sports such as riflery, rodeo, racing, flying, and more. A lot has been made about women being prevented from entering marathon races, and how Roberta Gibb (Bingay) wore a hooded sweatshirt to hide her participation in Boston's 1966 contest—coming in at three hours, twenty-one minutes, and forty seconds; the next year, Katherine Switzer openly entered the race and, by 2003, female finishers of the Boston Marathon made up 37 percent of the 17,030 total. By the late 1960s, women were entitled to carry the U.S. flag for the Olympics, and set records as jockeys, sailors, cyclists, even football, wrestling, and boxing.

Though this book aims to be inclusive, a great deal of research remains. Relative to women, Pam Creedon's (1994c, p. 139) list of "milestones" for women centers on "firsts":

1924	Judith Carey Waller produces football radio play-by-play on WMAQ
1937	Mrs. Harry Johnson broadcasts baseball for KFAB, Lincoln, Nebraska
1948	Sarah Palfrey Cooke hosts NBC's *Sportswoman of the Week*
1965	Donna de Varona becomes an ABC sports commentator
1973	Eleanor Riger is an ABC Sports producer; Anita Martini and Nelda Pena cover baseball All-Star, Kansas City
1974	Jane Chastain broadcasts NFL games on CBS; Anita Martini enters LA Dodgers' locker room in Houston Astrodome
1975	Phyllis George co-hosts *NFL Today* on CBS; the Super Bowl is hosted by Jane Chastain on CBS, Jeannie Morris on NBC
1976	Jayne Kennedy hosts a sports event on CBS;Mary Shane does TV play-by-play major league baseball in Chicago
1982	Mary Carillo and Andrea Kirby do first all-female tennis sportscasting
1983	Gayle Gardner is anchor on ESPN *SportsCenter*
1987	Cheryl Miller becomes a sports commentator on ABC; Andrea Joyce becomes a sports anchor on Top 10 WFAA-Dallas
1988	Gayle Gardner becomes a sports anchor for NBC; Gayle Sierens is play-by-play announcer of an NFL game for NBC
1990	Robin Roberts becomes an anchor/reporter on ESPN
1991	Nicole Watson becomes a producer for TBS Sports cable; Mimi Griffin broadcasts on-air analysis of men's NCAA basketball
1992	Robin Roberts becomes an Olympics commentator for ESPN

Feel free to update this, such as when Sally Jenkins of the *Washington Post* was named top sports columnist in 2001 by the Associated Press Sports Editors—the first woman to win the award, or Suzyn Waldman's becoming, in 2005, the first woman to work as a full-time MLB analyst. Although it is always tricky to cite key women sportscasters, these were some who led the way: Mary Carillo, Linda Cohn, Donna De Varona, Gayle Gardner, Andrea Joyce, Robin Roberts, Beth Ruyak, Hannah Storm, and Leslie Visser. "The thing about women sportscasters is that they all know each other," Sally Jenkins (1999, p. 80) has noted. "You might find them in a corner of the local sports bar or at a circular table in the Waldorf, explaining gimmick defenses, quoting the over-under and reciting baseball lore without once referring to an inning as a quarter."

Lou Schwartz (1999), president and founder of the American Sportscasters Association (ASA), has written a brief history of the profession, stating, "Women have come a long way in sportscasting; from just another 'Barbie-on-the-air' image to complement the sportscasting done by men, to today's qualified and respected professional hired for her skills and knowledge." Jeff Ryan (2001), writing in *The Village Voice* about Jane Chastain, claimed, "Female sportscasters have come a long way, baby. From 5:45 a.m. to 11 p.m. To be exact. . . These days, women are as much a part of sports broadcasting as reverse-angle replays. And sure, some of them are still hired strictly for their ability to make male viewers drool down the fronts of their officially licensed alternate road jerseys." Still, it gives us pause that *Playboy*'s poll of "America's Top 10 Sexiest Sportscasters" gets so much press (by the way, most recently Jill Arrington beat out Melissa Stark, and Lisa Derga Podsednik took top honors in *Stuff Magazine.* Lisa Guerrero of Fox Sports Net's *The Best Damn Sports Show Period* and more recently *MNF,* a former model, is also in contention).

"Other than the brief appearance of Sarah Palfrey Cooke on NBC in 1948, women's on-camera roles as sportscasters were extremely limited until the 1970s when—to keep their licenses—stations reached out to hire women and minorities," (Creedon, 1994c, p. 138). Creedon reminds us that the impetus for female participation in sports journalism sprang from legal matters. Her history goes on to describe how, when Billie Jean King insisted upon a female commentator for the famous 1973 "Battle of the Sexes"—when she beat Bobby Riggs, ABC hired tennis player Rosemary Casals. CBS hired skier Suzy Chaffee for its own *Battle of the Sexes* ten-week series of 1975. Other former athletes, such as swimmer Donna de Varona and figure skater Carol Heiss Jenkins followed soon thereafter. Above all, Jane Chastain's position for CBS Sports in 1974—the first female sports anchor on both national and local levels, covering both NFL and NBA beats, positions her as a barrier-breaking pioneer; when she was pregnant the next year, however, it won't surprise you that she was moved to covering sports like surfing and water skiing.

In 1998, Jim Spence declared Phyllis George "the most prominent of women sports broadcasters to date" (p. 175). Her entry into the male-dominated sphere was an inspiration for aspiring women lsuch as figure skaters-turned sportscasters Carol Heiss Jenkins and Peggy Fleming, tennis player-turned sportscaster Billie Jean King, sports producers Kathleen Sullivan (the first female to do a network sports broadcast) and the late Eleanor Riger (the first female network sports producer), Andrea Kirby (an ABC sports reporter who later formed her own business, Sports Media Group), and Gayle Gardner (an NFL play-by-play commentator for NBC and the first woman talent hired by ESPN, in 1983). Still, Spence comments about the former Miss America, Phyllis George, "When she failed to gain widespread acceptance, the cause suffered greatly. Let there be no question that a predominantly male audience has some resistance to hearing its sports from a female. That's male chauvinist piggism at its worst, but it's a fact." In all fairness, you might be interested to read George's own account of her years as a broadcast pioneer; her 2002 autobiography is titled *Never say Never: 10 Lessons to Turn You Can't into Yes I Can.*

Phyllis George may be credited with breaking the sportscasting gender barrier when, in 1975, she was hired on at CBS' *The NFL Today,* but, in truth, she was preceded by another, if lesser known, woman: Myrtle Power, who gained some fame as a baseball expert on *The $64,000 Question;* she was signed as a color commentator by CBS in the 1950s.

The Locker Room

The locker room is a guy's favorite room in the world. It even finishes ahead of that male mecca, the Den. Men love the locker room because there are hardly any chicks in there. The only ones allowed in are the occasional babe reporters, interviewing players after the Trauma and Spectacle of the Great Contest. The locker room used to be a total No Chicks Zone until 1978. Then babe journalists started suing over discrimination, and carrying microphones and tape recorders and notepads, and asking questions when they should have been writing for beauty magazines. Now the locker room has basically gone the way of fire departments and the Army. It's too bad about the Constitution. The problem with equal rights is that everybody gets them. (Jenkins, 1996, p. 120)

Then there is the issue of locker room coverage, a topic that has received a lot of attention (Curry, 2002; Fornoff, 1993; Fuller 1992a, c). Historically, the debate began when female sports journalists (Jane Gross of *Newsday* and Jennifer Quale of the *Times-Picayune*) were denied access to NBA locker rooms in 1975, exacerbated two years later when Melissa Ludtke of *Sports Illustrated* was shut out of the New York Yankee locker room and sued—culminating in a 1978 federal district court decision ruling that all reporters, regardless of gender, should be granted equal access. The case set a precedent for future gender bias cases in sports. Although some women sports journalists broke the wall, others were harassed, even physically ejected—Lesley Visser in particular can tell some hairy stories. Most people are familiar with what happened to *Boston Herald* reporter Lisa Olson in 1990, who endured some New England Patriots players making lewd comments and gestures, and who lined up for their "interviews" unclothed, which she described as "nothing less than mind rape." Although over the years the situation has certainly improved, we realize that it really has to do with privacy rights, gender bias, notions of respect and civility, discrimination in the workplace, concern over role models, and access itself.

Although the locker room issue was revived in 1999 when two avowedly devout Christians—Reggie White of the Green Bay Packers and Charlie Ward of the New York Knicks claimed that their religious beliefs made them uncomfortable with women in the locker room, and they lobbied to get the policy reversed, it remains. "The only women generally seen in NFL locker rooms are hard-working accredited print and electronic reporters," (Harvey Araton, 2004).

Michelle Kaufman (2003, p. 242), who has covered Olympic Games, World Cups, Pan Am Games, Super Bowls, Final Fours, NBA Finals, Stanley Cups, Open tennis tournaments, the World Series, and various college bowl games, includes an important side note in her discussion about the coverage of women's sports:

> Critics of women in the locker room often ask why women's locker rooms aren't open to male reporters. Truth is, they often are. The WNBA and Women's final Four have open-locker-room policies. The difference is that female athletes don't generally disrobe in front of reporters. They stay in their uniforms until interviews are complete, and once the reporters are gone, they shower and change. Male athletes have been unreceptive to that concept, claiming they can't wait to get their uniforms off.

Gender Orientation

Along with gender issues come concerns about homophobia in sports. "Perhaps because physically strong, powerful women call into question the concept of male dominance, athletic women throughout history have been characterized as less feminine or more 'mannish' than their less sporty sisters," (Andy Steiner on Pat Griffin 2000, p. 60). (Pat Griffin, former coach and athlete, (1998) wrote *Strong Women, Deep Closets: Lesbians and Homophobia in Sport.*) Other good resources include Cahn, 1993; Lenskyj, 2003; Pronger, 1990; Rogers, 1994; and Woog, 1998. Take the case of CBS commentator Ben Wright who, in 1996, declared that, "Lesbians . . . hurt women's golf." Of course this was the same golf announcer who also claimed "women are handicapped by having boobs."

ESPN, as has been pointed out earlier, actually bills itself as the "gay-friendly worldwide leader in sports" (Zeigler, 2007); to wit:

- ESPN first aired their groundbreaking *Outside the Lines* special, "The World of the Gay Athlete," on December 16, 1998. They followed that with a second *OTL* special, "The Gay Dilemma," on June 3, 2001.

- Luke Cyphers from *ESPN the Magazine* and ESPN producer Craig Lazarus participated in the first Gay and Lesbian Athletics Foundation conference in May of 2003.
- ESPN was a sponsor of the Gay Games in 2006, and ESPN Mobile sponsored a basketball team that participated in the Games; that team was captained by openly gay former *ESPN the Magazine* basketball editor LZ Granderson.
- ESPN has recruited at the conference for the National Lesbian and Gay Journalists Association since 2004.
- ESPN aired a five-minute segment over Memorial Day weekend 2005 about Andrew Goldstein, the openly gay lacrosse goalie at Dartmouth.
- ESPN was honored at the 2006 Commercial Closet's Images in Advertising Award for "Outstanding Business-To-Business Trade Ad."

More recently, following Minnesota Vikings' defensive lineman Esera Tuaolo's (2006) coming out (in 2002), the press and the public seem to be more empathic. The self-outing trend amongst athletes includes books by, amongst others, MLB player Billy Bean (2003), NFL veteran Roy Simmons (2005), and Olympics champion swimmer Mark Tewksbury (2006). ESPNU college football commentator Brian Kinchen was suspended for eluding to a comment as sounding "kinda gay." By comparison, this is nothing compared to ex-Miami Heat player Tim Hardaway's recent radio rant: "I hate gay people, so I let it be known. I don't like gay people and I don't like to be around gay people. I am homophobic. I don't like it. It shouldn't be in the world or in the United States. So yeah, I don't like it." And leave it to San Francisco to boast the first gay morning radio show, featuring "Greg, the Gay Sportscaster" on Energy 92.7 FM.

Cyd Zeigler (2007) asked, "In a sports industry that has largely ignored gay issues, in which very few professional sports teams offer same-sex domestic partner benefits, and from which some of the most homophobic public quotes have emerged in recent years, how has the 'worldwide leader' come to buck the trend and embrace diverse sexuality?" His answer to his own question: the sports leader is a business, after all.

RACE

Arguably, the media's portrayal of sport as one of only a limited range of opportunities for social and economic mobility for African-American working class youth also serves to reinforce the myth of natural Black athleticism. By effacing socioeconomic environment, cultural modeling, communal norms, and familial expectations in favor of genetic explanations for Black athletic success, the natural athlete myth suggests that African Americans possess innate physiological advantages while conversely lacking the necessary skills and intelligence to succeed in other occupational areas. (Grainger, Newman, and Andrews, 2006, p. 452)

Because we are a culture whose history is steeped in slavery, the issue of race is always with us. In sports sociology, the concept is called "unequal opportunity for equal ability," or the phenomenon whereby minorities need to prove themselves in order to participate.

Intricately tied up with sociopolitical aspects, racial aspects of sports have only recently been brought to a wider consciousness. Historians consider the 1938 boxing rematch between the Max Schmeling, a German who had no attachment to Nazi leanings but who was nevertheless associated with Hitler, and Joe Louis, an African American who came to represent hope for minorities when he won the title as a significant time marker. It is interesting how many blacks of that era have reported how clearly they remember following the fight on the radio (Fuller, 1992)—"one of *ours*," they cheered. How far we have gone when someone like ex-boxer George Forman is probably best known for his entrepreneurship in selling cooking grills carrying his name?

The subject of sports and race has drawn a great deal of academic attention (Bass, 2002; Billet and Formwalt, 1995; Bloom and Willard, 2002; Booth, 1998; Brooks and Althouse, 2000; Carrington and McDonald, 2001; Dawkins and Kinloch, 2000; Eisen and Wiggins, 1994; Entine, 2000; Garland and Rowe, 2001; Hoberman, 1997; Jarvie, 1991; King and Springwood, 2001; Kirsch, Harris, and Nolte, 2000; Lapchick, 1984, 1991, 2001; Miller and Wiggins, 2004; Ross,

2004; Saites, 1998; Shields, 1999; Shropshire, 1996; Spence, 2000; Tudor, 1997; Wiggins, 1997). It also concerns Native Americans. Kenneth L. Shropshire (1996, p. 12) reminds us that for the Rainbow Coalition for Fairness in Athletics, "The term [Washington] 'Redskins' is from an era when there was a bounty on Indian people and they were skinned and scalped. Eighty cents for a man's skin, 60 cents for a woman's skin and 20 cents for a child's skin . . . It is the most derogatory term that exists for Native Americans in the English language."

Right away you are probably thinking about Jackie Robinson's crossing the "color barrier" in 1945, the Civil Rights movement of the 1960s, including protests at the Olympic Games, boxing bouts including greats such as Joe Lewis, Jack Johnson, Muhammed Ali, versatile black athletes like Paul Robeson, legends like Jesse Owens, Magic Johnson, Wilma Rudolph, Serena Williams, and so many more. Then there is Tiger Woods, who famously has talked about his heritage as being "Ca-Bl-In-Asian" (Caucasian, black, Indian, and Asian).

Racism has many layers and levels. Smith and Henderson (2000) write about "stacking" in team sports—the physical placement of minorities at specific playing positions where their chances of success are lesser. There exists few minority owners of professional sports teams, few minority sports agents, few minority coaches, and few minority sportscasters who make it to the big time. Stuart Scott was the first black male anchor on ESPN's *SportsCenter,* and Robin Roberts certainly became a role model for future female sportscasters, but, overall we need to monitor race and ethnicity in key anchor roles.

Claims of racism have persisted in sportscasting. As was mentioned earlier, Howard Cosell continued to be criticized for the remark he made on *MNF* about a black player when he said, "That little monkey gets loose, doesn't he!" In 1988, Jimmy "the Greek" Snyder, a longtime sportscaster on CBS' *The NFL Today,* reopened this topic when he told a local television interviewer in Washington, DC, that black athletic superiority resulted from African Americans having been "bred to be that way since the days of slavery." Billy Packer drew some heat for calling Allen Iverson a "tough monkey" in a 1996 match between Georgetown and Villanova, but it was resolved. But don't forget Rush Limbaugh's resignation three days after making racial comments about Philadelphia Eagles quarterback Donovan McNabb. Clearly, the wider media monitors sportscaster comments.

Jocko Maxwell, author/compiler of *Great Black Athletes* (1972), is said to be the first African American to cross the color line as a sports announcer. Today, think of how many have been on air: Ahmad Rashad, Joe Morgan, Irv Cross, Stuart Scott, Fred Hickman, James Brown, Robin Roberts, brothers Bryant and Greg Gumbel, even O.J. Simpson in better days (see Lainson, 1998a).

> A consistent finding in studies surround sports commentary on white and black athletes is that (a) white athletes are frequently praised for their perceived "intellect" and m "leadership capacity," while (b) black athletes are often praised for being "naturally talented." A mediated conclusion that one could derive from such findings is that black athletes are *expected* to succeed athletically; conversely, white athletes are expected to have an innate ability to overcome seemingly insurmountable odds to accomplish their athletic stature. (Denham, Billing, and Halone, 2002, p. 315)

As to what determines "minority" continues to be reflected in our society; it is up to all of us to be aware of who is participating in sports, who is announcing those sports, and who is making those decisions.

DRUGS, GAMBLING, AND VIOLENCE

Modern sport has taken on an almost Manichaean character in which good coexists with evil; the evil is represented increasingly by the spread of the use of drugs amongst athletes eager to improve their performance and willing to risk all manner of chemical side-effects, or even direct effects in the attempt to build muscle, steady the hand, flush out body fluid, speed up the metabolism, or spark more aggression. There are drugs available that can assist in all these, but woe any athlete caught taking them. (Cashmore, 2005, p. 107)

Controversial and contradictory to what sports should be all about, drugs and doping wreak havoc both for individuals and organizations. Although performance-enhancing drugs have been around since the early days of sports, only in 1999 was the World Anti-Doping Agency (WADA) established by the International Olympic Committee; with a budget of $22 million, it is at least a first step toward "cleansing" the competitions. There has been quite a bit of interest in the issue (Boone, 2005; Burns, 2005; Dimeo, 2006; Mottram, 2005; O'Leary, 2001; Voy and Deeter, 1990; Wilson and Derse, 2001). Jim Palmer, who has covered Orioles games, is known for speaking out against steroid-using hitters; as such, we can only hope more sportscasters share his activism against products, including alcohol, which can affect real results.

Gambling

Originally associated with horse racing, cock fighting, animal baiting, billiards, boxing, shuffleboard, and sports suitable to betting, gambling today is a $200 billion business; although illegal in forty-nine states, the industry thrives. Don't for a minute think that it is limited to Las Vegas, or casinos that keep cropping up in the country; as Richard Hoffer (2007) points out, with the convenience of computers, or our local lottery dealer, we are betting more than ever on sports—and having a sporting good time doing it.

Sports gambling scandals date to the 1919 Chicago White Sox attempt to throw the World Series. What became known as the "Black Sox Scandal" was the theme of the movie *Eight Men Out* (1988). Other landmark events include a 1978 point-shaving scheme by mobsters in a Boston College basketball team, Pete Rose's ban from MLB for betting on his team (the Cincinnati Reds) while he was its manager, and any number of international incidents.

You can bet on the growth of gambling "anytime, night or day, dressed or not," argues Michael Real (2006, p. 177): "Like sports on the Web, gambling online has grown rapidly, most of it centered on sports. Between 1997 and 2003, the number of gambling Web sites grew from twenty-five to 1,800. During that time, Internet gambling losses grew from an estimated $300 million to somewhere between $3 billion and $6 billion."

Sports Violence

> Is violence in sport an essential ingredient that underpins its appeal to spectators? Does violence affect audience appreciation of media sports contests? . . . Does violence, when it occurs, enhance the entertainment value of these sports? (Gunter, 2006, p. 356)

How would you answer these questions? It is not as if sports violence is a new subject. Following are are some new concerns:

- As the media become evermore globalized, regional concerns for actions like hooliganism reach a wider audience.
- With a number of 24/7 sports television programs on air, both to fill space and to please consumers, more attention is being devoted to the topic of sports than ever before. Add to that the role of the Internet and our ability to access sports information instantaneously.
- Multimillion dollar contracts encourage the cult of celebrity, despite (or because of?) news about the number of star athletes who have been arrested for crimes ranging from assault to sexual battery or even murder.
- Bad-boy role models continue to command the most publicity.
- WWF has become the most popular program on television, especially for young boys, and NASCAR continues to be the fastest growing sport in popularity of attendance.

Against this backdrop, it behooves us to better understand how sports violence—whether inherent in the sport, such as boxing, or part of the play, such as hockey and football, or associated with spectator subcultures, such as with soccer, permeates our society. We know there is a growing literature on the subject of sports violence

(Benedict, 1997, 1998; Benedict and Yeager, 1998; Bryant, 1989; Dunning, 1999; Fuller, 1992f, 1994, 1999c, 2003a, 2005b; Giulianotti, Bonney, and Hepwarth, 1994; Goldstein, 1983; Gunter, 2006; Kerr, 2006; Leizman, 1999; Messner and Sabo, 1994; Murphy, Williams, and Dunning, 1990; Welch, 1997).

Whether biological, ecological, cognitive, and/or interactionist theoretical, approaches to the topic of sports violence are worthy of our attention.

Chapter 7

Practicum on Sportscasting

A would-be sports announcer would do well to learn all that he can of the different sports that are broadcast. The rules and requirements of the games must be thoroughly absorbed. He should study the phraseology that is distinctive of the game or sport, which he may use in his broadcasts if it is generally understood by sport fans and by the average listener. The sport pages of newspapers written by experts will form his textbook, for they will give him a diction that is picturesque and a style that is speedy. He should study the history of the sport and of those who have participated and gained renown. He must know the signs or gestures used by the officials to signify penalties, etc. But most of all, he must never forget that he is not watching a game for his own amusement, but is reporting it to listeners who are hanging on his word description.

(Abbot, 1941, p. 62)

BECOMING A SPORTSCASTER

So now we are down to it: How do you become a sportscaster? Have the rules changed since the era of the quotation? Although the various vignettes throughout this book by and about sportscasters are helpful, this section deals with the *skills* needed for sportscasting, sportscasting jobs, sportscasting preparation, a hint at the how-tos of it all, and encouragement for internships.

Sportscasters/Sportscasting

Sportscasting Skills

> Knowledge of sports cannot be faked. Sports fans are often experts themselves, and this means that an aspiring sportscaster must have a strong interest in, and knowledge of, the games to be reported. A sports anchor must be well informed about all sports, even activities he or she may not find personally appealing. (O'Donnell, Hausman, and Benoit, 1992, p. 218)

Some of the key skills needed for sportscasters include—if not necessarily in this order: Knowledge about, and enthusiasm for sport(s), a great voice, and even better hair. If you think this is a joke, or if you are only interested in radio or the Internet, just turn on your television to some sports show.

Let's return to the notion of voice; here, it is best if you have a pleasant-sounding, easy-to-understand voice, with good grammar and good timing, and clear, controlled pronunciation. Some people are naturals, but even they can improve from working with professionals in the speech industries. Utterback et al. (1990), for example, discuss basics like breathing, pitch, intonation, resonance, articulation, phonetics, and the like.

Although you do not need the "golden throat" that marked the early days of radio, you might want to work with a voice coach if you have an accent that needs modifying or if you want to improve the general timbre of your tone. Consider Cosell, who "had an unpleasant voice, its corrosive qualities further exacerbated by an accent that resonated with the sounds of his native Brooklyn. Cosell's voice grated on many listeners, not unlike the sound of fingernails being scratched along a blackboard" (Davies, 1994, p. 64). What did he do? He focused on a "tell it like it is" approach that became his stylistic strength.

What might you do? Take a course in public speaking. "A lot comes from Elocution lessons my mom made me take when I was ten years old," Curt Gowdy recalls (cited in Smith, 1998, pp. 260-261). Because you will want to get rid of clichés, one of the key things you can do is to at least beware of using sport sayings such as "It's a game of inches and seconds," "S/he's a natural" skier, shooter, hitter, or the like, "clutch player," "a team of destiny," "team effort," "killer instinct," "class team," "take them one game/one leg at a time," "willing to pay the price," and many more.

In Addition, draw on what you have learned in English classes, theater and drama, foreign languages, public relations and advertising courses, communications, marketing and management, and general liberal arts. To help you technically, it is assumed that you will be computer literate. Dick Enberg (2004, p. 38), who worked as both a college coach and an assistant professor of health education and safety, said: "As a broadcaster, you have to be entertaining, you have to be well informed, you have to be excited about what you know, and you have to have a sense of your audience—just like in the classroom."

Of course an integral part of your voice is what you say, and how you say it. A classic example is whether or not your delivery includes too many sports clichés, or whether you are depending too much on what other sportscasters say and do. Back in 1949, Stanley Woodward predicted that clichés would soon become extinct, but nearly four decades later Wanta and Leggett (1988, p. 82) found that they "nonetheless continue to creep into sports reporting. A baseball player hits a 'round-tripper,' a basketball player scores from 'the charity stripe,' and a football player 'explodes' downfield to catch a 'bomb' and 'hit paydirt.'" Using capacity theory, which deals with performance under pressure, the researchers examined thirty-four college football telecasters and found the following:

> Television sports announcers devote their attention to two tasks: processing information about the game on which they are reporting and communicating the pertinent information to the viewing audience. If announcers feel pressured by a game because it is developing unexpectedly, is very close, or involved highly regarded teams, then they must devote more attention to the game and less to their remarks. In this event announcers may fall back on terms with which they feel comfortable—clichés. (p. 83)

Miller (2000) states that broadcasters should build trust with fans; fans trust whatever the broadcaster tells them. Broadcasters who are perceived as untruthful risk losing effectiveness. Mary A. Hums

(2001), a professor of sports administration at the University of Louisville, has constructed some valuable tips for entering the field; in answer to the question *How do I get in the door?,* she suggests KEYS:

K - Knowledge
E - Experience
Y - Your hard work
S - Skills

Knowledge can come from both academic and industry resources; **E**xperience from voluntarism and internships; **Y**our hard work from knowing and being yourself, doing your homework, putting together professional materials, and having and strong spirit; and **S**kills include the following:

1. Initiative
2. Communication-oral/written skills
3. Organizational skills
4. Knowledge of industry segment
5. Ability to work in groups
5. People skills
6. Managing technology
7. Managing diversity

No doubt you have quite a bit of knowledge about sports. It is expected, in fact, that you read the sports section in various newspapers, listen to sports radio, watch sports television, reference sports online, talk with a number of people about sports, and maybe even are part of a sports chat group on the Web. If you don't, in fact, use multiple means for your sports outlets, you really need to know how valuable a multimedia approach can be to your career. Olbermann and Patrick offer "Top Ten Free Pieces of Advice to Other Sportscasters":

1. Stop saying "Hi, everybody!" Most people still listen to radio or watch TV by themselves. Subconsciously, when you say "Hi, everybody" to one guy sitting in a room alone, he thinks you're talking to everybody *else*. You're just underlining your own ego.

2. Never do an infomercial. Your career is over. You are done. Toast. Fried. We don't care if you're selling salad dressing that gives eternal life—you will never be taken seriously again.
3. Don't say "welcome back." The viewer didn't go anywhere: *You* did.
4. A game where the score is 21 to 21 is a tie game, or tied at 21, but saying it's a 21-21 tie is redundant and annoying.
5. Remember that the term "Super Bowl" is a *brand name,* not an adjectival phrase.
6. If a player has a slipped, bulging, or herniated disk and you've had an alcoholic beverage anytime in the preceding ninety-six hours, just say he has a "back injury."
7. Never read the name of a sponsor of an event or a stadium unless there's a gun pointed at your head. Just because *they* call it the Your-Name-Here Open doesn't mean *you* have to.
8. Don't say "grand slam homer." The only kind of grand slam in baseball is a homer. You might as well say "a run-scoring RBI."
9. Avoid the overly specific synonym for "beat." Better to say "defeated" ten times while you read a bunch of scores.
10. As Warner Wolf long ago pointed out, whatever *they* call it, since a ball hitting it is a *fair* ball, that thing sticking up in either corner of a baseball outfield logically *has* to be "the fair pole." (pp. 136-137)

"To become a sportscaster, first you must be responsible," suggests Scott Clark (n.d.). "You must also be a journalist. No matter the creativity, the flair, or the fun, the basics—who did what, when and where was it done—are always foremost. Then comes the hows, the how manys and the whys."

The part about "hair": of course, it is a fact of life that looks and grooming are important. Of course there is the old saw about having "a face that looks best on radio," but what we are talking about here is having a generally pleasant demeanor. Frank Deford famously described, in a 1983 *Sports Illustrated* profile, how Howard Cosell broke the mold of the ex-jock with a perfect face and perfect hair: "He is not the one with the golden locks or the golden tan, but the old one, shaking, sallow and hunched, with a chin whose purpose is not to exist as a chin but only to fade so that his face may, as the bow of a ship, break the waves and not get in the way of that voice."

As a neophyte, you probably will start out as production assistant, fact-finder, researcher, or cub reporter. Newcomers in radio often start by being asked to tape interviews and operate equipment, while beginners in television are go-fers on lots of levels. Take advantage of this time to talk to everyone involved in the production, learning everything from how scripting is done to what floor manager signals mean; at the least, it will help you appreciate what an art the process is. You probably will start out in a small station, or local community, moving on to larger, urban networks if you want.

Competition for sportscasting jobs, as you can well imagine, is keen. This book assumes that you are interested, so my goal is to help you as much as possible. Of course it helps to have some formal training from a communications course or a technical school. Best of all, though, is plain old experience. Brent Musburger (cited in Smith, 1998, p. 214) tells about what he learned from his early days at CBS: "Everybody was saying I talked too much, so I thought about it, looked at some tapes, and agreed. So you talk less. Then when you say something it means to much more."

If you are female, you may have already guessed that your chances of making it in the sportscasting field are especially difficult. Currently, fewer than 10 percent of our sportsjournalists are women; still, as in fields like medicine and law, those statistics are changing. Probably the best idea for all minorities interested in becoming sportscasters is to have your identity work in your behalf—whether it is gender, gender orientation, ethnicity, age, religious persuasion, or whatever.

Longtime sportscaster Gary Bender (1994, pp. 5-6) debunks some myths about the profession, e.g., needing a "radio" voice, looking like Mel Gibson or Cindy Crawford, being an ex-jock. Rather, he asks some key questions of would-be members of the profession: Do you have the ability to write? Do you have the ability to read? Are you expressive? Do you have a sense of time? Are you organized? Can you focus? Are you curious? Can you adapt rapidly to change? Do you get along well with people?

Sportscasting Jobs

> Sure, sportscasters get to interact with athletes, coaches and other high-profile members of the sports community on a regular basis, but the job is not all fun and games. These dedicated sports personalities arrive before the game and stay late after the game, wrapping up the post-event, interviewing players and preparing for the next game. They typically work long hours and weekends, depending upon their show's time slot and/or game time. Most sportscasters are avid sports fans who know a great deal about the industry. (Iovieno, 2001, p. 1)

Just as the sports photographer needs to have a thorough understanding of what he or she is covering, so too does the sportscaster need to be prepared. Oftentimes the hiring process includes interviews, an evaluation of your on-air presence, a chance for you to show your area(s) of expertise, and your overall delivery style.

Working conditions vary, with new sportscasters often having to learn as they "go with the flow." Hours can be irregular, depending on the sport and the season. Sometimes work time runs long, with breaks only intermittently. So, sportscasters need to be flexible, sometimes working late at night or early in the morning; alternatively, work time may be rigid, such as hosting a show for an entire morning. It might involve long commuting time, extensive travel, and/or oddly structured schedules.

Salaries for sportscasters can range from fairly low for learners to outrageously high for celebrities. Sometimes, part of the job description includes participation in various community events, such as emceeing sports banquets, visiting hospitals, attending local fairs, or greeting customers in sports stores. As might be expected, wages run higher for television than for radio.

Although the Federal Communication Commission cites statistics of some 78,000 people employed in commercial television, 50,000 in cable television, 10,000 in noncommercial television, and 16,000 at the major television networks, openings for the field of sportscasting remain quite closed. Typically those jobs are held by people who covet their positions, and who are loathe to giving them up. Furthermore, those positions are predominantly the result of self-creation. "The sports announcer has three constituencies to please in addition to the listener or viewer," Snyder and Spreitzer (1983, p. 218) remind us: "the owner of the sports franchise, the corporate sponsors who buy the advertising time, and the owner of the television or radio station."

Obviously, you are going to have quite a bit of competition, as careers in the sports industry are highly sought after. For starters, there are a number of places on the Internet you might try, such as the American Journalism Center in Washington, DC (www.aimajc.org); The Sports Internship (www.internships-usa.com); JobsInSports.com; SportsCareers.com; TeamJobs.com; WomenSportsJobs.com; the Asia American Journalists Association (www.aaja.org), SportscastingJobs .com, collegesports.com, or WorkInSports.com. Be aware, though: many are fee-based. Individual schools and states often have their own opportunities, such as the Florida Sports Foundation (www .flasports.com), or you might want to work with a team (my students have liked the Boston Bruins), the U.S. Olympic Committee, HBO Sports, and so many more.

Whatever your career choice, but particularly relative to sportscasting, it is always a good idea to be proactive. Consider what Len Berman did while he was a still a sophomore in college: He encouraged his fellow Syracuse classmates to sponsor the "First Annual College Sportscasting Conference," inviting people from other colleges to come hear Marv Albert and Marty Glickman, the latter giving a keynote offering this good advice: "When you're announcing, speak English, not jock talk."

Lots of successful sportscasters report their interest in the profession at an early age. Johnny Most (Carey, 2003, p. 2) shares how he would lie in bed, pretending to be broadcasting a Dodgers-Yankees game from Ebbets Field, using a glass or a hollow flashlight as a microphone: "I had memorized all the rosters—by name, by number, by position. I knew batting averages, earned run averages. I knew every player's nickname. I knew whether they were righty or southpaw. I could even tell you their hat and shoe size." If you think thirteen years of age is too young to be a sportscaster, maybe you don't know about Garrett MacDonald, a regular on the *Rocky Mount Sports Report/*

Early Edition. "Does he know college football? He can walk the walk and talk the talk. And talk and talk and talk," reports Dick Kreck (2004, p. E5). The trick, no matter your age, is knowing your stuff. "Certainly, an aspiring broadcaster of any sort must talk. But not just talk," declares Tom Hedrick (2000, p. 3). "The talk must have resonance and comfortable style (*voice*). The talk must have credibility and be informative (*preparation*). The talk must be entertaining and energetic (*style*)."

Beyond broadcasting, John R. Catsis (1996, pp. 51-52) suggests some extra employment opportunities for freelancers: announcing local teams on radio, working pay-per-view games, narrating videotapes for college and professional teams, authoring books and magazine articles, and "Going Hollywood"; relative to that last, you can note a number of instances in sportscaster profiles in this book where they have played either themselves or some scripted sportscaster.

Sportscasting Preparation

The Sports Business Research Network (www.sbrnet.com) provides a list of colleges and universities that are a good starting point if you are interested in learning more about the field; it includes business schools, public institutions, and private schools: University of Alabama, American International College, Appalachian State University, Arizona State University, Babson College, Bowling Green State University, University of Calgary, California University of Pennsylvania, Canisius College, Cazenovia College, University of Central Florida, University of Cincinnati, Colby Sawyer College, Colorado College, University of Colorado, Columbia Business School, Concordia University, Cornell University, Daniel Webster College, Dartmouth College, University of Dayton, University of Denver, DeSales University, Dowling College, Drexel University, Duquesne University, East Stroudsburg University, Elms College, Elon University, Emory University, Finger Lakes Community College, Florida Atlantic University, University of Florida, Fordham University, George Mason University, George Washington University, Georgetown University, University of Georgia, Harvard Business School, University of Illinois-Champaign/Urbana, Indiana State University, Indiana University, University of Iowa, John Carroll University, Kansas State University, Le Moyne College, Liberty University, Loyola College, Manhattanville College, Marist College, Marquette University, Massachusetts Institute of Technology, University of Massachusetts-Amherst, Menlo College, Metropolitan State College of Denver, Miami University of Ohio, Michigan State University, University of Minnesota, College Misericordia, Mitchell College, University of Montreal, Morehead State University, Mount Ida College, Mount Union College, Neumann College, University of Nevada-Las Vegas, University of New Hampshire, University of New Mexico, New York University, Nichols College, North Carolina State University, University of North Carolina-Chapel Hill, University of Northern Colorado, Northern Illinois University, Northern State University, Northwood University, University of Notre Dame, Ohio State University, Ohio University, University of Oregon, Penn State University, University of Pennsylvania, University of Pittsburgh, Point Park University, Princeton University, Rensselaer Polytechnic Institute, Rice University, University of Richmond, Sacred Heart University, Saint John Fisher College, Saint John's University, Saint Leo University, San Diego State University, Slippery Rock University, University of South Carolina, Southeastern University, Southern Illinois University/Carbondale and Edwardsville, University of Southern Mississippi, Southern New Hampshire University, Springfield College, Stanford Business School, State University of West Georgia, University of Tampa, Temple University, United States Sports Academy, University of Tennessee-Knoxville, Texas A&M University, Tulane University, Wake Forest University, Washington State University, Western New England College, University of West Florida, West Virginia University, Western Illinois University, University of Western Ontario, UCLA, University of Wisconsin-La Crosse, University of Wisconsin-Parkside, and Vanderbilt University. Also, some schools have specific programs, such as Northeastern University's Center for the Study of Sport in Society.

Other related fields some students might be interested in include sports marketing or management, sports psychology, physical education, coaching, communication, exercise and sports studies, human kinetics, kinesiology, leisure and tourism, sport sociology, sport ethics, sport public relations, sport law, and other related areas You are no doubt a candidate for sports journalism, which can mean print and/or electronic media. If you are serious about sportscasting, you need to know that there are technical contraptions with which you will be working; be sure to acquaint yourself with everything from microphones to mobile units, and it is a good idea to take a television production course somewhere along the line so that you will appreciate the process.

A number of good, recently published "sports careers" books are available (Field, 2004; Heitzmann, 2004; Mulligan and Mulligan, 1998; Plunkett, 2006); some are sportscasting-related (Bender, 1994; Catsis, 1996, Hedrick, 2000, Hitchcock, 1991, Schultz, 2002). A number of organizations that sports journalists might join exist, such as the American Federation of Television and Radio Artists (AFTRA), the American Sportscasters Association (ASA), the National Association of Broadcasting (NAB), the National Association of Broadcast Employees and Technicians (NABET), the National Sportscasters and Sportswriters Association (NSSA), the Radio and Advertising Bureau (RAB), the Radio Television News Directors Association (RTNDA), and the Writers' Guild of America (WGA).

Probably the best sportscasting preparation involves watching others at the job. Although you clearly want to keep your own distinctive style, it always helps to watch—and critique, other broadcasters. It's easy to watch television; another good source is on the Internet, including the *Sportscaster Chronicles*—where you can log on to "the great voices in radio and television history," at www.sportscaster chronicles.blogspot.com.

Don't get discouraged, even though landing your plum job might at times seem discouraging. At the end of his senior year, Len Berman (2005, p. 17) sent out "150 letters and resumes to the three networks in the top fifty markets. One hundred forty-seven stations ignored me."

It may be nasty of me to suggest it, but if you want a good laugh and if you don't want to be nominated for the dubious honor, you might want to check out Matt Lorch's "Worst sportscast in history," captured on YouTube, at http://www.kdotejebe/2007/03/15/worst-sportscast-in-history/.

There really is no such thing as "Sportscasters School." To date, it is not a course that is offered in an academic arena. The reason is simple: there are no textbooks. When I recently set out to teach such a course, I had to make up the entire course—including putting together relevant readings, inviting local sportscasters to speak to the class, constructing a practicum, teaching students to critique sportscasters on both radio and television.

Sportscasting How-Tos

So now you are ready to learn some of the hands-on approaches to actually being a sportscaster. You have reviewed some of the history of the topic, considered its financial implications, and better understand the role of the media. Now, your most important job is to connect with your audience(s). Remember, we Westerners tend to value the excitement of competitive sport—a luxury for many people around the world.

You can see how it behooves you to be aware of a wide range of topics relative to your audience members, ranging from their demographics (age, gender, race/ethnicity, education, socio-economic background, religion, and the like) to attitudes about drugs and doping, homophobia, statistics, personal stories, and so much more. Think of it this way: Because of the way the ratings systems works, they are your ultimate bosses.

One of your biggest challenges is making the decision on how humorous you might want to be. As in any other thing you do, you have to be natural. Even though you realize that your job per se is entertainment, it might suit your personality better to provide "infotainment." Try it all out, and see what works for you. "I think I learned how to broadcast in two ways," Marty Glickman (1996, p. 65) shares. "One was by watching Red Barber work an actual game off a ticker tape at the studio when the Dodgers were playing out of town. The other was by doing *Today's Baseball*." He offers these tips in what he calls "Guru Glickman's Primer" (pp. 177-180), abbreviated here:

- Know the game. Know the rules, the history, and the tradition of the event, the identities of the players, the officials, the coaches, the trainers, the doctors.
- Develop a philosophy of broadcasting. Determine for yourself what you are seeking to do. Your goal should be to have the listener or viewer see and *feel* the game as though he or she is present.
- Project. Although the microphone is only inches from your mouth, talk as though it is six to eight feet away from you. This will give your voice more assurance and strength.
- On radio, paint the word picture. Use descriptive words. A "great" catch can't be visualized. It might be a leaping, two-handed grab, an ankle-high catch running at top speed to the right. Use words like *right* and *left, high* and *low, arcing, wobbly, quivering, slanting,* and so on. Describe the principals: *angular, bulky, short, lean, sinewy, blond.*
- On TV, let the picture tell the story.
- Consider the listener/viewer. What is it he or she seeks? The score. The time remaining.
- Give down and yardage before every play in football. Every play is a new drama. The stage must be set. Down and yardage set the stage; score and time is the story line.
- Always remember that the game is the thing. Don't fill the air with irrelevance.
- Give meaning to your words.
- Voice control is important. Diction, timbre, accent, voice quality, clarity, pace, intensity, softness, excitement can all be achieved with voice control.
- Delete petty information, particularly numerical data, statistics.
- Beware of clichés.
- Don't embellish the graphics.
- Enjoy the event.

Part of your practicum, which began with various preparations, continues as each event requires it. Throughout, remain aware that your first responsibility is to your audience(s). Undoubtedly there will be conflicts about that, as various personnel might try to sway you in certain directions, but nothing beats a loyal following for your sportscasts. For veteran sportscaster Curt Gowdy (cited in Smith, 1995, p. 268), it doesn't matter whether you are broadcasting from radio or television; there are some basic rules: "An announcer has to call a game, identify players, give the count, how many outs, how many on, give the score. You can't give it enough. Sets tune in all the time. The first thing you want to know is who's ahead . . . The fundamentals haven't changed. Keep it simple. Do your homework. Give the score."

As you are into the actual broadcast, keep to what is going on, interpreting where appropriate. Play-by-play on radio requires much more accompanying detail than on television, when it is oftentimes best to let the drama speak for itself. If you are going to use statistics, be sure they are up to date and directly in front of you. For controversies, try to follow rules that your boss and/or organization might have—such as how to deal with injuries, or fights, or crazy spectator shenanigans. If you are working alone, be sure you have everything organized so you can concentrate on your delivery; if you have other sportscasters with you, be sure to share the banter and don't dominate—and if he or she makes mistakes, don't embarrass anyone outwardly, but maybe write out a note. Above all, it bears repeating that you are there for the fans.

One of the topics that comes up about sportscasters is whether or not they are "homers," or home-team rooters—Chicago reputedly having the most (Fuller, 1994)—such as when Red Kerr broadcasts the Chicago Bulls and calls the opponents the "bad guys." Some, like Johnny Most, are unabashedly biased, while others want to at least maintain a semblance of being nonbiased. "A 'homer', to me, is an announcer who tells you only half the story, the half he thinks the management of the club wants you to know," according to Harry Caray (1989, p. 193). Claiming not to be one, even though he was adored by so many Chicagoans, he added, "A homer sugar coats. He makes excuses for mistakes and errors and lousy play. He won't mention it if a player isn't hustling. When I'm at that ballpark broadcasting a game, I'm the eyes and ears for that fan at home. If I don't tell that fan the truth, the whole truth, and nothing but the truth, he or she isn't going to hear it. And the fan deserves to hear it" (p. 194).

Whether working for traditional broadcasting, such as radio and television, sportscasters write, read, and simultaneously analyze, critique, report, and dramatize sporting events. "For a broadcaster, nothing is as important—or as difficult to master—as describing what you see," Jon Miller (2000, p. 85) has observed. He uses as an example Bill King, who covered the NBA Warriors and the NFL Raiders before becoming the voice of the Oakland A's. King, with his trademark staccato-style of broadcasting, always described in detail the exact positions of players, who had possession, and who was guarding who.

As might be expected, a certain amount of anxiety is associated with sportscasting, especially in the early stages. Wanta and Leggett (1988, p. 82) have found that, "When the game is close, the outcome unexpected, or the teams prominent, announcers under stress rely on clichés in order to be able to maximize their attention to the game." Speaking openly about the stress that comes with the profession, such as memorizing names and numbers of players, Dick Enberg (2004, pp. xi-xii) shares:

> It would be interesting to monitor the blood pressure of an announcer as he calls a game. I'll bet it shoots up dramatically. To be able to speak for three hours off the top of your head, using a full range of emotions, is very demanding. All the while, the producer is giving instructions in your ear, adding to the challenge. And, like a defensive back in football, whose mistakes are right out in the open, I'm fully exposed. Everyone hears the verbal fumbles. There are no erasers on the microphone. There are no proofreaders.

A recurrent tip from successful sportscasters is "do your homework." Not to seem alarmist here, but it certainly makes sense to prepare yourself for any number of contingencies that might occur during your sportscast. There can be technical glitches, weather changes, scripting mix-ups, medical issues, accidents, even fatalities on the field. The best advice is for you to continue being yourself; you might spend some time thinking of how you might, for example, deal with a serious mishap during play—say, wondering whether someone has been paralyzed. Visualize it all from pre- to post- gametime.

Once you are established, it is also a good idea to put together a "tickler file," so named to "tickle" your memory about dates, people, and events. Whether you work best with Rolodex, Palm Pilot, or Blackberry-type instruments, hand-held text messenger, a crate with labeled folders, or simply a monthly calendar, it is a good idea to keep a list of key contact persons and annual sporting occurrences. You need to, in essence, become your own business agent.

Score sheets are *de rigueur* for sportscasters, and most fans are also familiar with them. In baseball, for example, the sportscaster should know these designations for defensive players: (1) pitcher, (2) catcher, (3) first base, (4) second base, (5) third base, (6) short-stop, (7) left field, (8) center field, and (9) right field.

Scorebooks, both during a season and afterward, for perspective, are invaluable. Scorebooks link players on the field with the fans in the stands, link sportscasters with their counterparts in sports journalism, and link families of fans. Just as you might on a bowling sheet, consider setting up your own code of scoring, such as the following:

BB = base on balls
D = double
F = fly
I = intercept
KO = knockout
L = left
R = right
/ (slash) = single
K = strike(out)

Phil Rizzuto, who was a Yankee ballplayer before becoming a broadcaster, had a simple system on a list of the lineup: one slash for at bat; on the other side of the name—a slash for a hit; two slashes to the left of a name and one to the right meant the player was one for two.

Internships

Perhaps my strongest suggestion for would-be sportscasters is to do an internship. According to www.sportscastingjobscom, "Almost everyone in the sports media industry began their career interning for someone, somewhere. By interning you'll make the contacts necessary for advancing to the ranks of the gainfully employed" (p. 3).

For starters, this is just the push you need to put together a resume. You might check out Exercise 7.3 for a sample, to get you going. Note that you should include your contact information—your complete name, postal address, telephone (including cell phone, if applicable), fax, e-mail, Web site, and anything else that might be relevant. Make sure you state your vocational goal, whether in front of or behind the broadcasting booth, and then first list your educational experience, including any extra courses that you might have had other than the degree-earning ones. Your work experience is important, indicating that you have held jobs and are dependable—so feel free to show your versatility in fields other than sport. Any volunteer/community involvement should also be documented, along with special skills that you have. Try to get everything typed on a single sheet of paper, and line up some references if you need them.

Work with advisors to determine what kind of internship might work best for you. During my tenure as Intern Chair, each year we arranged an Intern Fair, when community organizations and businesses came to talk to students about opportunities. It served several purposes, allowing local people and places to inform us about them and their activities, and providing students with a chance to both interview and to be interviewed. There were lots of "fits," or win-win situations.

By providing practical training not available in the classroom, internships are usually set up formally, with a contract specifying what both sides want and expect from the experience. Since school credit is often at stake, we set a standard whereby fifty hours of work would be equal to one credit hour; more likely, the project would involve 150 hours for 3 credits, but occasionally students would work in-depth during summertime or sometimes they would take the entire semester to work in New York City at HBO, the United Nations, or one of the networks, or at ESPN in Bristol, Connecticut. More typically, they would do their internships at a public access television center, at the *Boston Globe,* with advertising or public relations firms, at local radio stations, and other media outlets. One of my students even did an internship in Hawaii. My job was to monitor their work, being in continual contact with their assigned mentors, and although that usually meant on-site visitations you might correctly guess that most of that work remained local.

Media interns are usually not compensated, especially those done for college credit, but reimbursements for travel or allotments for meals sometimes are negotiated. We required a written journal in the form of a diary delineating what interns did, when and how, as well as an assessment of its value. Reciprocally, as you can see in Exercise 7.6, we performed an internship evaluation based on a number of criteria. Not only are internships valuable for learning about self, then, they also serve as great templates for future references.

All this preparation will help you as you enter the world of sportscasting, which can be a springboard to other challenges. Don't forget that former president Ronald Reagan, known as "The Great Communicator," started his career as a sportscaster!

SPORTS JOURNALISM: WRITING

Reporting is a companion skill to writing. Broadcasters who can generate story ideas, interview newsmakers, cull records, and observe and absorb the atmosphere and actions that surround the events and newsmakers they cover will be able to interpret events clearly for their listeners and viewers. (Gibson, 1991, p. xi)

Although you might think that sportscasters mostly need speaking skills, it is imperative that they also be good writers. Olbermann and Patrick (1997, p. 121) report that they each "write and ad-lib 10,000-20,000 words a week . . . You have to write well. You have to write quickly. Even if you wind up doing play-by-play or talk radio, where writing is not a vital portion of the job, the mental skills honed by writing are essential." For some sportscasters, it is simple. Here are some basic rules:

- Don't let anybody else do your work for you.
- Don't be afraid to ask.
- Verify your facts.
- Keep your promises.

A great example of critical writing can be found in Richard Sandomir's review of the 2006 running of the Kentucky Derby, which featured the then famously undefeated Barbaro: "Barbaro was coming up on the outside, then he took the lead. NBC's camera angle was perfect, and Barbaro was visibly adding to his advantage. But NBC switched to a much longer shot that made the horses appear as if they had leapt backward in an instant; the jarring cut created the peculiar illusion that the horses had not rounded the turn. The switch from the first angle, which was poised to display a lateral view of Barbaro's lead, to one that was so distant forced viewers to wait eight seconds to adjust their depth perception to see the extent of his lead." You can see how, as a sports journalist, you need to be aware of production terms and how important good writing skills can be.

The Web site eHow provides tips on becoming a sportswriter, (available at: http://www.ehow.com/how_15414_become-sportswriter .html) (Courtesy of eHow.com).

- Take writing courses in high school and college. Work on your high school and college newspaper, too.
- Every subject you study in school is helpful: history, political science, biology, etc. Major in journalism.
- Learn to type.
- Learn about sports. Watch and read about as many contests as possible.
- A great place to start is to cover high school sports for a local paper.
- Keep up to date by reading *Editor & Publisher* magazine, which has a classified-ad section listing openings in sports depart-

ments around the country. Subscribe to the *Columbia Journalism Review* as well.

- Read good writers—and not just in the newspaper sports sections and sports magazines.

"In many respects, writing for sports broadcasting is the same as writing for news, because most of the basics apply" (Brad Schultz, 2002, p. 58). He offers ten rules: (1) Use *active* voice ("the player caught the ball" rather than "the ball was caught"), (2) use proper grammar, (3) use simple words and numbers, (4) keep your writing clean and simple, (5) use solid reporting skills, (6) learn about more than just sports, (7) don't forget creativity and originality, (8) humanize your writing, (9) sometimes less is more, and (10) carefully consider outside elements (pp. 58-65).

It is expected that sports journalists will make every effort to remain objective about their reportage, keeping their biases about favorite sports teams and players hidden. They should be of a temperament that can deal with deadlines and pressures, and the most successful ones can get along easily with athletes, agents, coaches, managers, and any number of other sports-related people.

Let's use soccer as an example. Scott French (2003, pp. 54-55), senior editor at *Soccer America* magazine, gives this advice: "To write about soccer, you've got to understand the game; many soccer reporters in this country don't, and their copy is little more than descriptions of goals and assumptions based on match statistics." Furthermore, "A good game story is also a well-constructed critique of the game. It should explain how and why a result was achieved and what the result means in a larger context," he suggests that your story answer some simple questions:

- What happened?
- Why did it happen—what factors enabled it to happen?
- Did one team succeed or another team fail?
- Did the teams play well?
- Were there any major shifts in momentum?
- What spurred these shifts?

- How, if at all, did substitutions or the referee's decisions impact the match?
- How did each team play?
- What style of soccer did each employ?

Red Barber (1987), (answering questions that Don Huff, sports editor of *The Intelligencer* asks his colleagues), has some interesting responses. Here are the prompts: Most dramatic moment broadcast? Most unforgettable person? Any event you didn't cover you wish you had? Why is baseball the best sport to broadcast? Whom do you most admire in your profession? To the last, about his mentors, the legendary Barber responded, "I had excellent broadcasting partners—Al Hefner, Alan Hale, Connie Desmond, Ernie Harwell, Vin Scully, Jim Woods, Mel Allen, Phil Rizzuto, Joe Garagiola, and Jerry Coleman. They were men I worked with and traveled with and knew and respected. I doubt anyone worked with so many outstanding professionals." Welcome to the career!

SPORTS JOURNALISM: BROADCASTING

It's the best job in the world, isn't it? Traveling the globe, watching the big sporting events free from the best seats in the stadium, mingling with star players and athletes, seeing your byline in the newspapers or broadcasting to millions on radio and television, and being paid a lot of money for the privilege. That's the way many people see a sports writer's job. The reality can be rather different. Hard and demanding work to tight deadlines, long and unsocial hours (most of them worked in the evenings or at weekends), a lot of time spent in research and preparation, acquiring the same depth of knowledge about the sports you cover as the most fanatical or your readers or listeners, earning the trust of a wide range of contacts among players, coaches and administrators, and the skill to write accurately and entertainingly at great speed and often under difficult conditions. (Andrews, 2005, p. 1)

Career Moves

Chronologically, anchoring is the very last thing a sports broadcaster does with his show. It comes after the research and legwork, after the planning and preparation, and after all the shooting, producing, and writing. But anchoring is probably the single most important element of the entire process. Certainly, the other elements are important, but it takes good anchoring and good delivery to bring out the best in the writing and photography. A good sports anchor ties all the other elements together and communicates them in an interesting and entertaining way. It is five or so minutes that will make or break your entire sportscast and in some cases, an entire career. (Schultz, 2002, p. 95)

Radio sportscasters, who might work at the local, regional, or national network level, can count on a salary range from $20,000 to $750,000 (Field, 2004, p. 135). Depending on their skill level and the station's niche and needs, they might host a sports talk show, report on various sporting events, be a color commentator, or interview sports people. It is always a good idea not only to keep up with local sports, athletes, and fans, but also to be aware of what kind of programs and interviews the audience may want to hear. Much of this is also true about television sportscasters, although salary ranges are higher ($21,000 to more than a million); Shelly Field (2004, p. 132) would add that, "Most sportscasters are avid sports fans who both enjoy sports a know a great deal about the industry. Sportscasters are fortunate to work in an environment they love. They attend sports events and interview people in the sports industry." She offers these tips for entry:

1. Work with your college television station even if you can't get into the sports department. Hands-on experience will be useful.
2. If your college does not have a television station, work on the radio station. Try to get as much experience working in broadcasting as you can.
3. Job availabilities may be located in the newspaper's display or classified section. Look under heading classifications of Broad-

casting, Sportscaster, Television, Journalist, Sports, Reporter, or Sportswriter.

4. Get writing experience. Most sportscasters must write their own copy—at least at the beginning. Become a member of your college's newspaper. If you can, find a summer or part-time job working at a newspaper even if it isn't in the sports department. The experience will be worth it.

5. Look for a summer or part-time job at a local or cable radio station.

6. Many television stations and associations offer internships or training programs. Internships will give you on-the-job training and the opportunity to make important contacts. (pp. 133-134)

Television sports careers typically are on-camera (such as analyst, reporter, commentator, play-by-play sportscaster or color commentator, talk-show host, etc.), off-camera, and/or technical-oriented positions. Consider where you might best fit, and go from there. You might want to contact www.Sportscastingjobscom.

Production-wise, you should know that the average shot in news, drama, and in sports lasts for seven seconds, so use that as a parameter for what your audience expects. Additionally, even though a stadium may be panned at the beginning, television's typical camera distance is mid-shot to close-up. In terms of frequency, a mix of shots is used, such as atmosphere shots (giving a sense of space), reflexive shots (whether of players, fans, even, occasionally, announcers), and game shots of other participants, such as coaches, owners, managers, and others involved in the event.

Disclosing "The Game Behind the Game," Terry O'Neil (1989, p. 178) reveals that, "In the moments before air, one of the most critical decisions is finding an audio balance, such that (1) the producer hears everything in his headset; (2) the director hears everything in his headset, (3) both hear commentary through the speakers, and (4) the producer, director, and T.D. [technical director] hear each other in their 'open' ears. There is no explaining it," he comments, "but in the same way that [John] Madden sees what all twenty-two players do on every play, experienced production people hear every word that is said."

Be sure, before you begin commentary, that you know how to pronounce players' names. The best way to master this is simply by talking to each one individually, making sure you are following their suggestions. Do the same for owners, coaches, managers, and any other names you might be mentioning.

"Forget about Joe Morgan and Jon Miller, Al Michaels and John Madden, or any of the hack NBA announcers on TNT. Give me Mike Gordon and Tommy Heinsohn, Jerry Remy and Sean McDonough, or Jerry Trupiano and Joe Castiglione," rants Matthew Ouelette (2003). "Why? Because they aren't bickering egoists who care more about themselves than the game they're calling."

Interviews

As a would-be sportscaster, interviews will be an important part of your career. First of all, you will undoubtedly be interviewed to get the job. This is your opportunity to demonstrate how hireable you are, and also your chance to ask questions about potential places where you might work. In your preparation for the (probably formal) interview, be sure to have your materials lined up—like your resume, a demo tape, letters of recommendation, and anything else that might help your cause. Be sure you have done your homework, so you know about the organization and the job. And be sure to spend some time on your appearance for the interview; even if the climate is really informal, don't even think about cut-off jeans. You need to present yourself as someone who can get the job done and someone with whom others will want to work.

Once you are employed as a sportscaster, part of your job will be interviewing other people—athletes, coaches, managers, owners, trainers, even players' families and friends. Whether those interviews are pre- or postgame, whether they take place at a sporting venue or at a news conference, whether they will be live or delayed, and maybe edited, a few general rules hold. Mainly, what message(s) do you want your audience to learn? If there are controversial or complex issues to be discussed, be sure you have both your interviewee and audience with you—which is to say, don't talk down to them, but don't talk above them, either. Be alert to what might be newsworthy, and timely—try to stay away from simple, superficial questions. Use your own style, and keep it conversational. "Sports journalism is not only about what performers do on the field of play, but what they and their coaches and administrators say off it," Phil Andrews (2005, p. 104) reminds us—which is why cultivating contacts is such an important role.

Phil Schaap (2001, p. 433), who worked as a sports journalist for *Newsweek* and the *Herald Tribune* before becoming an ABC correspondent and host of ESPN's *The Sports Reporters,* discloses what he considers his simple interviewing strength: "I try to allow people to be themselves, to reveal themselves. I don't want them to put on a show. I don't want them to say what they think they *should* say. I try to relax them. I try to be probing, but not confrontational." One of Len Berman's (2005, p. 233) least favorite interviews is what he terms the "coaching deathwatch": "It's tough to interview a coach who everyone knows will soon be fired. But you still have to ask the questions, and the poor coaches still have to answer them."

Usually, you have the perspective of the whole field. In a single glance, not unlike at the circus, you can see the players, their coaches, even their managers, officials, and fans. Typically, there is even a scoreboard for your reference(s).

SPECIFIC SPORTS(CASTING)

People ask me to compare baseball and football. With each, you have to keep the whole picture in front of you. You put yourself in the place of the guy at home and say, 'What does that person need to know to enjoy the game a little more?' What can't he know without your telling him, informing him, leading him to the next situation?

The biggest difference is pace. Football occurs in five-second bursts. You have a play, then 40 seconds of whatever you want: a replay or anecdote or analysis. Baseball's more conversational, especially with a partner that you're able to work off well. In baseball, the play often seems incidental to your stories. In football, you're always stopping because you have to see if a pass goes 50 yards downfield, a run breaks off tackle, or a measurement. A lot of things break narrative. I don't mean a guy won't hit a home run in the middle of a story in baseball. It's just that the flow and texture of the game lend themselves to easy listening, as it were.

We live in a highlights world. But anyone who knows baseball realizes you need continuity within a game—the seamless flow. Baseball's not just a highlights sport. Something to consider as the game tries to rediscover what it is and has to offer. (Michaels, cited in Smith, 1995, p. 265)

Although the field for sportscasting is huge, discuss some of the sports that you are *most likely* to encounter: baseball, basketball, boxing, football, golf, hockey, horse racing, tennis, track and field. Your input on these and others is highly encouraged. "Baseball dominates the historical memory of the United States in a powerful way that is mirrored by football in Europe. However, the fastest-growing sports are snowboarding and mountain hiking, and the leading sports in terms of new media coverage are bull riding and bass fishing," John Sweeney (2007, p. 3).

Baseball

"Baseball is the best arguing game," declares Jon Miller (2000, p. 57). "If you're passionate about baseball, you argue." The game allows plenty of time to unfold, giving the announcer the opportunity to bring in information and interpret events as they transpire.

Being a baseball broadcaster, according to Dick Enberg (2004, p. 93) involves special skills: "Because the game moves at such a leisurely pace, the announcer is fully exposed. He not only needs to have plenty of anecdotes and stories at his disposal, it's critical that he thoroughly understands the nuances of the game . . . No sport reveals your lack of knowledge like baseball." It also allows good access to the players: "Media are allowed to hang around the batting cage for well over an hour during batting practice, asking questions, listening in on conversations, bantering with the players. You can also wander in and out of the locker rooms and dugouts."

Each sportscaster has his or her own unique style; many people consider Red Barber as their favorite. Consider his dialogue here taken from the 1936 World Series:

> Dick Bartell up, and this is a tight ball game and certainly a splendid exhibition of what a World Series ball game should be. Hadley winds up. Delivers . . . Bartell takes inside on the letters for ball one. The first pitch of the fourth inning. Bartell stands there with his left foot right up against the plate, his right foot crouched underneath him. The pitch. Dick swings . . . It's a high foul behind third. Rolfe is underneath in the coach's box, waiting, and squeezes it for the out. And Rolfe, after he caught that foul behind third base, shook his head very wryly as though to wring the tears out of his eyes. The sky overhead in a very beautiful robin's-egg blue with, as the boys say, very few angels in the form of clouds in it. It's a very tough sky for the players to look into. And left field at Yankee Stadium is the sun garden. (cited in Edwards, 1993, p. 66)

"Baseball provides an additional challenge to announcers because of the slowness of the game," John R. Catsis (1995, p. 244) has noted. "Extensive preparation is the only solution. There are no shortcasts. By doing homework, a broadcast will sound smooth and have a minimum of dead air. Most professional baseball announcers will put in a full workday preparing for and broadcasting each game." Catsis offers this checklist (p. 245):

1. Gather basic information
   a. Annual media guide
   b. Media notes from each team, highlighted by a colored marker pen
   c. Pregame conversations with players, coaches, managers, and other broadcasters
2. Detail starting pitchers, often on 3" × 5" cards
   a. Records for the year
   b. Types of pitches each throws

3. Obtain starting lineups
   a. Note recent hitting streaks
   b. Note previous game performance for each player on both teams
   c. Reference season-to-date records for each player, highlighting significant games
4. Gather general information on the opposing team
   a. Home and road records
   b. Recent team trends and streaks
   c. Overall team trends

Basketball

> One muff at the mike is committed by every basketball announcer in the country in virtually every game. The offensive player makes a head fake. The defensive player foolishly responds by jumping. The offensive player either sneaks in for an easy basket or gets fouled by the defensive player on his way down. And the announcer criticizes the defensive player for "leaving his feet." (Hirsch, 1994, p. 52)

Even if you have played a certain sport, announcing it can change the complexion of how you see the game. For example, Dick Enberg (2004, p. 50) describes how basketball looks so different close up: "You get a real feel for how big the players are, how strong they are, how quick they are, and how powerful they are as shot blockers and rebounders. They're incredibly better than they appear on television."

Announcing basketball at first can seem loaded with lots of obstacles, as you have to keep track of players, plays, points, and any number of issues that need attention; the good part, at least, is that you can concentrate on specifics. "Basketball, from the announcer's standpoint, can almost become nightmarish in its complexity. Listeners want the announcer to keep track of how many fouls a player has, how many rebounds, and how many points each player has scored in the game so far," O'Donnell, Hausman, and Benoit (1992, pp. 220-221) have noted. eHow suggests steps on becoming a basketball sportscaster (available at: (http://www.ehow.com/how_16611_prepare-basketball-broadcast.html) (Courtesy of eHow.com):

- Receive media guides on the teams.
- Check your and set up files for each team you work with.
- Study information about players and coaches. Become familiar with names and statistics.
- Watch early season games.
- Pay attention to what is happening in basketball. Read the sports section of your newspaper, and other publications.
- Be familiar with teams outside your normal coverage area.
- Update yourself just prior to the broadcast.

"Basketball is a *flow* sport," John R. Hitchcock (1991, p. 70) asserts. "The action is basically continuous. There is little time to stop and analyze what is going on. To learn to do basketball play-by-play, start by describing where the ball is on the court and where it goes (top of the circle to the left wing to the baseline left)."

Boxing

> Boxing entails the ability to do speculation and analysis. Since almost all boxing broadcast today is televised, the play-by-play commentator must be able to do much more than relay reports of who hit whom. The broadcasters must analyze the bout to determine why one fighter's style makes him vulnerable to the punches of the other or whether one fighter is being tired by body blows. It is also necessary to speculate, for example, whether a contestant's jabs are piling up points with the judges. (O'Donnell, Hausman, and Benoit, 1992, p. 221)

Encouraging analysis of how a bout is developing, boxing by definition depends on speculating about style. "Radio's roots were in the boxing ring," David J. Halberstam (1999, p. 1) reminds us. "Naturally, one-punch round knockouts are about as much fun for a broadcaster as laryngitis," Marv Albert (1993, p. 82) has noted. Usually live, in real time, it behooves the broadcaster to be on top of his or her game. Wondering, during his early telecasts of boxing, what the spots were on his sports coat, Dick Enberg (2004, p. 49) quickly figured it out: "From a distance, you don't realize how ferocious the punches are, but I was often no more than three feet away. From there, you not only hear the punches, you hear the reaction to them and you see the spray that flies off the fighters." His suggestion: don't wear white.

Football

> Football on television is an analyst's medium, because of how far the game has come from a technical point of view. Unlike other sports, the football analyst is extraordinarily significant because it is such a replay-geared sport. What makes a good one? You start with the entertainment value—showing the viewer something he doesn't know and get out in time for the next play. Knowledge: Seeing many things on the same play. (Albert, cited in Smith, 1998, p. 93)

With so many players on the field at the same time, football sportscasting brings its own unique challenges. Although you may have memorized the names, the possible plays, and even understand the many accompanying statistics associated with the sport, sometimes the best thing is to just let the play speak for itself. "Football is perfect for television because it is an ongoing series, neatly timed, with a careful balance between continuity and change," Phil Patton (1984, p. 4). "It preserves and destroys, abandons and introduces characters like a good soap opera." For Sean McDonough, "Football is the easiest sport to broadcast—there's a natural rhythm with your partner. The play starts, and the play-by-play person speaks. When it's over, the analyst steps in" (cited in Smith, 1998, p. 269). Tom Hedrick (2000, p. 89) offers a six-step summary for football coverage on radio:

1. Learn the players both by numbers and by physical characteristics for immediate recognition.
2. Give down-and-distance and yard line before every snap, and the ball carrier or passer and receiver, and the tackler on every play. If you can pick up a key blocker, that's a bonus.

3. Give the score at least every 1 1/2 minutes, and recap the story line every 10-15 minutes so that the listener dialing in and out will know what has happened when he has just joined the broadcast.
4. Work in advance with your color commentator and define your roles specifically. Determine a system for knowing who will talk when.
5. Describe every play so the listener can visualize explicitly what is happening at the stadium.
6. Check your tapes after the broadcast to be sure you have covered the basics on each play. Determine whether you gave the score enough. Listen for clichés.

Golf

On the one hand, covering golf is the easiest gig in sportswriting, everything is spoon fed and you have the day to mind your words and build your piece from the bottom up. Yet it is the most dispiriting job—the job that requires you to travel the most to see the least, the job where the depressing sameness of the environment must gnaw at your soul. (Humphries, 2003, p. 95)

Melanie Hauser (2003, p. 82) of the Golf Writers Association of America suggests that golf is clearly not as cushy to cover as some people might think:

To begin with, golf is the only sport where the action doesn't unfold in front of you—or in four quarters, two halves, or three sets. There's no court or field, but rather 18 holes, a driving range, a putting green, a locker room, and, more often than you'd think, a parking lot where learning everything you need to know for the day can and will take place.

Dick Enberg (2004, p. 229) agrees: "You never see a golf shot in person. Like the audience at home, you're watching it on television. Your back is even to the eighteenth hole, simply a background for the on-camera close ups to prove to the audience that you're really where you say you are." Their cautions are well taken: As the sports journalist, you need to cover a huge distance and numerous players. Hauser offers an important perspective:

> Golf isn't just birdies, bogeys, and world rankings. Sure, you need to know the basics—all the terms, how far most players can hit a 3-iron or wedge, and a hook from a slice—but you also have to deal with technology issues such as the design of golf balls and clubs, plus sponsorships, purses, course design, PGA and LPGA Tour regulations, and just about anything else you can think of surrounding the game. And playing the game—or at least attempting to—is another must. (p. 84)

It never hurts to maintain a sense of humor covering a sport where the sportscaster is nearly always filling time. Ralph Kiner (1987), a former slugger who became a sportscaster for the New York Mets, recalls an early assignment for a Bing Crosby National Pro-Am golf tournament: Paired on air with his longtime friend Phil Harris, who asked him if he knew Gay Brewer, he responded, "I thought he was a fag winemaker from Modesto" (p. xi). Luckily, both the sponsor and ad agency were pleased with his quick reactions.

Hockey

> Hockey presents unique challenges in description. It features rapid, continuous action but light scoring (like soccer) and audience unfamiliarity (the game mostly is associated with Canada and a few specific climes in the United States). Also, the puck [is] small and often hidden from view. The late satirical columnist Jim Murray of the *Los Angeles Times* wrote that all goals scored in hockey were figments of the imagination. "I defy anyone," he wrote, "to tell me that they actually saw a hockey puck go into the net." (Hedrick, 2000, p. 135)

A fast-paced sport where both the announcer and the audience need to follow the puck, hockey presents its own challenges. Play-by-players need to cover the entire expanse of the rink, rapidly reporting vivid details on radio and allowing action to evolve on television. Declaring him "one of the greatest hockey announcers of all time," Tom Hedrick (2000, p. 135) reports how the late Dan Kelly, veteren caller for the St. Louis Blues, shared with him the "two key elements in calling hockey: (1) instant recognition of players, and (2) accurate description of every pass, every movement of a game filled with rapid and swirling movements." "Hockey is challenging," declares O'Donnell, Hausman, and Benoit (1992, p. 221). "By the time the announcer has told the audience who is in possession of the puck, the game has moved to the other end of the rink."

Horse Racing

According to Jack Whitaker (1998, p. 158), "Horse racing offers the wondrous world of past-performance charts and a language that is both colorful and sparse." HorseRacing TV, a subsidiary of Magna Entertainment Corporation (MEC), provides twenty-four-hour viewing of thoroughbred, harness, and quarter horse racing in the United States and Canada. Its posting of odds and results is rife with gambling potential. Judy Delin (2000, p. 40) points out how horse racing has its own vocabulary, including words such as *furlongs, make the running, breast girth, cap, soft/fast ground,* and *divots;* its commentary links clauses together, and it is speedy—so sportscasters might be using something over 188 words per minute.

Tennis

Tennis is the most overanalyzed sport on television. Just let the viewer watch the game . . . let it breathe. (Collins, cited in Hedrick, 2000, p. 141)

"This may surprise you, but if there's one sport where you *don't* need an intruder like me, it's tennis," writes Dick Enberg (2004, p. 211). "Of all sports, tennis least requires an announcer. It's absolutely the simplest TV sport of all to call. It's played in a small, defined area, usually contested between only two competitors, and any good chair umpire offers a reliable call. Those of us in the booth fill in with personal stories and strategy, while fans at home can get the basics by watching the screen and listening to the umpire." Andrew Billings (2003, p. 52) reports on how inescapable gender bias is in women's tennis reportage: "Female athletes remain the underdogs. They aren't strong enough, they aren't quick enough, they can't leap high enough."

Track and Field

> The people in the track community are the best commentators on the sport. We regular announcers are very dependent upon their knowledge because of our minimal exposure to the sport. The analyst plays a huge role. All I am there for is to tell you who's in the race, identify their jersey numbers, perhaps a little bit of info on them as they get into the starting blocks . . . basically set the scene. I let the analyst jump in and dictate the race of event, say who is in the lead coming down the stretch and the likely contenders challenging from behind. (Twibell, cited in Hedrick, 2000, p. 147)

Depending on how many competitors there are, sportscasters can squirm trying to keep an eye on all the action, but it's always a good idea to follow one or two runners.

SPORTS PSYCHOLOGY

Obviously, sports psychology is part and parcel of your whole experience. Although we may associate it with attitude, we all know that mental approach is critical both for practical and training purposes. Concerned with both mental and physical factors affecting sports performance, the general field includes everything from relaxation and visualization to goal-setting and concentration, and more. Established as an area of study by Norman Triplett of Indiana University, who studied solo cyclists versus those in pairs, research labs have been in existence since the 1920s, and today's research ranges from therapeutic aids to theories about coaches and competition.

There are two major organizations in the field: the North American Society for the Psychology of Sport and Physical Activity (www

.naspspa.org) and the International Society of Sports Psychology, which publishes the *International Journal of Sport Psychology*. In addition, there is also a great deal of scholarly work in the field (Anshel, 1994; Butler, 1996; Cox, 1990; Diamant, 1991; Goldstein, 1983; Horn, 1992; Kremer and Scully, 1994; Mechikoff, 1987; Murphy, 1995; Roberts, Spink, and Pemberton, 1986; Russell, 1993; Sheik and Korn, 1994; Singer, Hausenblas, and Janelle, 2001; Stein and Hollwitz, 1994; Todhunter, 2000;.Van Raalte and Brewer, 1996; Wann, 2001; Zimmerman and Reavill, 1998).

Once you consider psychology relative to sportscasting, it will help you realize the perspective(s) of your audience members. Mainly, you need to know there are fans rooting for both sides, and you should be careful about not being accused of showing your own biases. "Every person needs someone to teach him about broadcasting," declares Jim Kaat (cited in Smith, 1995, p. 269) "[Gene Kirby said] 'If you're doing play-by-play and say, "There's a ball in the corner, it's trouble,"—ask yourself, "Trouble for *whom*?" Don't be a homer.'"

Notice that my approach here has skirted around the negative. It's a good thing to be pumped up before a performance, but if you have followed the various suggestions here you don't need to worry about "Mike Fright"; rather, it will all flow naturally. If you still have any apprehensions, though, let me refer you to my co-authored book *Communicating Comfortably: Your Guide to Overcoming Speaking and Writing Anxieties* (Fuller and Shilling, 1990).

Psychology can also be applied to yourself. "The single most important requirement for somebody wanting to get into broadcasting is *perseverance*," (Marty Glickman, 1996, p. 184). "Stay with it, and you will become a member of the broadcasting labor force in some capacity."

"It's hard to tell young people anything," Red Barber wrote in 1970 (p. 11). "That's all right. We have to learn for ourselves. But I'm sorry to see kids today flip on their transistor radios without thinking, listen to the toneless beat, the mumbled voices, and the hard-sell commercials, and take it all for granted." How much things change, and how much things don't change.

Chapter 8

Future Concerns and Considerations about Sports and Sportscasting

The nature of television's presentation and coverage of sporting events has undergone dramatic shifts in recent years. The presence of 24-hour-a-day sports channels and the development of sports-news channels were early markers of sea changes in sports television. More recently, the introduction of specialized magazines and web sites derived from televised sports, the "discovery" of women's sports, the ascendancy of motor sports and wrestling, the "wars" over network contracts for sports coverage, and many other tremblings are manifestations of a ferment that is occurring in what has historically been one of the most tradition-bound genres of television. These dramatic changes all merit systematic study in their own right. They must be studies as phenomena that may well alter the way the "Sovereign Consumer" of the information age uses and enjoys sports.

(Bryant and Raney, 2000, p. 172)

When you consider where we are going with sports, sportscasters, and sportscasting, the puzzle clearly comes together: there is a symbiosis between sport history, economics, audiences, media, and society. Not unlike how sports teams and leagues are interdependent with their owners, fellow players, franchises, fans, and sociopolitical frameworks and constraints, you no doubt "get it," but wonder what might be next.

Sportscasters/Sportscasting

"The work of a television sportscaster is an odd job. It is neither art nor science, neither common labor nor honored profession," William O. Johnson Jr. wrote in 1971 (p. 192). "To criticize its practice, or its practitioners, is difficult and perhaps even unfair, since it really has no strict standards or firm procedures by which one can make documentable judgments. Beyond bad grammar, mispronounced names, or perhaps a cheap haircut, one may have trouble finding either a norm or a means for complaint. The sportscaster is easier to define by what he is not than by what he is. He is not quite a journalist, not quite a carnival barker, not quite an orator or an interlocutor or master of ceremonies or trained seal. Yet he is a little of all of them." Except perhaps for the assumption that the television sportscaster would be a male, we have to question what is different from this observation from three decades ago.

Are sportscasters a cultural reflection of television's dominance? Are they an elite group, who speak "boothtalk" (Jackson, 1986, p. 45); do they inform audiences, or entertain them? Is sportscasting a "profession," as such? What are the rules and roles for women and minorities to break into the field? What is the relationship between sportscasting and celebrityhood? Between sportscasting and sponsors? But most of all, what role do sportscasters play for audiences, for us sports fans? Hopefully this book begins addressing some of these issues.

John Sweeney, founder and director of the Sports Communication Program at the University of North Carolina at Chapel Hill, considers "10 controversial issues confronting the sports industry" in the January/February 2007 issue of *The Futurist* that have important implications for sportscasting. Identifying branding, ever-diversifying media, and ever-changing sports choices, the women's revolution, haves and have-nots, environmental concerns, engineered athletes, technological advances for audiences from satellites and the Internet, and the moral connections therein. What follows is a discussion about technology, sports stadiums, politics and legalities, ethics, and you and the future of sports/sportscasting. Although this is the final chapter in the book, it is meant to be the beginning of careers and continuing analysis of the field.

TECHNOLOGY

Imagine that all of the ballplayers in a sports stadium wear a small device that senses location (through the Global Positioning System or local electrical field sensing) and transmits DIS packets over a wireless network. Similar sensors are embedded in gloves, balls, bats and even shoes. A computer server in the stadium feeds telemetry inputs into a physically based articulated human model that extrapolates individual body and limb motions. The server also maintains a scene database for the stadium complete with textured images of the edifice, current weather, and representative pictures of fans in the stands. Meanwhile, Internet users have browsers that can navigate and view the stadium from any perspective. Users can also tune to multicast channels providing updated player positions and postures along with live audio and video. Statistics, background information, and multimedia home pages are available for each player. Online fan clubs and electronic mail lists let fans trade opinions and even send messages to the players. Thus any number of remote fans might supplement traditional television coverage with a live interactive computer-generated view. Perhaps the most surprising aspect of this scenario is that all component software and hardware technologies exist today. (Brutzman, Macedonia, and Zyda, 1997, p. 118)

Today, we can access sporting events on our personal computers, cell phones, and pagers, and soon, on our iPods, broadband, wireless, and on-demand. Media have evolved to where we are never without knowledge of our favorite teams and players. Smith and Westerbeek (2004) suggest we may soon have genetically engineered athletes, and virtual stadiums beaming into our living rooms.

In an era of Fantasy Baseball and Fantasy Football, the role of technology hardly has limits; consider, for example, the GoFlyCam that was introduced at the Sydney Olympics, a tiny camera made to monitor the action for track-and-field, mountain biking, and kayaking. Think about wireless technology, cell phones, computerized data, fiber optic networks, twenty-four-hour television sports coverage, video production centers, mobile telephony, interactive biosks, electronic turnstiles at ballparks, cameras built into hockey pucks and helmets, TelePrompTers spitting out stats, instant replay, the Telestrator that allows us to follow game plans, high-definition TV (HDTV), and much, much more. Technologically, it is literally a whole new ball game. Already, the Buffalo Bills and their fans can get updates through a deal with Verizon (Schaff, 2004, p. 149), and it is only a matter of time before some sports sponsor decides to offer "streaming" via customers' phone message spaces. "Better cameras can see farther and in less light than those used in television's early years, thus allowing such widely dispersed sports as golf and even sailing to be telecast," (Neal-Lunsford, 1992, p. 75). "Miniature cameras are now routinely installed in race cars, affording a view that previously could be seen only by the driver."

Consider baseball: "The national pastime has fallen prey to the national obsession—technology," according to Peter H. Lewis (2000, p. C1). "Fiber optic networks handle torrents of data flowing from voice and data links, concession stands, scoreboards, security cameras, sound systems, interactive kiosks and video production centers." He suggests it needs to change its name to "databaseball." An interactive software service called ChoiceSeat, "Lets fans call up photos, scouting reports and statistics for any player; to see a graphical representation of the position, type and speed of every pitch; to view replays from different camera angles; to follow scores of other games, and even to watch the regular live TV broadcast of the game in front of them—just like at home."

Fuller (forthcoming) has pointed out how, technologically, some sports innovations have been inspired by sportscasting: "Maybe it began with the Goodyear Blimp, but we now have cameras built into hockey pucks and helmets, TelePrompTers that can spit out statistics and clever sayings, strategically placed cameras in places like catchers' masks or racing cars, instant replay that is sometimes more interesting than the actual play." Since it was introduced for NBC's 1965 Rose Bowl football game, technology for the slow-motion ("slo-mo") videodisc recorder has been advanced by a helical-scan VTR that can record and save game plays. Now, video recorded on hard computer digital disks allows for nearly split-second repeats.

The Telestrator, a software item that, since its debut in 1981, allows commentators to add pen marks to televised images such that viewers can follow along with game diagrams, has set a standard. Although many sportscasters use it, the Telestrator remains mostly associated with John Madden.

"During the week, coaches sit down to a coaching station—typically a Macintosh computer hooked up to Avid Sports' SportsPro and SportsView video-management systems. Every station is connected via fiber-optic network funneling video through the system," (Chris Oakes, 1999). Check out some of the businesses that have joined the process: Sportsvision, FoxTrax technology, InMotion Technologies, StroMotion, ModelGolf, and more. Similarly, you might want to log on to sportsline.com, espn.com, cnnsi.com, wwf.com, majorleague baseball.com, nascar.com, nfl.com, nba.com, or sportingnews.com, and/or any number of "Sportscasting-related Web sites" listed in Appendix 9.

"NASCAR telecasts evolved from hours of left turns into a carnival of in-car views from banked turns, enhanced sound from the 750-horsepower cars and data about miles an hour and revolutions per minute," Richard Sandomir (2001, p. 8) has noted. "ESPN viewers can take viewers through the path of a bat in the strike zone and measure home runs distance. HBC distinguished one Olympic swimmer from another at the 2000 Summer Games by their nations' flags digitally inserted beneath them in their lanes." A veteran sportswriter, Sandomir sees television sports becoming more like video games than sportscasting in the future. It gives new meaning to the term, "Take me out to the ballgame."

As sportscasters well know, all this technological achievement comes with a price. Now, for example, games need to accommodate the "TV time out" especially for football and basketball, adjusted schedules, "breaking news"/potential interruptions, and the like.

SPORTS STADIUMS

Nearly 70 teams in the four major professional sports in the United States built new stadiums and arenas in the past two decades. About a dozen additional facilities are under construction, and many of the remaining franchises are interested in renovating an existing structure or building a new facility. Funding a new sports facility generally involved local public officials developing a financial package subject to a public vote. These projects are among the largest and most expensive public works a community might undertake. They have often been politically controversial. (Brown, 2002)

More than 100 venues are home to teams from MLB, NBA, NFL, NHL, MLS, and the WNBA; about one-third are privately owned. Stadium construction is at an all-time high, such that their numbers may soon double; in 2002, there was a projected cost of $7.8 billion for them, according to Lee and Chun (2002). Although money can be gleaned from sports merchandising, franchising, and endorsements, one of the more recent sources is from building stadiums that can be named for corporations or businesses, or from simply changing names of already-existing ones. By contrast, it is understood that this building boom is not manifested from need of seating space or need for repairs or replacements; rather, all the construction is yet another means to increase cash flow for inflated salaries and the costs of business. Though a new stadium might initially increase audiences, those attendees will soon discover that the real target is luxury box buyers.

Only four stadiums have hosted a Super Bowl and a World Series: Dolphin Stadium in Miami Gardens, Florida (Super Bowls XXIII, XXIX, XXXIII, and XLI plus the 1997 and 2003 World Series); The Los Angeles Coliseum in Los Angeles, California (Super Bowls XXII, XXXII, and XXXVII plus the 1984 and 1998 World Series); and The Hubert H. Humphrey Metrodome in Minneapolis, Minnesota (Super Bowl XXVI plus the 1987 and 1991 World Series). Of those, only Qualcomm Stadium hosted both in the same year (1998). Still, sports franchises have figured out how to use their monopolistic power over local governments—promising profits while extracting financial aid.

If you wonder, and worry, about stadiums being a classic example of the divisions of wealth relative to sports and sportscasting, you might want to research the topic more. Bleacher bloom helps increase the franchise value and those who can afford it certainly enjoy the fancy skyboxes and restaurants, but few families can afford to go to games. In 1994 Dean V. Baim wrote *The Sports Stadium As a Municipal Investment*, arguing for the home team; times clearly have changed since then. To get you started on learning more, you might check out Cagan and De Mause (1998), Delaney and Eckstein (2003), Noll and Zimbalist (1997). And you might be interested to know that the Sports Medium Stadium-Arena TV Advertising Network has recently announced plans to offer on-screen graphic, animation, audio, and video. Everyone, it would seem, is invested in our sports viewing. For now, your assignment is to note how often sportscasters (have to?) mention the names of their stadiums.

POLITICS AND LEGALITIES

Like all other journalists, those who specialize in sport must abide by the laws of the country in which they operate and in which their work is published or broadcast. Sports journalists will not find themselves constrained by legal considerations as often as crime correspondents or court reporters, but they cannot afford to be complacent about legal issues. (Andrews, 2005, p. 170)

As in every profession, sportscasting is infused with politics. Some of it comes from sportscasters' backgrounds, where their relationship(s) with various team players and/or leagues can't help but color their feelings. Try as they might to remain unbiased, we often can't help but pick up subtle intonation. David Rowe (1999, p. 104) points out how broadcast commentators can "get criticized not only for their technical failings and banalities, but also for bringing political issues (usually inadvertently) to the surface."

Then, too, there is office politics. We can only picture how rookies are treated, as opposed to pampered celebrity sportscasters. Who is the boss of whom? It might have to do with the "politics of the body" (Choi, 2000; Cole, Loy, and Messner, 1993; Fuller, 1999b; Guttman, 1996; Hargreaves, 2001; Lenskyj, 1994, 2000; Real, 1999; Rowe, 1995; Weitz, 2002).

Or, politics may be specific to sports and issues ranging from racism and/or sexism to national interests (Allison, 1993, 2006; Andrews and Jackson, 2001; Baker and Boyd, 1997; Barry, 2001; Blackshaw, 2002; Booth, 1998; Festle, 1996; Horrell, 1968; Houlihan and White, 2002; Jackson and Andrews, 2003; Sage, 1990; Theberge, 2000; Vinokur, 1988; Wilson and Derse, 2001). Think about boycotts of Olympic Games, or unbalanced coverage of international events, or worse—omissions.

A wide variety of books about national pastimes are available (Billet and Formwalt, 1995; Chandler, 1988; Szymanski and Zimbalist, 2005; Tomlinson and Young, 2006). Of course, there is a good deal of scholarship on nationalism and sports (Arnaud and Riordan, 1998; Baimer, 2001; Donnelly, 1997; Fuller, 2004b, 2007; Gruneau and Whitson, 1993; Hoberman, 1986; Hong, 2006; Houlihan, 1994; Larson and Park, 1993; Ingham and Loy, 1993; Maguire, 1999, 2005; Porter, 2004; Senn, 1999; Stark, 1997; Thoma and Chalip, 1996; Tomlinson and Young, 2006; Wilcox, 1994; Wilson, 1994).

Should audiences be able to expect nonbiased description and interpretation, or should audiences be subjected to team-preferred sportscasters? In the one camp is Bob Prince of KDKA, the Pirates broadcaster known as the Prince of Homers, who states: "We are not journalists as such. We are part-reporter and part-entertainer. We are there to make our rooters happy—and the other teams' rooters mad" (cited in Durslag, 1975, p. 2). Surely Johnny Most makes no pretense of objectivity regarding being a Celtics fan, and his many supporters appreciate sharing that passion. Jim McKay feels very strongly about objectivity:

> Reporting, I think, is simply the communication to someone not on the scene of a given event, a happening. The reporter's job is to tell as clearly and accurately as he can the facts of the situation and, in the case of television, to explain the meaning of the visual image on the screen. More subtly, I think the reporter must communicate the mood of the moment. What is the inner emotional reaction to the scene, in the words of one who is there?" (1973, p. 212)

John Madden (1984) has been quoted as joking that he knows he has done a good job on a game when each team complains about his favoring the other. And then too it can backfire, as with Patriot audience dislike of Bob Griese as their sportscaster because of his long-time association with the Dolphins. "Every sportscaster (and broadcaster) should know the laws and rules that govern what is allowed to go over the air and where trouble areas may occur for the individual and the station. Think before you speak," warns John R. Hitchcock (1999, p. 24).

Because it is, or at least can become, so complicated, there are a number of legal issues surrounding sport. Following is a list of books written about the topic give you an idea of what a large field it is: Berry and Wong, 1993; Blackshaw, 2002; Boyle, Flood, and Kevin, 2004; Champion, 1993; Condon et al., 2004; Cotton and Wilde, 1997; Cozzillio and Levinstein, 1997; Dougherty, 1994; Fotiades, 1989; Greenberg, 1993; Greenfield and Osborn, 2000; Hladczuk, 1991; Jarvis and Coleman, 1999; Jones, 1999; Lowe, 1995; Mitten, David, Smith, and Berry, 2005; O'Leary, 2001; Quirk, 1996; Shropshire, 1990; Tokarz, 1986; Weiler, 2000; Weiler and Roberts, 1993; Wong, 1994; Wong and Wilde, 1994; Yasser, 1985; Yasser, McCurdy, and Goplerud, 1990. Between contract law, intellectual property law, antitrust law, labor law, and more laws, you begin to realize how complicated this all can get. "Sports reporters and editors sometimes are confronted with legally ticklish situations," Douglas A. Anderson (1994, p. 285) reminds us:

- Should they report that a football player had been indicted for illegal drug use if the athlete's attorney threatens a libel suit?
- Should they report that a high school basketball player is being benched because he violated training rules? What would happen if the young man's parents brought a libel suit?
- Should they write a column about the inept way a volleyball tournament was conducted? Can opinions that cause embarrassment to officials be freely expressed?
- Should they publish information provided by an anonymous source? If the information is published, would a reporter have to reveal the source if called upon to do so in court?

Sports law, which might include anything from tort liability to contracts, keeps evolving as issues such as privacy, player-agent relations, drugs and drug testing, and anti-trust enter the marketplace. The Sports Lawyers Association (SLA), "a non-profit, international, professional organization whose common goal is the understanding, advancement and ethical practice of sports law," has more than 1,000 current members. Its mission is threefold:

- To provide educational opportunities and disseminate data and information regarding specific areas of sports law.
- To provide a forum for lawyers representing athletes, teams, leagues, conferences, civic recreational programs, educational institutions, and other organizations involved in professional, collegiate, Olympic, and amateur sports. SLA's role is to foster the discussion of legal problems affecting sports law and to promote the exchange of a variety of perspectives and positions.
- To promote and, where necessary, establish rules of ethics for its members involved in sports law.

Environmentally, we worry about sports that might not respect our landscapes, and encourage advocacy that demands golf course architects work within proscribed concerns for biodiversity, ski resort owners use caution against possible pollutions, hill and mountain climbing concerns respect our heritage, sea sports operators monitor fish and fresh air, and that all our activities think green. Legally and morally, we hope that countries and consumers work with legislators to protect our natural resources.

ETHICS

Most people are guided by a code of ethics regardless of their walk of life. But, because they are in the public eye, sportscasters have to be particularly cautious of how they conduct themselves. (Bender, 1994, p. 207)

If you are going into the profession for free tickets and other freebies, forget it. Journalism ethics, enforced at most publications, forbids the accepting of gifts. "Almost every day, broadcast reporters face ethical decisions that range from correcting errors and reacting courteously to newsmakers to intrusions on grief-stricken victims and respecting the rights of accused persons to fair trials," Roy Gibson (1991, p. 272) reminds us.

Though some people would argue that the term "media ethics" is an oxymoron, you should know that, as a member of the profession, they are actually paramount. We all know the value of credibility to one's audience, and so it behooves sportscasters to be aware of potential conflicts of interest—even the *appearance* of conflict of interest. Toward that end, avoid being accused of favoritism, or manipulated by various team owners, players, or administrators; don't get involved in point spreads, don't misrepresent yourself, and don't accept special favors. If you are covering an event, buy your own ticket—or at least have your company sponsor you.

Pete Rose has become the poster child for what can happen in sports gambling. Of course we all know that betting with bookies is against the law, but even legal betting, such as at racetracks, is best not performed at a venue you are going to cover. There is a growing literature on ethics and sport (Arnold, 1997; Berlow, 1994; DeSensi and Rosenberg, 1996; Jones, 1992; Loland, 2006; Lumpkin, Stoll, and Beller, 2003; McNamee and Parry, 1998; Shogan, 1999; Tannsjo and Tamburrini, 2000; Whannel, 2002.

Remember the advice about not having favorites? That advice can be doubly important if you bet on a team, such as baseball, football, or basketball; you might hold a grudge against them if they lose. Although we all have biases, and sports favorites, keep some opinions in check. Len Berman (2005, p. 192) confesses, "I like to think that my broadcasts have always been impartial. But I know that when I called Celtics games, friends who are Knicks fans would tell me that my broadcasts were pro-Celtic." Celtics sportscaster Johnny Most (in Carey, 2003, p. 48) felt the same way: "I saw that there was nothing wrong with rooting for the team you're covering. And from that point on, I've never felt I had to defend myself to anyone, including the holier-than-thou-media critics. Hey, how can you *not* root for guys with whom you're around 24 hours a day, guys you travel with, eat with, socialize with?" Following are the current *Ethical Guidelines of the Associated Press Sports Editors* (APSE):

1. The newspaper pays its staffer's way for travel, accommodations, food, and drink.
   a. If a staffer travels on a chartered team plane, the newspaper should insist on being billed. If the team cannot issue a bill, the amount can be calculated by estimating the cost of a similar flight on a commercial airline.
   b. When services are provided to a newspaper by a pro or college team, those teams should be reimbursed by the newspaper. This includes providing telephone, typewriter or fax service.
2. Editors and reporters should avoid taking part in outside activities or employment that might create conflict of interest or even appearance of a conflict.
   a. They should not serve as an official scorer at baseball games.
   b. They should not write for team or league media guides or other team or league publications. This has the potential of compromising a reporter's disinterested observations.
   c. Staffers who appear on radio or television should understand that their first loyalty is to the paper.
3. Writers and writers' groups should adhere to APME and APSE standards: No deals, discounts or gifts except those of insignificant value or those available to the public.
   a. If a gift is impossible or impractical to return, donate a gift to charity.
   b. Do not accept free memberships or reduced fees for memberships. Do not accept gratis use of facilities, such as golf courses or tennis courts, unless it is used as part of doing a story for the newspaper.
   c. Sports editors should be aware of standards of conduct of groups and professional associations to which their writers belong and the ethical standards to which those groups adhere, including areas such as corporate sponsorship from news sources it covers.
4. A newspaper should not accept free tickets, although press credentials needed for coverage and coordination are acceptable.

5. A newspaper should carefully consider the implications of voting for all awards and all-star teams and decide if such voting creates a conflict of interest.
6. A newspaper's own ethical guidelines should be followed, and editors and reporters should be aware of standards acceptable for use of unnamed sources and verification of information obtained other than from primary news sources.
   a. Sharing and pooling of notes and quotes should be discouraged. If a reporter uses quotes gained secondhand, that should be made known to the readers. A quote could be attributed to a newspaper or to another reporter.
7. Assignments should be made on merit, without regard for race or gender.

Guidelines can't cover everything. Use common sense and good judgment in applying these guidelines in adopting local codes.

Pulitzer Prize-winner Howard Rosenberg of the *Los Angeles Times* was critical about jingoistic sportscasters' reportage of the 1984 Olympic Games: "Winning is finishing first. Everything else is losing. Agree? If so, you may be watching too much Olympicsvision on ABC. There are many nations whose teams at the Summer Olympics will not break into TV here. That's because they are unlikely to win a gold medal" (cited in Fischer, 1995, p. 122). In terms of the ethics of sportscasting, media on media, it would be difficult to find a better case for our First Amendment.

YOU AND THE FUTURE OF SPORTSCASTERS/SPORTSCASTING

As we consider the future, we should recall our sporting past. Remember that baseball began in the 1870s, around the time that hockey was started. James Naismith invented basketball in 1891, while the American form of football, a variant of English rugby, took its present form at the turn of the century. As we move ahead, it is frightening to see so many "reality" programs on television, and we can worry about returning to the 1970's attempts at "trash sports." In the 1970s, there were many TV shows with celebrities matched up in sports like tennis or golf; they pale by comparison to today's fare, but by now you have learned how ratings rule.

One of the key ways of maintaining your professional integrity, and reputation, is by having strict standards for getting and citing sources. Put out your personal barometer, and try to get material that your audience can relate to and use. Ethics can be situational, but when it comes to sportscasting you can help keep the field above board.

"I've always been concerned about the motivation for television criticism, but the longer I've been in the industry, the more I've been able to accept the necessity for it and the positive impact it can have," (Jim Spence, 1988, p. 307). "These days I think the print media, with its probing and picking, serves a useful function in many areas, not least in keeping the electronic media on its toes." Yet another field you might consider, is sports photography.

In the January 2005 issue of *The Futurist,* Robin Gunston, chairman of Futures Thinking (www.futurestrust.org.nz), identified key trends that will shape sports in the twenty-first century:

- Sports have become an entertainment business. As a result, stadiums have become billboards, athletes have become celebrities, and competitions have become sense-bombarding experiences.
- An emerging trend that seems likely to continue is the demise of team sports and the ascendance of individual sports. This trend seems closely associated with changes to work-life balance and the culture of individualism apparent in most of Generation X. The serious fitness addict or sporting person is turning more to individual pursuits—such as triathlons, marathons, the personal fitness regimen at the gym, and Ironman competitions—to achieve prowess.
- The majority of team sports, including baseball, basketball, soccer, and rugby, are in professional leagues and managed as business franchises. Business owners, however much they may like a sport or a club, want one thing above all else: a better-than-normal rate of return on their investment.

- The trend for sports people to enhance their performance through substances is not a modern one. Both coaches and pharmaceutical interests have been trying to find drugs that avoid detection.
- New directions in sports could emerge as a result of the development of high-technology equipment. Sports are no longer just pastimes. They are big business. Over a twenty-year period, there has been a 10,000 percent increase in sports sponsorship, affecting every possible sport imaginable. Without sponsors, there will be no teams or individual superstar athletes.
- Another strong influence on the shape of modern sports is the ongoing conflict between amateurs and professionals.

Anticipating growth in niche sports, along with continuing support for and interest in the wide array of sports that we already enjoy—both as spectators and as participants, we can clearly assume that sportscasters and sportscasting will remain with the industry for a long time. My own personal hope is for the following: expanded languages for sportscasting, such as in ESPN Deportes Spanish-language broadcasts, inclusion of disabled persons in all aspects of sport, and a continuing concern for ethical conduct.

As you will notice from Appendix 2 "Autobiographies, Biographies, and Books About Sportscasters," a number of sports biographies have had help from sportswriters and many sports books in general have been ghostwritten outright for various athletes and coaches. Because you undoubtedly have a way with words, you may at some point be approached to help out in this way, but be aware that you take your chances if you enter into financial arrangements with anyone or any field you may be covering.

Roberta E. Pearson (1988, p. 15) includes announcers' predictive function to several others (e.g., establishing interpretive frameworks, remembrance, description, and summary, demonstrating how they "act as narrators, selecting, ordering, and interpreting events). In performing the prediction function, the announcers act as readers, marshalling the information which the 'text' of the game has provided up to that point, and sharing it with the viewer in the form of graphically displayed statistics and replays, which presumably have predictive capacity."

Although we cannot completely predict the future of sportscasting, we can easily see that its role will continue to evolve. As sports (Lipsyte, 1991) and sportscasting continue to become more recognized as academic subjects, and as we as spectator-consumers continue to become more critical, my strong prediction is that our experiences can only keep us all scoring well.

Appendix 1

Acronyms

ABC	American Broadcasting Company
ACC	Atlantic Coast Conference
BCS	Bowl Championship Series
CATV	Community Antenna Television (cable television)
CBS	Columbia Broadcasting System
ESPN	Entertainment and Sports Programming Network
HBO	Home Box Office
MLB	Major League Baseball
MSG	Madison Square Garden
NAB	National Association of Broadcasters
NASCAR	National Association of Sports Cars of America
NBA	National Basketball Association
NBC	National Broadcasting Company
NCAA	National Collegiate Athletic Association
NESN	New England Sports Network
NFL	National Football League
NHL	National Hockey League
OG	Olympic Games
PGA	Professional Golfers Association
YES	Yankee Entertainment and Sports Network

Appendix 2

Autobiographies, Biographies, and Books about Sports Journalists

Albert, Marv with Rick Reilly (1993). *I'd love to but I have a game: 27 years without a life.* New York: Doubleday.

Allen, Mel (1964). *You can't beat the hours.* New York: Harper and Row.

Allen, Mel with Frank Graham, Jr. (1959). *It takes heart.* New York: Harper and Brothers.

Barber, Red (1947). *When all hell broke loose in baseball.* Garden City, NY: Doubleday & Co.

Barber, Red (1970). *The broadcasters.* New York: Dial Press.

Barber, Red (1997). *Rhubarb in the catbird seat.* Lincoln, NB: Bison Books.

Bender, Gary with Michael L. Johnson (1994). *Call of the game: What really goes on in the broadcast booth.* Chicago, IL: Bonus Books.

Berkow, Ira (1986). *Red: A biography of Red Smith.* New York: Times Books.

Berman, Len (2005). *Spanning the world: The crazy universe of big time sports, all-star egos, and Hall of Fame bloopers.* New York: William Morrow.

Borelli, Stephen (2005). *How about that! The life of Mel Allen.* Champaign, IL: Sports Publishing.

Bradshaw, Terry with David Fisher (2001). *It's only a game.* New York: Atria.

Bradshaw, Terry with David Fisher (2002). *Keep it simple.* New York: Atria.

Brickhouse, Jack (1996). *A voice for all seasons.* Chicago, IL: Contemporary.

Brickhouse, Jack with Jack Rosenberg and Ned Colletti (1986). *Thanks for listening.* South Bend, IN: Diamond Communications.

Buck, Jack (2003). *Forever a winner.* Champaign, IL: Sports Publishing.

Buck, Jack with Bob Rains and Bob Broeg (1997). *That's a winner!* Champaign, IL: Sagamore Publishing.

Sportscasters/Sportscasting

Cannon, James J. (1978). *Nobody asked me, but . . . The world of Jimmy Cannon.* New York: Holt, Rinehart.

Caray, Harry with Bob Verdi (1989). *Holy cow!* New York: Villard Books.

Carey, Mike with Jamie Most (2003). *High above courtside: The lost memoirs of Johnny Most.* Champaign, IL: Sports Publishing.

Castiglione, Joe with Douglas B. Lyons (2004). *Broadcast rites and sites: I saw it on the radio with the Boston Red Sox.* Lanham, MD: Taylor Trade Publishing.

Coleman, Ken (1973). *So you want to be a sportscaster: The techniques and skills of sports announcing by one of the country's most experienced broadcasters.* Brist, UK: Hawthorn.

Coleman, Ken and Valenti, Dan (1982). *Diary of a sportscaster.* Pittsfield, MA: Literations.

Coleman, Ken and Valenti, Dan (2000). *Talking on air: A broadcaster's life in sports.* Champaign, IL: Sports Publishing.

Cope, Myron (2002). *Double yoi! A revealing memoir by the broadcaster/writer.* Champaign, IL: Sports Publishing.

Cosell, Howard (1974). *Like it is.* Chicago, IL: Playboy Press.

Cosell, Howard with Peter Bonaventre (1985). *I never played the game.* New York: William Morrow and Company, Inc.

Cosell, Howard with Mickey Herskowitz (1973). *Cosell.* Chicago, IL: Playboy Press.

Cosell, Howard with Shelby Whitfield (1991). *What's wrong with sports.* New York: Simon & Schuster.

Costas, Bob (2001). *Fair ball: A fan's case for baseball.* New York: Broadway Books.

Costas, Bob with Buzz Bissinger (1998). *Costas on baseball.* New York: Broadway.

Cousy, Bob with Albert Hirshberg (1958). *Basketball is my life.* Englewood Cliffs, NJ: Prentice Hall.

Deford, Frank (2000). *The best of Frank Deford: I'm just getting started.* Chicago, IL: Triumph Books.

Drysdale, Don with Bob Verdi (1990). *Once a bum, always a Dodger: My life in baseball from Brooklyn to Los Angeles.* New York: St. Martin's Press.

Dunphy, Don (1988). *Don Dunphy at Ringside.* New York: H. Holt.

Edwards, Bob (1993). *Fridays with Red (Barber): A radio friendship.* New York: Simon and Schuster.

Eisenstock, Alan (2001). *Sports talk: A journey inside the world of sports talk radio.* New York: Pocket Books.

Elston, Gene (2005). *The wide world of sports: Over a century of amusing stories and quotes.* Bloomington, IN: Authorhouse.

Enberg, Dick with Jim Perry (2004). *On my!* Champaign, IL: Sports Publishing.

Feherty, David (2003). *Somewhere in Ireland, a village is missing an idiot.* New York: Rugged Land.

Franklin, Pete with Terry Pluto (1988). *You could argue but you'd be wrong.* Chicago, IL: Contemporary Books.

Garagiola, Joe (1990). *Baseball is a funny game.* New York: HarperCollins.

Garner, Joe (1999). *And the crowd goes wild: Relive the most celebrated sporting events ever broadcast.* Naperville, IL: Sourcebooks.

Garner, Joe (2000). *And the fans roared: The sports broadcasts that kept us on the edge of our seats.* Naperville, IL: Sourcebooks.

Gifford, Frank (1976). *Gifford on courage.* New York: Evans.

Gifford, Frank with Harry Waters (1993). *The whole ten yards.* New York: Random House.

Glickman, Marty (1996). *Fastest kid on the block.* Syracuse, NY: Syracuse University Press.

Gowdy, Curt with Al Hirshberg (1966). *Cowboy at the mike.* Garden City, NY: Doubleday & Co.

Gowdy, Curt with John Powers (1993). *Seasons to remember: The way it was in American sports, 1945-1960.* New York: HarperCollins.

Graham, Frank, Jr. (1981, 2003). *A farewell to heroes.* Carbondale, IL: Southern Illinois University Press.

Greenberg, Mike (2006). *Why my wife thinks I'm an idiot: The life and times of a sportscaster dad.* New York: Villard.

Green, Tim (1997). *The dark side of the game: My life in the NFL.* New York: Warner.

Greenwald, Hank (1997). *This copyrighted broadcast.* San Francisco, CA: Woodford Press.

Hamilton, Milo, Schlossberg, Dan, and Ibach, Bob (2006). *Making airwaves: 60 years at Milo's microphone.* Champaign, IL: Sports Publishing.

Harmon, Merle with Sam Blair (1998). *Merle Harmon stories.* Arlington, TX: Reid Publishing.

Harwell, Ernie (1985). *Tuned to baseball.* South Bend, IN: Diamond Communications.

Harwell, Ernie (1991). *Ernie Harwell's diamond gems.* Ann Arbor, MI: Momentum.

Harwell, Ernie (2001). *Stories from my life in baseball.* Detroit, MI: Detroit Free Press.

Harwell, Ernie (2002). *The Babe signed my shoe.* South Bend, IN: Diamond Communications.

Harwell, Ernie (2004). *Life after baseball.* Detroit, MI: Detroit Free Press.

Hearn, Chick and Springer, Steve (2004). *Chick: His unpublished memoirs and the memories of those who loved him.* Chicago, IL: Triumph Books.

Hodges, Russ (1952). *Baseball complete.* New York: Grosset and Dunlop.

Hodges, Russ (1963). *My Giants.* New York: Doubleday.

Hubbell, Ralph (1975). *Come Walk with Me.* Englewood Cliffs, NJ: Prentice-Hall.

Hughes, Libby (2005). *Ronald Reagan: From sports to movies to politics.* iUniverse.

Jackson, Tom with Woodrow Paige (1987). *Blitz: An autobiography.* New York: NTC/Contemporary.

Johnston, Daryl (2005). *Watching football: Discovering the game within the game.* Globe Pequot.

Keegan, Tom (2002). *Ernie Harwell.* Chicago, IL: Triumph Books.

Kiner, Ralph with Joe Gergen (1987). *Kiner's korner: At bat and on the air: My 40 years in baseball.* New York: Arbor House.

Kornheiser, Tony (2003). *I'm back for more cash: a Tony Kornheiser collection (Because you can't take two hundred newspapers into the bathroom).* New York: Villard.

LaRussa, Tony, Carole Buck, Joe Buck, and Julie Buck (2003). *Jack Buck: Forever a winner.* Champaign, IL: Sports Publishing, Inc..

Lawler, Jerry with Doug Asheville (2003). *It's good to be king . . . sometimes.* New York: World Wrestling Entertainment Books.

Levine, Ken (1993). *It's gone! . . . No, wait a minute. . .: Talking my way into the big leagues at 40.* New York: Villard Books.

Lupica, Mike (1988). *Shooting from the Lip: Essays, columns, quips, and gripes in the grand tradition of dyspeptic sports writing.* Chicago, IL: Bonus Books.

Madden, John (1988). *One size doesn't fit all.* New York: Villard Books.

Madden, John with Dave Anderson (1984). *Hey, wait a minute, I wrote a book!* New York: Villard Books.

Madden, John with Dave Anderson (1996). *All Madden: Hey, I'm talking pro football!* New York: HarperCollins.

Matthews, Denny with Matt Fulks (2006). *Tales from the Royals dugout.* Champaign, IL: Sports Publishing

Matthews, Denny with Fred White and Matt Fulks (1999). *Play by play: 25 years of Royals on radio.* Lenexa, KS: Addax Publishing Group.

Matthews, Denny with Matt Fulks (2006). *Tales from the Royals dugout.* Champaign, IL: Sports Publishing.

McCarver, Tim with Ray Robinson (1987). *Oh, Baby, I Love It!* New York: Villard Books.

McKay, Jim (1973). *My wide world.* New York: Macmillan Publishing Co.

McKay, Jim (1998). *The real McKay: My wide world of sports.* New York: Dutton.

Miller, Jon with Mark Hyman (1998). *Confessions of a baseball purist: What's right— and wrong—with baseball, as seen from the best seat in the house.* Baltimore, MD: Johns Hopkins University Press.

Nelson, Lindsey (1985). *Hello everybody, I'm Lindsey Nelson.* New York: William Morrow and Co.

Nelson, Lindsey with Al Hirshberg (1966). *Backstage at the Mets.* New York: The Viking Press.

Olbermann, Keith and Dan Patrick (1997). *The big show: Inside ESPN's SportsCenter.* New York: Pocket Books.

Oppenheim, Louis (Ed.) (1994). *Chris names: An illustrated guide to Chris Berman's unique characterizations of sports personalities.* Kansas City, MO: Andrews & McMeel.

Packer, Billy (1999). *Why we win: Great American coaches offer their strategies for success in sports and life.* New York: McGraw-Hill.

Packer, Billy with Roland Lazenby (1986). *Hoops: Confessions of a college basketball analyst.* New York: Contemporary Books.

Petterchak, Janice A. (1996). *Jack Brickhouse: A voice for all seasons.* Chicago, IL: Contemporary Books.

Peyer, Tom and Hart Seely (Eds.) (1997). *O Holy Cow: The selected verse of Phil Ruzzuto.* New York: Ecco Press.

Rashad, Ahmad with Peter Bodo (1988). *Rashad: Vikes, mikes and something on the backside.* New York: Penguin.

Remy, Jerry with Corey Sandler (2004). *Watching baseball: Discovering the game within the game.* Guilford, CT: Globe Pequot.

Reynolds, Bill (2005). (Bob) *Cousy: His life, career, and the birth of big-time basketball.* New York: Simon and Schuster.

Rice, Grantland (1954). *The tumult and the shouting: My life in sport.* New York: Barnes.

Russo, Chris and St. John, Allen (2006). *Mad dog hall of fame: The ultimate top-ten rankings of the best in sport.* New York: Doubleday.

Schaap, Dick (2001). *Flashing before my eyes: 50 years of headlines, deadlines, and punchlines.* Waterville, Maine: Thorndike Press.

Schemmel, Jerry with Kevin Simpson (1996). *Chosen to live: The inspiring story of Flight 232 survivor Jerry Schemmel.* Redwood City, CA: Victory Publishing.

Sherrod, Blackie (1988). *The Blackie Sherrod collection.* Dallas, TX: Taylor Publishing.

Smith, Curt (1978). *America's Dizzy Dean.* Bloomington, MN: Bethany Press.

Smith, Curt (1992). *Voices of the game: The acclaimed chronicle of baseball broadcasting.* New York: Fireside Publishing.

Smith, Curt (1995). *The storytellers: From Mel Allen to Bob Costas: 60 years of baseball tales from the broadcast booth.* New York: Macmillan.

Smith, Curt (1998). *Of mikes and men: From Roy Scott to Curt Gowdy: Broadcast tales from the pro football booth.* Lanham, MD: Diamond Communications.

Smith, Curt (2005). *Voices of summer: Baseball's greatest announcers.* New York: Carroll and Graf.

Stern, Bill (1949). *Bill Stern's favorite baseball stories.* Garden City, NY: Blue Ribbon Books.

Stone, Steve with Barry Rozner (1999). *Where's Harry? Steve Stone remembers his years with Harry Caray.* Dallas: Taylor Publishing.

Storm, Hannah and Mark Jenkins (2002). *Go girl: Raising healthy, confident, and successful girls through sports.* Naperville, IL: Sourcebooks.

Stram, Hank with Lou Sahadi (1986). *They're playing my game.* New York: William Morrow.

Summerall, Pat (2006). *Summerall: On and off the air.* Chicago, IL: Nelson.

Thompson, Chuck with Gordon Beard (1996). *Ain't the beer cold!* South Bend, IN: Diamond Communications.

Thornley, Stew (1991). *Holy cow! The life and times of Halsey Hall.* Cambridge, MN: Nodin Press.

Uecker, Bob with Mickey Herskowitz (1982). *Catcher in wry.* New York: Penguin.

Vitale, Dick with Curry Kirkpatrick (1988). *Vitale: just your average bald, one-eyed basketball wacko who beat the ziggy and became a PTP'er.* New York: Simon and Schuster.

Vitale, Dick with Dick Weiss (2003). *Dick Vitale's living dream: Reflections on 25 years sitting in the best seat in the house.* Champaign, IL: Sports Publishing.

Whitaker, Jack (1998). *Preferred lies and other tales: Skimming the cream of a life in sports.* New York: Simon and Schuster.

Wolf, Warner with William Taaffe (1983). *Gimme a break!* New York: McGraw-Hill.

Wolf, Warner with Larry Weisman (2000). *Let's go to the videotape! All the plays—and replays—from my life in sports.* New York: Warner Books.

Wolfe, Rich and Castle, George (1998). *I remember Harry Caray.* Champaign, IL: Sports Publishing, Inc.

Wolff, Bob (1992). *It's not who won or lost the game: It's how you sold the beer.* Lanham, MD: Diamond Communications.

Appendix 3

Sportscasters: A Partial Listing

Kenny Albert
Marv Albert
Mel Allen
Joe Angel
Greg Anthony
Richie Ashburn
Red Barber
Johnny Bench
Chris Berman
Len Berman
Bonnie Bernstein
Bud Blattner
Terry Bowden
Terry Bradshaw
Bob Brenly
Thom Brennaman
Marty Brennaman
Jack Brickhouse
Tom Brookshier
James Brown
Jack Buck
Joe Buck
Buck Canel
Harry Caray
Skip Caray
Mary Carillo
Herb Carneal
Joe Castiglione
Tom Cheek
Don Cherry
Gil Clancy

Eric Clemons
Linda Cohn
Jerry Coleman
Ken Coleman
Cris Collingsworth
Bud Collins
Myron Cope
Howard Cosell
Bob Costas
Bob Cousy
Irv Cross
Randy Cross
Bill Curry
Howard David
Dizzy Dean
Dan Dierdorf
Mike Ditka
John Dockery
Jerry Doggett
Jimmy Dudley
Don Drysdale
Don Dunphy
Ian Eagle
Bob Elson
Gene Elston
Mike Emrick
Dick Enberg
Julius Erving
David Feherty
Roy Firestone
Peggy Fleming

Lanny Frattare
Joe Garagiola
Gayle Gardner
Joe Gibbs
Frank Gifford
Earl Gillespie
Jerry Glanville
Marty Glickman
Bob Golic
Curt Gowdy
Jim Gray
Tim Green
Hank Greenwald
Lisa Guerrero
Bryant Gumbel
Greg Gumbel
Pat Haden
Halsey Hall
Milo Hamilton
Tom Hammond
Kevin Harlan
Merle Harmon
Ken Harrelson
Ernie Harwell
Chick Hearn
Tom Heinsohn
Dan Hicks
Russ Hodges
Mark Holtz
Pat Hughes
Jim Hunter
Ted Husing
Keith Jackson
Tom Jackson
Jaime Jarrin
Ron Jaworski
Ernie Johnson
Daryl Johnston
Charlie Jones
Jim Kaat
Harry Kalas
Len Kasper
George Kell

Ralph Kiner
Tony Kornheiser
Andrea Kremer
Tony Kubek
Jim Lampley
Jerry Lawler
Cawoof Ledford
Ken Levine
Vince Lloyd
Verne Lundquist
John Madden
Paul Maguire
Mark Malone
Dan Marino
Ned Martin
Denny Matthews
Bill McAtee
Tim McCarver
Tim McCormick
Arch McDonald
Sean McDonough
John McEnroe
Al McGuire
Jim McKay
Larry Merchant
Don Meredith
George Michael
Al Michaels
Matt Millen
Johnny Miller
Jon Miller
Van Miller
Monte Moore
Ted Moore
Joe Morgan
Johnny Most
Anthony Munoz
Bob Murphy
Brent Musburger
Jim Nantz
Lindsey Nelson
David Niehaus
Keith Olbermann

Merlin Olsen
Don Orsillo
Billy Packer
Ron Pitts
Bob Prince
Mel Proctor
Felo Ramírez
Jay Randolph
Ahmad Rashad
Ronald Reagan
Beasley Reece
Pee Wee Reese
Jerry Remy
Phil Rizzuto
Robin Roberts
Ted Robinson
John Rooney
Sam Rosen
Bill Russell
Byrum Saam
Billy Sample
Ron Santo
Jerry Schemmel
Chris Schenkel
Ray Scott
Vin Scully
Lon Simmons
Phil Simms
Ken Singleton
Dewayne Staats

Melissa Stark
Bob Starr
John Sterling
Bill Stern
Jackie Stewart
Dick Stockton
Hannah Storm
Hank Stram
Pat Summerall
Joe Theismann
Chuck Thompson
Mike Tirico
Al Trautwig
Bob Trumpy
Jerry Trupiano
Ty Tyson
Bob Uecker
Dave Van Horne
Lesley Visser
Dick Vitale
Murray Walker
Bill Walton
Pam Ward
Pete Weber
Jack Whitaker
Ken Wilson
Warner Wolf
Bob Wolff
Dave Zinkoff

Appendix 4

Sportscasting-related Journals, Periodicals, Magazines, Newspapers, and E-zines

A

ABC Sports (http://sports.espn.go.com)
Aethlon: The Journal of Sport Literature
American Journal of Sports Medicine
American Sports WebZine
Arena Review
Athletic Business
Athletic Insight: The Online Journal of Sport Psychology
Athletic Journal
Australian Society for Sports History

B

Black Sports
British Journal of Sports Medicine

C

Canadian Journal of Applied Sport Science
Culture, Sport, Society
Cybersport

D

Daily Mail online newsletter (London)
Daily Sport Newspaper

E

ESPN The Magazine
eSports Media Group
Ethics in Sport
European Journal of Sport Science

F

Fitnessmanagement.com
Fox Sports (msn.foxsports.com)

G

Gender, Sport and Society Forum (GSSF)
GNEXT Entertainment

H

Her Sports
Howard Bloom's SBN (sportsbusinessnews.com)
Human Kinetics

I

Inside Sport
International Bulletin of Sports Information
International Journal of the History of Sport
International Journal of Sport Nutrition and Exercise Metabolism
International Journal of Sport Psychology
International Review for the Science of Sport
International Review for the Sociology of Sport (IRSS)
International Review of Sport Sociology
International Sports Journal
iPlayOutside

J

Japanese Journal of Sociology of Sport
Jewish Sports
Journal of Applied Sports Psychology
Journal of Athletic Training
Journal of Broadcasting & Electronic Media
Journal of the Philosophy of Sport (JPS)
Journal of Science and Medicine in Sport
Journal of Sport and Social Issues (JSSI)

Journal of Sport Behavior
Journal of Sport History
Journal of Sport and Exercise Psychology (JSEP)
Journal of Sport Management (JSM)
Journal of Sport Rehabilitation
Journal of Sports Economics
Journal of Sports Science and Medicine

L

La Gazzetta dello Sport (Italy)
Legalball
Leisure Sciences
Leisure Studies: The Journal of the Leisure Studies Association
L'Equipe (France)

M

Managing Leisure
Marca (Spain)
Media and Communications Studies (MCS)
Medicine & Science in Sports & Exercise
MetroSport (Greece)
Mind Sports Worldwide
MinorLeagueNews.com

N

N.A.S.S.S. newsletter (North American Society for the Sociology of Sport)
National Sport Information Centre: SportScan
Nemzeti Sport (Hungary)
Newcastle University Sport Newsletter (UK)
New Zealand Academy Of Sport Newsletter
North American Society for Sport History Newsletter

O

Olympian
Olympic Message
Olympic Review
Olympika: The International Journal of Olympic Studies

P

Palaestra
Play and Culture
Psychology and Sociology of Sport
Psychology of Sport and Exercise

Q

Quest (The official journal of the National Association for Kinesiology and Physical Education in Higher Education)

R

Real Sports
Record (Portugal)
Research Quarterly for Exercise and Sport

S

Scandinavian Journal of Medicine & Science in Sports
Science & Sports
SeeJaneRunSports
Seton Hall Journal of Sport Law
Silent Sports
Sky Sportzine
The Sociology of Sport Journal (SSJ)
Sovietski Sport (Russia)
Spirit of Sport
Sport
Sport (Slovakia)
Sport Business (UK)
SportBusiness.com
Sport and Fitness Index
Sport, Education and Society
Sport Ekspress (Russia)
Sport Ethics (Australian)
Sport First (UK)
Sport History Review
Sport in Society
Sport Management Magazine
Sport Marketing Quarterly (SMQ)
Sport and Recreation Information Group (SPRIG)
Sport and Technology
Sport History Review (SHR)

The Sport Journal (www.thesportjournal.org)
The Sport Psychologist (TSP)
SportScan
The Sporting News
Sports Illustrated/CNN
Sports 'n Spokes (wheelchair sports)
SportScience (sportsci.org)
Sportzblitz Sports Magazines
Sports Business Research Network
The Sports Critics
Sports Engineering
SportsFan
Sports Jones
SportsLetter
Sports Medicine
SportsNews
Sportspages.com
Sports Weekly
Sports Worlds
Sportsweb (Norway)
SportzBlitz
SportZine
Street and Smith's Sports Annuals
Street and Smith's Sports Business Journal
SUNY Brockport Sport E-Newsletter

T

TouSports (Switzerland)
Tour de Sport

U

United Athletes

W

Women in Sport and Physical Activity Journal
Women's Sports and Fitness
Women'Sports Wire

Appendix 5

Sportscasting-related Resources for Racial Minorities

African American in Sports: Black American History
www.africanaonline.com/sport_golden_area.htm

African American Sports websites: Blacks and Sports Directory
www.blackrefer.com/sports2.html

African-Americans in the Sports Arena: Long Island University, C.W. Post campus
www.liu.edu/cwis/cwp/library/aaitsa.htm

Asian Sports Stars & Athletes: Richard E. Lapchick and ESPN
www.asian-nation.org/sports.shtml

Black Athlete Sports Network
www.blackathlete.com

Blackbaseball.com: Negro Baseball Leagues
www.blackbaseball.com

Black College Football Online: Historically Black Colleges and Universities (HBCU)
www.onnidan.com

Black College Sports
www.blackcollegesports.org

Black College Sports Online
www.blackcollegesportsonline.com

Black Sports Agents Association
www.blacksportsagents.com

Black Sports Network
www.blacksportsnetwork.com

Sportscasters/Sportscasting

Black Women in Sport Foundation
www.blackwomeninsport.org

Hampton Roads African American Sports Hall of Fame
www.hraashf.org/index.php

The History of Jim Crow: African American "Firsts" in Sports
www.jimcrowhistory.org/geography/sports.htm

Inside Black College Sports
www.ibcsports.com

It's a Black Thang: African American Sports-Related Artwork
www.itsablackthang.com

Javanoir: A Selected Guide to African-American Resources on the Internet
www.javanoir.net/guide/sports.html

National Black Sports and Entertainment Hall of Fame
http://harlemdiscover.com/halloffame

Negro Leagues Baseball Museum
www.nlbm.com

Onnidan's Black College Sports Online Front Page
www.onnidan.com

Seeing Black
www.seeingblack.com/x122302/2002sports.shtml

The Struggle of the Black Athlete: Afro-American Web Ring
www.geocities.com/dblimbrick

The SWAC Page Network (TSPN): Rashad Communications
www.swacpage.com

The Urban Connection: Black Sports
www.urbanconnect.com/sports.htm

Appendix 6

Sportscasting-related Resources for Women

Association for Women in Sports Media (AWSM)
www.awsmonline.org

Black Women in Sport Foundation
www.blackwomeninsport.org

Canadian Association for the Advancement of Women and Sport and Physical Activity (CAAWS)
www.caaws.ca

Feminist Internet Gateway: Women and Girls in Sport
www.feminist.org/gateway/feministgateway-results.asp?category1 = sports

Gender Equity in College Sports
http://chrobnicle.com/stats/genderequity

Gender Equity in Sports: University of Iowa libraries
http://bailiwick.lib.uniowa.edu/ge

Gender, Sport and Society Forum
www.gssf.co.nr

Go, Girl! magazine

Japanese Association for Women in Sport
www.jws.or.jp

Just Sports for Women

The Many Faces of Jane Curry: "Nice Girls Don't Sweat"
www.usfamily.net/webdllund/jac/faces.htm

Melpomene Institute: Women's and Girls' Health and Physical Activity
www.melpomene.org

Sportscasters/Sportscasting

Mindspring Sports Links
http://library.scsu.ctstateu.edu/womenbib.html#Cat27

Moms on Boards: Surf, Snow, Wake, Skate, Body, etc.
www.momsonboards.com

National Women's Law Center, Washington, D.C.
www.nwlc.org

Pink Phoenix Dragon Boat Team: Breast Cancer Survivors
www.pinkphoenix.org

Pretty Tough Sports—Everything for the Female Athlete
www.prettytough.com

Real Sports Magazine
www.real-sports.com/homepage.htm

Real Women in Sports
www.realwomeninsports.com

SheLovesSports.Com
www.shelovessports.com

Silent Edge (advocacy for figure skaters, including news of sexual abuse and harassment in sports)
www.silent-edge.org

Smith College: Women, including Sendra Berenson and Dorothy Sears Ainsworth papers
www.smith.edu/libraries/libs/archives

Sports Jones Magazine
www.sportsjones.com

Tucker Center for Research on Girls and Women in Sport, University of Minnesota
http://education.umn.edu/tuckercenter

Women IN Xtreme Sports
www.winxs.net

Womenspace: Canadian Women's Internet Directory
http://directory.womenspace.ca

Women's Exercise Network
http://womensexercisenetwork.com

Women's Sports Foundation: New York (founded in 1974 by Billie Jean King)
www.womenssportsfoundation.org/cgi-bin/iowa/index.html

Women's Sports Foundation: UK
www.wsf.org.uk

Women's Sports Net
www.womenssportsnet.com

Women's Sports Wire
www.womensportswire.com

WomenSport International
www.sportsbiz.bz/womensportinternational

Women Sports Online: Celebrating the Achievement of the Female Athlete
www.womensportsonline.com

WWW Women's Sports Page, University of Texas

Appendix 7

Sportscasting-related Schools, Libraries, Museums, and Archives

Note: many colleges and universities have sports-related documents; you might check them out individually at SIRC Sport Research: http://www .sirc.ca/online_resources/sportquest_physed.cfm)

Amateur Athletic Foundation of Los Angeles: Avery Brundage Collection, Ralph Miller Golf Collection, USATF National Track and Field Research Library, Olympian Oral Histories, etc.
www.aafla.org

Boston (MA) Public Library: Boston Tradition in Sports
www.bpl.org/research/special/collections.htm

Center for the Study of Sport in Society—Northeastern University, Boston, MA
www.sportinsociety.org

Centre for the Sociology of Sport, Leicester University, Leicester, UK
www.le.ac.uk/sociology/css

International Association for Sports Information (IASI)
www.iasi.org

International Association of Sports Museums and Halls of Fame (IASMHF)
www.sportshalls.com

Library of Congress: Baseball cards, Jackie Robinson papers, Wesley Branch Rickey papers, etc.
www.loc.gov/rr/mss

Marquette University Law School National Sports Law Institute
http://law.marquette.edu/cgi-bin/site.pl?21308pageID = 160

Sportscasters/Sportscasting

National Baseball Hall of Fame and Museum Archives, Cooperstown, NY
www.baseballhalloffame.org

National Sporting Library, Middleburg, VA: Horse and Field sports
www.nsf.org

New York Public Library: turnverein, Yankees Baseball, Spalding Collection, etc.
www.nypl.org/digital

North American Sport Library Network (NASLIN)
www.naslin.org

Open Archives Initiative (OAI), University of Illinois at Urbana-Champaign
www.openarchives.org

Smith College: women, including Sendra Berenson and Dorothy Sears Ainsworth papers
www.smith.edu/libraries/libs/archives

Sport and Recreation Information Group (SPRIG)
www.sprig.org.uk

The Sporting News Research Center: 1.2 million photos, media guides, and clipping files on individuals and subjects
www.sportingnews.com/archives/research

Springfield College: Luther Halsey Gulick, Larry O'Brien, and other papers, James Naismith scrapbook, American Alliance for Health, Physical Education, Recreation and Dance (AAHPERD) archives, etc.
www.spfldcol.edu/homepage/library.nsf/home

Tucker Center for Research on Girls and Women in Sport, University of Minnesota
http://education.umn.edu/tuckercenter

UNESCO Archives Portal
www.unesco.org/webworld/portal_archives

United States Sports Academy, Daphne, Alabama
www.ussa.edu

University of Idaho: Repositories of primary sources
www.uidaho.edu/special-collections/nuentry.htm

University of Minnesota: Tucker Center for Research on Girls and Women in Sport
http://education.umn.edu/tuckercenter

Wharton Sports Business Initiative, University of Pennsylvania, Kenneth Shropshire, Director; sportsbusiness@wharton.upenn.edu
http://wsb.wharton.upenn.edu

World Sport Publishers' Association, Aachen, Germany
www.meyer-meyer-sports.com/wsa

Appendix 8

Sportscasting-related Web Sites

http://www.abcsports.com: ABC sports
www.americansportscasters.com: American Sportscasters Association (ASA)
www.amstat.org/sections/sis/pages.html: sports statistics
www.armorytrack.com: National Track and Field Hall of Fame
www.baseballlibrary.com: baseball
www.boa.org.uk: British Olympic Association
http://cbc.ca/sports/hockey: Hockey Night in Canada
http://cbs.sportsline.com/u/cbs/sports: CBS sports, including bios on CBS
    sportscasters
www.cricinfo.com: cricket
www.cstv.com: College Sports TV
http://msn.espn.go.com: ESPN on MSN
www.ezinesandnewsletters.com: general
www.fifa.com: Federation Internationale de Football Association
www.formula1.com: Formula 1
www.foxsports.com: Fox sports
http://www.jimrome.com: Jim Rome Show
www.jse.sagepub.com: Journal of Sports Economics
http://www.kdotejebe/2007/03/15/worst-sportscast-in-history: Worst sports-
    cast in history
www.lta.org: Lawn Tennis Association
www.lpga.com: Ladies Professional Golf Association
www.majorleaguebaseball.com: Major League Baseball
www.marketingpower.com: American Marketing Association
www.minorleaguebaseball.com: Minor League Baseball
http://www.motoworld.com: MotoWorld online
http://msn.espn.go.com/thisissportsscenter: ESPN on MSN, This is Sports-
    Center
http://msn.foxsports.com: Fox Sports
www.msnbc.com/news/nfl_front.asp: MSNBC Sports-NFL
www.nascar.com: National Association for Stock Car Racing

Sportscasters/Sportscasting

www.nba.com: National Basketball Association
www.ncaa.org: National Collegiate Athletic Association
http://www.nesn.com: New England Sports Network
www.nfl.com: National Football League
www.nhl.com: National Hockey League
www.olympics.com: official website of the Olympic Movement
www.pba.org: Professional Bowlers Association
www.pga.com: Professional Golfers Association
http://www.racelineonline.com: Raceline
www.reporter.org/beat/sports.html: maintained by Investigative Reporters
   and Editors
www.rfu.com: Rugby Football Union
www.salisburync.gov/snna: National Sportscasters and Sportswriters Hall
   of Fame
www.sportaccord.com: The International Sports Convention
www.sportcal.com: The business site for sport
www.sportbusiness.com: Sport Business Group
www.sportbusinessnews.com: Howard Bloom's SBN
www.sportingnews.com: "The experts' choice."
www.sportonair.com: Sport on Air, UK
http://www.sportsbyline.com: Sports Byline
www.sports.com: "The first word in sports betting since 1996."
www.sportscasterchronicles.blogspot.com: Sportscaster Chronicles
www.sportseditor.com: online sports editors, producers, and writers
http://sports.espn.go.com/sports/tvlistings/schedule?network = 30: ABC
   Sports
www.sports.co.uk: sport in the United Kingdom
www.sportscommissions.org: National Association of Sports Commissions
http://sportsillustrated.cnn.com: Sports Illustrated
www.sportsjones.com: "A guide to the best, worst, & strangest sports stuff
   on the Web."
www.sports-law.blogspt.com: Sports law blog
www.sportsline.com: CBS
www.sportslinkscentral.com/Sports_Business/sports_marketing.htm:
   Sportslink Central
www.SportsLizard.com: sports collectibles
www.sportsmagazines.net: auto racing, basketball, billiards, bodybuilding,
   cycling, equestrian, extreme sports, martial arts, rowing, scuba diving,
   skateboarding, soccer, surfing, swimming and diving, windsurfing
www.sportsmarketingnetwork.com: National Sports Marketing Network
www.sportsmuseum.org: New England Sports Museum
http://www.sportsnetowrk.com: Sports Network
http://www.sportsontv.net: Sports on TV

www.sportspages.com: maintained by Rich Jones
http://sportsticker.com: Sports Ticker
http://www.sportswriters.net: Sports Writers
www.talksport.net: Talksport Radio, UK
www.teammarketing.com: Team Marketing Report
www.thebigproject.co.uk/sport_bott.htm: Formula 1
www.thefa.com: The Football Association
http://www.tsn.ca: The Sports Network
www.ucalgary.caa/library/ssportsite: scholarly site, for sports researchers
www.uefa.com: Union of European Football Association
www.usoc.org: United States Olympic Team
www.wnba.com: Women's National Basketball Association
http://www.wwsbi.org: Women's Sports Broadcasting, Inc.
http://www.wwe.com: World Wrestling Entertainment

Appendix 9

Sports Halls of Fame

Alabama Sports Hall of Fame, 2150 Richard Arrington Jr. Blvd. N., Birmingham, AL, 35203; 205/323-6665 (www.ashof.org)

Alberta Sports Hall of Fame, 30 Riverview Park, Red Deer, Alberta T4N lE3, Canada; 403/341-8614 (www.albertasportshalloffame.com)

America's Clogging Hall of Fame, c/o Earl Powell, President; 828/891-3435 (www.achf.hof)

America's Cup Hall of Fame, Herreshoff Marine Museum, One Burnside Street, Bristol, RI, 02809; 401/253-5000 (www.herreshoff.org)

The Armory Foundation (www.armorynyc.org), 216 Fort Washington Avenue, New York, NY, 10032; 212/923-1803

Australian Racing Museum and Hall of Fame, Federation Square, Melbourne, Australia (www.racingmuseum.com.au)

Bay Area Sports Hall of Fame, 235 Montgomery Street, 12th Floor, San Francisco, CA, 94104; 415/352-8835 (www.bashof.org)

Braves Museum and Hall of Fame, Turner Field, Atlanta, GA; 404/614-2311 (www.atlanta.braves.mlb.com)

Burnaby Sports Hall of Fame, 3676 Kensington Avenue, Burnaby, British Columbia V5B 4Z6, Canada (www.burnabysportshalloffame.ca)

Canada's Sports Hall of Fame, 115 Princes/ Boulevard, Exhibition Place, Toronto, Ontario M6K 3C3, Canada 416/260-6789 (www.cshof.ca)

Canadian Football Hall of Fame and Museum, 58 Jackson Street West, Hamilton, Ontario L89 lL4, Canada; 905/528-7566 (www.footballhof.com)

Cincinnati Reds Hall of Fame, 100 Main Street, Cincinnati, OH, 45202; 513/765-7000 (www.cincinnati.reds.mbl.com)

College Football Hall of Fame, 111 South St. Joseph Street, South Bend, IN; 800/440FAME (www.collegefootball.org)

Colorado Ski and Skateboard Hall of Fame, Vail Transportation Center, Vail, CO, 81657; 970/476-1876

Colorado Sports Hall of Fame, Invesco Field at Mile High, Denver, CO, 80204; 720/258-3535 (www.coloradosports.org)

Cycling Hall of Fame, 9101 Stuart Street, Westminster, CO, 80031 (www .cyclinghalloffame.com)

Delaware Sports Museum and Hall of Fame, Frawley Stadium, 801 South Madison Street, Wilmington, DE, 19801; 302/425-3263 (www .desports.org)

Drum Corps International Hall of Fame, 470 South Irmen Drive, Addison, IL, 60101; 630/628-7888 (www.dci.org.org/fame)

Finnish Hockey Hall of Fame, Vaprikki, PO Box 487, 33101 Tampere, Finland; 03/31466966 (www.tampere.fi/jaakiekkomuseo)

Formula One Hall of Fame Web site (www.formula1.com/archive/halloffame)

Georgia Sports Hall of Fame, 301 Cherry Street, Macon, GA, 31208; 478/752-1585 (www.gshf.org)

Greater Buffalo Sports Hall of Fame, HSBC Arena, Buffalo, NY, 14203; (www.buffalosportshallfame.com)

Greater Peoria Sports Hall of Fame, 110 N.E. Water Street, Peoria, IL, 61602; 309/674-4255 (www.gpshof.org)

Greater Syracuse Sports Hall of Fame, One Tex Simone Driver, Syracuse, NY, 13208; 315/470-1826 (www.syracusehalloffame.com)

Greater Victoria Sports Hall of Fame, PO Box 39015, James Bay, Victoria V8X 4M8 Canada; 250/384-1648 (www.gvshof.ca)

Green Bay Packers Hall of Fame, 1265 Lombardi Avenue, Green Bay, WI, 54304; 920/569-7512 (www.packers.com/hall_of-fame)

Hall of Fame Dance Challenge, 3160 Haggerty, Suite F., West Bloomfield, MI, 48323, 866/Dance99 (www.halloffamedance.com)

Hampton Roads African American Sports Hall of Fame, PO Box 3635, Norfolk, VA, 23514; 757/366-8766 (www.hraashf.org)

Harness Racing Museum and Hall of Fame, 240 Main Street, Goshen, NY, 10924; 845/294-6330 (www.harnessmuseum.com)

High Banks Hall of Fame, PO Box 264, Belleville, KS, 66935; 785/527-2526 (www.highbanks-museum.org)

Hockey Hall of Fame, BCE Place, 30 Yonge Street, Toronto, Ontario M5E lX8, Canada 416/360-7765 (www.hhof.com)

Indiana Baseball Hall of Fame, 1436 Leopold Street, Jasper, IN, 47546; 812/482-2262 (www.indbaseballhalloffame.org)

Indiana Basketball Hall of Fame, One Hall of Fame Court, New Castle, IN, 47362; 765/529-1891 (www.hoopshall.com)

Indianapolis Motor Speedway Hall of Fame Museum, 4790 West 16th Street, Indianapolis, IN, 46222; 317/492-678 (www.indianapolismotor speedway.com/museum)

Intercollegiate Tennis Association Women's Tennis Hall of Fame, College of William and Mary, Williamsburg, VA, 23187; 757/221-3331 (www.wm .edu/tenniscenter)

International Association of Sports Museums and Halls of Fame, PO Box 3093, Ponte Vedra, FL, 32004; 904/955-0126 (www.sportshalls.com)

International Bowling Museum and Hall of Fame, 111 Stadium Plaza, St. Louis, MO, 63102; 314/231-6340 (www.bowlingmuseum.com)

International Boxing Hall of Fame, 1 Hall of Fame Drive, Canastoga, NY, 13032; 315/697-7095 (www.ibhof.com)

International Federation of Bodybuilders and Fitness, 1630 Valmarie Avenue, Ottawa, Ontario K2C 1W1, Canada 613/321-1785 (www.ifbb .com)

International Frisbee Hall of Fame, Houghton County Historical Museum, 5500 Highway M-26, Lake Linder, MI, 49945 (www.sas.it.mtu .edu/~dkwalika/frisbee/Hall.html)

International Game Fish Association Hall of Fame, 300 Gulf Stream Way, Dania Way, FL, 33004; 954/922-4212 (www.igfa.org)

International Jewish Sports Hall of Fame (www.jewishsports.net) Regional Halls of Fame: West Hills, CA; Washington, DC, Chicago, IL; Rockville, MD; West Bloomfield, MI; St. Louis, MO; Wayne and West Orange, NJ; Canton, Cleveland, and Columbus, OH; Commack and Rochester, NY; Philadelphia and Pittsburgh, PA; Providence, Rhode Island; Milwaukee, WI.

International Swimming Hall of Fame, One Hall of Fame, Ft. Lauderdale, FL, 33316; 954/462-6536 (www.ishof.org)

International Tennis Hall of Fame, 194 Bellevue Avenue, Newport, RI, 02840; 401/849-3990 (www.tennisfame.com)

Juggling Hall of Fame, 289 Surrey Street, San Francisco, CA, 94131; 415/337-8693 (www.juggling.org)

Kansas Sports Hall of Fame, 238 North Mead. Wichita, KS, 67202; 316/262-2038 (www.kshof.org)

The Manitoba Sports Hall of Fame, 450 Portage Avenue, Winnipeg, Manitoba R3C OE7 Canada 204/774-0002 (www.halloffame.mb.ca)

Mississippi Sports Hall of Fame, 1152 Lakeland Drive, Jackson, MS, 39236; 601/982-8264 (www.msfame.com)

The Missouri Sports Hall of Fame, 3861 E. Stan Musial Drive, Springfield, MO, 65809; 417/889-3100 (www.mosportshalloffame.com)

The Motorcycle Hall of Fame Museum, 13515 Yarmouth Street, Pickerington, OH, 43147; 614/856-2222 (www.motorcyclemuseum.org)

Motorsports Hall of Fame, P.O. Box 194, Novi, MI, 48376-0194; 800/250-RACE (www.mshf.com)

The Mountain Bike Hall of Fame, 331 Elk Avenue, Crested Butte, CO, 81224; 800/454-4505 (www.mtnbikehalloffame.com)

Mountaineer Sports Hall of Fame, Western State College, Gunnison, CO, 81231; 970/943-2079 (www.western.edu/ath/hall_fame)

Museum of Polo and Hall of Fame, 9011 Lake Worth Road, Lake Worth, FL, 33467; 561/969-3210 (www.polomuseum.com)

Naismith Memorial Basketball Hall of Fame, 1000 West Columbus Avenue, Springfield, MA; 413/781-6500 (www.hoophall.com)

National Aviation Hall of Fame, PO Box 31096, Dayton, OH, 45437; 937/256-0944 (www.nationalaviation.blade6.donet.com)

National Baseball Hall of Fame, 25 Main Street, Cooperstown, NY, 13326; 888/HALL-OF-FAME (www.baseballhalloffame.org)

National Bow Hunters Hall of Fame, PO Box 511, Squaw Valley, CA, 93675; 559/332-2535 (www.bowhuntershalloffame.com)

National Cowboy Hall of Fame and Western Heritage Museum, 1700 N.E. 63rd Street, Oklahoma City, OK, 73111; 405/478-2250 (www.national cowboymuseum.org)

National Cowgirl Museum and Hall of Fame, 1720 Gendy Street, Fort Worth, TX, 76107; 817/336-4475 (www.cowgirl.net)

National Distance Running Hall of Fame, 114 Genesee Street, Utica, NY, 13502; 315/724-4525 (www.distancerunning.com)

National Fresh Water Fishing Hall of Fame, 10360 Hall of Fame Drive, Hayward, WI, 54843; 715/634-4440 (www.freshwater-fishing.org)

National Italian American Hall of Fame, 1431 West Taylor Street, Chicago, IL, 60607; 312/226-5566 (www.niashf.org)

National Museum of Dance and Hall of Fame, 99 South Broadway, Saratoga Springs, NY, 12866; 518/584-4515 (www.dancemuseum.org)

National Museum of Racing and Hall of Fame, 191 Union Avenue, Saratoga Springs, NY, 12866; 800/JOCKEY4 (www.racingmuseum.org)

National Soccer Hall of Fame, 18 Stadium Circle, Oneonta, NY, 13820; 607/432-3351 (www.soccerhall.org)

National Softball Hall of Fame, 2801 N.E. 50th Street, Oklahoma City, OK, 73111; 405/424-5266 (www.softball.org)

National Sprint Car Hall of Fame and Museum, One Sprint Capital Place, Knoxville, IA, 50138; 800/874-4488 (www.sprintcarhof.com)

National Wrestling Hall of Fame, 405 W. Hall of Fame, Stillwater, OK, 74075; 405/377-5243 (www.wrestlinghalloffame.org)

National Youth Sports Hall of Fame, 201 South Capital Avenue, Indianapolis, IN, 46225; 317/829-5777 (www.nyscorp.org)

New Jersey Sports Hall of Fame, Meadowlands Sports Complex, East Rutherford, NJ, 07073; 201/460-4377 (www.sportshalloffamenj.org)

New Zealand Sports Hall of Fame, Railway Station, Anzac Avenue, Dunedin, New Zealand (www.nzhalloffame.co.nz)

North Carolina Auto Racing Hall of Fame, 119 Knob Hill Road, Lakeside Park, NC, 28117; 704/663-5331 (www.ncarhof.com)

Nova Scotia Sport Hall of Fame, The Metro Centre, 1800 Argyle Street, Halifax, Nova Scotia B3J 3N8, Canada; 902/421-1266 (www.novascotia sporthalloffame.com)

Bobby Orr Hall of Fame, Two Bay Street, Parry Sound, Ontario P2A lS3, Canada; 877/746-4466 (www.bobbyorrhalloffame.com)

Philadelphia Sports Hall of Fame Foundation, 410 Waverly Road Wyncote, PA, 19095; 215/886.6657 (www.phillyhof.org)

Pinball Hall of Fame, 3330 E. Tropicana, Las Vegas, NV, 89121 (www.pinballmuseum.org)

Professional Wrestling Hall of Fame and Museum, PO Box 434, Latham, NY, 12110; 518/842-0022 (www.pwhf.org)

Pro Football Hall of Fame, 2121 George Halas Driver NW, Canton, OH, 44708; 330/456-8207 (www.profootballhof.com)

ProRodeo Hall of Fame, 101 ProRodeo Drive, Colorado Springs, CO, 80919; 719/528-4761 (http://prorodeo.org/hof)

Rose Bowl Hall of Fame, 391 South Orange Grove Boulevard, Pasadena, CA, 91184; 626/449-4100 (www.tournamentofroses.com)

Scholar Athlete Hall of Fame, Institute for International Sport, 3045 Kingstown Road, Kingstown, RI, 02881; 401/874-2375 (www.internationalsport.com/sa_hof)

Scottish Sports Hall of Fame, Chambers Street, Edinburgh, Scotland (www.sshf.co.uk)

The Show Jumping Hall of Fame, 38 Mechanic Street, Foxboro, MA, 02035; (www.showjumpinghalloffame.net)

Snowmobile Hall of Fame, PO Box 720, St. Germain, WI, 54558; 715/542-4488 (www.snowmobilehalloffame.com)

South Dakota Sports Hall of Fame, Box 88602, Sioux Falls, SD, 57109; 605/336-6715 (www.sdshof.com)

Stanford Athletics Hall of Fame, Stanford University, Stanford, CA, 94305 (www.gostanford.sctv.com)

State of Oregon Sports Hall of Fame, 321 Salmon Street, Portland, OR 97204; 503/227-7466 (www.ohwy.com/ore/o/oresport.htm)

St. Louis Cardinals Hall of Fame Museum, 111 Stadium Plaza, St. Louis, MO, 63102; 314/231-6340 (www.cardinals.mlb.com)

Surfers' Hall of Fame, 411 Olive Avenue, Huntington Beach, CA, 92648; 714/960-3483 (www.surfingmuseum.com/hall_of_fame.html)

Ted Williams Museum and Hitters Hall of Fame, Tropicana Field, St. Petersburg, FL (www.twmuseum.com)

Tennessee Sports Hall of Fame, 501 Broadway, Nashville, TN, 37203; 616/242-4750 (www.tshf.net)

Texas Ranger Hall of Fame and Museum, 100 Texas Ranger Trail, Waco, TX, 76706; 254/750-8631 (www.texasranger.org)

Texas Sports Hall of Fame, 1108 S. University Parks Drive, Waco, TX, 76706; 800/567-9561 (www.tshof.org)

Trapshooting Hall of Fame, 601 National Road, Vandalia, OH; 937/898-4638 (www.traphof.org)

UCLA Athletics Hall of Fame, PO 24044, Los Angeles, CA, 90024; (www.uclabruings.sctv.com)

University of Iowa Athletics Hall of Fame, Roy G. Karro Building, Iowa City, IA, 52242; 319/384-1031 (www.hawkeyesports.cstv.com)

University of Massachusetts Athletics Hall of Fame, Mullins Center, Amherst, MA; 413/545-4379 (www.umassathletics.cstu.com)

U.S. Bicycling Hall of Fame, 1 Hunterdon Street, Somerville, NJ, 08876; 908/393-9384 (www.usbhof.com)

U.S. Hockey Hall of Fame, 801 Hat Trick Avenue, Eveleth, MN, 55734; 218/744-5167 (www.ushockeyhall.com)

U.S. Lacrosse Hall of Fame, 113 West University Parkway, Baltimore, MD, 21210; 410/235-6882 (www.uslacrosse.org)

U.S. National Ski Hall of Fame and Museum, 610 Palms Avenue, Ishpeming, MI, 49849; 906/485-6323 (www.skihall.com)

UBC Sports Hall of Fame, 6081 University Boulevard, Vancouver, British Columbia V6T lZl; 604/687-2381 (www.ubcportshalloffame.com)

USA Field Hockey Hall of Fame. 1 Olympic Plaza, Colorado Springs, CO, 80909; 719/866-4567 (www.usfieldhockey.com)

Virginia Sports Hall of Fame, 206 High Street, Portsmouth, VA, 23705; 757/398-8031 (www.virginiasportshalloffame.com)

Volleyball Hall of Fame, 444 Dwight Street, Holyoke, MA, 01040; 413/536-0926 (www.volleyhall.org)

Water Ski Hall of Fame, 1251 Holy Cow Road, Polk City, FL, 33868; 863/324-2472 (www.waterskihalloffame.com)

Western Pennsylvania Sports Museum (www.sports.pghhistory.org)

Women's Basketball Hall of Fame, 700 Hall of Fame Drive, Knoxville, Tennessee 37915 865/633-9000 (www.wbhof.com)

Women Divers Hall of Fame, 2753 Broadway, New York, NY, 10025 (www.wdhof.org)

World Boxing Hall of Fame, 6657 45th Street, Riverside, CA, 92509 (www .wbhf.org)

World Chess Hall of Fame, 13755 SW 119th Avenue, Miami, FL, 33186; 786/242-HALL (www.excaliberelectronics.com).

World Figure Skating Museum and Hall of Fame, 20 First Street, Colorado Springs, CO 80906 719/635-5200 (www.worldskatingmuseum.org)

World Golf Hall of Fame, One World Golf Place, St. Augustine, Florida 32092 904/940-4123 (www.wgv.com)

World Kite Museum and Hall of Fame, 303 Sid Snyder Drive, Long Beach, Washington 98631 360/642-4020 (www.worldkitemuseum.com)

World Sports Humanitarian Hall of Fame, 1910 University Drive, Bronco Stadium, Boise State University, Boise, Idaho 83707 208/343-7224 (www .sportshumanitarian.com)

Appendix 10

Sports Networks

ABC
www.abc.com

CBS
www.cbs.com

ESPN
www.espn.go.com

ESPN Star Sports
www.espnstar.com

FOX: FSN (Fox Sports Network), FOX College Sports, FOX Soccer Channel, Speed Channel, Fuel, FOX, FX, FOX News)
www.FOXSports.com

NBA Entertainment
450 Harmon Meadow Blvd., Secaucus, NJ, 07094, 201/865-1500

NBC
www.nbc.com

NESN (New England Sports Network)
www.boston.com/sports/nesn

Oxygen Sports
www.oxygen.com/sports

PGA
www.pga.com/home

Sports Business Research Network
http://www.sbrnet.com

Sports webcasting
http://www.sportsjuice.com

Sportscasters/Sportscasting

Turner Sports
One CNN Center, 13 South Tower, Atlanta, GA 30303, tnt@turner.com
www.turnerinfo.com

Versus
www.versus.com/sports

YES Network
Yankees Entertainment and Sports Network, The Chrysler Building, 405
Lexington Avenue, 36th Floor, New York, NY 10174-3699, 646/487-3600;
fax 646/487-3612 info@yesnetwork.com
www.yesnetwork.com

Appendix 11

Sports and Sportscasting-related Organizations

African Association for Health, Physical Education, Recreation, Sport and Dance (AFAHPER), University of Botswana. Contact: Dr. Moni Wekesa
wekesam@noka.ub.bw

American Academy of Kinesiology and Physical Education (AAKPE)
www.aakpe.org

American Alliance for Health, Physical Education, Recreation and Dance (AAHPERD)
www.aahperd.org

American Association of University Professors
www.aaup.org

American Board of Sport Psychology (ABSP)
www.americanboardofsportpsychology.org

American College of Sports Medicine (ACSM)
www.acsm.org

American Medical Society for Sports Medicine (AMSSM)
www.newamssm.org

American Sportscasters Association
www.americansportscasters.com

Asian American Journalists Association
www.aaja.org

Association for the Advancement of Applied Sport Psychology (AAASP)
www.aaasponline.org/index.php

Sportscasters/Sportscasting

Association for Professional Basketball Research (APBR)
www.hometown.aol.com/bradleyrd/apbr.html

Association for Women in Sports Media (AWSM)
www.awsmonline.org

Australian Society for Sports History (ASSH)
www.sporthistory.org

British Society of Sports History (BSSH): publisher of *Sports Historian*
www2.umist.ac.uk/sport/SPORTS%20HISTORY/index2.html

Canadian Association for the Advancement of Women and Sport and Physical Activity (CAAWS)
www.caaws.ca

Canadian Association for Health, Physical /education, Recreation and Dance (CAHPERD)
www.cahperd.ca

Center for the Study of Sport in Society (CSSS), Northeastern University
360 Huntington Avenue, Boston, MA 02115

Citizenship Through Sports Alliance: character, sportsmanship and fair play
www.sportsmanship.org

European Academy of Sport Science (EAS)
www.lsb-nrw.de/eads

European Association for Sociology of Sport (EASS)
www.univie.ac.at/sportsoz

European Committee for Sport History
www.cesh.info

European Fair Play Movement (EFPM)
www.fairplayeur.com

European Federation of Sport Psychology
www.fepsac.org

European Women and Sport: network
www.ews-online.com

Federation of Gay Games
584 Castro Street, San Francisco, CA 94114

Feminist Majority Foundation
www.feminist.org/sports

Finnish Society for Research in Sport and Physical Education
www.lts.fi

Football Writers' Association of American (FWAA)
www.sportswriters.net/fwaa

Forum for the Analysis of Sport Technology (FAST): international ethics research
www.fast.paisley.ac.uk

French Society of Sport Psychology
www.unicaen.fr/unicaen/sfps/droite.html

Gay Games
19 West 21st Street, #1202, New York, NY 10010

Hellenic Society of Sport Psychology (HSSP)
www.phed.uoa.gr/sportpsy/hssp

Hockey Research.com
www.hockeyresearch.com

Institute for International Sport (IIT), University of Rhode Island
www.internationalsport.com/index.html

Intergovernmental Committee for Physical Education and Sport (CIGEPS)
www.unesco.org/education/educprog/eps/EPSanglais/HOMEang.htm

International Association of Computer Science in Sport (IACSS)
www.iacss.org

International Association for the Philosophy of Sport (IAPS)
www.iaps.net

International Association of Sport Kinetics (IASK)
www.sportkinetics.com

International Committee for Fair Play
www.fairplayinternational.org

International Council of Sport Science and Physical Education (ISCPES): publishes *International Sports Studies*
www.iscpes.org

International Federation of Sports Medicine: 100+ associations
www.fims.org/fimss/frames.asp

International Olympic Committee IOC—Comite International Olympique)
Chateau de Vidy, 1007 Lausanne, Switzerland

International Skiing History Association (ISHA)
www.skiinghistory.org

International Society for the History of Physical Education and Sport (ISHPES)
www2.umist.ac.uk/sport/SPORTS%20HISTORY/ishpes.html

International Society of Football Scholars (ISFS)
www.footballstudies.com

International Society of Olympic Historians (ISOH)
www.isoh.org/index.html

International Society for Sport Psychiatry (ISSP)
www.mindbodyandsports.com/issp

International Society of Sport Psychology (ISSP)
www.fitinfotech.com/ISSP/index.tpl

International Sociology of Sport Association (ISSA)
http://u2.u-strasbg.fr/issa

International Sport and Culture Association (ISCA)
www.isca-web.org

International Sports Engineering Association (ISEA)
www.sportengineering.co.uk

International Sports Organization for the Disabled (ISOD)
www.is-od.com/default.htm

International Sports Press Association: 25,000+ sports journalists
www.aips-media.com

International Working Group on Women and Sport (IWG)
www.iwg-gti.org

Japan Society of Sport Sociology (JSSS)
www.jsss.org

Japanese Association for Women in Sport
www.jws.or.jp

Korean Society for the Sociology of Sport (KSSS)
www.ksss.org

National Association of Broadcasters (NAB)
www.nab.org

National Association for Girls and Women in Sport (NAGWS)
www.aahperd.org/nagws

National Association for Sport and Physical Education (NASPE)
www.aahperd.org/naspe/template.cfm

National Association of Sports Officials (NASO)
www.naso.org

National Center on Physical /activity and Disability (NCPAD), University of Illinois
www.ncpad.org

National Institute for Sport Science and Safety (NISSS)
www.nisss.org

National Lesbian & Gay Journalists Association
www.nlgia.orgs

National Sporting Goods Association
www.nsga.org

The National Sportscasters and Sportswriters Hall of Fame
www.salisburync.gov/nssa

National Sports Marketing Network (NSMN)
www.sportsmarketingnetwork.com

Native American Journalists Association
www.naja.com

A. C. Nielsen
www.acnielsen.com

North American Snowsports Journalists Association (NASJA)
www.nasja.org

North American Society for Psychology and Physical Activity (NASPSPA)
www.naspspa.org

North American Society for Sport History (NASSH)
www.naash.org

North American Society for the Sociology of Sport (NASSS)
www.nasss.org

North East Asian Society for History of Physical Education and Sport
sanada@taiiju.tsukuba.ac.jp

Philosophic Society for the Study of Sport
Department of Physical Education, Recreation, and Health, Kean College of New Jersey, Union, NJ 07083

The Poynter Institute: for journalists
www.poynter.org

Professional Football Researchers Association (PFRA)
www.footballresearch.com

Radio-Television News Directors Association and Foundation (RTNDA)
www.rtnda.org

Research Committee on Sociology of Sport, International Sociological Association
www.ucm.es/info/isa/rc27.htm

Society for American Baseball Research (SABR)
www.sabr.org

Society for International Hockey Research, Kingston, Ontario, Canada
www.sihrhockey.org

Special Olympics International
1350 New York Avenue NW, #500, Washington, DC 20005

Sport Marketing Association (SMA); publishes *Sport Marketing Quarterly* (SMQ)
www.sportmarketingassociation.com

Sports Ethics Institute (SEI)
www.sportsethicsinstitute.org

Sports Intelligence Unit, Vingsted, Denmark
www.playthegame.org

Sports Literature Association (SLA)
www.uta.edu/english/sla/index.html

Tucker Center for Research on Girls and Women in Sport, University of Minnesota
http://education.umn.edu/tuckercenter

U.S. National Senior Sport Organization (USNSO)
14323 South Outer 40 Road #N300, Chesterfield, MO 63017

U.S. Olympic Committee (USOC)
One Olympic Plaza, Colorado Springs, CO 80909

Women in Sports Careers
www.wiscfoundation.org

Women Sports Broadcasting, Inc.
www.wsbi.org

Women's Sports Foundation: New York
www.womenssportsfoundation.org/cgi-bin/iowa/index.html

Women's Sports Foundation: UK
www.wsf.org.uk

WomenSport International
www.sportsbiz.bz/womensportinternational.com

WomenSport International Task Force on Sexual Harassment
www.de.psu.edu/wsi

Women's Sport Legends online
www.wslegends.org

World Commission of Science and Sports (WCSS)
www.wcss.org.uk

World Federation of Athletic Training and Therapy (WFATT)
www.wfatt.org

Appendix 12

Worldwide Sports

Aerobics
Archery
Auto racing
Badminton
Baseball
Basketball
Bicycling (road, racing, mountain, touring)
Billiards/snooker
Bocce Ball (wooden balls)
Body building
Boomerang
Bowling
Boxing
Broomball
Camel racing
Camogie (a field sport using curved sticks)
Canoeing
Cheerleading
Climbing (rock, ice)
Crew
Cricket
Croquet
Cross country
Curling
Cycling
Darts
Diving
Extreme sports
Fencing

Field hockey
Figure skating
Fishing (fly fishing, sport fishing)
Flying
Football
Gaelic
Gay Games
Goalball
Golf
Goodwill Games
Gymnastics
Handball
Horse racing
Horseback riding, jumping
Hunting
Ice hockey, ringette, and roller hockey
Ice skating
Inline skating
Jai Alai
Jet skiing
Judo
Kabaddi
Kayaking
Korfball
Lacrosse
Laser games
Lumberjack
Marathons
Martial arts
Motor sports
Multi-sports

Sportscasters/Sportscasting

Netball
Olympic Games
Orienteering
Paddleball
Paintball
Paralympics
Petanque
Platform tennis
Polo
Racing cars
Racquetball
Rodeo
Rope skipping
Rounders
Rowing
Rugby
Running
SCUBA diving
Sailing
Sepak Takraw
Shooting
Skateboarding
Skating
Skiing
Snowboarding
Snowmobiling
Soccer
Softball
Speed skating
Squash
Surfing
Swimming
Table tennis
Tae Kwon Do
Tchoukball
Team handball
Tennis
Track and field
Triathlons
Ultimate Frisbee
Volleyball
Walking
Water polo and other water sports
Waterskiing
Weight lifting
Windsurfing
Wrestling

Glossary

Atlantic Coast Conference (ACC): Founded on May 8, 1953 at Greensboro, North Carolina, its original charter members were Clemson, Duke, Maryland, North Carolina, North Carolina State, South Carolina, and Wake Forest. Georgia Tech was accepted in 1978, Florida State in 1991, University of Miami and Virginia Polytechnic Instate and State University in 2004, and Boston College in 2005.

Big 12 schools: Baylor, Colorado, Iowa State, Kansas, Kansas State, Missouri, Nebraska, Oklahoma, Oklahoma State, Texas, Texas A&M, Texas Tech

Big 12 sports: baseball, men's basketball, women's basketball, cross country, football, golf, gymnastics, soccer, softball, swimming and diving, tennis, track, volleyball, wrestling

BCS: Bowl Championship Series—part of the NCAA

color commentator: called "the summariser" in England, this broadcaster helps the play-by-play announcer by providing fill-in information such as biographical data, statistics, strategies, and various reports on athletes, coaches, and teams. S/he can also add colorful, even humorous pieces.

"Fighting Irish": University of Notre Dame football team

Green Jacket: traditionally worn by winner of the Masters golf tournament

play-by-play broadcaster: "the voice" of a sporting event

Southeast Conference (SEC): Alabama, Arkansas, Auburn, Florida, Georgia, Kentucky, LSU, Mississippi State, Ole Miss, South Carolina, Tennessee, and Vanderbilt

Yellow Jersey/yellow bracelet: popularized by Lance Armstrong, winner of the Tour de France and cancer survivor.

Sportscasters/Sportscasting

References

Aamidor, Abraham (Ed.) (2003). *Real sports reporting*. Bloomington: Indiana University Press.

Abbot, Waldo (1941). *Handbook of broadcasting*. New York: McGraw-Hill.

Adams, Terry and C.A. Tuggle (2004). ESPN *SportsCenter* and coverage of women's athletics: 'It's a boy's club.' *Mass Communication & Society,* Volume 7, Number 2: 237-248.

Adler, Larry (1992). *Football coach quotes: The wit, wisdom, and winning words of leaders on the gridiron*. Jefferson, NC: McFarland & Company.

Albert, Marv with Rick Reilly (1993). *I'd love to but I have a game: 27 years without a life*. New York: Doubleday.

Allen, Maury (Ed.) (1971). *Voices of sport*. New York: Grosset and Dunlap.

Allen, Mel (1959). *It takes heart*. New York: HarperCollins.

Allison, Lincoln (Ed.) (1993). *The changing politics of sport*. Manchester: Manchester University Press.

Allison, Lincoln (2006). *The global politics of sport: The role of global institutions in sport*. Oxford, UK: Routledge.

Amis, John (2005). *Global sport sponsorship*. Oxford, UK: Berg Publishing.

Anderson, Douglas A. (1994). *Contemporary sports reporting,* 2nd ed. Chicago, IL: Nelson-Hall.

Anderson, William B. (2001.) Does the cheerleading ever stop? Major league baseball and sports journalism. *Journalism & Mass Communication Quarterly,* Volume 78, Number 2 (Summer): 355-382.

Andrews, David L. (Ed.) (2001). *Michael Jordon, Inc: Corporate sport, media culture, and late modern America*. Albany: State University of New York Press.

Andrews, David L. (2004). Sport in the late capitalist moment. In Trevor Slack (Ed.), *The commercialization of sport* (London: Routledge): 3-28.

Andrews, David L. (2006). *Sport-commerce-culture: Essays on sport in late capitalist America*. New York: Peter Lang.

Andrews, David L. and Steven J. Jackson (Eds.) (2001). *Sports stars: The cultural politics of sporting celebrities*. London: Routledge.

Andrews, David L. and Stephen Wagg (2006). *East plays west: Sport and the Cold War*. New York: Routledge.

Andrews, Peter (1987). The art of sportswriting. *Columbia Journalism Review* (May/June): 25-30.

Sportscasters/Sportscasting

Andrews, Phil (2005). *Sports journalism: A practical guide*. London: Sage.

Angell, Roger (1972). *Five seasons: A baseball companion*. New York: Simon and Schuster.

Angell, Roger (1999). The bard in the booth [Tim McCarver]. *The New Yorker* (September 6): 28-32.

Anshel, Mark H. (1994). *Sport psychology: From theory to practice*. Scottsdale, AZ: Gorsuch Scarisbrick.

Arabe, Katrina C. (2004). Sporting goods market ahead of the game. Available online: www.news.thomasnet.com.

Araton, Harvey (2004). Chauvinism lives in the locker room. *The New York Times* (November 21): S9.

Archer, Gleason L. (1971). *History of radio to 1926*. New York: Arno Press and the *New York Times*.

Aris, Stephen (1990). *Sportsbiz: Inside the sports business*. London: Hutchinson.

Arledge, Roone (2003). *Roone: A memoir*. New York: HarperCollins.

Arnaud, Pierre and James Riordan (Eds.) (1998). *Sport and international politics*. London: E. and FN Spon.

Arnold, Peter J. (1997). *Sports, ethics, and education*. London: Cassell.

Arron, Simon and Mark Hughes (2003). *The complete book of Formula One*. Osceola, WI: Motorbooks International.

Auletta, Ken (1991). *Three blind mice: How the TV networks lost their way*. New York: Random House.

"AWSM tribute to Mary Garber." (ND). Available online: www.awsmonline.org/Garber.htm.

Bain, Dean V. (1994). *The sports stadium as a municipal investment*. Westport, CT: Greenwood Press.

Bairner, Alan (2001). *Sport, nationalism, and globalization: European and North American perspectives*. Albany: State University of New York Press.

Baker, Aaron (2003). *Contesting identities: Sports in American film*. Urbana, IL: University of Illinois Press.

Baker, Aaron and Todd Boyd (Eds.) (1997). *Out of bounds: Sports, media, and the politics of identity*. Bloomington, IN: Indiana University Press.

Baker, William J. (2000). *If Christ came to the Olympics*. Sydney: University of New South Wales Press.

Bale, John (1994). *Landscapes of modern sport*. Leicester, UK: Leicester University Press.

Bale, John (2002). *Imagined Olympians: Body culture and colonial representations in Rwanda*. Minneapolis, MN: University of Minnesota Press.

Baran, Stanley J. (ND). Sports and television. Museum of Broadcast Communications. Available online: www.museum.tv/archives/etv/S/htmlS/sportsandte/htm.

Barber, Red (1970). *The broadcasters*. New York: Dial Press.

Barber, Red (1987). Culling great moments and people from 57 years of sportscasting. *The Christian Science Monitor* (August 27): 16.

Barber, Red (1997). *Rhubarb in the catbird seat*. Lincoln, NB: Bison Books.

Barcelona, Bob (2004). Looking beyond jockocracy. *National Recreation and Park Association*. (January) available online: www.nrpa.org.

Barnett, Steven (1990). *Games and sets: The changing face of sport on television*. London: British Film Institute.

Barney, Robert K., Stephen R. Wenn, and Scott G. Martyn (2002). *Selling the five rings: The International Olympic Committee and the rise of Olympic commercialism*. Salt Lake City: University of Utah Press.

Barnouw, Erik (1966). *A tower in Babel: A history of broadcasting in the United States to 1933*. New York: Oxford University Press.

Barnouw, Erik (1968). *The golden web: A history of broadcasting in the United States 1933 to 1953*. New York: Oxford University Press.

Barnouw, Erik (1970). *The image empire: A history of broadcasting in the United States from 1953*. New York: Oxford University Press.

Barry, John M. (2001). *Power plays: Politics, football, and other blood sports*. Jackson, MS: University Press of Mississippi.

Bass, Amy (Ed.) (2005). *In the game: Race, identity, and sports in the twentieth century* New York: Palgrave Macmillan.

Baughman, Cynthia (Ed.) (1995). *Women on ice: Feminist essays on the Tonya Harding/Nancy Kerrigan spectacle*. New York: Routledge.

Bean, Billy with Chris Bull (2003). *Going the other way: Lessons from a life in and out of Major-League baseball*. New York: Marlowe & Company.

Beard, Adrian (1998). *The language of sport*. New York: Routledge.

Bender, Gary with Michael L. Johnson (1994). *Call of the game: What really goes on in the broadcast booth*. Chicago, IL: Bonus Books.

Benedict, Jeff (1997). *Public heroes, private felons: Athletes and crimes against women*. Boston: Northeastern University Press.

Benedict, Jeff (1998). *Athletes and acquaintance rape*. Thousand Oaks, CA: Sage.

Benedict, Jeff (2000). *Out of bounds: Inside the NBA's culture of rape, violence, and crime*. Boston: Northeastern University Press.

Benedict, Jeff and Don Yeager (1998). *Pros and cons: The criminals who play in the NFL*. New York: Warner Books.

Berkow, Ira (1986). *Red: A biography of Red Smith*. New York: Times Books.

Berlow, Lawrence H. (1994). *Sports ethics: A reference handbook*. Santa Barbara, CA: ABC-Clio.

Berman, Len (2005). *Spanning the world: The crazy universe of big time sports, all-star egos, and Hall of Fame bloopers*. New York: William Morrow.

Bernstein, Alina (2002). Is it time for a victory lap?: Changes in media coverage of women in sport. *International Review for the Sociology of Sport*, Volume 37, Numbers 3-4: 515-428.

Bernstein, Alina and Neil Blain (Eds.) (2003). *Sport, media, culture: Global and local dimensions*. London: F. Cass.

Berri, David J., Martin B. Schmidt, and Stacey L. Brook (2006). *The wages of wins: Taking measure of the many myths in modern sport.* Stanford, CA: Stanford University Press.

Berry, Robert C. and Glenn M. Wong (1993). *Law and business of the sports industries: Common issues in amateur and professional sports.* Westport, CT: Praeger.

Betancourt, Marian (2001). *Playing like a girl: Transforming our lives through team sports.* Chicago, IL: Contemporary Books.

Bilby, Kenneth (1986). *The General: David Sarnoff and the rise of the communications industry.* New York: Harper and Row.

Billet, Bret L. and Lance J. Formwalt (1995). *America's national pastime: A study of race and merit in professional baseball.* Westport, CT: Praeger.

Billings, Andrew C. (2003). Dualing genders: Announcer bias in the 1999 U.S. Open tennis tournament. In Robert S. Brown and Daniel J. O'Rourke (Eds.) *Case studies in sport communication.* Westport, CT: Praeger: 51-62.

Billings, Andrew C. (2007). *Olympic media: Behind the scenes at the biggest show on television.* New York: Routledge.

Birrell, Susan and Cheryl Cole (Eds.) (1994). *Women, sport, and culture.* Champaign, IL: Human Kinetics.

Birrell, Susan and Mary G. McDonald (Eds.) (2000). *Reading sport: Critical essays on power and representation.* Boston, MA: Northeastern University Press.

Bissell, Kimberly L. (2006). Game face: Sports reporters' use of sexualized language in coverage of women's professional tennis. In Linda K. Fuller, (Ed.), *Sport, rhetoric, and gender: Historical perspectives and media representations* (171-184). New York: Palgrave Macmillan.

Blackshaw, Ian (2002). *Mediating sports disputes: National and international perspectives* New York: Springer.

Blake, A. (1996). *Body language: The meaning of modern sport.* London: Lawrence & Wishart.

Blue, Adrianne (1987). *Grace under pressure: The emergence of women in sport.* London: Sidgwick and Jackson.

Bloom, John and Michael Nevin Villard (Eds.) (2002). *Sports matters: Race, recreation, and culture.* New York: New York University Press.

Blumenthal, Howard J. and Oliver R. Goodenough (1991). *This business of television.* New York: Billboard Books.

Blumenthal, Kare (2005). *Let me play: The story of Title IX: The law that changed the future of girls in America.* New York: Atheneum Publishers.

Bolton, Clyde (2005). *Stop the presses (so I can get off): Tales from forty years of sportswriting.* Tuscaloosa, AL: Fire Ant Books/University of Alabama Press.

Bonjean, Chris (2005, August 9). Film recalls Yao Ming's bounce into the NBA. *Sun Times.* Available online:www.chinadaily.com.

Boone, William T. (2005). *Is sports nutrition for sale?: Ethical issues and professional concerns for exercise physiologists.* Waltham, MA: Nova Biomedical.

Booth, Douglas (1998). *The race game: Sport and politics in South Africa.* London: F. Cass.

Booth, Douglas (2006). *The field: Truth and fiction in sport history.* New York: Routledge.

Borelli, Stephen (2005). *How about that! The life of Mel Allen.* Champaign, IL: Sports Publishing.

Bowen, William G., Sarah A. Levin, James L. Shulman, Colin G. Campbell, Susanne C. Pichler, and Martin A. Kurzweil. 2003. *Reclaiming the game: College sports and educational values.* Princeton, NJ: Princeton University Press.

Boyd, Todd (2003). *Young, Black, rich and famous: the rise of the NBA, the Hip Hop invasion and the transformation of American culture.* New York: Doubleday.

Boyd, Todd and Kenneth L. Shropshire (Eds.) (2000). *Basketball Jones: America above the rim.* New York: New York University Press.

Boyer, Peter J. (1988). *Who killed CBS?* New York: Random House.

Boyle, Raymond (2006). *Sports journalism: Context and issues.* London: Sage.

Boyle, Raymond and Richard Haynes (2000). *Power play: Sport, media, and popular culture.* Harlow: Pearson Education Ltd.

Boyle, Raymond and Richard Haynes (2004). *Football in the new media age.* London: Routledge.

Boyle, Raymond, Peter Flood, and Deirdre Kevin (Eds.) (2004). Sport and the media: Recent economic, legal, and technological developments. *Trends in Communication,* Volume 12, Issue 2 & 3 (September).

Brabazon, Tara (2006). *Playing on the periphery: Sport, identity and memory.* London: Routledge.

Brackenridge, Celia H. (2001). *Spoilsports: Understanding and preventing sexual exploitation in sport.* London: Routledge.

Brackenridge, Celia H. (2002). Men loving men hating women: The crisis of masculinity and violence to women in sport. In Sheila Scranton and Anne Flintoff (Eds.) *Gender and sport: A reader.* London: Taylor and Francis: 255-268.

Brackenridge, Celia H. and Kari Fasting (Eds.) (2002). *Sexual harassment and abuse in sport: International research and policy perspectives.* London: Whiting and Birch.

Bradshaw, Terry with David Fisher (2001). *It's only a game.* New York: Atria.

Bradshaw, Terry with David Fisher (2002). *Keep it simple.* New York: Atria.

Breslin, Jimmy (1991). *Damon Runyon: A life.* New York: Ticknor and Fields.

Brickhouse, Jack (1996). *A voice for all seasons.* Chicago, IL: Contemporary.

Brookes, Rod (2002). *Representing sport.* London: A Hodder Arnold Publication.

Brooks, Christine M. (1994). *Sports marketing: Competitive business strategies for sports.* Englewood Cliffs, NJ: Prentice Hall.

Brooks, Dana and Ronald Althouse (Eds.) (2000). *Racism in college athletics: The African American athlete's experience,* 2nd edition. Morgantown, WV: Fitness Information Technology.

Brown, Clyde (2002). The political scorecard of professional sports facility referendums in the United States, 1984-2000. *Journal of Sport and Sports Issues,* Volume 26, Number 3: 248-267.

Brown, Robert S. and Daniel J. O'Rourke (Eds.) (2003). *Case studies in sport communication.* Westport, CT: Praeger.

Buck, Jack (2003). *Forever a winner.* Champaign, IL: Sports Publishing.

Buck, Jack, Rob Rains, and Bob Broeg (1997). *That's a winner.* Champaign, IL: Sagamore.

Broun, Heywood Hale (1979). *Tumultuous merriment.* New York: Richard Marek.

Bruccoli, Matthew J. and Layman, Richard (1976). *Ring W. Lardner: A descriptive bibliography.* Pittsburgh, PA: University of Pittsburgh Press.

Brummett, Barry and Margaret Carlisle Duncan (1990). Theorizing without totalizing: Specularity and televised sports. *The Quarterly Journal of Speech,* Volume 76, Number 3 (August): 227-246.

Brutzman, Donald P., Michael R. Macedonia, and Michael J. Zyda, "Internetwork Infrastructure Requirements for Virtual Environments." (1997). In NII 2000 Steering Committee, *White Papers: The unpredictable certainty: Information infrastructure through 2000.* Washington, DC: National Academy Press: 110-122.

Bryant, Jennings (1989). Viewers' enjoyment of televised sports violence. In Lawrence A. Wenner (Ed.), *Media, sports, & society.* Newbury Park, CA: Sage: 270-289.

Bryant, Jennings, Dan Brown, Paul W. Comisky, and Dolf Zillmann (1982). Sports and spectators: Commentary and appreciation. *Journal of Communication,* Volume 32, Number 1: 109-119.

Bryant, Jennings and Andrea M. Holt (2006). A historical overview of sports and media in the United States. In Arthur A. Raney and Jennings Bryant (Eds.) *Handbook of sports and media.* Mahwah, NJ: Lawrence Erlbaum: 21-43.

Bryant, Jennings and Arthur A. Raney (2000). Sports on the screen. In Dolf Zillman And Peter Vorderer (Eds.), *Media entertainment: The psychology of its appeal.* Mahwah, NJ: Lawrence Erlbaum: 153-174.

Burns, Christopher N. (Ed.) (2005). *Doping in sports.* Waltham, MA: Nova Biomedical.

Burris, Susan (2006). She got game, but she don't got fame. In Linda K. Fuller (Ed.) *Sport, rhetoric, and gender: Historical perspectives and media representations.* (85-96). New York: Palgrave Macmillan.

Burstyn, Varda (1999). *The rites of men: Manhood, politics, and the culture of sport.* Toronto: University of Toronto Press.

Butler, Richard J. (1996). *Sport psychology in action.* Oxford: Butterworth-Heineman.

Cagan, Joanna and Neil De Mause (1998). *Field of schemes: How the great stadium swindle turns public money into private profit.* Monroe, ME: Common Courage Press.

Cahn, Susan K. (1993). From the 'muscle moll' to the 'butch' ballplayer: Mannishness, lesbianism, and homophobia in U.S. women's sport. *Feminist Studies* 19: 343-365.

Cahn, Susan K. (1994). *Coming on strong: Gender and sexuality in twentieth century women's sport*. New York: Free Press.

Cannon, James J. (1978). *Nobody asked me, but. . .The world of Jimmy Cannon*. New York: Holt, Rinehart.

Caray, Harry with Bob Verdi (1989). *Holy cow!* New York: Villard Books.

Carey, Mike with Jamie Most (2003). *High above courtside: The lost memoirs of Johnny Most*. Champaign, IL: Sports Publishing.

Carpenter, Linda Jean and R. Vivian Acosta (2004). *Title IX*. Champaign, IL: Human Kinetics.

Carpenter, Linda Jean and R. Vivian Acosta (2006). *Women in intercollegiate sport: A longitudinal, national study: Twenty nine year update, 1977-2006*. Available online: http://webpages.charter.net/womeninsport.

Carrington, Ben and Ian McDonald (Eds.) (2001). *'Race,' sport, and British society*. London: Routledge.

Cashmore, Ellis (2005). *Making sense of sport*, 4th edition. New York: Routledge.

Cashmore, Ellis and Andrew Parker (2003). One David Beckham? Celebrity, masculinity, and the soccerati. *Sociology of Sport Journal* (20): 214-231.

Castiglione, Joe with Douglas B. Lyons (2006). *Broadcast rites and sites: I saw it on the radio with the Boston Red Sox*. Lanham, MD: Taylor Trade Publishing.

Catsis, John R. (1995). *Sports broadcasting*. Chicago, IL: Nelson-Hall.

Chad, Norman (1990). Sounding off on the voices of America. *The National Sports Daily* (September 28): 18.

Chambers, Deborah, Linda Steiner, and Carole Fleming (2002). *Women and journalism*. New York: Routledge.

Chambers, Marcia (1995). *The unplayable lie: The untold story of women and discrimination in American golf*. New York: Pocket Books.

Champion, Walter T., Jr. (1993). *Sports law in a nutshell*. St. Paul, MN: West Pub.

Chandler, Joan M. (1988). *Television and national Sport: The U.S. and Britain*. Urbana, IL: University of Illinois Press.

Chastain, Brandi (2004). *It's not about the bra: Play hard, play fair, and put the fun back Into competitive sports* New York: Collins.

Choi, Precilla Y.L. (2000) *Femininity and the physically active woman*. London: Routledge.

Choi, Sungwook (2005). Hyper-commercialism in U.S. sports media. Taipei, Taiwan. International Association of Media and Communication Research.

Clark, Scott (ND). So you want to become a sportscaster. Available online: http://www.americansportscastersonline.com/soyouwanttobe.html.

Clarke, Gill (2002). Outlaws in sport and education? Exploring the sporting and education experiences of lesbian physical education teachers. In Sheila

Scranton and Anne Flintoff (Eds.) *Gender and sport: A reader.* London: Taylor and Francis: 209-221.

Clarke, Gill and Barbara Humberstone (Eds.) (1997). *Researching women and sport.* Houndmetts, UK: Macmillan.

Coakley, Jay (2003). *Sport in society: Issues and controversies.* 8th edition. St. Louis, MO: McGraw-Hill.

Coakley, J. and E. Dunning (Eds.) (2000). *Handbook of sports studies.* London: Sage.

Cocchiarale, Michael and Scott D. Emmert (Eds.) (2004). *Upon further review: Sports in American literature.* Westport, CT: Praeger.

Cohen, Greta L. (Ed.) (1993). *Women in sport: Issues and controversies.* London: Sage.

Colangelo, Jerry and Len Sherman (1999). *How you play the game: Lessons for life from the billion-dollar business of sports.* Saranac Lake, NY: AMACOM/American Management Association.

Cole, Cheryl, John Loy, and Mike Messner (Eds.) (1993). *Exercising power: The making and remaking of the body.* Albany, NY: SUNY Press.

Coleman, Ken (1973). *So you want to Be a sportscaster: The techniques and skills of sports announcing by one of the country's most experienced broadcasters.* Brist, UK: Hawthorn Books.

Coleman, Ken and Valenti, Dan (1982). *Diary of a sportscaster.* Pittsfield, MA: Literations.

Coleman, Ken and Valenti, Dan (2000). *Talking on air: A broadcaster's life in sports.* Champaign, IL: Sports Publishing.

Collins, Timothy (2004). *The piranha club: Power and influence in Formula One.* London: Virgin Books.

Condon, Creighton O'M., James W. Quinn, Kelly Charles Crabb, John M. Genga, Joel A. Katz, Kent Newsome, Bonnie E. Berry, Barry B. Langberg, Joshua J. Kaufman, David A. Gurwin, Arnold P. Peter, Roger L. Armstrong, and M. Robert Dushman (2004). *The legal side of entertainment, sports, and media.* Boston, MA: Aspatore Books.

Conrad, Mark (2006). *The business of sports: A primer for journalists.* Mahwah, NJ: Laurence Erlbaum.

Considine, Tim (1982). *The Language of Sport.* New York: World Almanac.

Consoli, John (2004, February 4). ESPN cancels successful *Playmakers* drama. Available online: http://mediaweek.printthis.clickability.com

Cook, Philip S., Douglas Gomery, and Lawrence W. Lichty (Eds.) (1992). *The future of news: Television, newspapers, wire services, newsmagazines.* Baltimore, MD: Johns Hopkins University Press.

Cope, Myron (2002). *Double yoi! A revealing memoir by the broadcaster/writer.* Champaign, IL: Sports Publishing.

Cosell, Howard (1974). *Like it is.* Chicago, IL: Playboy Press.

Cosell, Howard with Peter Bonaventre (1985). *I never played the game*. New York: William Morrow and Company, Inc.

Cosell, Howard with Mickey Herskowitz (1973). *Cosell*. Chicago, IL: Playboy Press.

Cosell, Howard with Shelby Whitfield (1991). *What's wrong with sports*. New York: Simon & Schuster.

Costa, D.M. and S.R. Guthrie (Eds.) (1994). *Women and sport: Interdisciplinary perspectives*. Champaign, IL: Human Kinetics.

Costas, Bob (1998). *Costas on sports*. New York: Bantam.

Costas, Bob (2001). *Fair ball: A fan's case for baseball*. New York: Broadway Books.

Cotton, Doyice J. and T. Jesse Wilde (1997). *Sport law for sport managers*. Dubuque, Iowa: Kendall/Hunt.

Cousy, Bob with Albert Hirshberg (1958). *Basketball is my life*. Englewood Cliffs, NJ: Prentice Hall.

Coventry, Barbara Thomas (2004). On the sidelines: Sex and racial segregation in television sports broadcasting. *Sociology of Sport Journal,* Volume 21: 322-341.

Covil, Eric C. (ND). Radio and its impact on the sports world. Available online: www.americansportscastersonline.com/radiohistory.html.

Cowan, Thomas H. (1950). *Reminiscences*. Unpublished.

Cox, Richard H. (1990). *Sport psychology: Concepts and applications*. Dubuque, Iowa: William C. Brown.

Cozzillio, Michael J. and Mark S. Levinstein (1997). *Sports law: Cases and materials*. Durham, NC: Carolina Academic Press.

Crawford, Garry (2005). *Consuming sport*. New York: Routledge.

Crawford, Garry and Victoria K. Gosling (2004). The myth of the 'Puck Bunny.' *Sociology,* Volume 38, Number 3: 477-493.

Crawford, Scott A.G.M. (2004). *Serious sport: J.A. Mangan's contribution to the history of sport*. London: Frank Cass.

Creedon, Pamela J. (Ed.) (1994a). *Women, media and sport: Challenging gender values*. Thousand Oaks, CA: Sage.

Creedon, Pamela J. (Ed.) (1994b). Women in toyland: A look at women in American Newspaper sports journalism. In Pamela J. Creedon (Ed.), *Women, media and sport: Challenging gender values*. (67-107). Thousand Oaks, CA: Sage.

Creedon, Pamela J. (Ed.) (1994c). From whalebone to spandex: Women and sports Journalism in American magazines, photography and broadcasting. In Pamela J. Creedon (Ed.), *Women, media and sport: Challenging gender values*. (108-158). Thousand Oaks, CA: Sage.

Creedon, Pamela J. and Stanley T. Wearden (2000). Media coverage of U.S. women's sports: A critical analysis of trends and changes. International Association of Mass Communication Research, Singapore.

Cronin, Mike and David Mayall (Eds.) (1998). *Sporting nationalisms*. Oxford, UK: Taylor & Francis, Inc.

Crosset, Todd W. (1995). *Outsiders in the clubhouse: The world of women's profes-sional golf.* Albany, NY: State University of New York Press.

Crouser, Dick (1983). *'It's unlucky to be behind at the end of the game' and other great sports retorts.* New York: William Morrow.

Cummins, R. Glenn (2006). Sports fiction: Critical and empirical perspectives. In Arthur A. Raney and Jennings Bryant (Eds.) *Handbook of sports and media.* Mahwah, NJ: Lawrence Erlbaum: 185-204.

Cuneen, Jacquelyn and M. Joy Sidwell (1994). *Sport management: Field experi-ences.* Morgantown, WV: Fitness Information Technology.

Curry, Timothy Jon (2002). Fraternal bonding in the locker room: A profeminist analysis of talk about competition and women. In Sheila Scranton and Anne Flintoff (Eds.) *Gender and sport: A reader.* London: Taylor and Francis: 169-187.

Curtis, Bryan (2006). Prime-time wisenheimer. *Play* (September): 40.

Curtis, Bryan (2007). Simply marvelous. *Play* (March): 28.

Daddario, Gina (1998). *Women's sport and spectacle: Gendered television cover-age and the Olympic Games.* Westport, CT: Praeger.

Davidson, Judith A. (Ed.) (1993). *Sport on film and video: The North American So-ciety for Sport History guide.* Metuchen, NJ: Scarecrow.

Davies, Richard O. (1994). *America's obsession: Sports and society since 1945.* Fort Worth: Harcourt Brace.

Davis, Laurel R. (1997). *The swimsuit issue and sport: Hegemonic masculinity in Sports Illustrated.* Albany, NY: State University of New York Press.

Dawkins, Marvin P. and Kinloch, Graham C. (2000). *African American golfers dur-ing the Jim Crow era.* Westport, CT: Praeger.

Deford, Frank (1987). *The world's tallest midget: The best of Frank Deford.* Boston, MA: Little, Brown & Company.

Deford, Frank (2000). *The best of Frank Deford.* Chicago: Triumph Books.

Delaney, Kevin J. and Rick Eckstein (2003). *Public dollars, private stadiums: The battle over building sports stadiums.* New Brunswick, NJ: Rutgers University Press.

Delin, Judy (2000). *The language of everyday life.* London: Sage.

de Morgas Spa, Miquel, Nancy K. Rivenburgh, and James F. Larson (1995). *Televi-sion in the Olympics.* London: John Libbey.

Dempsey, J.M., Paul Gullifor, William Raffel, and Max Utsler (2007). Sports talk radio in America: Today and tomorrow. Popular Culture Association, Boston, MA.

Denham, Bryan E., Andrew C. Billings, and Kelby K. Halone (2002). Differential accounts of race in broadcast commentary of the 2000 NCAA men's and women's Final Four basketball tournaments. *Sociology of Sport Journal,* Vol-ume 19: 315-332.

DeSensi, Joy T. and Danny Rosenberg (1996). *Ethics in sports management.* Morgantown, WV: Fitness Information Technology.

Diamant, Louis (Ed.) (1991). *Psychology of sport, exercise, and fitness: Social and personal issues.* New York: Hemisphere Pub.

Dimeo, Paul (Ed.) (2006). *Drugs, alcohol and sport.* New York: Routledge.

Dinan, John (1998). *Sports in the pulp magazines.* Jefferson, NC: McFarland.

Donnellan, Nanci with Neal Karle (1996). *The babe in toyland* (by The Fabulous Sports Babe). New York: Regan Books.

Donnelly, Peter (Ed.) (1997). *Taking sport seriously: Social issues in Canadian sport.* Toronto: Thompson.

Dougherty, Neil J. (1994). *Sport, physical activity, and the law.* Champaign, IL: Human Kinetics

Drinkwater, Barbara L. (Ed.) (2000). *Women in sport: Volume VIII, Encyclopedia of sports medicine.* Cambridge, MA: Blackwell.

Drysdale, Don with Bob Verdi (1990). *Once a bum, always a Dodger: My life in baseball from Brooklyn to Los Angeles.* New York: St. Martin's Press.

Duncan, Joyce (2004). *Sport in American culture: From Ali to X-games.* Santa Barbara, CA: ABC-CLIO.

Duncan, Margaret Carlisle and Barry Brummett (1987). The mediation of spectator sport. *Research Quarterly for Exercise and Sport,* Volume 58, Number 2: 168-177.

Duncan, Margaret Carlisle and Michael Messner (2000). *Gender in televised sports: 1989, 1993, and 1999.* Los Angeles, CA: Amateur Athletic Foundation.

Dunnavant, Keith (2004). *The fifty-year seduction: How television manipulated college football, from the birth of the modern NCAA to the creation of the BCS.* New York: T. Dunne Books.

Dunning, Eric (1999). *Sport matters: Sociological studies of sport, violence, and civilisation.* London: Routledge.

Dunning, Eric, Dominic Malcolm, and Ivan Waddington (Eds.) (2006). *Sport histories: Figurational studies of the development of modern sports.* London: Routledge.

Dunphy, Don (1988). *Don Dunphy at ringside.* New York: Henry Holt.

Durslag, Melvin (1975). I don't care who wins, as long as *We* do!: An unblushing defense of announcers who root for the home team. *TV Guide* (May 17): 21-3.

Dyreson, Mark (1998). *Making the American team: Sport, culture, and the Olympic experience.* Urbana, IL: University of Illinois Press.

Eastman, Susan Tyler and Andrew C. Billings (2000). Sportscasting and sports Reporting: The power of gender bias. *Journal of Sport and Social Issues,* Volume 24, Number 2: 192-214.

Eastman, Susan Tyler and Andrew C. Billings (2004). Biased voices of sports: Racial and gender stereotyping in college basketball. *Howard Journal of Communication,* Volume 12, Number 4 (October): 183-201.

Edwards, Bob (1993). *Fridays with Red (Barber): A radio friendship.* New York: Simon and Schuster.

Egendorf, Laura K. (Ed.) (1999). *Sports and athletes: Opposing viewpoints*. San Diego, CA: Greenhaven Press.

Eggerton, John (2005). ESPN to track product placements. *Broadcasting & Cable* (Mary 9).

Ehrenreich, Barbara (2006). *Dancing in the streets: A history of collective joy*. New York: Metropolitan Books.

Eisen, George and David K. Wiggins (Eds.) (1994). *Ethnicity and sport in North American history and culture*. Westport, CT: Greenwood.

Eisenstock, Alan. (2001). *Sports talk: A journey inside the world of sports talk radio*. New York: Simon and Schuster.

Eitzen, D. Stanley (1999). *Fair and foul: Beyond the myths and paradoxes of sport*. Oxford: Rowman and Littlefield.

Eitzen, D. Stanley (Ed.) (2004). *Sport in contemporary society: An anthology*. 7th ed. Boulder, CO: Paradigm Publishers.

Elder, Donald (1956). *Ring Lardner: A biography*. Garden City, NY: Doubleday.

Elderkin, Phil (1993). A sportswriter's writer (Jim Murray). *The Christian Science Monitor* (July 6): 14.

Elderkin, Phil (2006). Red Auerbach, an off-court legend. *The Christian Science Monitor* (October 30): 2.

Elias, Norbert and Eric Dunning (1986). *The quest for excitement: Sport and leisure in the civilizing process*. New York: Basil Blackwell.

Elston, Gene (2005). *The wide world of sports: Over a century of amusing stories and quotes*. Bloomington, IN: Authorhouse.

Enberg, Dick with Jim Perry (2004). *Oh my!* Champaign, IL: Sports Publishing.

Enriquez, Jon (2002). Coverage of sports. In W. David Sloan and Lisa Mullikin Parcell (Eds.), *American journalism history: Principles, practices*. Jefferson, NC: McFarland: 198-208.

Entine, Jon (2000). *Taboo: Why black athletes dominate sports and why we are afraid to talk about it*. New York: Public Affairs.

Evey, Stuart and Irv Broughton (2004). *Creating an empire: The no-holds barred story of power, ego, money, and vision that transformed a culture*. Chicago, IL: Triumph Books.

Falk, Gerhard (2005). *Football and American identity* Binghamton, NY: The Haworth Press.

Feherty, David (2003). *Somewhere in Ireland, a village is missing an idiot*. New York: Rugged Land.

Festle, Mary Jo (1996). *Playing nice: Politics and apologies in women's sports*. New York: Columbia University Press.

Field, Shelly (2004). *Career opportunities in the sports industry*. 3rd edition. New York: Checkmark Books.

Findling, John E. and Kimberly D. Pelle (Eds.) (1996). *Historical dictionary of the modern Olympic movement*. Westport, CT: Greenwood Press.

Finn, Gerry P.T. and Richard Guilianotti (Eds.) (2000). *Football culture: Local contests, global visions.* London: Frank Cass.

Fischer, Heinz-Dietrich (1995). *Sports journalism at its best: Pulitzer prize-winning articles, cartoons, and photographs.* Chicago, IL: Nelson-Hall Publishers.

Fixx, James F. (1981). *Jackpot!* New York: Random House.

Fizel, John, Elizabeth Gustafson, and Lawrence Hadley (Eds.) (1999). *Sports economics: Current research.* Westport, CT: Praeger.

Fleder, Rob (Ed.) (2003). *Fifty years of great writing: Sports Illustrated, 1954-2004.* New York: Sports Illustrated Books.

Foer, Franklin (2004). *How soccer explains the world: An unlikely theory of globalization.* New York: Harper Perennial.

Football Television Briefing Book (1981). Shawnee Mission, KS: NCAA Football TV Commission.

Ford, Richard (1986). *The sportswriter.* New York: Vintage.

Fornoff, Susan (1993). *Lady in the locker room.* Champaign, IL: Human Kinetics.

Fort, Rodney D. (2006). *Sports Economics,* 2nd edition. Englewood Cliffs, NJ: Prentice Hall.

Fotiades, John M. (1989). *You're the judge: How to understand sports, torts & courts.* Worcester, MA: Edgeworth and North Books.

Fountain, Charles (1993). *Sportswriter: The life and times of Grantland Rice.* New York: Oxford University Press.

Franklin, Pete with Terry Pluto (1988). *You could argue but you'd be wrong.* Chicago: Contemporary Books.

Freeman, Michael (2002). *ESPN: The uncensored history.* Dallas, TX: Taylor.

French, Scott (2003). Soccer. In Abraham Aamidor (Ed.), *Real sports reporting.* (Bloomington: Indiana University Press): 40-60.

Fulks, Matt (1998). *The sportscaster's dozen: Off the air with southeastern legends.* Indianapolis, IN: Masters Press.

Fuller, Linda K. (1987a). Researching women and the Olympics. *The Starting Line,* Canadian Association for the Advancement of Women and Sport (Summer): 11+.

Fuller, Linda K. (1987b). Olympics access for women: Athletes, organizers, and sports journalists. *The olympic movement and the mass media: Past, present and future issues.* International Conference Proceedings, The University of Calgary. (Calgary, Alberta, Canada: Hurford Enterprises Ltd.): 4/9-4/18.

Fuller, Linda K. (1989). The business of sportscasting. International Conference on Sports Business, University of South Carolina, Columbia, S.C.

Fuller, Linda K. (1990a). The baseball movie genre: At bat or struck out? *Play & Culture* 3 (February): 64-74.

Fuller, Linda K. (1990b). Images of Olympians in film. International Communication Association, Dublin, Ireland.

Fuller, Linda K. (1990c). An American audience for the Seoul Summer Olympics. International Association for Mass Communication Research, Lake Bled, Yugoslavia.

Fuller, Linda K. (1991). 'Triumph of the underdog' in baseball films. In Paul Loukides and Linda K. Fuller (Eds.), *Beyond the Stars 11: Plot conventions in American popular film* (Bowling Green, OH: Popular Press, 1991): 53-60.

Fuller, Linda K. (1992a). Reporters' rights to the locker room. Union for Democratic Communications, Trent University, Peterborough, Ontario, Canada.

Fuller, Linda K. (1992b). Remembering radio: Work in progress on oral history, International Association for Mass Communication Research, Guaruja, Brazil.

Fuller, Linda K. (1992c). Reporters rights in the locker room. *Feminist Issues,* Volume 12, No. 1 (Spring): 39-45.

Fuller, Linda K. (1992d). Magic in the media: An analysis and survey on the sports story of our times. International Society for Comparative Physical Education and Sport Conference, University of Houston, Texas.

Fuller, Linda K. (1992e). *The Cosby Show: Audiences, impact, implications.* Westport, CT: Greenwood Press.

Fuller, Linda K. (1992f). Sportstalk/wartalk/patriotismtalk/mentalk: Super Bowl XXV. International Association for Mass Communication Research, Guaruja, Brazil.

Fuller, Linda K. (1994a). Chicago sportscasters. Popular Culture Association, Chicago, IL.

Fuller, Linda K. (1994b). The Magic Johnson Media phenomenon: An interdisciplinary analysis and survey. In Linda K. Fuller and Lilless McPherson Shilling (Eds.), *Communicating About Communicable Diseases.* (Amherst, MA: Human Resource Development Press): 155-176.

Fuller, Linda K. (1994c). The business of sportscasting. In Peter J. Graham (Ed.), *Sport Business: Operational and Theoretical Aspects* (Dubuque, IA: Wm. C. Brown): 251-261.

Fuller, Linda K. (1995a). *The not-so-'Rocky' road: Philadelphia films about sports.* Philadelphia, PA, Popular Culture Association.

Fuller, Linda K. (1995b). The 'Sultan of Swat' on the silver screen. A Conference Commemorating the 100th Birthday of Babe Ruth, Hofstra University, Hempstead, NY.

Fuller, Linda K. (1996). Olympic documentary films. In John E. Findling and Kimberly D. Pelle (Eds.), *Historical dictionary of the modern olympic movement* (Westport, CT: Greenwood Press): 404-414.

Fuller, Linda K. (1997a). Trekking rhetoric: Magazine accounts of the May, 1996 Mount Everest disaster. Popular Culture Association, San Antonio, TX.

Fuller, Linda K. (1997b). The sporting life in Pennsylvania caught on celluloid. *Pennsylvania History,* Volume 43, No. 4 (Autumn): 543-548.

Fuller, Linda K. (1997c). We can't duck the issue: Imbedded advertising is increasing in the motion pictures. In Katherine T. Frith (Ed.), *Undressing the ad: Reading culture in advertisements* (New York: Peter Lang): 117-138.

Fuller, Linda K. (1999a). Disney's ducks: A film series to advertise an NHL franchise. Popular Culture Association, Orlando, FL, 1998.

Fuller, Linda K. (1999b). Single-sex health clubs: Political, economic, psychological, and socio-cultural implications. Women's Studies for a New Millennium colloquium, Southern Connecticut State University, New Haven, CT.

Fuller, Linda K. (1999c). Super Bowl speak: Subtexts of sex and sex talk in America's annual sports extravaganza. In Meta G. Carstarphen and Susan C. Zavoina (Eds.), *Sexual rhetoric: Media perspectives on sexuality, gender, and identity* (Westport, CT: Greenwood Press): 161-173.

Fuller, Linda K. (2000). The gym/gyn health club issue. Popular Culture Association New Orleans, LA.

Fuller, Linda K. (2001). Miller time? Time (and ratings) will tell how long Dennis Miller will rate as a sportscaster on *MFN*. Popular Culture Association, Philadelphia, PA.

Fuller, Linda K. (2003a). (Un)necessary roughness: A review of sports violence. Northeast Popular Culture Association, Worcester State College, Worcester, MA.

Fuller, Linda K. (2003b). Teaming gender with the language of sport. National Communication Association, Miami, FL.

Fuller, Linda K. (2004a). Fictionalizing (American) football: A case study of the television show *Playmakers*. International Association for Media and Communication Research Conference, Porto Alegra, Brazil.

Fuller, Linda K. (Ed.) (2004b). *National days/National ways: Historical, political, and religious celebrations around the world.* Westport, CT: Greenwood.

Fuller, Linda K. (2005a). Jockocracy revisited and revisioned: A case study of a 30-years-ago sports media panic. International Association for Media and Communication Research Conference, Taipei, Taiwan.

Fuller, Linda K. (2005b). The warlike, violent language of sport. Boston, MA Northeastern University.

Fuller, Linda K. (Editor) (2006a). *Sport, rhetoric, and gender: Historical perspectives and media representations.* New York: Palgrave Macmillan.

Fuller, Linda K. (2006b). The vamp, the homebody, and the upstart: Women, language, and baseball films. In Linda K. Fuller (Ed.), *Sport, rhetoric, and gender: Historical perspectives and media representations.* (New York: Palgrave Macmillan): 185-197.

Fuller, Linda K. (2006c). Sports celebrity-hood seen in a positive light: The case of Yao Ming and HIV/AIDS in China. Popular Culture Association, Atlanta, Georgia.

Fuller, Linda K. (Ed.) (2007a). *Community media: International perspectives.* New York: Palgrave Macmillan).

Fuller, Linda K. (Ed.) (2007b). Pat Tillman: Sport hero/martyr as militaristic symbol of the Iraq/Afghanistan war. International Association for Media and Communication Research Conference. Paris, France.

Fuller, Linda K. (Forthcoming). @*nalog to zine$: An encyclopedia of telecommunications in popular culture.* Cresskill, NJ: Hampton Press.

Fuller, Linda K. and Lilless McPherson Shilling (1990). *Communicating comfortably: Your guide to overcoming speaking and writing anxieties.* Amherst, MA: Human Resource Development Press.

Fuller, Linda K. and Mark D. West (2001). Toward a typology of theoretical grounding for computer content analysis. In West, Mark D. (Ed.), *Theory, method, and practice in computer content analysis.* (77-94). Westport, CT: Ablex.

Garagiola, Joe (1990). *Baseball is a funny game.* New York: HarperCollins.

Garber, Mary (1994). Women and children are not admitted to the press box. In Ron Rappaport (Ed.), *A kind of grace: A treasury of sportswriting by women.* Berkley, CA: Zenobia Books:377-384.

Garland, Jon and Michael Rowe (2001). *Racism and anti-racism in football.* Houndmills, Basingstoke: Palgrave.

Garner, Joe (1999). *And the crowd goes wild.* Naperville, IL: Sourcebooks.

Garner, Joe (2000). *And the fans roared: The sports broadcasts that kept us on the edge of our seats.* Naperville, IL: Sourcebooks.

Garrison, Bruce (1987). The evolution of professionalism in sports reporting. *The olympic movement and the mass media: Past, present, and future issues.* International Conference Proceedings, The University of Calgary. (Calgary, Alberta, Canada: Hurford Enterprises Ltd.): 3/23-3/27.

Garrison, Bruce with Mark Sabljak (1990). *Sports reporting.* Ames, IA: Iowa State University Press.

Gavora, Jessica (2002). *Tilting the playing field: Schools, sports, sex and Title IX.* New York: Encounter Books.

Geismar, Maxwell (Ed). (1963). *The Ring Lardner reader.* New York: Scribners.

Gems, Gerald R. (2006). *The athletic crusade: Sport and American cultural imperialism.* Lincoln: University of Nebraska Press.

George, Nelson (1999). *Elevating the game: Black men and basketball.* Lincoln, NE: University of Nebraska Press.

George, Phyllis (2002). *Never say never: 10 lessons to turn you can't into yes I can.* New York: McGraw-Hill.

Gerber, Ellen W. (Ed.) (1974). *The American woman in sport.* Reading, MA: Addison- Wesley.

Gerdy, John R. (2002). *Sports: The all-American addiction.* Jackson, MS: University of Mississippi Press.

Gibson, Heather (2006). *Sport tourism.* New York: Routledge.

Gibson, Roy (1991). *Radio and television reporting.* Boston, MA: Allyn and Bacon.

Gifford, Frank (1976). *Gifford on courage.* New York: Evans.

Gifford, Frank with Harry Waters (1993). *The whole ten yards.* New York: Random House.

Giulianotti, Richard, Norman Bonney, and Mike Hepwarth (Eds.) (1994). *Football, violence, and society identity.* London: Routledge.

Giulianotti, Richard (Ed.) 2004. *Sport and modern social theorists: Theorizing homo ludens.* New York: Palgrave Macmillan.

Glickman, Marty (1996). *Fastest kid on the block*. Syracuse, NY: Syracuse University Press.

Goff, Brian L. and Robert D. Tollison (Eds.) (1990). *Sportometrics*. College Station, TX: Texas A&M University Press.

Gogol, Sara (2002). *Hard fought victories: Women coaches making a difference*. Terra Haute, IN: Cardinal Publishing Group.

Goldenson, Leonard H. and Marvin J. Wolf (1991). *Beating the odds: The untold story behind the rise of ABC*. New York: Charles Scribner's Sons.

Goldman, Robert and Stephen Papson (1998). *Nike culture*. London: Sage.

Goldstein, Jeffrey H. (Ed.) (1983). *Sports violence*. New York: Springer-Verlag.

Goodman, Ellen (1998). Super Bowl sends testosterone raging. *Union News* (January 29): A11.

Gopnik, Adam (2007). The sporting scene: The unbeautiful game. *The New Yorker* (January 8): 38-43.

Gordon, Jeff (2003). Covering hockey. In Abraham Aamidor (Ed.), *Real sports reporting*. (Bloomington: Indiana University Press): 26-39.

Gorman, Jerry and Kirk Calhoun (1994). *The name of the game: The business of sports*. New York: John Wiley & Sons.

Gorn, Elliott J. and Warren Goldstein (2004). *A brief history of American sports*. Urbana: University of Illinois Press.

Gowdy, Curt (1966). *Cowboy at the mike*. New York: Doubleday.

Graham, Frank, Jr. (1981, 2003). *A farewell to heroes*. Carbondale, IL: Southern Illinois University Press.

Graham, Peter J. (Ed.) (1994). *Sport business: Operational and theoretical aspects*. Madison, WI: WCB Brown & Benchmark.

Graham, Stedman, Joe Jeff Goldblatt, and Lisa Delphy Neirotti (2001). *The ultimate guide to sports marketing*. New York: McGraw-Hill.

Grainger, Andrew, Joshua I. Newman, and David L. Andrews (2006). In Arthur A. Raney and Jennings Bryant (Eds.) *Handbook of sports and media*. Mahwah, NJ: Lawrence Erlbaum: 447-467.

Grant, Randy R., John Leadly, and Zenon Zygmont (2007). *Economics of intercollegiate sports*. Hackensack, NJ: World Scientific Publishing Company.

Grafton, Chris and Ian Jones (2003). *Research methods for sports studies*. New York: Routledge.

Gratton, Chris and Harry Arne Solberg (2007). *The economics of sports broadcasting*. New York: Routledge.

Green, Tim (1997). *The dark side of the game: My life in the NFL*. New York: Warner.

Greenberg, Judith E. (1997). *Getting into the game: Women and sports*. New York: Franklin Watts.

Greenberg, Martin J. (1993). *Sports law practice*. Charlottesville, VA: Michie Co.

Greenberg, Mike (2006). *Why my wife thinks I'm an idiot: The life and times of a sportscaster dad*. New York: Villard.

Greenfield, Steve and Guy Osborn (Eds.) (2000). *Law and sport in contemporary society.* London: Frank Cass.

Greenwald, Hank (1997). *This copyrighted broadcast.* San Francisco, CA: Woodford Press.

Griffin, Pat (1998). *Strong women, deep closets: Lesbians and homophobia in sport.* Champaign, IL: Human Kinetics.

Grout, Jeff, Sarah Perrin, and Clive Woodward (2006). *Mind games: Inspirational lessons from the world's finest sports stars.* Knoxville, TN: Capstone.

Gruneau, Richard (1999). *Class, sports, and social development.* Champaign, IL: Human Kinetics.

Gruneau, Richard and David Whitson (1993). *Hockey night in Canada: Sport, identities, and cultural politics.* Toronto, ON: Garamond Press.

Gunston, Robin (2005). The future of sport. *The Futurist* (January).

Gunter, Barrie (2006). Sport, violence, and the media. In Arthur A. Raney and Jennings Bryant (Eds.) *Handbook of sports and media.* Mahwah, NJ: Lawrence Erlbaum: 353-364.

Gunther, Marc (1994). *The house that Roone built: The inside story of ABC News.* Boston, MA: Little, Brown.

Gunther, Marc and Bill Carter (1988). *Monday night mayhem: The inside story of ABC's Monday Night Football.* New York: Beech Tree Brooks.

Guttman, Allen (1978). *From ritual to record: The nature of modern sports.* New York: Columbia University Press.

Guttman, Allen (1986). *Sports spectators.* New York: Columbia University Press.

Guttman, Allen (1988). *A whole new ball game: An interpretation of American sports.* Chapel Hill, NC: The University of North Carolina Press.

Guttman, Allen (1991). *Women's sports: A history.* New York: Columbia University Press.

Guttman, Allen (1992). *The Olympics: A history of the modern games.* Urbana, IL: University of Illinois Press.

Guttman, Allen (1996). *The erotic in sports.* New York: Columbia University Press.

Hafner, Everett (1989). *Sports riddles.* New York: Viking Kestrel.

Halberstam, David J. (1999). *Sports on New York radio: A play-by-play history.* Lincolnwood, IL: Masters Press.

Hall, M. Ann (1996). *Feminism and sporting bodies: Essays on theory and practice.* Champaign, IL: Human Kinetics.

Hallmark, James R. (2006). We don't glow, we sweat: The ever changing commentary about women's athletics. In Linda K. Fuller (Ed.) *Sport, rhetoric, and gender: Historical perspectives and media representations.* (159-168). New York: Palgrave Macmillan.

Hamil, Sean, Jonathan Michie, Christine Oughton, and Steven Warby (Eds.) (2006). *The changing face of the football business.* London: Frank Cass.

Hamm, Mia (2000). *Go for the goal: A champion's guide to winning in soccer and life.* New York: Quill/HarperCollins.

Harmon, Merle (1998). *Merle Harmon stories*. Dallas: Sam Blaire and Bob Lilly.

Hauser, Melanie (2003). Golf. In Abraham Aamidor (Ed.), *Real sports reporting*. (Bloomington: Indiana University Press): 81-93.

Hamilton, Milo, Schlossberg, Dan, and Ibach, Bob (2006). *Making airwaves: 60 years at Milo's microphone*. Champaign, IL: Sports Publishing.

Hargreaves, Jennifer (1994). *Sporting females: Critical issues in the history and sociology of women's sports*. London: Routledge.

Hargreaves, Jennifer (2001). *Heroines of sport: The politics of difference and identity*. London: Routledge.

Harper, William A. (1999). *How you played the game: The life of Grantland Rice*. Columbia, MO: University of Missouri Press.

Harris, Fran (2001). *Summer madness: Inside the wild, wacky, wonderful world of the WNBA*. San Jose, CA: Authors Choice Press.

Harris, Janet C. (1994). *Athletes and the American hero dilemma*. Champaign, IL: Human Kinetics.

Hartman-Tews, Ilse and Gertrude Pfister (Eds.) (2003). *Sport and women: Social issues in international perspective*. London: Routledge.

Harwell, Ernie (1985). *Tuned to baseball*. South Bend, IN: Diamond Communications.

Harwell, Ernie (1991). *Ernie Harwell's diamond gems*. Ann Arbor, MI: Momentum.

Harwell, Ernie (2001). *Stories from my life in baseball*. Detroit, MI: Detroit Free Press.

Harwell, Ernie (2002). *The Babe signed my shoe*. South Bend, IN: Diamond Communications.

Harwell, Ernie (2004). *Life after baseball*. Detroit, MI: Detroit Free Press.

Hearn, Chick and Springer, Steve (2004). *Chick: His unpublished memoirs and the memories of those who loved him*. Chicago, IL: Triumph Books.

Hedrick, Tom (2000). *The art of sportscasting: How to build a successful career*. South Bend, IN: Diamond Communications.

Heitzmann, William Ray (2004). *Careers for sports nuts and other athletic types*, 3rd edition. New York: McGraw-Hill.

Helfand, Lewis (2005). Sportscaster salaries. Available online: http://www.ask men.com.

Helitzer, Melvin (1996). *The dream job: $port$ publicity, promotion and marketing*. Athens, OH: University Sports Press.

Heller, Dick (2003). Gionfriddo caught DiMaggio by surprise. *The WashingtonTimes*, March 24.

Hemphill, Dennis and Caroline Symons (Eds.) (2002). *Gender, sexuality, and sport: A dangerous mix*. Petersham, NSW, Australia: Walla Walla Press.

Heywood, Leslie (2000). *Pretty good for a girl: An athlete's story*. Minneapolis, MN: University of Minnesota Press.

Heywood, Leslie and Shari L. Dworkin (2003). *Built to win: The female athlete as cultural icon*. Minneapolis, MN: University of Minnesota Press.

Higgs, Robert J. (1995). *God in the stadium: Sports and religion in America.* Lexington, KY: University Press of Kentucky.

Higham, James (2004). *Sport tourism destinations: Issues, opportunities and analysis.* Burlington, MA: Butterworth-Heinemann.

Hilton, Christopher (2003). *Inside the mind of the Grand Prix driver: The psychology of the fastest men on earth: Sex, danger and everything else.* Somerset, UK: J. H. Haynes.

Hinch, Thomas and James E. S. Higham (2004). *Sport tourism development.* Clevedon, UK: Channel View Books.

Hirsch, Alan (1994). Sports 'muffs' at the mike. *Media History Digest,* Volume 14, Number 1 (Spring-Summer): 51-52.

Hirshberg, Charles (2004). *ESPN 25: 25 mind-bending, eye-popping, culture morphing years of highlights.* New York: ESPN Books.

Hitchcock, John R. (1991). *Sportscasting.* Boston, MA: Focal Press.

Hladczuk, John (Comp.) (1991). *Sports law and legislation: An annotated bibliography.* New York: Greenwood Press.

Hnida, Katie (2006). *Still ticking: My dramatic journey as the first woman to play division 1 college football.* New York: Scribner.

Hoberman, John (1986). *The Olympic crisis: Sport, politics, and the moral order.* New Rochelle, NY: A.D. Caratzas.

Hoberman, John (1997). *Darwin's athletes: How sport has damaged Black America and preserved the myth of race.* New York: Mariner Books.

Hoberman, John (2005). *Testosterone dreams: Rejuvenation, aphrodisia, doping.* Berkeley, CA: University of California Press.

Hoffer, Richard (2007). *Jackpot nation: Rambling and gambling across our landscape of luck.* New York: HarperCollins.

Hoffman, Marilyn (1984). Women sports stars tackle broadcast journalism. *Christian Science Monitor* (August 2): 27.

Hofmann, Dale and Martin J. Greenberg (1989). *Sport$biz: An irreverent look at big business in pro sports.* Champaign, IL: Leisure Press.

Holtzman, Jerome (1974). *No cheering in the press box.* New York: Holt, Rinehart and Winston.

Hong, Fan (2006). *Sport, nationalism and orientalism: The Asian Games.* London: Routledge.

Horn, Thelma S. (Ed.) (1992). *Advances in sport psychology.* Champaign, IL: Human Kinetics.

Horne, John (2006). *Sport in consumer culture.* Houndmills, Basingstoke, Hampshire: Palgrave Macmillan.

Horne, John, Alan Tomlinson, and Gary Whannel (1999). *Understanding sport: An introduction to the sociological and cultural analysis of sport.* London: E. and F.N. Spon.

Horowitz, Ira (1974). Sports Broadcasting. In Roger C. Noll (Ed.), *Government and the sports business.* Washington, DC: Brookings Institution.

Horrell, Muriel (comp.) (1968). *South Africa and the Olympic Games*. Johannesburg, South Africa: South African Institute of Race Relations.

Houlihan, Barrie (1994). *Sport and international politics*. New York: Harvester Wheatsheaf.

Houlihan, Barrie and Anita White (2002). *Politics of sports development*. New York: Routledge

Howard, Dennis R. and John L. Crampton (1995). *Financing sport*. Morgantown, WV: Fitness Information Technology.

Howe, David (2003). *Sport, professionalism and pain: Ethnographies of injury and risk*. London: Routledge.

Howell, Colm D. (2001). *Blood, sweat and cheers: Sport and the making of modern Canada*. Toronto: University of Toronto Press.

Hubbell, Ralph (1975). *Come walk with me*. Englewood Cliffs, NJ: Prentice-Hall.

Hudson, Simon (Ed.) (2002). *Sport and adventure tourism*. Binghamton, NY: The Haworth Press.

Hughes, Mark and Simon Arron (2003). *The complete book of Formula One*. Osceola, WI: Motorbooks.

Hughes, Pat with Bruce Miles (2007). *Harry Caray: Voice of the fans*. Naperville, IL:sourcebooks.

Hughson, John and Marcus Free (2006). Paul Willis, cultural commodities, and collective sport fandom. *Sociology of Sport Journal* (20): 214-231.

Hughson, John, David Inglis, and Marcus Free (2004). The uses of sport: A critical study. *Sport in Society*, Volume 9, Number 3: 483-485.

Humphries, Tom (2003). *Laptop dancing and the nanny goat mambo: A sportswriter's year*. Dublin: Pocket Books Townhouse.

Hums, Mary A. (2001). Myths and realities: What employers in the sport industry look for. Available online: http://155.33.32.224/csss/disability/challenge2001 .pdf.

Hums, Mary A. and Joanne C. Maclean (2004). *Governance and policy in sport organizations*. Scottsdale, AZ: Holcomb Hathaway.

Huppertz, Nancy (2002, March 13). The importance of language. Available online: http://www.gogirlgo.com.

Husing, Ted (1935). *Ten years before the mike*. New York: Farrar & Rinehart.

Inabinett, Mark (1994). *Grantland Rice and his heroes*. Knoxville, TN: University of Tennessee Press.

Ingham, Alan G. and John W. Loy (Eds.) (1993). *Sport in social development: Traditions, transitions, and transformations*. Champaign, IL: Human Kinetics.

Iovieno, Stephanie (2001). Sportscaster. Available online: http://www.womens sportsfoundation.org.

Ireland, Mary Lloyd (Ed.) (2002). *The female athlete*. Philadelphia, PA: Saunders.

Ismond, Patrick (2003). *Black and Asian athletes in British sport and society: A sporting chance*. London: Palgrave Macmillan.

Jackson, Herb (1986). Watch 'em single coverage the wide receivers and collision the quarterback! *TV Guide* (March 8): 45-6.

Jackson, Steven J. and David L. Andrews (Eds.) (2003). *Sport, culture, and advertising: Identities, commodities and the politics of representation.* Westport, CT: Greenwood.

Jackson, Tom with Woodrow Paige (1987). *Blitz: An autobiography.* New York: NTC/Contemporary.

Jarvie, Grant (1991). *Sport, racism, and ethnicity.* London: Falmer.

Jarvie, Grant (2006). *Sport, culture and society: An Introduction.* London: Routledge.

Jarvie, Grant and Joseph Maguire (1994). *Sport and leisure in social thought.* London: Routledge.

Jarvis, Robert M. and Phyllis Coleman (1999). *Sports law: Cases and materials.* St. Paul, MN: West Group.

Jeanrenaud, Claude and Stefan Kesenne (Eds.) (2006). *The economics of sport and the media.* Cheltenham, UK: Edward Elgan.

Jenkins, Henry (1997). Never trust a snake: WWF wrestling as masculine melodrama. In Aaron Baker and Todd Boyd (Eds.) (1997). *Out of bounds: Sports, media, and the politics of identity.* Bloomington, IN: Indiana University Press: 48-78.

Jenkins, Sally (1996). *Men will be boys: The modern woman explains football and other amusing male rituals.* New York: Doubleday.

Jenkins, Sally (1999). Women have invaded the men's club of TV sportscasters, but who let them in? *Sports Illustrated* (June 17): 78-85.

Jennings, Kenneth M. (1990). *Balls and strikes: The money game in professional baseball.* New York: Praeger.

Jhally, Sut (1989). Cultural studies and the sports/media complex. In Lawrence A. Wenner, (Ed.), *Media, sports, & society.* (Newbury Park, CA: Sage): 70-95.

Johnson, William O., Jr. (1971). *Super spectator and the electric lilliputians.* Boston, MA: Little, Brown & Co.

Johnston, Daryl (2005). *Watching football: Discovering the game within the game.* Guilford, CT: Globe Pequot.

Jones, Donald, with Elaine L. Daly (1992). *Sports ethics in America: A bibliography, 1970-1990.* Westport, CT: Greenwood.

Jones, Ian (2003). *Research methods for sports studies.* New York: Routledge.

Jones, Michael E. (1999). *Sports law.* Upper Saddle River, NJ: Prentice-Hall.

Jones, Robyn L. and Kathleen M. Armour (Eds.) (2000). *Sociology of sport: Theory and practice.* Boston: Longman.

Jozsa, Frank P., Jr. (2003). *American sports empire: How the leagues breed success.* Westport, CT: Praeger.

Jozsa, Frank P., Jr. (2006). *Big sports, big business: A century of league expansions, mergers, and reorganizations.* New York: Praeger.

Kahn, Roger (2000). *A flame of pure fire: Jack Dempsey and the Roaring 20s.* New York: Harcourt Brace.

Kane, Mary Jo (1996). Setting a course for college athletics: Media coverage of the post Title 1X female athlete: A feminist analysis of sport, gender, and power. *Duke Journal of Gender Law & Policy,* Volume 3, Number 1: 105-117.

Kanner, Bernice (2003). *The super bowl of advertising: How the commercials won the game.* New York: Bloomberg Press.

Katz, Jackson and Sut Jhally (1999). Crisis in masculinity. *Boston Globe* (May 2).

Kaufman, Michelle (2003). Covering women's sports: Fair play? In Abraham Aamidor (Ed.), *Real sports reporting.* (Bloomington: Indiana University Press): 233-243.

Keegan, Tom (2002). *Ernie Harwell: My 60 years in baseball.* Chicago: Triumph Books.

Kenyon, Gerald S. and John W. Loy (1965). Toward a sociology of sport. *Journal of Health, Physical Education and Recreation,* Volume 36, Number 24-25: 68-69.

Kerr, John H. (2006). *Rethinking aggression and violence in sport.* New York: Routledge.

Kew, Frank (1997). *Sport: Social problems and issues.* Oxford: Butterworth-Heinemann.

Kindred, Dave (2006). *Sound and fury: Two powerful lives, one fateful friendship.* New York: Free Press.

Kiner, Ralph with Joe Gergen (1987). *Kiner's korner: At bat and on the air: My 40 years in baseball.* New York: Arbor House.

King, C. Richard and Charles Fruehling Springwood (2001). *Beyond the cheers: Race as a spectacle in college sport.* Albany, NY: State University of New York Press.

Kirby, Sandra, Lorraine Greaves, and Olena Hankinsky (2001). *The dome of silence: Sexual harrassment and abuse in sport.* New York: Zed Books.

Kirsch, George B., Othello Harris, and Claire E. Nolte (Eds.) 2000. *Encyclopedia of ethnicity and sports in the United States.* Westport, CT: Greenwood.

Klatell, David A. and Norman Marcus. (1988). *Sports for sale: Television, money, and the fans.* New York: Oxford University Press.

Klein, Naomi (2000). *No logo: Taking aim at the brand bullies.* Vintage Canada.

Koppett, Leonard. (1994). *Sports illusion, sports reality: A reporter's view of sports, journalism and society.* Champaign, IL: University of Illinois Press.

Koppett, Leonard. (2003). *The rise and fall of the press box.* Toronto: Ontario: SportClassic Books.

Kornheiser, Tony (1995). Cosell told itlike it was, like only he could. *Washington Post* (April 24).

Kornheiser, Tony (2003). *I'm back for more cash: a Tony Kornheiser collection* (Because you can't take two hundred newspapers into the bathroom). New York: Villard.

Kramer, Staci D. (1987). The rewritten rules of sports journalism. *New York Times* (August 2): S9.

Kreck, Dick (2004). 13-year old's acumen blitzes sports network. *The Union* (December 7): E4-5.

Kremer, John and Deirdre M. Scully (1994). *Psychology in sport.* London: Taylor & Francis.

Kugelmass, Jack (Ed.) (2007). *Jews, sports, and the rites of citizenship.* Urbana, IL: University of Illinois Press.

Kuiper, Koenraad (1996). *Smooth talkers: The linguistics performance of auctioneers and sportscasters.* Mahwah, NJ: Lawrence Erlbaum.

Lainson, Suzanne (1998a). Television sportscasters (African American). Available online: http://www.onlinesports.com/sportstrust/sports44.html.

Lainson, Suzanne (1998b). What sportscasters earn. Available online: http://www.onlinesports.com/sportstrust/sports45.html.

Lapchick, Richard (1984). *Broken promises: Racism in American sports.* New York: St. Martin's.

Lapchick, Richard (1991). *Five minutes to midnight: Race and sports in the 1990s.* Madison, WI: University of Wisconsin Press.

Lapchick, Richard (1996). *Sport in society: Equal opportunity or business as usual?* Thousand Oaks, CA: Sage.

Lapchick, Richard (2001). *Smashing barriers: Race and sport in the new millennium.* National Book Network.

Lapchick, Richard (2005). 2004 racial and gender report card. Available: http://www.bus.ucf.edu/sport/public/downloads/2004_Racial_Gender_Report_Card.pdf.

Lapchick, Richard E., Jessica Bartter, Jennifer Brenden, Stacy Martin, Drew Tyler, and Brian Wright (2006). *100 heroes: People in sports who make this a better world.* Victoria, Australia: NCAS Publishing.

Larson, James F. and Heung-Soo Park (1993). *Global television and the politics of the Seoul Olympics.* Boulder, CO: Westview Press.

Larussa, Tony, Carole Buck, Joe Buck, and Julie Buck (2003). *Jack Buck:forever a winner.* Champaign, IL: Sports Publishing, Inc.

Laurel, David (2003). Mark Lewis says 'I've got you babe.' *Professional Sports.*

Lawler, Jennifer (2002). *PUNCH! Why women participate in violent sports.* Terre Haute, IN: Wish Publishing.

Lawler, Jerry with Doug Asheville (2003). *It's good to be king . . . sometimes.* New York: World Wrestling Entertainment Books.

Lee, Soonhwan and Hyosung Chun (2002). Economic values of professional sport franchises in the United States. *Sport Journal,* Volume 5, No. 3.

Leeds, Michael and Peter von Allmen (2004). *The economics of sports,* 2nd ed. Boston, MA: Addison Wesley.

Leizman, J. (1999). *Let's kill 'em: Understanding and controlling violence in sports.*

Lanham, MD: University Press of America.

Lenskyj, Helen Jefferson (1986). *Out of bounds: Women, sport and sexuality.* Toronto: Garamond.

Lenskyj, Helen (1994). *Women, sport and physical activity: Selected research themes.* Gloucester, Ontario: Sport Information Resource Centre.

Lenskyj, Helen Jefferson (2000). *Inside the Olympic industry: Power, politics, and activism.* Albany, NY: State University of New York Press.

Lenskyj, Helen Jefferson (2003). *Out on the field: Gender, sport and sexualities.* Toronto, ON: Women's Press.

Leonard, Wilbert Marcellus 11. (1993). *A sociological perspective of sport,* 4th ed. New York: Maxwell Macmillan.

Lester, Robin (1995). *Stagg's university: The rise, decline, and fall of big-time football at Chicago.* Urbana, IL: University of Illinois Press.

Levine, Ken (1993). *It's gone! . . . No, wait a minute . . . : Talking my way into the big leagues at 40.* New York: Villard Books.

Levine, Peter (1993). *Ellis Island to Ebbets Field: Sport and the American Jewish experience.* New York: Oxford University Press.

Lewis, Michael (2003). *Moneyball: The art of winning an unfair game.* New York: W. W. Norton & Company.

Lewis, Peter H. 2000. "Baseball stadiums go high-tech." *Union-News* (April 24): C1+.

Lipsky, Richard (1981). *How we play the game: Why sports dominate American life.* Boston, MA: Beacon Press.

Lipsyte, Robert (1975). *SportsWorld: An American dreamland.* New York: Quadrangle.

Lipsyte, Robert (1991). Sports are more than games in the groves of academe. *The New York Times* (November 24): 10.

Littlewood, Thomas B. (1990). *Arch: A promoter, not a poet.* Ames, IA: Iowa State UP.

Littman, Jonathan (2000). *The beautiful game: Sixteen girls and the soccer season that changed everything.* New York: Harper Perennial.

Loland, Sigmund (2006). *Fair play in sport: A moral norm system.* London: Routledge.

Longman, Jere (2000). *The girls of summer: The U.S. women's soccer team and the championship that changed everything.* New York: HarperCollins.

Looney, Douglas S. (2000). Who's the best-ever behind the mike? Classy Jim McKay. *The Christian Science Monitor* (May 12): 12.

Lovinger, Jay (2003). *The gospel according to ESPN: The saints, saviors, and sinners of sports.* New York: Hyperion.

Lowe, Marie R. (1998). *Women of steel: Female bodybuilders and the struggle for self-definition.* New York: New York University Press.

Lowe, Stephen R. (1995). *The kid on the sandlot: Congress and professional sports, 1910-1922.* Bowling Green, OH: Bowling Green State University Popular Press.

Lowry, Brian (2006, Feb 5.). Booya? Sportscasters' commentary lost in translation. Available online: http://variety.com.

Lumpkin, Angela, Sharon Kay Stoll, and Jennifer M. Beller (2003). *Sport ethics: Applications for fair play.* Boston, MA: McGraw-Hill.

Lupica, Mike (1988). *Shooting from the lip: Essays, columns, quips, and gripes in the grand tradition of dyspeptic sports writing.* Chicago, IL: Bonus Books.

MacClancy, Jeremy (Ed.) (1996). *Sport, identity, and ethnicity.* Oxford, UK: Berg.

MacDonald, J. Fred (1979). *Don't touch that dial!: Radio programming in American life from 1920 to 1960.* Chicago: Nelson-Hall.

Madden, John (1988). *One size doesn't fit all.* New York: Villard Books.

Madden, John with Dave Anderson (1984). *Hey, wait a minute, I wrote a book!* New York: Villard Books.

Madden, John with Dave Anderson (1996). *All Madden: Hey, I'm talking pro football!* New York: HarperCollins.

Maguire, Joseph (1999). *Global sport: Identities, societies, civilizations.* Cambridge, UK: Polity Press.

Maguire, Joseph (2005). *Power and global sport zones of prestige, emulation and resistance* London: Routledge.

Mahan, Janielle L. (2004). *Female sportscaster credibility: Has appearance taken precedence?* Chicago, IL, National Communication Association.

Majumdar, Boria and Fan Hong (Eds.) (2006). *Modern sport the global obsession.* Oxford, UK: Routledge.

Mandelbaum, Michael (2004). *The meaning of sports: Why Americans watch baseball, football, and basketball, and what they see when they do.* New York: Public Affairs.

Mandell, Richard D. (1987). *The Nazi Olympics.* Urbana, IL: University of Illinois Press.

Mangan, J.A. (1987). *From fair sex to feminism: Sport and the socialization of women in the industrial and post-industrial eras.* London: Frank Cass.

Mangan, J.A. and Roberta J. Park (Eds.) (1987). *From 'Fair Sex' to feminism: Sport and the socialization of women in the industrial and post-industrial eras.* London: F. Cass.

Markula, Pirkko (Ed.) (2005). *Feminist sports studies: Sharing experiences of joy and pain.* Albany: State University of New York Press.

Markula, Pirkko and Richard Pringle (2006). *Focault, sport and exercise: Power, knowledge and transforming the self.* New York: Routledge.

Martzke, Rudy (2000). DeVarona fights for fairness on principle $50M age, sex suit vs. ABC 'hardest thing I've ever done.' *USA Today* (September 7): 3C.

Masteralexis, Lida Pike, Carol A. Barr, and Mary A. Hums (Eds.) (2004). *Principles and practices of sports management.* 2nd ed. Gaithersburg, MD: Aspen.

Matchett, Steve (2000). *The mechanic's tale: Life in the pit-lanes of Formula One.* London: Orion Publishing.

Matthews, Denny with Matt Fulks (2006). *Tales from the Royals dugout.* Champaign, IL: Sports Publishing.

Matthews, Denny with Fred White and Matt Fulks (1999). *Play by play: 25 years of Royals on radio.* Lenexa, KS: Addax Publishing Group.

Mawson, Marlene (2006). Sportswomanship: The cultural acceptance of sport or women versus the accommodation of cultured women in sport. In Fuller (ed.), Sport, rhetoric, and gender: Historical perspectives. New York: Palgrave MacMillan. 19-30.

Maxwell, Jocko (1972). *Great black athletes.* Largo, FL: Snibbe Publications.

Mayeux, Peter E. (1991). *Broadcast news: Writing and reporting.* Dubuque, IA: Wm. C. Brown Publishers.

McAllister, Matthew P. (1996). *The commercialization of American culture: New advertising, control and democracy.* Thousand Oaks, CA: Sage.

McCarthy, Perry. (2003). *Flat out, flat broke: Formula 1 the hard way!* Somerset, UK: J. H. Haynes.

McCarver, Tim with Ray Robinson (1987). *Oh, baby, I love it!* New York: Villard.

McChesney, Robert W. (1989). Media made sport: A history of sports coverage in the United States. In Lawrence A. Wenner (Ed.), *Media, sports, & society.* Newbury Park, CA: Sage: 49-69.

McComb, David G. (2004). *Sports in world history.* New York: Routledge.

McDonald, Mark A. and George R. Milne (1999). *Cases in sports marketing.* Sudbury, MA: Jones and Bartlett.

McEntegart, Pete, L. Jon Wertheim, Gene Menez, and Mark Bechtel (2002). The top 100 sports books of all time. *Sports Illustrated* (December 16): 128-148.

McKay, Jim (1973). *My wide world.* New York: Macmillan Publishing Co.

McKay, Jim (1998). *The real McKay: My wide world of sports.* New York: Dutton.

McKay, Jim, Michael A. Messner, and Don Sabo (Eds.) (2000). *Masculinities, gender relations and sport: Research on men and masculinities.* Thousand Oaks, CA: Sage.

McNamee, Graham (1926). *You're on the air.* New York: Harper & Bros.

McNamee, Mike J. and S. Jim Parry (Eds.) (1998). *Ethics and sport.* London: E. and F.N. Spon.

McPherson, Barry D., James E. Curtis, and John W. Loy, John W. (1989). *The social significance of sports.* Human Kinetics Books: Champaign, IL.

Mechikoff, Robert A. with Virginia Evans (1987). *Sport psychology for women.* New York: Harper & Row.

Mechikoff, Robert and Michael Real (1990). *Deep fan: Mythic identification, technology, and advertising in spectator sports.* Bled, Yugoslavia, International Association for Mass Communication Research.

Messner, Michael A. (1992). *Power at play: Sports and the problem of masculinity.* Boston, MA: Beacon Press.

Messner, Michael A. (2002). *Taking the field: Women, men and sports.* Minneapolis, MN: University of Minnesota Press.

Messner, Michael A., Margaret Carlisle Duncan, and Cheryl Cooky (2003). Silence, Sports bras, and wrestling porn: Women in televised sports news and highlights shows. *Journal of Sport and Social Issues,* Volume 27, Number 1: 38-51.

Messner, Michael A., Margaret Carlisle Duncan, and Kerry Jensen (1993). The gendered language of televised sports. *Gender and Society,* Volume 7: 121-137.

Messner, Michael A. and Donald F. Sabo (Eds.) (1990). *Sport, men, and the gender order: Critical feminist perspectives.* Champaign, IL: Human Kinetics.

Messner, Michael A. and Donald F. Sabo (1994). *Sex, violence & power in sports.* Freedom, CA: The Crossing Press.

Messner, Michael A., Donald F. Sabo, and Jim McKay (Eds.) (2000). *Masculinities: Gender relations and sport.* Thousand Oaks, CA: Sage.

Michener, James A. (1976.) *Sports in America.* New York: Random House.

Miller, Ashley (nd). Sports writer. Available: http://www.womenssportsfoundation.org.

Miller, Jon with Mark Hyman (2000). *Confessions of a baseball purist: What's right—and wrong—with baseball, as seen from the best seat in the house.* Baltimore, MD: Johns Hopkins University Press.

Miller, Lorik (1997). *Sport business management.* Gaithersburg, MD: Aspen.

Miller, Patrick B. and David K. Wiggins (Eds.) (2004). *Sport and the color line: Black athletes and race relations in twentieth-century America.* New York: Routledge.

Miller, Richard K. (2005). *The 2006 sports business market research handbook.* Loganville, GA: Richard K. Miller & Associates.

Miller, Toby (2001). *SportSex.* Philadelphia, PA: Temple University Press.

Miller, Toby, Geoffrey Lawrence, Jim McKay, and David Rowe (2001). *Globalization and sport: Playing the world.* London: Sage.

Miller, Tom (2004). From the high beam. (March).

Milne, George R. and Mark A. McDonald (1999). *Sports management: Managing the exchange process.* Sudbury, MA: Jones and Bartlett.

Miloch, Kimberly S., Paul M. Pedersen, Michael K. Smucker, and Warren A. Whisenant (2005). The current state of women print journalists: An analysis of the status and careers of females in newspapers sports departments. *Public Organization Review,* Volume 5, Number 3 (September): 219-232.

Mitrook, Michael A. and Noelle Haner Dorr (2001). *Women in sports broadcasting: Credibility in the ears of the public.* Washington, DC, Association for Education in Journalism and Mass Communication.

Mitten, Matthew J., Timothy Davis, Rodney K. Smith, and Robert C. Berry (2005). *Sports law and regulation: Cases, materials, and problems.* New York: Aspen Publishers.

Mittman, Dick (2003). Auto racing. In Abraham Aamidor (Ed.), *Real sports reporting.* (Bloomington: Indiana University Press): 71-80.

Mizell, Hubert (2003). Time to hand Madden's crown to Collinsworth. *St. Petersburg Times* (Jan. 12).

Molzon, Bill (ND). Television's sports heritage: The early days of TV sports. Available: http://americansportscastersonline.com/waynesbergarticle.html.

Mondello, Michael (2006). Sports economics and the media. In Arthur A. Raney and Jennings Bryant (Eds.) *Handbook of sports and media*. Mahwah, NJ: Lawrence Erlbaum: 277-294.

Montville, Leigh (1993). Cherry bombs. *Sports Illustrated* (March 29): 59-66.

Morgan, William J. (1994). *Leftist theories of sport: A critique and reconstruction*. Urbana, IL: University of Illinois Press.

Morgan, William J. (2006). *Why sports morally matter*. New York: Routledge.

Morse, Margaret (1983). Sport on television: Replay and display. In E. Ann Kaplan (Ed.), *Regarding television: Critical approaches—an anthology*. (University Publications of America, Inc.): 4-66.

Morton, Gerald W. and George O'Brien (1985). *Wrestling with rasslin'*: Ancient sport to American spectacle. Bowling Green: Bowling Green State University Popular press.

Mott, Frank Luther (1962). *American journalism: A history, 1690 to 1960*. New York: Macmillan.

Mottram, David R. (Ed.) (2005). *Drugs in sport*. New York: Routledge.

Mullen, Lawrence J. and Dennis W. Mazzocco (2000). Coaches, drama, and technology: Mediation of Super Bowl broadcasts from 1969 to 1997. *Critical Studies in Media Communication*, Volume 17, Number 3 (September): 347-363.

Mulligan, Joseph F. and Kevin T. Mulligan (1998). *Sports journalism careers*. Chicago, IL: VGM Career Horizons.

Mullin, Bernard J., Stephen Hardy, and William A. Sutton (1993). *Sport marketing*. Champaign, IL: Human Kinetics.

Munslow, Alun and Murray G. Phillips (Eds.) (2005). *Deconstructing sport history: A postmodern analysis*. Albany, NY: State University of New York Press.

Murphy, Patrick, John Williams, and Eric Dunning (1990). *Football on trial: Spectator violence and development in the football world*. London: Routledge.

Murphy, Shane M. (Ed.) (1995). *Sport psychology interventions*. Champaign, IL: Human Kinetics.

Murray, Jim (1993). *Jim Murray: An autobiography*. New York: Macmillan.

National Broadcasting Company (1985). *The great communicators of sports*. New York: SportsWorld.

Neal-Lunsford, Jeff (1992). Sport in the land of television: The use of sport in network prime-time schedules 1946-1950. *Journal of Sport History*, Vol. 19, No. 1 (Spring): 56-76.

Nelson, Lindsey (1966). *Backstage at the Mets*. New York: Viking.

Nelson, Lindsey (1985). *Hello everybody, I'm Lindsey Nelson*. New York: Beech Tree.

Nelson, Mariah Burton (1991). *Are we winning yet? How women are changing sports and sports are changing women*. New York: Random House.

Nelson, Mariah Burton (1994). *The stronger women get, the more men love football: Sexism and the American culture of sports*. Orlando, FL: Harcourt Brace.

Nichols, William, Patrick Moynahan, Allan Hall, and Janis Taylor (2001). *Media relations in sport.* Morgantown, WV: Fitness Information Technology.

Nicholson, Matthew (2006). *Sport and the media: Managing the nexus.* Burlington, MA: Butterworth-Heineman.

Noll, Roger G. and Andrew Zimbalist (Eds.) (1997). *Sports, jobs, and taxes: The economic impact of sports teams and stadiums.* Washington, DC: Brookings Institution Press.

Noverr, Douglas A. and Laurence E. Ziewacz (1983). *The games they played: Sports in American history, 1865-1980.* Chicago, IL: Nelson-Hall.

Oakes, Chris. 1999 (January 7). "Smart Video = Smart Football." Available online: www.wired.com.

O'Donnell, Lewis B., Carl Hausman, and Philip Benoit (1992). *Announcing: Broadcast communicating today,* 2nd ed. Belmont, CA: Wadsworth.

Oglesby, Carole A., Doreen L. Greenberg, Ruth Louise Hall, Karen L. Hill, Frances Johnston, and Sheila Easterby (Eds.) (1999). *Encyclopedia of women and sport in America.* Westport, CT: Oryx.

Olbermann, Keith and Dan Patrick (1997). *The big show: Inside ESPN's Sports Center.* New York: Pocket Books.

O'Leary, John (Ed.) (2001). *Drugs and doping in sport: Socio-legal perspectives.* London: Cavendish.

The Olympic movement and the mass media: Past, present and future issues. (1989). Calgary, Alberta, Canada: Hurford Enterprises Ltd.

O'Neill, Terry (1991). *The game behind the game: High stakes, high pressure in TV sports.* New York: St. Martin's.

Oppenheim, Louis (Ed.) (1994). *Chris names: An illustrated guide to Chris Berman's unique characterizations of sports personalities.* Kansas City, MO: Andrews & McMeel.

Ordman, Virginia L. and Dolf Zillman (1994). Women sports reporters: Have they caught up? *Journal of Sport and Social Issues,* Volume 18, Number 1: 66-75.

O'Reilly, Jean and Susan K. Cahn (Eds.) (2007). *Women and sports in the United States: A documentary reader.* Boston: Northeastern University Press.

Oriard, Michael (1991). *Sporting with the gods: The rhetoric of play and game in American culture.* Cambridge, UK: Cambridge University Press.

Oriand, Michael (1993). *Reading football: How the popular press created an American spectacle.* Chapel Hill, NC: University of North Carolina Press.

Oriand, Michael (2001). *King football: Sport and spectacle in the golden age of radio, newsreels, movies and magazines.* Chapel Hill, NC: University of North Carolina Press.

Ouellette, Matthew (2003, Oct 19). Local sports announcers: Yay or Nay? Available online: www.dailyutahchronicle.com.

Packer, Billy with Roland Lazenby (1986). *Hoops: Confessions of a college basketball analyst.* New York: Contemporary Books.

Paley, William S. (1979). *As it happened: A memoir.* Garden City, NJ: Doubleday.

Paper, Lewis J. (1987). *Empire: William S. Paley and the making of CBS.* New York: St. Martin's Press.

Parkhouse, Bonnie L. (Ed.) (1991). *The management of sport: Its foundation and application.* St. Louis: Mosby Year Book.

Parks, Janet B., Beverly R. Zanger, and Jerome Quarterman (Eds.). (1998). *Contemporary sports management.* Champaign, IL: Human Kinetics.

Patton, Phil (1984). *Razzle-dazzle: The curious marriage of television and professional football.* Garden City, NY: The Dial Press.

Pearson, Roberta E. (1988). *Take me out to the ballgame: The narrative structure and reception of televised baseball.* London, England, International Television Studies Conference.

Pemberton, Cynthia Lee A. and Donna de Varona (2002). *More than a game: One woman's fight for gender equity in sport.* Boston, MA: Northeastern University Press.

Perinbanayagam, Robert (2007). *Games and sports in everyday life: Dialogues and narratives of the self.* Boulder, CO: Paradigm Publishers.

Perrin, Dennis (2000). *American fan: Sports mania and the culture that feeds it.* New York: Spike.

Peterson, Bill. 2000 (March 23-29). Sports: Boom, boom, out go the lights. *Best of Cincinnati,* Vol. 6, Issue 18.

Petterchak, Janice (1996). *Jack Brickhouse: A voice for all seasons.* Chicago: Contemporary Books.

Peyer, Tom and Seely (1997). *O Holy cow: The selected verse of Phil Rizzuto* New York: Ecco/HarperCollins.

Phillips, Murray G. (Ed.) (2005). *Deconstructing sport history: A postmodern analysis.* Albany, NY: State University of New York Press.

Picart, Caroline Joan (2006). *From ballroom to dancesport: Aesthetics, athletics, and body culture.* Albany, NY: State University of New York Press.

Pitts, Brenda G. and David K. Stotlar (1996). *Fundamentals of sports marketing.* Morgantown, WV: Fitness Information Technology.

Plunkett, Jack W. (2006). *Plunkett's sports industry almanac 2007: Sports industry market research, statistics, trends and leading companies.* Houston, TX: Plunkett Research Ltd.

Poindexter, Ray (1966). *Golden throats and silver tongues: The radio announcers.* New York: Oxford University Press.

Polley, Martin (2007). *Sports history: A practical guide.* New York: Palgrave Macmillan.

Porter, Dilwyn (2004). *Sport and national identity in the post-war world.* London: Routledge.

Porto, Brian L. (2003). *A new season: Using Title IX to reform college sports.* Westport, CT: Praeger.

Povich, Shirley, Lynn Povich, Maury Povich, David Povich, and George Solomon (Eds.) (2005). *All those mornings at the Post: The twentieth century in sports.* Washington, DC: Public Affairs.

Powers, Ron (1984). *Super tube: The rise of television sports.* New York: Coward-McCann.

Prebish, Charles S. (1993). *Religion and sport: The meeting of sacred and profane.* Westport, CT: Greenwood.

Preuss, Holger (2000). *Economics of the Olympic games: Hosting the games, 1972-2000.* Petersham, NSW: Wala Walla Press.

Price, Joseph L. (Ed.) (2001). *From season to season: Sports as American religion.* Macon, GA: Mercer University Press.

Pronger, Brian (1990). *The age of masculinity: Sports, homosexuality, and the meaning of sex.* New York: St. Martin's.

Putnam, Douglas T. (1999). *Controversies of the sports world.* Westport, CT: Greenwood.

Queenan, Joe (2003). *True believers: The tragic inner life of sports fans.* New York: Henry Holt.

Quinlan, Sterling (1979). *Inside ABC: American Broadcasting Company's rise to power.* New York: Hastings House.

Quirk, Charles (Ed.) (1996). *Sports and the law: Major legal cases.* New York: Garland.

Quirk, James and Rodney Fort (1999). *Hard ball: The abuse of power in pro team sports.* Princeton, NJ: Princeton University Press.

Rader, Benjamin G. (1983). *American sports: From the age of folk games to the age of spectators.* Englewood Cliffs, NJ: Prentice-Hall, Inc.

Rader, Benjamin G. (1984). *In its own image: How television has transformed sports.* New York: Macmillan.

Rader, Benjamin G. (2004). *American sports: From the age of folk games to the age of televised sports,* 5th ed. Englewood Cliffs, NJ: Prentice-Hall, Inc.

Rail, Genieva (Ed.) (1998). *Sport and postmodern times.* Albany, NY: State University of New York Press.

Raney, Arthur A. and Jennings Bryant (Eds.) (2006). *Handbook of sports and media.* Mahwah, NJ: Lawrence Erlbaum.

Rappaport, Ron (1994). *A kind of grace: A treasury of sportswriting by women.* Berkley, CA: Zenobia Books.

Rashad, Ahmad with Peter Bodo (1988). *Rashad: Vikes, mikes and something on the backside.* New York: Penguin.

Rasmussen, Bill (1983). *Sports junkies rejoice! The birth of ESPN.* Hartsdale, NY: QV Publishing.

Real, Michael (1989). *Super media: A cultural studies approach.* Newbury Park, CA: Sage.

Real, Michael (1998). MediaSport: Technology and the commodification of postmodern sport. In Lawrence A. Wenner (Ed.), *MediaSport* (New York: Routledge): 14-26.

Real, Michael (1999). Aerobics and feminism: Self-determination or patriarchal hegemony? In Randy Miller and Toby Miller (Eds.), *SportCult*. Minneapolis, MN: University of Minnesota Press.

Real, Michael (2006). Sports online: The newsest player in mediasport. In Arthur A. Raney and Jennings Bryant (Eds.) *Handbook of sports and media*. Mahwah, NJ: Lawrence Erlbaum: 171-184.

Reidenbaugh, Lowell (1985). *The Sporting News: First hundred years, 1886-1986*. St. Louis, MO: The Sporting News.

Rein, Irving, Philip Kotler, and Ben Shields (2006). *The elusive fan: Reinventing sports in a crowded marketplace*. New York: McGraw-Hill.

Remy, Jerry with Corey Sandler (2004). *Watching baseball: Discovering the game within the game*. Guilford, CT: Globe Pequot.

Reynolds, Bill (2005). *Cousy: His life, career, and the birth of big-time basketball*. New York: Simon and Schuster.

Rhoden, William C. (2006). *Forty million dollar slaves: The rise, fall, and redemption of the black athlete*. New York: Crown.

Ricchiardi, Sherry (2005). Offensive interference. *American Journalism Review* (Dec/Jan). Available: http://www.ajr.org/article_printable.asp?id = 3788.

Rice, Grantland (1954). *The tumult and the shouting: My life in sport*. New York: Barnes.

Riess, Steven A. (Ed.) (1998). *Sports and the American Jew*. Syracuse, NY: Syracuse University Press.

Ritchie, Brent W. and Daryl Adair (Eds.) (2004). *Sport tourism: Interrelationships, impacts and issues*. Oxon, UK: Multilingual Matters.

Roberts, Glyn C., Kevin S. Spink, and Cynthia C. Pemberton (1986). *Learning experiences in sport psychology*. Champaign, IL: Human Kinetics.

Robertson, Nan (1992). *The girls in the balcony: Women, men and The New York Times*. New York: Random House.

Robins, J. Max (1988). NBC's year to be a big sport. *Channels of Communication* (June): 74-5.

Robinson, Laura (2002). *Black tights: Women, sport, and sexuality*. New York: HarperCollins.

Robinson, Matthew J., Mary A. Hums, R. Brian Crow, and Dennis R. Phillips (2001). *Profiles of sport industry professionals: The people who make the games happen*. Sudbury, MA: Jones and Bartlett.

Robinson, Tom (2004). *Sports tourism: An introduction*. Boston, MA: Thomson Learning.

Robinson, Tom, Sean Gammon, and Ian Jones (2003). *Sports tourism: An Introduction*. London: Continuum.

Roche, Maurice (Ed.) (1998). *Sport, popular culture and identity*. Aachen: Meyer and Meyer Verlag.

Roche, Maurice (2001). *Mega-events and modernity: Olympics and expos in the growth of global culture*. London: Routledge.

Rogers, Susan Fox (Ed.) (1994). *Sportsdykes: Stories from on and off the field*. New York: St. Martin's Press.

Rose, Ava and James Friedman (1997). Television sports as mas(s)culine cult of distraction. In Aaron Baker and Todd Boyd (Eds.) *Out of bounds: Sports, media, and the politics of identity*. Bloomington, IN: Indiana University Press: 1-15.

Rosentraub, Mark S. (1997). *Major League losers: The real cost of sports and who's paying for it*. New York: Basic.

Ross, Charles K. (Ed.) (2004). *Race and sport: The struggle for equality on and off the field*. Jackson, MS: University of Mississippi Press.

Rothenbuhler, Eric W. (1988). The living room celebration of the Olympic Games. *Journal of Communication*, Volume 38, Number 4 (Autumn): 61-81.

Rowe, David (1995). *Popular cultures: Rock music, sport, and the politics of pleasure*. London: Sage.

Rowe, David (1999). *Sport, culture and the media: The unruly trinity*. London: Sage.

Rowe, David and Geoffrey Laurence (Eds.) (2000). *Tourism, leisure, sport, and critical perspectives*. Cambridge University Press.

Rudd, Alyson (1999). *Astroturf blonde: Taking on the men at their own game*. London: Headline Publishing Group.

Russell, Gordon W. (1993). *The social psychology of sport*. New York: Springer-Verlag.

Russo, Chris and Allen St. John (2006). *Mad dog hall of fame: The ultimate top-ten rankings of the best in sport*. New York: Doubleday.

Ryan, Chris (2003). *Recreational tourism: Demand and impacts*. Celevedon, UK: Channel View Publications.

Ryan, Jeff (2001). A woman's place: Jane Chastain, sports broadcasting trailblazer. Available online: http://villagevoice.com.

Ryan, Joan (1995). *Little girls in pretty boxes: The making and breaking of elite gymnasts and figure skaters*. New York: Doubleday.

Sabo, Donald F. and Joe Panepinto (1990). In Michael Messner and Donald F. Sabo (Eds.) *Sport, men, and the gender order: Critical feminist perspectives*. (Champaign, IL: Human Kinetics): 115-126.

Sage, George H. (1990). *Power and ideology in American sport: A critical perspective*. Champaign, IL: Human Kinetics.

Saites, Gary A. (Ed.) (1998). *African Americans in sport: Contemporary themes*. New Brunswick, NJ: Transaction.

Salter, David F. (1996). *Crashing the old boys' network: The tragedies and triumphs of girls and women in sports*. Westport, CT: Praeger.

Sandomir, Richard (1991). Sports through the cozy prism of television. *The New York Times* (December 1): H31.

Sandomir, Richard (1995). Bob Costas calls it as he regretfully sees it.. *The New York Times* (October 8): H36.

Sandomir, Richard (2001). Graphics giving telecasts a look like video games. *The New York Times* (April 15): SP 1+

Sandomir, Richard (2006). In perspective, Derby coverage fell short. *The New York Times* (May 9): C17.

Sandoz, Joli (Ed.) (1997). *A whole other ball game: Women's literature on women's sport*. New York: Noonday Press.

Sandoz, Joli and Joby Winans (Ed.) (1999). *Whatever it takes: Women on women's sport*. New York: Farrar, Straus, and Giroux.

Sandvoss, Cornel (2003). *A game of two halves: Football fandom, television and globalisation*. London: Routledge.

Scannell, Paddy (1991). *Broadcast talk*. London: Sage.

Scarrott, Martin (Ed.) (1999). *Sport, leisure and tourism information sources: A guide for researchers*. Butterworth-Heinemann.

Schaap, Dick (2001). *Flashing before my eyes: 50 years of headlines, deadlines, and punchlines*. Waterville, ME: Thorndike Press.

Schaaf, Phil (1995). *Sports marketing: It's not just a game anymore*. Amherst, NY: Prometheus Books.

Schaaf, Phil (2004). *Sports, Inc.: 100 years of sports business: Event evolution, global properties, sponsorship, franchise relocation, radio and television, stadium issues, endorsements*. Amherst, NY: Prometheus Books.

Schemmel, Jerry (1996). *Chosen to live*.Redwood, CA: Victory Publishing.

Schlossberg, Howard (1996). *Sports marketing*. Cambridge, MA: Blackwell Business.

Schultz, Brad (2002). *Sports broadcasting*. Boston: Focal Press.

Schuster, Joseph (1989). Beers with . . . Dan Dierdorf. *Sport* (December): 17-19.

Schwartz, Dona (1998). *Contesting the Super Bowl*. New York: Routledge.

Schwartz, Lou (1999). Women in sportscasting: A brief history. Available online: http://www.americansportscasters.com/women.html.

Scranton, Sheila and Anne Flintoff (Eds.) (2002). *Gender and sport: A reader*. London: Taylor and Francis.

Scully, Gerald W. (1995). *The market structure of sports*. Chicago, IL: University of Chicago Press.

Segrave, Jeffrey and Donald Chu (Eds.) (1988). *Olympic games in transition*. Champaign, IL: Human Kinetics.

Segrave, Jeffrey O., Katherine L. McDowell, and James G. King 111. (2006). Language, gender, and sport: A review of the research literature. In Linda K. Fuller, (Ed.), *Sport, rhetoric, and gender: Historical perspectives and media representations* (31-52). New York: Palgrave Macmillan.

Senn, Alfred Erich (1999). *Power, politics, and the Olympic games*. Champaign, IL: Human Kinetics.

Shank, Matthew D. (1999). *Sports marketing: A strategic perspective*. Upper Saddle River, NJ: Prentice Hall.

Shea, Jim (2000). The king: How ESPN changes everything. *Columbia Journalism Review* (January/February). Available online: http://archives.cjr.org/year/00/1/king.asp.

Sheehan, Richard G. (1996). *Keeping score: The economics of big-time sports*. South Bend, IN: Diamond Communication.

Sheikh, Anees A. and Errol R. Korn (Eds.) (1994). *Imagery in sports and physical performance*. Amityville, NY: Baywood Pub.

Sherrod, Blackie (1988). *The Blackie Sherrod collection*. Dallas, TX: Taylor Pub.

Shields, David (1999). *Black planet: Facing race during an NBA season*. New York: Crown.

Shipnuck, Alan (2006). *The battle for Augusta National: Hootie, Martha, and the masters of the universe*. New York: Simon and Schuster.

Shogan, Debra (1999). *The making of high-performance athletes: Discipline, diversity, and ethics*. Toronto: University of Toronto Press.

Shropshire, Kenneth L. (1990). *Agents of opportunity: Sports agents and corruption in collegiate sports*. Philadelphia, PA: University of Pennsylvania Press.

Shropshire, Kenneth L. (1996). *In black and white: Race and sports in America*. New York: New York University Press.

Shropshire, Kenneth L. and Davis, Timothy (2003). *The business of sports agents*. Philadelphia, PA: University of Pennsylvania Press.

Simmons, Roy with Damon DiMarco (2005). *Out of bounds*. New York: Carroll & Graf.

Simon, Rita (Ed.) (2005). *Sporting equality: Title IX thirty years later*. New Brunswick, NJ: Transaction.

Simon, Robert L. (1991). *Fair play: Sports, values, and society*. Boulder, CO: Westview Press.

Simson, Vyv and Andrew Jennings (1992). *The lord of the rings. Power, money, and drugs in the modern Olympics*. London: Simon and Schuster.

Singer, Robert N., Heather A. Hausenblas, and Christopher M. Janelle (Eds.) (2001). *Handbook of sports psychology*. New York: John Wiley & Sons.

Singer, Stephen (1987). The best sportscasters on television. *TV Guide* (November 21): 5-6.

Slack, Trevor (Ed.) (2004). *The commercialization of sport*. Oxon, UK: Routledge.

Slide, Anthony (1991). *The television industry: A historical dictionary*. Westport, CT: Greenwood Press.

Smart, Barry (2005). *The sport star: Modern sport and the cultural economy of sporting celebrity*. Newbury Park CA: Sage Publications.

Smith, Aaron and Hans Westerbeek (2004). *The sport business future*. New York: Palgrave Macmillan.

Smith, Curt (1978). *America's Dizzy Dean.* Bloomington, MN: Bethany Press.

Smith, Curt (1987). *Voices of the game: The first full-scale overview of baseball broadcasting, 1921 to the present.* South Bend, IN: Diamond Communications.

Smith, Curt (1992). *Voices of the game: The acclaimed chronicle of baseball broadcasting.* New York: Fireside Publishing.

Smith, Curt (1995). *The storytellers: From Mel Allen to Bob Costas: 60 years of baseball tales from the broadcast booth.* New York: Macmillan.

Smith, Curt (1998). *Of mikes and men: From Roy Scott to Curt Gowdy: Broadcast tales from the pro football booth.* Lanham, MD: Diamond Communications.

Smith, Curt (2005). *Voices of summer: Baseball's greatest announcers.* New York: Carroll and Graf.

Smith, Earl and Debra A. Henderson (2000). Stacking in the team sport of intercollegiate baseball. In Dana Brooks and Ronald Althouse (Eds.), *Racism in college athletics: The African American athlete's experience,* 2nd edition. Morgantown, WV: Fitness Information Technology: 65-83.

Smith, Lissa (Ed.) (1998). *Nike is a goddess: The history of women in sports.* New York: Atlantic Monthly Press.

Smith, Ronald A. (2001). *Play-by-play: Radio, television, and big-time college sport.* Baltimore: The Johns Hopkins University Press.

Smith, Sally Bedell (1990). *In all his glory: The life of William S. Paley.* New York: Simon and Schuster.

Snyder, Eldon E. and Elmer A. Spreitzer (1983). *Social aspects of sports,* 2nd ed. Englewood Cliffs, NJ: Prentice-Hall.

Sowell, Mike (2006). A woman in a man's world: 'Annie Laurie,' one of America's first sportswriters. In Linda K. Fuller, (Ed.), *Sport, rhetoric, and gender: Historical perspectives and media representations* (65-70). New York: Palgrave Macmillan.

Spanberg, Erik (2003). Field of dreams. *The Christian Science Monitor* (October 16): 14-15.

Spence, Christopher M. (2000). *The skin I'm in: Racism, sports and education.* Halifax, NS: Fernwood Publications.

Spence, Jim with Dave Diles (1988). *Up close and personal: The inside story of network television sports.* New York: Atheneum Publishers.

Sperber, Murray (2001). *Beer and circus: How big-time college sports is crippling undergraduate education.* New York: Owl Books.

Standeven, Joy and Paul DeKnop (1999). *Sport tourism.* Champaign, IL: Human Kinetics.

Stanley, Gregory Kent (1996). *The rise and fall of the sportswoman: Women's health, fitness, and athletics, 1860-1940.* New York: Peter Lang.

Stanton, Tom (2002). *The final season: Fathers, sons, and one last season in a classic American ballpark.* New York: St. Martin's Griffin.

Stark, Steven D. (1997). *Telenation: The television shows and events that made us who we are.* New York: Free Press.

Starr, Mark (2006). Sports: My favorite years. *Newsweek* (August 14): 44-56.

Staudohar, Paul D. (Ed.) (2000). *Diamond mines: Baseball and labor.* Syracuse, NY: Syracuse University Press.

Staudohar, Paul D. and James A. Mangan (Eds.) (1991). *The business of professional sports.* Urbana, IL: University of Illinois Press.

Stauffer, Kathleen and Greg J. Cylkowski (1994). *Womansport: The women's sports bible.* Little Canada, MN: Athletic Achievements.

Stein, Murray and John Hollwitz (Eds.) (1994). *Psyche and sports.* Wilmette, IL: Chiron Pub.

Steiner, Andy (1995). *A sporting chance: Sports and gender.* Minneapolis, MN: Lemer Publishing Group.

Steiner, Andy (2000). Pat Griffin: She says that in the world of sports, closets have no place. *Utne Reader* (January-February): 60-61.

Stern, Bill (1949). *Bill Stern's favorite baseball stories.* Garden City, NY: Blue Ribbon Books.

St. John, Warren (2004). *Rammer jammer yellow hammer: A journey into the heart of fan mania.* New York: Crown.

St. John, Warren (2005). That sports guy thrives online. *The New York Times* (November 20): 1, 17.

Stoldt, G. Clayton, Stephen W. Dittmore, and Scott E. Branvold (2006). *Sport public relations: Managing organizational communication.* Champaign, IL: Human Kinetics.

Stone, Steve (1999). *Where's Harry: Steve Stone remembers his years with Harry Caray.* Lanham, MD: Taylor Trade Publishing.

Storm, Hannah and Mark Jenkins (2002). *Go girl: Raising healthy, confident, and successful girls through sports.* Naperville, IL: Sourcebooks.

Stotlar, David K. (1993). *Successful Sports Marketing.* Madison, WI: WCB Brown and Benchmark.

Stram, Hank with Lou Sahadi (1986). *They're playing my game.* New York: William Morrow.

Sugar, Bert Randolph (1978). *The thrill of victory: The inside story of ABC sports.* New York: Hawthorn Books.

Sugden, John (Ed.) (2002). *Power games: A critical sociology of sport.* New York: Routledge.

Suggs, Welch (2006). *A place on the team: The triumph and tragedy of Title IX.* Princeton, NJ: Princeton University Press.

Summerall, Pat (2006). *Summerall: On and off the air.* Chicago, IL: Nelson.

Svensson, Anders (2004). *Media sport: New technology on a local level—an audience perspective.* Porto Alegra, Brazil, International Association for Media and Communication Research.

Sweeney, John (2007). SportsCast: 10 controversial issues confronting the sports industry. *The Futurist* (January 1).

Szymanski, Stefan and Andrew Zimbalist. (2005). *National pastime: How Americans play baseball and the rest of the world plays soccer.* Brookings Institution Press.

Talbot, Margaret (2002). Playing with patriarchy: The gendered dynamics of sports organizations. In Sheila Scranton and Anne Flintoff (Eds.) *Gender and sport: A reader.* London: Taylor and Francis: 277-291.

Talen, Julie (1986). How the camera changes the game. *Channels of Communication* (April): 50-5.

Tannsjo, Torbjorn and Claudio Tamburrini (Eds.) (2000). *Values in sport: Elitism, nationalism, gender equality and the scientific manufacture of winners.* London: E. and FN Spon.

Teitelbaum, Stanley H. (2005). *Sports heroes, fallen idols.* Lincoln, NE: University of Nebraska Press.

Tewksbury, Mark (2006). *Inside out: Straight talk from a gay jock.* New York: Wiley.

Theberge, Nancy (1981). A critique of critiques: Radical and feminist writings on sport. *Social Forces,* Vol. 60, No. 2: 341-353.

Theberge, Nancy (2000). *Higher goals: Women's ice hockey and the politics of gender.* Albany, NY: State University of New York Press.

Thoma, James E. and Laurence Chalip (1996). *Sport governance in the global community.* Morgantown, WV: Fitness Information Technology.

Thompson, Chuck with Gordon Beard (1996). *Ain't the beer cold!* South Bend, IN: Diamond Communications.

Thornley, Stew (1991). *Holy cow! The life and times of Halsey Hall.* Cambridge, MN: Nodin Press.

Todhunter, Andrew (2000). *Dangerous games: Ice climbing, storm kayaking, and other adventures from the extreme edge of sports.* New York: Doubleday.

Tokarz, Karen (1986). *Women, sports, and the law: A comprehensive research guide to sex discrimination in sports.* Buffalo, NY: W.S. Hein.

Toma, J. Douglas (2003). *Football U: Spectator sports in the life of the American university.* Ann Arbor, MI: University of Michigan Press.

Tomlinson, Alan and Christopher Young (Eds.) (2006). *National identity and global sports events.* Albany, NY: State University of New York Press.

Towers, Wayne M. (1981). World Series coverage in New York City in the 1920's. *Journalism Monographs,* 73 (August): 4-5.

Trope, Mike and Steve Delsohn (1987). *Necessary roughness.* Chicago: Contemporary.

Trujillo, N. (1991). Hegemonic masculinity on the mound: Media representations of Nolan Ryan and the American sports culture. *Critical Studies in Mass Communication,* Vol. 8 (September): 290-308.

Trumbull, Alison (2003). Woman in a man's world: Pam Ward and the register of sportscasting talk. Perception and Realization in Language and Gender Research. Michigan State University.

Tuana, Nancy (Ed.) (2002). *Revealing male bodies.* Bloomington, IN: Indiana UP.

Tuaolo, Esera (2006). *Alone in the trenches: My life as a gay man in the NFL.* Naperville, IL: Sourcebooks.

Tudor, Deborah V. (1997). *Hollywood's vision of team sports: Heroes, race, and gender.* New York: Garland.

Tuggle, Charles A. (1997). Differences in television sports reporting of men's and women's athletics: ESPN *SportsCenter* and CNN *Sports Tonight. Journal of Broadcasting and Electronic Media,* 41: 14-24.

Turco, Douglas Michele, Roger S. Riley, Kamilla Swart (2002). *Sport tourism.* Morgantown, WV: Fitness Information Technology.

Turco, Mary (1999). *Crashing the net: The U.S. women's olympic ice hockey team and the road to gold.* New York: HarperCollins.

Turner, Beverley (2005). *The pits: The real world of Formula One.* London: Atlantic.

Uecker, Bob with Mickey Herskowitz (1982). *Catcher in wry.* New York: Penguin.

Underwood, John (1984). *Spoiled sport: A fan's notes on the troubles of spectator sports.* Boston, MA: Little, Brown & Company.

U.S. Olympic Committee (1996). *Olympism: A basic guide to the history, ideals, and sports of the Olympic movement.* Glendale, CA: Griffin Pub.

Utterback, Ann, Susan L. Stolov, and Barbara J. Scherokman (1990). *Broadcast voice handbook: How to polish your on-air delivery.* Chicago, IL: Bonus Books.

Van Bottenburg, Maarten (2001). *Global games.* Champaign, IL: University of Illinois Press.

Van Der Wagen, Lynn (2002). *Event management: For tourism, cultural, business, and sporting events.* Englewood Cliffs, NJ: Prentice-Hall.

VanderZwaag, Harold T. (1998). *Policy development in sports management.* Westport, CT: Praeger.

Van Raalte, Judy L. and Britton W. Brewer (Eds.) (1996). *Exploring sport and exercise.* Washington, D.C.: American Psychological Association.

Vecsey, Geroge (1989). *A year in the sun: The games, the players, the pleasure of sports.* New York: Times Books.

Vincent, John (2004). Game, sex, and match: The construction of gender in British newspaper coverage of the 2000 Wimbledon Championships. *Sociology of Sport Journal,* Volume 21, Number 4: 435-456.

Vincent, John (2005). Equitable media coverage of female and male athletes: Is there a solution? *The New P. E. & Sports Dimension* (April), #34; Available: http://www.sports-media-org/newdimension8.htm.

Vinokur, Martin Barry (1988). *More than a game: Sports and politics.* New York: Greenwood.

Vitale, Dick with Curry Kirkpatrick (1988). *Vitale: Just your average bald, one-eyed basketball wacko who beat the ziggy and became a PTP'er.* New York: Simon and Schuster.

Vitale, Dick with Dick Weiss(1995). *Holding court: Reflections on the game I love.* Indianapolis, IN: Masters Press.

Vitale, Dick with Dick Weiss (2003). *Dick Vitale's living dream: Reflections on 25 years sitting in the best seat in the house.* Champaign, IL: Sports Publishing.

Volkwein-Caplan, Karin and Gopal Sankaran (2001). *Sexual harassment in sport: Issues, impact, and challenges.* Aachen: Meyer and Meyer Verlag.

Voy, Robert and Kirk D. Deeter (1990). *Drugs, sport and politics.* Leeds, UK: Human Kinetics Europe.

Walsh, Christopher J. (2006). *No time outs: What it's really like to be a sportswriter today.* Lanham, MD: Taylor Trade Publishing.

Wann, Daniel L., Merrill J. Melnick, Gordon W. Russell, and Dale G. Pease (2001). *Sport fans: The psychology and social impact of spectators.* New York: Routledge.

Wanta, Wayne (2006). The coverage of sports in print media. In Arthur A. Raney and Jennings Bryant (Eds.) *Handbook of sports and media.* Mahwah, NJ: Lawrence Erlbaum: 105-115.

Wanta, Wayne and Dawn Leggett (1988). 'Hitting paydirt': Caapacity theory and sports announcers' use of clichés. *Journal of Communication,* Volume 38, Number 4 (Autumn): 82-89.

Warburton, Terrence L. (1987). Sports and the media: The evolution of sportscasting. Popular Culture Association, Montreal.

Wascovich, Terence R. (1993). *The sports marketing guide.* Cleveland, OH: Points Ahead Inc.

Watkins, Sid (1997). *Life at the limit: Triumph and tragedy in Formula One.* London: Pan.

Watson, Mary Ann (1998). *Defining visions: Television and the American experience since 1945.* Fort Worth, TX: Harcourt Brace.

Weed, Mike and Chris Bull (2003). *Sports tourism: Participants, policy and providers.* Burlington, MA: Butterworth-Heinemann.

Weidman, Lisa M. (1998). *In the Olympic tradition: Sportscasters' language and female athleticism.* Baltimore, MD. Association for Education in Journalism and Mass Communication.

Weiler, Paul C. (2000). *Leveling the playing field: How the law can make sports better for fans.* Cambridge, MA: Harvard University Press.

Weiler, Paul C. and Gary R. Roberts (1993). *Cases, materials and problems on sports and the law.* St. Paul, MN: West Pub.

Weiller, Karen, Catriona Higgs, and Christy Greenleaf (2004). Analysis of television media commentary of the 2000 Olympic Games. *Media Report to Women* (Summer): 14-21.

Weiss, Ann E. (1993). *Money games: The business of sports.* Boston, MA: Houghton Mifflin.

Weiss, Don and Chuck Day (2002). *The making of the Super Bowl: The inside story of the world's greatest sporting event.* New York: McGraw-Hill.

Weitz, Rose (Ed.) (2002). *The politics of women's bodies: Sexuality, appearance, and behavior.* New York: Oxford University Press.

Welch, Michael (1997). Violence against women by professional football players: A gender analysis of hypermasculinity, positional status, narcissism, and entitlement. *Journal of Sport and Social Issues* (21): 392-411.

Wenner, Lawrence A. (Ed.) (1989). *Media, sports, & society.* Newbury Park, CA: Sage.

Wenner, Lawrence A. (Ed.) (1998). *MediaSport.* New York: Routledge.

Westerbeek, Han and Aaron Smith (2003). *Sport business in the global marketplace.* New York: Palgrave Macmillan.

Whannel, Garry (1992). *Fields in vision: Television sport and cultural transformation.* London: Routledge.

Whannel, Garry (2002). *Media sports stars: Masculinities and moralities.* London: Routledge.

Whitaker, Jack (1998). *Preferred lies and other tales: Skimming the cream of a life in sports.* New York: Simon and Schuster.

White, Philip and Kevin Young (Eds.). (2006). *Sport and gender in Canada,* 2nd ed. London: Oxford University Press.

Wiggins, David K. (1995). *Sport in America: From wicked amusement to national obsession.* Champaign, IL: Human Kinetics.

Wiggins, David K. (1997). *Glory bound: Black athletes in a white America.* Syracuse, NY: Syracuse University Press.

Wilcox, Ralph (Ed.) (1994). *Sport in the global village.* Morgantown, WV: Fitness Information Technology.

Williams, Alan (ND). Death of the jockocracy. Available: www.dumbesttv.cheeb .com/willaims2.html.

Williams, Huntington (1989). *Beyond control: ABC and the rise of the networks.* New York: Atheneum.

Williams, Jason with Steve Friedman (1999). *Loose balls: Easy money, hard fouls, cheap laughs, and true love in the NBA.* New York: Doubleday.

Wilson, John (1994). *Playing by the rules: Sport, society, and the state.* Detroit, MI: Wayne State University Press.

Wilson, Wayne (Ed.) (1999). *Children and sports media.* Los Angeles, CA: Amateur Athletic Foundation of Los Angeles.

Wilson, Wayne and Edward Derse (Eds.) (2001). *Doping the elite sport: The politics of drugs in the Olympic movement.* Champaign, IL: Human Kinetics.

Wilstein, Steve (2001). *Associated Press sports writing handbook.* New York: McGraw-Hill.

Wise, Suzanne (1994). *Social issues in contemporary sport: A resource guide.* New York: Garland.

Wojciechowski, Gene (1990). *Pond scum and vultures: America's sportswriters talk about their glamorous profession.* New York: Macmillan.

Wolf, Warner with Larry Weisman (2000). *Let's go to the videotape! All the plays—and replays—from my life in sports*. New York: Warner Books.

Wolf, Warner with William Taaffe (1983). *Gimme a break!* New York: McGraw-Hill.

Wolfe, Rich and George Castle (1998). *I remember Harry Caray*. Champaign, IL: Sports Publshing.

Wolff, Bob (1992). *It's not who won or lost the game: It's how you sold the beer*. Lanham, MD: Diamond Communications.

Wong, Glenn M. (1994). *Essentials of amateur sports law*. Westport, CT: Praeger.

Wong, Glenn M. and T. Jesse Wilde (1994). *The sport lawyer's guide to legal periodicals: An annotated bibliography*. Buffalo, NY: W.S. Hein.

Woodward, Stanley (1949). *The sports page*. New York: Simon and Schuster.

Woog, Dan (1998). *Jocks: True stories of America's gay male athletes*. Los Angeles, CA: Alyson Books.

Wushanley, Ying (2004). *Playing nice and losing: The struggle for control of women's intercollegiate athletics, 1960-2000*. Syracuse University Press.

Yardley, Jonathan (1977). *Ring: A biography of Ring Lardner*. New York: Random House.

Yasser, Raymond L. (1985). *Torts and sports: Legal liability in professional and amateur athletics*. Westport, CT: Quorum Books.

Yasser, Ray, James R. McCurdy, and C. Peter Goplerud (1990). *Sports law: Cases and materials*. Cincinnati, OH: Anderson.

Yiannakis, Andrew and Merrill J. Melnick (Eds.) (2001). *Contemporary issues in sociology of sport*. Champaign, IL: Human Kinetics.

Yost, Mark (2006). *Tailgating, sacks, and salary caps: How the NFL became the most successful sports league in history*. New York: Kaplan Business.

Young, Kevin (Ed.) (2007). *Sporting bodies, damaged selves*. Amsterdam: Elsevier.

Young, Kevin and Kevin Wamsley (Eds.) (2005). *Global Olympics: Historical and sociological studies of the modern games*. Amsterdam: JAI Press.

Youngblut, Shelly (1998). *The quotable ESPN*. New York: Hyperion.

Zagacki, Kenneth S. and Dan Grano (2005). Radio sports talk and the fantasies of sport. *Critical Studies in Media Communication,* Volume 22, Number 1 (March): 45-63.

Zang, David W. (2004). *Sportswars: Athletes in the age of aquarius*. Fayetteville: University of Arkansas Press.

Zeigler, Cyd, Jr. (2007). The gay-friendly worldwide leader in sports. Available online: www.outsports.com/news/2007/0117espn.htm.

Zimbalist, Andrew (1994). *Baseball and billions*. New York: Basic Books.

Zimbalist, Andrew (2001). *Unpaid professionals: Commercialism and conflict in big-time college sports*. Princeton, NJ: Princeton University Press.

Zimbalist, Andrew (2003). *May the best team win: Baseball economics and public policy*. Washington, DC: Brookings Institution Press.

Zimmerman, Jean and Gil Reavill (1998). *Raising our athletic daughters: How sports can build self-esteem and save girls' lives*. New York: Doubleday.

ABOUT THE AUTHOR

Linda K. Fuller, PhD, has taught sportscasting for the Communications Department of Worcester State College for several years. In addition to journal articles on the baseball film genre, she has done extensive research and is published on topics such as the Olympic Games, locker room issues, Magic Johnson, the Super Bowl, Dennis Miller and Monday Night Football, Yao Ming, Pat Tillman, and sport violence. She is the author or co-author of more than 20 books and 250+ publications, including *Sport, Rhetoric, and Gender: Historical Perspectives and Media Representations* (2006) and *Community Media: International Perspectives* (2007). Professor Fuller has been awarded Fulbrights to teach in Singapore and to do AIDS-related research in Senegal, and she is currently a Senior Fellow at Northeastern University.

Index